Railwaymen, Politics and Money

Railwaymen, Politics and Money

The Great Age of Railways in Britain

ADRIAN VAUGHAN

JOHN MURRAY
Albemarle Street, London

To Ron and Jo
for their kindness

First published in 1997
by John Murray (Publishers) Ltd,
50 Albemarle Street, London W1X 4BD

A catalogue record for this book is available from the British Library

ISBN 0-7195-5150-1

Typeset in 11/13 pt Stempel Garamond by
Servis Filmsetting Ltd, Manchester

Printed and bound in Great Britain by
The University Press, Cambridge

Contents

Contents

Illustrations

The author and publisher wish to acknowledge the following for permission to reproduce illustrations: Plate 1, 7, 10, 11, 12, 15, 17, 18, 19, 20, 23, 24 and 30, National Railway Museum; 2, Science musem; 3, 4, 5 and 6, National Portrait Gallery; 8, Adrian Vaughan Collection; 9, 16, 21, 22, 28 and 29, GWR/Adrian Vaughan Collection; 13, Phyllis Youngman; 14, H.C. Casserly, courtesy of R.M. Casserly; 25 and 26, W.L. Kenning/Adrian Vaughan Collection; 27, *Punch*.

Acknowledgements

I AM INDEBTED TO the following kind friends for their help in preparing this book and am glad to acknowledge: Philip Atkins, Librarian, NRM; Ed Bartholomew, Photographic Curator, NRM; Mike Harding, Curator of Machines, Science Museum; Mary Murphy, Archivist at the Institution of Civil Engineers, and also the library staff there; Paul Goldstein, House of Lords Record Office, and staff at the House of Commons Information Office; Miss J.M. Kinsey, Librarian Official Publications, University of East Anglia; Nick Lee, Curator, Bristol University Library Special Collections; Pat Southern, Newcastle Literary & Philosophical Society; Alan Pearce, Hackworth Museum; Terry Knight, Crewe Public Library; Steve Dyke, Darlington Railway Centre; Amanda Doran, *Punch* Library; Richard Tinker, Railway Heritage Trust. Thanks are also due to the staff at Derby Reference Library; Leicester University Library; Science Museum Picture Library; Llanelli Library; Liverpool Record Office; Swindon Reference Library; Truro Reference Library; Suffolk County Record Office; Norwich Reference Library; Institute of Transport Library; Darlington Local Studies Library.

I should also like to thank Philip and Rosemary Bagwell, Bill and Jill Bradshaw and Richard Joby for their kind instruction and encouragement; John Murray for waiting so long for this book; at John Murray Ltd, Grant McIntyre, my Editor-in-Chief, Gail Pirkis and Caroline Westmore; Roger Hudson and Ingrid Grimes for their editorial assis-

Acknowledgements

tance; Alan Peck for his contribution on Gooch and Disraeli; Peter Jordan and Steve Joice for the use of their private libraries; my good friends Ron and Jo Price and my sister Frances for their generous hospitality when I am in London; and the Royal Literary Fund for its generous support. Last, but by no means least, I – and everyone who reads and enjoys this book – am indebted to my dear wife Susan, who supported me through thick and thin during the five long years this book took to come to a conclusion.

Maps

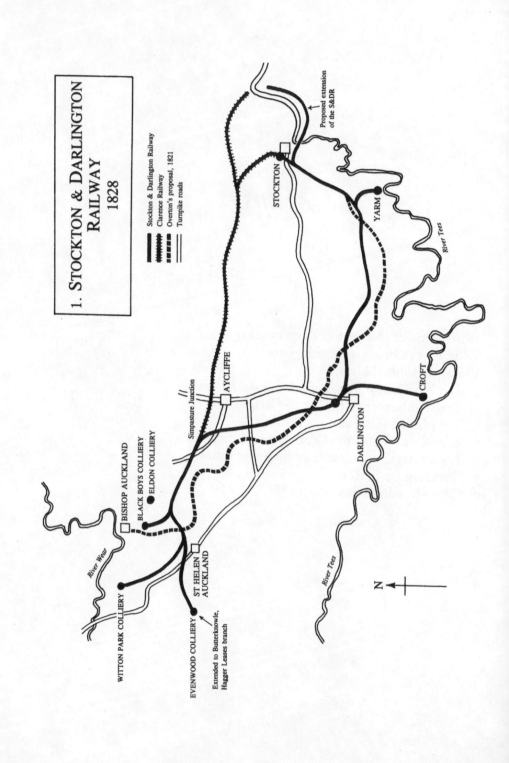

1. STOCKTON & DARLINGTON RAILWAY 1828

Stockton & Darlington Railway
Clarence Railway
Overton's proposal, 1821
Turnpike roads

Proposed extension of the S&DR

STOCKTON

YARM

River Tees

AYCLIFFE

Simpasture Junction

BISHOP AUCKLAND
BLACK BOYS COLLIERY
ELDON COLLIERY

River Wear

WITTON PARK COLLIERY

ST HELEN AUCKLAND

EVENWOOD COLLIERY

Extended to Butterknowle, Hagger Leases branch

DARLINGTON

CROFT

River Tees

N

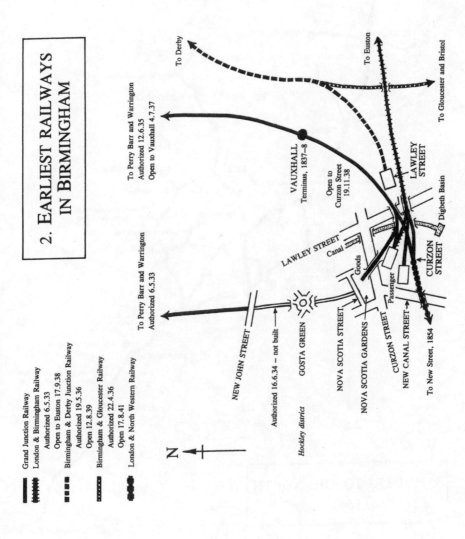

2. EARLIEST RAILWAYS IN BIRMINGHAM

To Derby

To Euston

To Gloucester and Bristol

To Perry Barr and Warrington
Authorized 12.6.35
Open to Vauxhall 4.7.37

VAUXHALL
Terminus, 1837–8

Open to
Curzon Street
19.11.38

LAWLEY
STREET

Digbeth Basin

LAWLEY STREET
Canal

Goods

CURZON
STREET

To Perry Barr and Warrington
Authorized 6.5.33

Passenger

NEW JOHN STREET

Authorized 16.6.34 – not built   GOSTA GREEN

NOVA SCOTIA STREET

NOVA SCOTIA GARDENS

CURZON STREET

NEW CANAL STREET

To New Street, 1854

Hockley district

N

Grand Junction Railway
London & Birmingham Railway
    Authorized 6.5.33
    Open to Euston 17.9.38
Birmingham & Derby Junction Railway
    Authorized 19.5.36
    Open 12.8.39
Birmingham & Gloucester Railway
    Authorized 22.4.36
    Open 17.8.41
London & North Western Railway

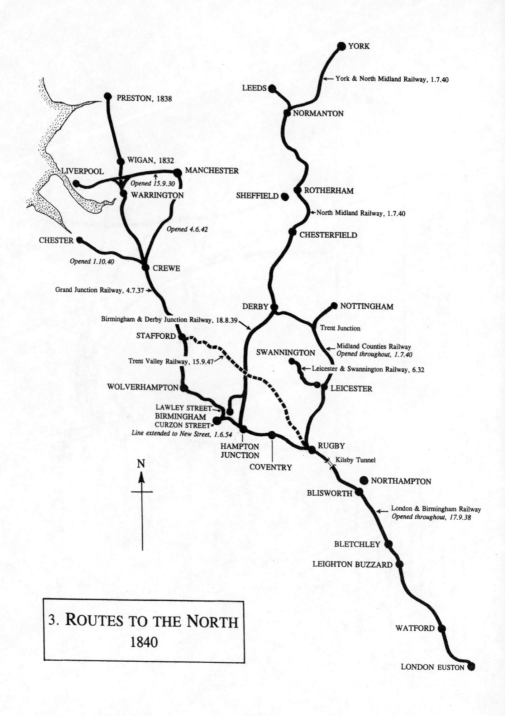

YORK

← York & North Midland Railway, 1.7.40

LEEDS

NORMANTON

PRESTON, 1838

WIGAN, 1832

↑ Opened 15.9.30

LIVERPOOL MANCHESTER

WARRINGTON

SHEFFIELD ROTHERHAM

← North Midland Railway, 1.7.40

Opened 4.6.42

CHESTER

CHESTERFIELD

Opened 1.10.40

CREWE

Grand Junction Railway, 4.7.37 →

DERBY NOTTINGHAM

Trent Junction

Birmingham & Derby Junction Railway, 18.8.39

STAFFORD

Midland Counties Railway
Opened throughout, 1.7.40

SWANNINGTON

Trent Valley Railway, 15.9.47 →

← Leicester & Swannington Railway, 6.32

WOLVERHAMPTON

LEICESTER

LAWLEY STREET
BIRMINGHAM
CURZON STREET
Line extended to New Street, 1.6.54

RUGBY

HAMPTON
JUNCTION

Kilsby Tunnel

COVENTRY

N

NORTHAMPTON

BLISWORTH

← London & Birmingham Railway
Opened throughout, 17.9.38

BLETCHLEY

LEIGHTON BUZZARD

3. ROUTES TO THE NORTH
1840

WATFORD

LONDON EUSTON

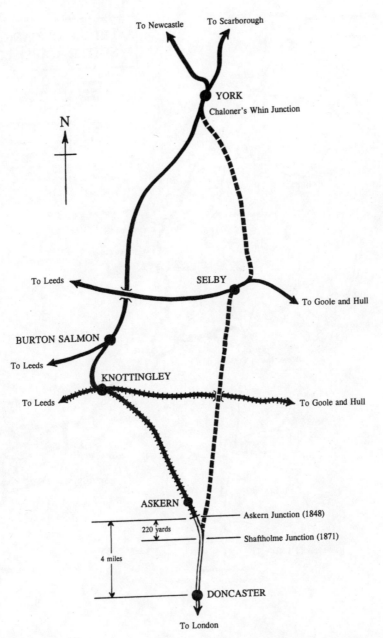

To Newcastle

To Scarborough

YORK

Chaloner's Whin Junction

N

To Leeds

SELBY

To Goole and Hull

BURTON SALMON

To Leeds

KNOTTINGLEY

To Leeds

To Goole and Hull

ASKERN

Askern Junction (1848)

220 yards

Shaftholme Junction (1871)

4 miles

DONCASTER

To London

Great Northern Railway route to York via Knottingley
and Burton Salmon, 1848–71

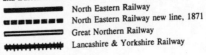

North Eastern Railway

North Eastern Railway new line, 1871

Great Northern Railway

Lancashire & Yorkshire Railway

4. THE NER'S NEW LINE, YORK–DONCASTER 1871

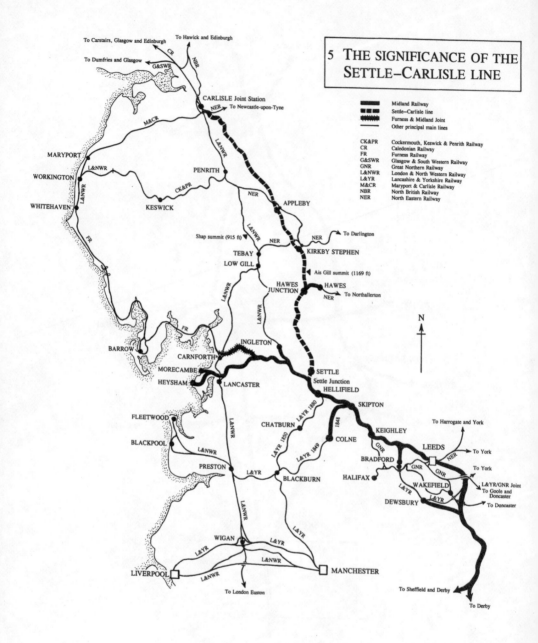

Midland Railway
Settle–Carlisle line
Furness & Midland Joint
Other principal main lines

CK&PR	Cockermouth, Keswick & Penrith Railway
CR	Caledonian Railway
FR	Furness Railway
G&SWR	Glasgow & South Western Railway
GNR	Great Northern Railway
L&NWR	London & North Western Railway
L&YR	Lancashire & Yorkshire Railway
M&CR	Maryport & Carlisle Railway
NBR	North British Railway
NER	North Eastern Railway

To Carstairs, Glasgow and Edinburgh
To Hawick and Edinburgh
To Dumfries and Glasgow
CR
NBR
G&SWR

CARLISLE Joint Station
NER — To Newcastle-upon-Tyne

M&CR
MARYPORT
L&NWR
WORKINGTON
L&NWR
WHITEHAVEN
L&NWR
PENRITH
NER
CK&PR
KESWICK
APPLEBY

FR

Shap summit (915 ft)
L&NWR
NER
NER
To Darlington
TEBAY
NER
KIRKBY STEPHEN
LOW GILL
Ais Gill summit (1169 ft)
HAWES JUNCTION
HAWES
NER
To Northallerton

BARROW
FR
L&NWR
L&NWR

INGLETON
CARNFORTH
MORECAMBE
HEYSHAM
LANCASTER
SETTLE
Settle Junction
HELLIFIELD
SKIPTON

L&YR 1880
1848
To Harrogate and York

FLEETWOOD
CHATBURN
KEIGHLEY
L&YR 1880
COLNE
LEEDS
To York
BLACKPOOL
L&YR 1849
GNR
L&NWR
BRADFORD
NER
To York
L&YR 1850
GNR
PRESTON
L&YR
HALIFAX
GNR
L&YR/GNR Joint
WAKEFIELD
To Goole and Doncaster
L&YR
DEWSBURY
L&YR
To Doncaster

L&NWR
BLACKBURN

L&YR
WIGAN
L&YR
L&YR
LIVERPOOL
L&NWR
L&NWR
MANCHESTER
To London Euston
To Sheffield and Derby
To Derby

N

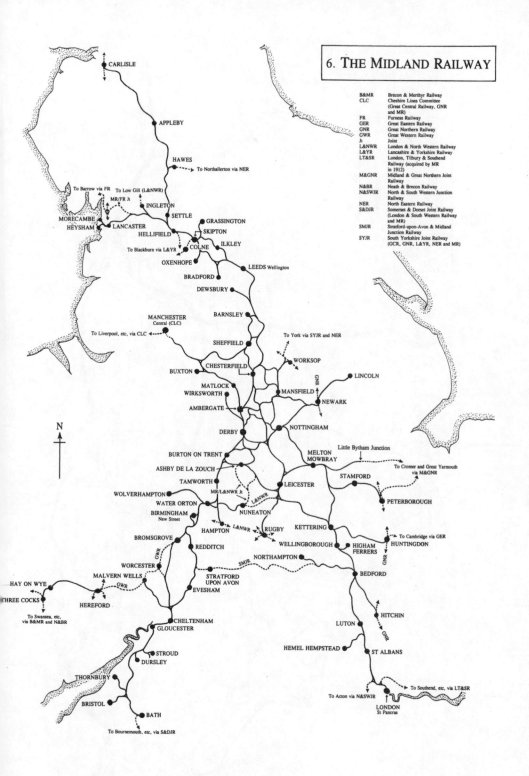

6. THE MIDLAND RAILWAY

B&MR   Brecon & Merthyr Railway
CLC   Cheshire Lines Committee
              (Great Central Railway, GNR
              and MR)
FR   Furness Railway
GER   Great Eastern Railway
GNR   Great Northern Railway
GWR   Great Western Railway
Jt   Joint
L&NWR   London & North Western Railway
L&YR   Lancashire & Yorkshire Railway
LT&SR   London, Tilbury & Southend
              Railway (acquired by MR
              in 1912)
M&GNR   Midland & Great Northern Joint
              Railway
N&BR   Neath & Brecon Railway
N&SWJR   North & South Western Junction
              Railway
NER   North Eastern Railway
S&DJR   Somerset & Dorset Joint Railway
              (London & South Western Railway
              and MR)
SMJR   Stratford-upon-Avon & Midland
              Junction Railway
SYJR   South Yorkshire Joint Railway
              (GCR, GNR, L&YR, NER and MR)

CARLISLE

APPLEBY

HAWES

To Northallerton via NER

To Barrow via FR

To Low Gill (L&NWR)

MR/FR Jt

INGLETON

SETTLE

GRASSINGTON

MORECAMBE

HEYSHAM

LANCASTER

HELLIFIELD

SKIPTON

ILKLEY

To Blackburn via L&YR

COLNE

OXENHOPE

BRADFORD

DEWSBURY

LEEDS Wellington

BARNSLEY

MANCHESTER
Central (CLC)

To Liverpool, etc, via CLC

SHEFFIELD

To York via SYJR and NER

BUXTON

CHESTERFIELD

WORKSOP

MATLOCK

WIRKSWORTH

MANSFIELD

LINCOLN

AMBERGATE

NEWARK

DERBY

NOTTINGHAM

BURTON ON TRENT

MELTON
MOWBRAY

Little Bytham Junction

ASHBY DE LA ZOUCH

TAMWORTH

STAMFORD

To Cromer and Great Yarmouth
via M&GNR

WOLVERHAMPTON

MR/L&NWR Jt

LEICESTER

PETERBOROUGH

WATER ORTON

L&NWR

BIRMINGHAM
New Street

NUNEATON

BROMSGROVE

HAMPTON

L&NWR

RUGBY

KETTERING

To Cambridge via GER

REDDITCH

WELLINGBOROUGH

HIGHAM
FERRERS

HUNTINGDON

WORCESTER

SMJR

NORTHAMPTON

HAY ON WYE

MALVERN WELLS

STRATFORD
UPON AVON

BEDFORD

THREE COCKS

GWR

EVESHAM

HEREFORD

HITCHIN

To Swansea, etc,
via B&MR and N&BR

CHELTENHAM

LUTON

GLOUCESTER

STROUD

HEMEL HEMPSTEAD

ST ALBANS

DURSLEY

THORNBURY

To Southend, etc, via LT&SR

BRISTOL

To Acton via N&SWJR

BATH

LONDON
St Pancras

To Bournemouth, etc, via S&DJR

N

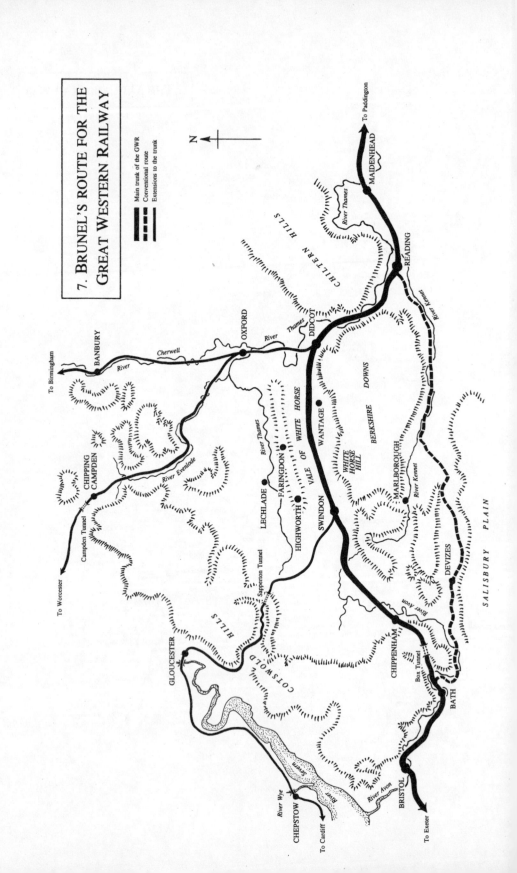

7. BRUNEL'S ROUTE FOR THE GREAT WESTERN RAILWAY

Main trunk of the GWR
Conventional route
Extensions to the trunk

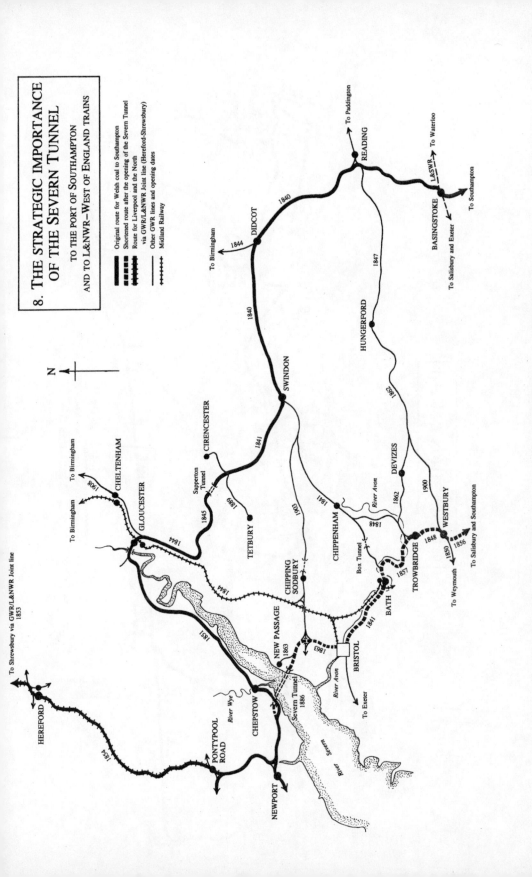

8. THE STRATEGIC IMPORTANCE
OF THE SEVERN TUNNEL
TO THE PORT OF SOUTHAMPTON
AND TO L&NWR–WEST OF ENGLAND TRAINS

Original route for Welsh coal to Southampton
Shortened route after the opening of the Severn Tunnel
Route for Liverpool and the North
via GWR/L&NWR Joint line (Hereford-Shrewsbury)
Other GWR lines and opening dates
Midland Railway

N

To Shrewsbury via GWR/L&NWR Joint line
1853

HEREFORD

River Wye

PONTYPOOL
ROAD

1851

NEWPORT

CHEPSTOW

Severn Tunnel
1886

River Severn

River Wye

To Birmingham

To Birmingham

CHELTENHAM

1908

GLOUCESTER

1844

1844

Sapperton
Tunnel

1845

1889

CIRENCESTER

TETBURY

1841

SWINDON

1840

1840

DIDCOT

1844

To Birmingham

READING

To Paddington

1851

1861

NEW PASSAGE
1863

1863

CHIPPING
SODBURY

1903

1841

CHIPPENHAM

Box Tunnel

1841

BATH

1857

1841

BRISTOL

To Exeter

River Avon

1848

River Avon

TROWBRIDGE

1848

DEVIZES

1862

1862

1900

1850

1856

WESTBURY

To Salisbury and Southampton

To Weymouth

HUNGERFORD

1847

L&SWR

BASINGSTOKE

To Salisbury and Exeter

To Waterloo

To Southampton

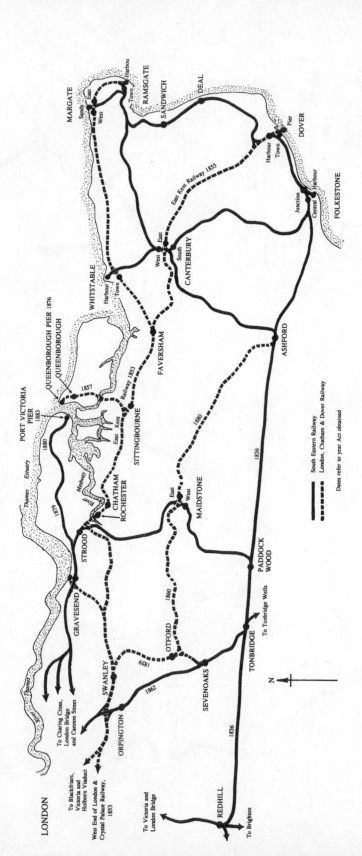

9. COMPETITION IN KENT

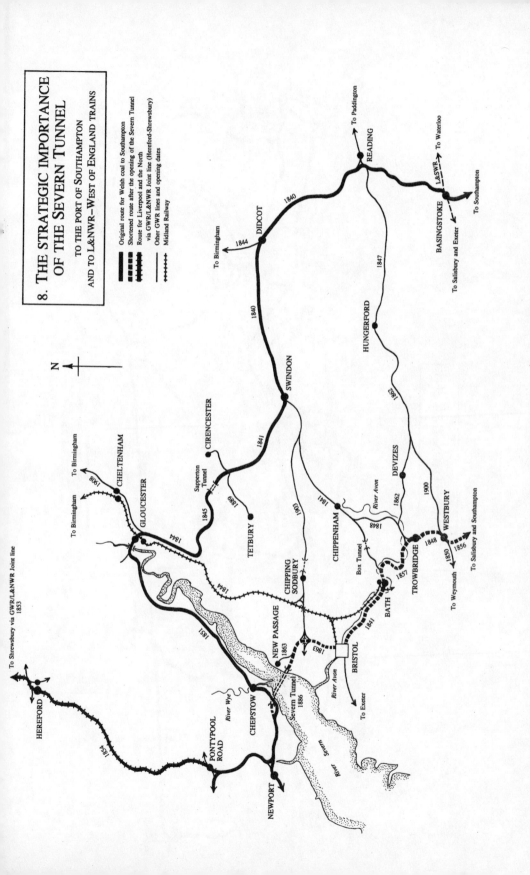

8. THE STRATEGIC IMPORTANCE OF THE SEVERN TUNNEL

TO THE PORT OF SOUTHAMPTON
AND TO L&NWR—WEST OF ENGLAND TRAINS

Original route for Welsh coal to Southampton
Shortened route after the opening of the Severn Tunnel
Route for Liverpool and the North
via GWR/L&NWR Joint line (Hereford-Shrewsbury)
Other GWR lines and opening dates
Midland Railway

N

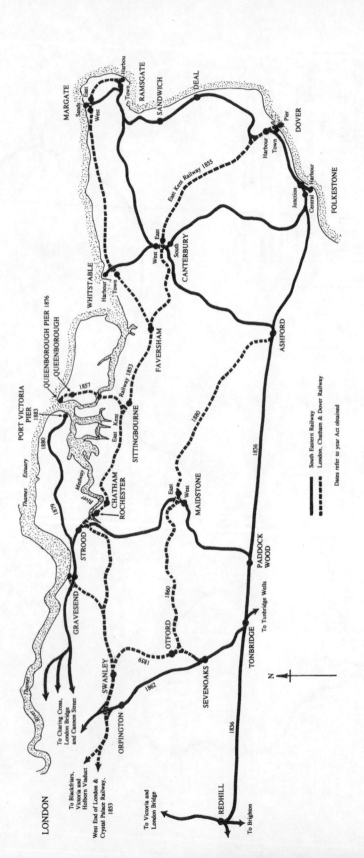

9. COMPETITION IN KENT

LONDON

Thames Estuary

River Thames

River Medway

To Charing Cross,
London Bridge
and Cannon Street

West End of London &
Crystal Palace Railway,
1853

To Blackfriars,
Victoria and
Holborn Viaduct

PORT VICTORIA
PIER 1883

QUEENBOROUGH PIER 1876
QUEENBOROUGH

1880

1879

1857

East Kent
Railway 1853

STROOD

CHATHAM
ROCHESTER

SITTINGBOURNE

FAVERSHAM

WHITSTABLE

Harbour
Town

West
East

MARGATE

Sands
East
West

Harbour
Town

RAMSGATE

SANDWICH

DEAL

Pier

DOVER

Harbour
Town

Junction

Central   Harbour

FOLKESTONE

East Kent Railway 1855

South
CANTERBURY

ASHFORD

1880

GRAVESEND

SWANLEY

ORPINGTON

1862

1859

OTFORD

1860

East
West
MAIDSTONE

PADDOCK
WOOD

To Tunbridge Wells

TONBRIDGE

SEVENOAKS

1836

1836

REDHILL

To Victoria and
London Bridge

To Brighton

N

South Eastern Railway

London, Chatham & Dover Railway

Dates refer to year Act obtained

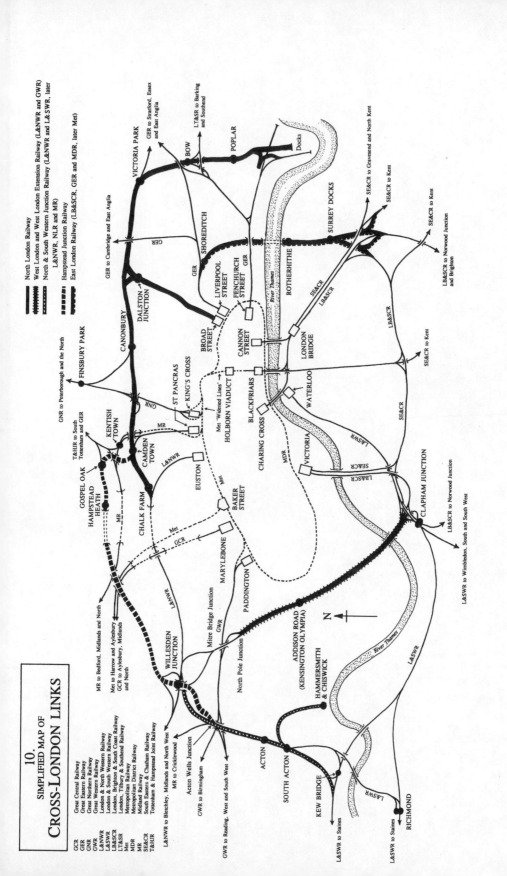

10.
SIMPLIFIED MAP OF
CROSS-LONDON LINKS

GCR   Great Central Railway
GER   Great Eastern Railway
GNR   Great Northern Railway
GWR   Great Western Railway
L&NWR   London & North Western Railway
L&SWR   London & South Western Railway
LB&SCR   London, Brighton & South Coast Railway
LT&SR   London, Tilbury & Southend Railway
Met   Metropolitan Railway
MDR   Metropolitan District Railway
MR   Midland Railway
SE&CR   South Eastern & Chatham Railway
T&HJR   Tottenham & Hampstead Joint Railway

North London Railway
West London and West London Extension Railway (L&NWR and GWR)
North & South Western Junction Railway (L&NWR and L&SWR, later L&NWR, NLR and MR)
Hampstead Junction Railway
East London Railway (LB&SCR, GER and MDR, later Met)

I

Early Railways

THE ANCIENT ROMAN Empire had perfected a technique of building roads which was used in Britain to create a 'chariotway' system of roads. Two parallel lines of stone paving, truly and smoothly laid, enabled a horse, running along the grass strip between, to haul a carriage at a brisk pace for many miles, with little if any discomfort to the traveller. The Romans departed these shores in 410 AD and thereafter travel reverted to its former state: roads became mud tracks, wider or narrower, rutted, precipitous, bumpy and dangerous. Since it was the rich who travelled by wheeled vehicle it is surprising that, through all the centuries, no effective technique was developed for the creation of comfortable roads.

It was not until 1660 that the first regular stage-coach service started; running between Oxford and London, it took 12 hrs on a good, dry day. By 1662 Britain was blessed with six scheduled stage-coach services – one John Crosdell of the Charterhouse is reported as commenting that this was six too many![1] There was still a lack of road-building technique, of organization and of laws necessary to maintain roads as a secure and certain means of long-distance communication. This required co-operation, co-ordination and centralization. Anything more than a purely local company, maintaining 20–30 miles of road, would have been opposed as a 'monopoly'. In 1663 magistrates in the counties of Hertford, Huntingdon and Cambridge obtained an Act to charge tolls on their sections of the

Great North Road from London and York – described in the Act as 'ruinous and impassable', though in Roman times they had been solidly paved.

The example of these pioneers was not immediately followed by a rush of visionary entrepreneurs, eager to 'turnpike' the entire route; and indeed, the idea was treated scornfully by many. In 1671 Sir Henry Herbert declared: 'If a man were to propose to convey us regularly from London to Edinburgh in 7 days – should we not vote to consign him to Bedlam?'[2] Thirty years later, a few more Turnpike Trust Acts had been passed but there was still no great rush to build toll roads. The first regular stage-coach service from London to Edinburgh began in 1706, starting from the Black Swan in Holborn, along the Great North Road via Huntingdon, Stamford, Doncaster and York, and promising to reach Edinburgh in four days.[3] To get to Edinburgh on time remained, however, a remarkable piece of good fortune – overturned or crashed coaches were a normal feature of road travel in the best of weather; in bad weather, travel ceased. Even under favourable conditions, to complete such a long journey by stage-coach was a great feat of endurance for the traveller, and many were confined to bed for several days after a road journey from London to York.

During the period 1740–70 there was something of a 'mania' for turnpiking existing main roads and for building new roads. A turnpike company would own a mere 20 miles of road, and the maintenance of that would be divided into short contract lengths, so quality tended to vary within one turnpike and along the entire route of the road; but at least some sort of orderly control was established. The famous traveller–chronicler Arthur Young estimated that some 18 per cent of turnpike road mileage was maintained to 'excellent' standards; a similar percentage he classed as 'vile'.

In the absence of a proper system of construction no roads could withstand heavy use by large freight vehicles – much less steam road carriages. The three best-known road builders of the late eighteenth and early nineteenth century were John ('Blind Jack') Metcalf, (1717–1810), Thomas Telford (1757–1834) and John Loudon McAdam (1756–1836). Telford and McAdam each devised precise specifications for making hard road surfaces; McAdam, Surveyor of Roads in Bristol, spread his technique nationwide with such success that he was voted a grant of £10,000 by a grateful Parliament. It had taken Britain 1400 years to discover a system equal to that used by the Romans.

As the main roads were improved, so stage-coach journeys became faster. The Exeter–London coach of 1688 was advertised to cover the distance in four days; in 1788 its owner claimed two days, and by 1832, 17½ hrs: a speed of 10 mph. By 1820 the Turnpike Trust system had been applied to virtually all trunk roads and many miles of cross-country roads. The advent of macadamized roads ushered in the so-called Golden Age of coaching; McAdam believed that the coming of railways was a tragedy.

Improved roads inevitably gave rise to more coach operators, and thus, to competitive timings and prices. This was excellent for passengers but bad for the coach proprietors, who clamoured for a reduction in road tolls – although such a reduction at a time of increasing traffic would have been detrimental to road surfaces. Competition also increased the operators' haulage costs because higher speeds demanded extra horses, while the life of a horse was shortened through the over-exertion required to enable their owners to compete.

By the mid-eighteenth century companies were operating daily freight services between London and Liverpool, York and Scotland, using the muddy roads and also water transport. The inland waterways were circuitous and slow, and canals froze in winter, while in summer water became too low; sea-borne traffic, too, was at the mercy of the forces of nature. In 1786 William Murdoch (1754–1839), an employee of James Watt, built a viable, high-pressure steam road carriage but Watt forbade him to continue with a steam-engine system in competition with his own. Between 1786 and 1804 several other inventors produced workable steam road carriages. What was lacking was a road strong enough to withstand their weight.

Just who invented the 'railroad' (as railways were original called) is a matter of dispute. In 1597 Sir Francis Willoughby, a coal-mine owner of Woollaton Hall, Nottinghamshire, had laid a track of wooden beams over which ran wooden wagons with flanged wheels.[4] At this time, the collieries of Northumberland and Durham used similar railroads to carry coal down to navigable water more effectively than by pack-horse. Cast-iron, flanged wheels running on wooden 'edge-rails' were in use on Durham wagonways in 1760, when they were mentioned by Bishop Pococke.[5] Nicholas Wood's treatise on railways gives the credit to a Mr Reynolds, the owner of an ironworks at Coalbrookdale in Shropshire who, in 1767, made cast-iron rails with the flange on the rail, rather than on the wheels.

Benjamin Outram (1761–1805) cast his first 'Outram' plates at his iron foundry in Ripley, Derbyshire, in 1785. This was the first system for laying an iron way, using standard components. The plates were L-shaped, about 5 ft long, with a running surface about 4 in. wide and with parallel ribs underneath for strengthening; they were laid on timber cross-sleepers, with the upright part of the 'L' back to back, like book-ends, and acted as a guide to the wheels, which did not therefore have to be specially flanged. Lines constructed with Outram plates were known as 'tramways', and the labourers who laid the plates were known as 'platelayers'.

The great disadvantage of the Outram plate was that the wagon wheels struck or rubbed against the upright part while the broad running surface and the angle between it and the upright accumulated a deposit of mud and stones sufficient to impede progress and even to derail wagons. William Jessop (1745–1814), a leading canal engineer, and a partner with Outram in the Ripley foundry, subsequently re-designed the 'edge-rail', using only cast iron: each rail was 3 ft long and reinforced by a 'fish-bellied' underside. The rails had a 'foot' at each end through which they were nailed to heavy stone blocks bedded into the earth; these blocks were drilled and a wooden insert hammered home to form a grip for the metal spike. Jessop used this system on a railway to connect Nanpanton with the canal at Loughborough, about 3½ miles away.

Cast iron is brittle and is liable to break when stressed or when struck sharply; thus the rails frequently broke at the ends, where there was a gap between one rail and the next, or where the stone blocks sub-sided under pressure and the track was uneven. For this eventuality, Jessop in 1797 invented the cast-iron 'chair', into which the broken rail was placed, and wedged with a block of oak; the 'chair' was then spiked into the stone block. Soon this became the standard way to hold the rail ends.

Jessop's system found less favour than Outram's – perhaps because the latter was the better salesman, or because the Outram system enabled common carts of varying gauge to use it. Jessop's edge-rail system was adopted in the north-east, but Outram's tramway was installed almost everywhere else. (The Monmouthshire Railway of 1796, from Pontnewydd, near Pontypool, to Blaeavon ironworks; Samuel Homfray's Pen-y-darran tramway of 1803, from the Abercynon Basin to Merthyr and Dowlais; and the Ruabon Brook tramway of 1805, built by the Ellesmere Canal Co. from Pontcysyllte to Acrefair, are some examples.) The 4½-mile tramway from Denby colliery to the canal at Little Eaton was to have been laid with Jessop's

rails, but after intense lobbying from Outram the proprietors purchased his technically inferior system. The line was opened in 1799; it
was laid to a gauge of 4 ft 6 in. and was single with passing loops; the
movable plates, to switch wagons from one line to another, were called
'pointers', soon shortened to 'points': a term which continues to this
day.

Rails of cast iron could be formed relatively cheaply: ironstone was
heated and the iron ran out of it into moulds. If, however, the white-
hot block of cast iron was forced back and forth between rollers, rails
of worked or 'wrought' iron were produced, which were far more
resilient and flexible, and better able to withstand a sharp blow or
heavy loading. The first wrought-iron rails were used at Bedlington
colliery, in Durham, in 1805. Short, feeder railways, usually from a colliery, quarry, foundry or factory to a waterway, were encouraged by
Jessop's and Outram's systems; by 1798 Outram was suggesting long-
distance railways.

The first railway to be constructed for public use – the Surrey Iron
Railway – was built as an alternative to canalizing a river, important as
a power source to factories along its banks. Authorized by Parliament
on 21 May 1801 to provide 'for the populous neighbourhood . . . a
cheap and easy communication for the conveyance of coals, corn and
other goods and merchandise to and from the Metropolis and other
places', the line was opened on 26 July 1803. It ran northwards from
Pitlake Meadow in Croydon to the Ram Field on the Thames at
Wandsworth, where a dock was made. It passed close to the River
Wandle, on which stood mills and factories in need of better transport;
these, it was hoped, would provide the railway with a profitable traffic.
Its Engineer William Jessop, assisted by his brother Josiah, designed it
as a double track, using Outram plates laid to a gauge of 4 ft between
the backs of the uprights of the plates. These were laid on stone sleepers of such dimensions that, when the railway was taken up, they were
used as kerbstones.

Perhaps Jessop did not use his own edge-rail system here because
the Surrey Iron Railway was to be a public highway, an iron turnpike
road, which had therefore to accommodate the maximum number of
'gauges' of road vehicles. Haulage was by 'horse, ass, mule or donkey'.
Its superiority over road haulage was that it could remain open
throughout the year and that it enabled a single horse to haul, at
walking speed and without undue effort, trains weighing up to 55
tons.[6]

In 1800 Watt's patent on steam-engines expired and a Cornishman, Richard Trevithick (1771–1833), set out to realize his own ideas for a steam-engine. The result was first demonstrated on the Pen-y-darran tramway, Merthyr, on 15 February 1804. It had a single horizontal cylinder, 4¾ in. in diameter, with a 3-ft stroke with a flywheel to swing the connecting rod and crank over the dead spot at the end of the piston's stroke. The boiler carried steam at 40 lb psi. The machine hauled 10 tons of iron nine miles along the tramway at 5 mph.[7]

Samuel Homfray, owner of the line, graciously permitted Trevithick to use his track but made Trevithick pay all expenses. His engine was the first to possess three features most vital to the future development of steam locomotion: its boiler generated steam at high pressure; it ran on smooth wheels, and depended for its traction on the weight of the engine pressing the wheels to the tram plate (the tractive effort of the engine was enhanced by having the wheels coupled together); and it discharged its exhaust steam upwards inside its chimney from the base. There was no attempt at making a jet 'blast pipe', but the enlivening effect on the fire of each rush of exhaust steam through the chimney was at once noted: the coal or coke burned much more fiercely and raised steam faster.

Samuel Homfray was not impressed with what he had seen, because Trevithick's engine broke the plates of the track, built only for animal haulage. That might have been an end of the matter had not Christopher Blackett, the owner of the Wylam colliery, 8 miles west of Newcastle, heard what Trevithick's engine had achieved – probably from the Gateshead engineer, John Steele, who had assisted Trevithick with his engine at Pen-y-darran. Blackett asked Steele to build him such a machine, but on condition that he need not buy it if it did not please him. Steele accordingly built a close copy of Trevithick's engine. It weighed 5 tons, and was thus too heavy for the wooden rails of the Wylam colliery track, so Blackett refused to buy it, leaving Steele to recoup his losses as best he might. Blackett nevertheless replaced his wooden track with cast-iron tram plates, and in 1808 he approached Trevithick for an engine but the latter replied that he was no longer in that business. Although Steele was still at work, Blackett allowed the matter to rest without consulting him again.[8]

On 10 April 1811 John Blenkinsop, part-owner of Middleton colliery, Leeds, patented a locomotive system using a 'rack and pinion' type of drive with a patent rail. He then commissioned Matthew Murray, a native of Stockton-on-Tees and the brain behind the Leeds engineering firm of Fenton, Wood, Murray & Jackson, to build such a machine. The resulting locomotive was given its first run with eight wagons of coal on 24 June 1812. It had two cylinders mounted vertically, partly within the boiler and along its centre line. It was carried on four wheels and, between them, a cogged pair which engaged in lugs cast into the side of the rails. Exhaust steam vented directly to atmosphere. In September 1813 two of Blenkinsop's engines were set to work on the Kenton & Coxlode wagonway, County Durham, where they were seen by George Stephenson.[9] They were successful in routinely hauling 67½ tons of coal at 3 mph,[10] but with the cumbersome geared drive from the cylinders to the pinion wheel and the big pinion which engaged ponderously in the special rail, they could not have been developed into high-speed engines. Trevithick's smooth-wheeled, weight-adhesion principle was clearly the way forward.

The man who was to convert the railway steam-locomotive into a reliable machine and to devise most, if not all, of the improvements to the locomotive from 1812 to 1829 was Timothy Hackworth, born in Wylam village on 22 December 1786. The son of the Wylam colliery Foreman Blacksmith, Hackworth was apprenticed to his father in 1802. Two years later his father died and Christopher Blackett took over supervision of the boy's apprenticeship. In 1807 Hackworth himself became Foreman Blacksmith at Wylam, where, in 1811, with some assistance from the mine Manager, William Hedley, he designed and built the colliery's first locomotive. The *Wylam Grasshopper* – so called because of the alternating rise and fall of the two beams, propelled by the vertical cylinders – was a smooth-wheeled machine, driven by and coupled through gears. (The actual construction was shared by Jonathan Foster, a fine mechanic who later became Enginewright at Wylam.[11]) The engine was somewhat heavy for the iron plateway, and in 1813 the Hackworth/Hedley partnership produced the *Wylam Dilly*, a 'grasshopper' engine whose weight was distributed over eight wheels grouped into two sets of four, mounted on bogies beneath the main frame.

The man who would convince sceptical capitalists that the steam-locomotive was indeed the future motive power for railways and who came to be regarded as the 'Father of Railways', and also of the locomotive, was George Stephenson, also born at Wylam, on 9 June 1781. Stephenson was the son of Robert, a stoker on a stationary engine at Wylam colliery. The colliery horse-drawn tramway, carrying coal to the Tyne, passed the door of their hovel so the boy was familiar with the rumble of iron wheels from the earliest age. He worked on local farms from the age of eight until, at thirteen, his father got him a better-paid job sorting coal at Dewleyburn colliery. By the time he was seventeen, he was Engineman, with his father as his assistant; he was now able to afford evening lessons in reading and writing from the Wylam schoolmaster Robin Cowens, and in 1800, he began to learn arithmetic from Andrew Robertson of New Burn. In 1802 he moved to Willington Quay as Engineman, where he met Frances Henderson, whom he married that September; Frances gave birth to their only son, Robert, on 16 October 1803.[12] He also met the engineer Robert Hawthorn, with whom he had many valuable conversations regarding steam-engines.

In 1812 Stephenson was appointed Enginewright at Killingworth colliery, about 7 miles north of Newcastle. He was in charge of erecting and maintaining several stationary steam-engines, and received the relatively large sum of £100 a year, which enabled him to send his son away to Newcastle for a formal education. Stephenson had also to look after his blind father, and he supplemented his income by mending shoes, clocks and watches.

At that time, coal-mining was extremely hazardous because of the constant influx of gas into the tunnels and the lack of any light other than a naked flame. After a terrible explosion at the Felling pit in 1812, William Clanny, MD, designed a safety lamp and read a paper on it to the Royal Society on 20 May 1813.[13] The lamp was constructed that year and, despite its relative bulkiness, for many years enjoyed popularity among miners from as far afield as Staffordshire and Durham. However, the mine owners were not entirely satisfied and invited Sir Humphrey Davy to study the problem. In 1814 there was a devastating underground explosion at the Killingworth pit. Stephenson, the colliery Engineer, was spurred to make his own gas-proof lamp. On 4 and again on 30 November 1814, he demonstrated a lamp, in gas, underground, at Killingworth.[14] Davy demonstrated *his* lamp on a table at the Royal Society in London on 3 November that same year. In 1816, after an investigation, it was Davy who received a prize of 500 guineas as the inventor of the miners' safety lamp.

In 1814 Killingworth colliery's coal was still hauled by oxen. Stephenson had seen Blenkinsop's engines at work at Coxlode colliery line, and was reported to have been less than impressed with their design and performance. He was also well acquainted with Timothy Hackworth's work at Wylam – and with John Steele. Stephenson was sure he could make an engine for Killingworth, and was given the necessary permission by Killingworth's owner, Lord Ravensworth.

This engine – the *Blucher* – began running on 25 July 1814. Its wheels were placed 4 ft 8 in. apart, since that was the gauge width of the Killingworth colliery tracks. The *Blucher* could haul 30 tons up a one-in-450 gradient at 5 mph, and reduced by twenty the number of horses required to carry coal to the shipping point. It was no more than an amalgam of ideas taken from the engines of Trevithick, Blenkinsop and Hackworth and perpetuated Blenkinsop's fault of allowing exhaust steam to vent to atmosphere direct, rather than being discharged into the chimney to draw up the fire. Without any such 'draw', the *Blucher*'s single-flue boiler did not maintain steam pressure for long periods of exertion.

In 1815 Stephenson built a second engine incorporating important, new ideas invented by Ralph Dodd, mine Manager at Killingworth, and Dodd's nephew Isaac.[15] The clumsy – and frictional – cog-wheel drive and coupling system was dispensed with. The cylinders were still placed vertically within the boiler but at each end. The leading cylinder drove the leading pair of wheels, and the trailing cylinder the rear pair of wheels, by means of connecting rods from the piston crosshead to cranks on each wheel. Dodd's patent had included a coupling rod between the wheels to combine their tractive effort, but the system required this coupling rod to work on the cranked axles, under the boiler. Forged crank axles were at that time too difficult to manufacture and so instead, each axle carried a sprocket around which ran a coupling chain. This engine discharged its exhaust steam into the chimney but not with any precision, merely as a way of reducing to some extent the noise of the exhaust. However, some 'drawing' of the fire did result. The absolutely vital concept of the coned exhaust jet, or 'blast pipe', was to be Hackworth's invention, more than a decade later.[16] Stephenson's Killingworth engines were no more cost-effective than horses. They remained unimproved for twelve years.[17]

Stephenson then had to consider how to lay a track strong enough to stand the locomotive's weight. Michael Longridge, owner of the Bedlington ironworks, had been offered cheap coal for his works by the owner of Bedlington colliery if he, Longridge, would provide the rails for a colliery railway. Longridge had declined, knowing that the brittleness of cast-iron rails made them uneconomic. Stephenson, however, drew Longridge's attention to the Tindall Fell Railway, near Brampton, County Durham, which had been laid between 1808 and

1812 with 3½ miles of 1½ × 1½ in. wrought-iron rail. These more flexible rails had proved to be durable, although they were too narrow and wore grooves in the wagon wheels.[18] Delighted, Longridge gave Stephenson the job of laying out and supervising the construction of the new railway, and agreed to roll a supply of rails. Stephenson was rewarded with a partnership in the colliery company, but his greater reward lay in his burgeoning reputation. He had capitalized on his natural expertise as an engine doctor to become a constructor of loco-motive engines, and now he would enable entrepreneurs to increase their entire business – he could deliver the whole railway, from survey to track and locomotives.

Stephenson was enthusiastically encouraged by William James (1771–1837). Born at Henley-in-Arden, the son of a solicitor, James was in 1799 Land Agent and Surveyor for the Earl of Warwick, for whom he was laying out railways between canals and the Earl's coal-mines. In 1803 James witnessed Richard Trevithick's locomotive experiment on the Pen-y-darran tramway and was very impressed. The following year, while carrying out survey work on lands between Liverpool and Manchester, James realized that the best place to try out a locomotive-hauled railway would be between the factories of Manchester and Lancashire and their port of Liverpool. In 1808 he published his proposal for a 'General Railroad Company'[19] to build a national trunk railway network including (among other routes) a line from Liverpool to Manchester through Warrington, and another south, from Warrington to Birmingham and London.

By 1816 James was rich and influential: he owned collieries in West Bromwich, Swadlincote and Coventry and also the tolls on the Upper Avon Navigation between Evesham and Stratford. He was Engineer of the Stratford Canal from his own Upper Avon Navigation to a junc-tion at King's Norton with the complex of canals in Birmingham. Around 1819 or 1820, he and the equally far-sighted Thomas Gray (1787–1848) of Nottingham made fresh proposals for a company to build a national trunk railway network: a 'Central Junction Railway or Tramroad' of 4 ft 8½ in.-gauge line, because it was intended to use Stephenson locomotives. It would run from the Stratford-on-Avon Canal basin, to Moreton-in-Marsh, and thence to the Thames at Chelsea via Oxford, Thame, Uxbridge and Paddington; joining this trunk near Shipston-on-Stour would be a line from the Oxfordshire ironstone country and the Coventry coalfields.

Lord Redesdale, the local landowner, and the Midlands industrialist

Lord Dudley were both in favour of the scheme, and James was its Engineer. An Act for the first section from Stratford-on-Avon to Moreton-in-Marsh was obtained on 28 May 1821, only six weeks after the Stockton & Darlington Act. In July, James urged the Stratford & Moreton Railway Directors to use wrought-iron rails and to buy Stephenson's locomotive *Invention*. The Directors felt that, at £440, the engine was expensive, and sent one of their number, John Greaves (a local merchant), to the north-east to investigate the relative costs of horse or locomotive haulage. His report came out absolutely in favour of horses and rope haulage. He could only see locomotives as they then were, and failed to realize their potential; and his parochial view of the S&MR was equally limited. The Directors then asked John Urpeth Rastrick,[20] a versatile civil and mechanical engineer, for his opinion. He too recommended horse haulage – but only because James had designed the route with gradients steeper than Rastrick (or Stephenson) believed could be surmounted by locomotive power. One wonders why James had not consulted Stephenson on this vital point; on the other hand, one wonders why Stephenson did not rise to the challenge and make a more powerful locomotive: the gradients James envisaged were by no means steep. James lost his position to Rastrick, who became Engineer of the S&MR in 1823. The 17 miles from Stratford to Moreton was opened, horse-drawn over wrought-iron rails on stone blocks, on 5 September 1826.

In 1823 James journeyed to Canterbury, where merchants were considering improvements to the River Stour as far as the coast at Sandwich. James persuaded them to allow him to design a railway northwards to Whitstable and to build a harbour there, only 6 miles from Canterbury. The Act for the line, to James's plan, was obtained in 1825. James had, however, chosen his ground badly; he would have done better with a route down the Stour valley. Going north to Whitstable his railway had to climb, then descend, steeply on gradients of 1 in 50 and even 1 in 28. As a result the line was stationary engine- and rope-hauled except for 1¾ miles. By the time of gaining the Act, James was already bankrupt, his health had failed, and he received no assistance from Stephenson, the man he had championed. Thus William James departed the railway scene into poverty and obscurity, while the Canterbury & Whitstable Railway was completed by Stephenson.

2

The Stockton & Darlington Railway

THE NORTH-EAST OF England, and County Durham in particular, had been an important coalfield for hundreds of years. In the
Middle Ages the mines were sited close to the rivers Tyne, Wear
and Tees. Because the technology to drain them was lacking, these
early mines were shallow and thus, they were soon exhausted, so that
new pits had to be sunk, further from the waterways.

In 1725 coal from the Etherley colliery, near Bishop Auckland, cost
2½d at the pit head for one bushel (80 lb) and 8d on the street in
Darlington, 12 miles away. It was carried by trains of pack-horses or
mules, ten or twelve animals per ton of coal, to the staithes on the River
Tees at Stockton. The Tees Navigation Company maintained the river
– somewhat ineffectually – as a commercial waterway from the sea to
Stockton, and the water was shallow at the upper end. At Stockton coal
sometimes had to be tipped into keels which carried it down river to
deeper water, where it would be reloaded on to colliers and taken to
east-coast ports and, principally, London. Transport and labour costs
made the fuel very expensive.

In the north of Durham, on the Tyne, there were some wagonways
between the mines and the river, most notably the Tanfield line with
its 48-ft-tall embankment and 102-ft-span Tanfield Arch. Throughout
the eighteenth and early nineteenth centuries there had been plans for

canals between Auckland and the Tees, indeed between Newcastle and Carlisle, which had come to nothing largely because of the problem of the 'wayleave'. Most of County Durham was in the hands of a few great magnates and farmed out to their tenants, who demanded large sums of money annually in return for allowing wagonways or canals to cross their lands. This system was little better than highway robbery. In 1729 a Parliamentary Inquiry was mounted into the impositions of William Ramsay and William Cotesworth, tenants of the Bishop of Durham in the Wickham and Gateshead manors; it was stated that these men had 'played the tyrant over their neighbours, made themselves masters of the wayleaves and took £3,000 p.a. from the colliery, which was ⅓th more than the colliery owner got'.[1] The wayleave system was as much responsible for the inflated price of coal as the inadequate methods of transporting it, and high-priced coal increased the cost of every manufactured item.

In May 1818, the Earl of Strathmore, the owner of the Evenwood colliery, west of Bishop Auckland, proposed to build a canal to the Tees over land compulsorily purchased under statutory powers. The route was blatantly self-interested – from his own colliery directly to the river at Portrack, near Stockton.

Stockton people were delighted with the proposal but the businessmen of Darlington, Yarm and the other bypassed places were alarmed to be placed at such a disadvantage. A Committee, mainly comprising Quaker businessmen, was formed to oppose the 'Northern line' of the canal, and included Yarm citizens Thomas Meynell, Jeremiah Cairns (his steward) and Benjamin Flounders, a gentleman of independent means, Jonathan Backhouse and Edward Pease of Darlington, Leonard Raisbeck of Stockton and Henry Stobart of Bishop Auckland. They set out to raise support for a canal from Auckland through Darlington to the River Tees, with a branch to Yarm. Soon afterwards, Cairns's relation George Overton, who had engineered the Pen-y-darran and other tramways in South Wales, wrote advising Cairns to construct an iron way. The Committee agreed, and the earliest written mention of the 'Stockton & Darlington Railway' was in a letter from one Richard Jackson to Jonathan Backhouse, dated 21 September 1818.

On 13 November 1818, the S&DR Committee called a General Meeting of shareholders in Darlington to persuade them of the merits of a tramway or a railway, rather than a canal. (It must be remembered that while canals were then conventional and profitable, a lengthy, *public* iron way was a leap into the unknown.) Backhouse and Pease argued successfully for an iron way of some sort. The Committee's proposal was for an expenditure of £113,000 for the main line and three branches, and estimated the profit at 15 per cent per annum. Since they did not know what the running costs would be, this was exceedingly optimistic, though it was noted that the Sirhowy tramway, built in 1802 as part of the Monmouthshire Canal, paid 18 per cent a year. Pease took the unusually honest and practical step of playing down estimates of maximum income in favour of an assured 5 per cent. In careful, though conjectural, detail he showed how an iron way could not fail to earn a minimum of 5 per cent for its investors.

The Meeting was persuaded to support the Committee in its plans for an iron way from the Auckland collieries to Stockton, with a branch to Darlington and Yarm; Pease's nineteen-year-old son Joseph wrote the Prospectus, and within seven days £25,000 had been subscribed towards the estimated cost of the line. Some 24 per cent of the total required was provided by Norwich Quaker bankers: the Barclays, Birkbecks, and in particular the Gurneys (who were related by marriage to the Pease family). The iron way proposal even won over most of the 'Northern line' canal supporters; there remained, however, a rump of opposition to the S&DR which re-formed to agitate for a direct railway line from Auckland to the Tees, and whose obstruction tended to increase the legal costs of the S&DR.

The type of iron way was not decided when the first Stockton & Darlington Railway Bill for 'making and maintaining a railway or tramroad from the river Tees at Stockton to Witton Park colliery with several branches' went before Parliament early in 1819. Opposing the Bill were the protagonists of the direct 'Northern line', the Trustees of the turnpike roads in the area, and the carriers who used them. The most formidable opponents of the scheme included the local wayleave owner Lord Eldon, and the Earl of Darlington. The latter, an ardent foxhunter, feared his hunting would be spoiled and was more concerned about this than the loss of his wayleave income.[2] Lord Eldon questioned why the land had to be sold, and asked what was wrong with the wayleave system (to which the answer must surely have been: nothing at all, if you happened to be Lord Eldon).

Eldon was worried that the railway company, in getting possession of a ribbon of land, would act in as rapacious a manner as his noble self: 'If the soil on which the railway is built belongs to the railway, and if there is a seam of coal passing beneath the railway, then this too will belong to the railway and the owner must stop his workings or the railway *may make him pay what they please* for passing under their line.'[3]

The Bill was lost, by 93 to 106 votes, on 5 April 1819. Far from being discouraged by the result, the Committee was pleased with the strength of support and determined to try again in 1820. Meanwhile it was also active in disarming the opposition. The route was altered to avoid the Earl of Darlington's foxhunting land, and Lord Eldon was bought off with substantial compensation. The protagonists of the 'Northern line' agreed, on 9 December 1819, to give up their plan in consideration of the S&DR Committee's promising to restrict their tolls to 2d per ton/mile for coal to be sold locally and ½d per ton/mile for export coal. The Prospectus for this Bill contained a passage which has a contemporary ring, even today:

> The cost of carriage of coal will be halved for a district of 40,000 people. A great nuisance will be removed from the roads by removing the numerous one-horse carts and carrying horses and asses which now infest them, for about ¹⁄₁₀th of this number on rail.

The S&DR Bill was lodged in Parliament for the Session of 1820, and included a clause to extend the proposed Evenwood branch 4 miles further westwards to Hagger Leases Lane, close to Butterknowle and Copley collieries, which were owned by the Revd Luke Prattman.[4] On 29 January 1820 the death of King George III stopped Parliamentary business in Private Bills. The Committee determined to return in 1821 and meanwhile they revised their plan for the line of railway and strengthened their support in Durham. The proposed Hagger Leases branch was dropped, so that the line would terminate at the Earl of Strathmore's[5] Evenwood colliery. (Presumably Strathmore did not want Prattman to compete with him and would otherwise have opposed the Bill.) Lord Barrington was persuaded to become a shareholder, and the Trustees of the Darlington–Bishop Auckland turnpike were bought out.

Having removed the main opposition the Committee expected a walk-over in Parliament in 1821, but they almost failed to get through the door. Parliamentary Standing Orders required that a company should deposit four-fifths of the capital required to build the line before the Bill was presented. The Committee found itself £7000 short of this amount, and the entire sum was loaned as a mortgage by the Darlington mill-owner Edward Pease, who had already subscribed £3000 in shares. Thereafter, the Bill had a clear run and received the

Royal Assent on 19 April 1821, the twenty-first Railway Act to be passed since 1800.

The now-famous title is something of a misnomer – Darlington was barely half-way along the route, and was in any case on a branch line. The authorized line was for a main line of 26¾ miles, from Witton Park colliery, west of Bishop Auckland, to Stockton-on-Tees, with four branches: to Coundon (north-west of Bishop Auckland); to Norless House (West Auckland to Evenwood); to Darlington; and to Yarm (south of Stockton). The whole system amounted to 36¾ miles. The official seal of the new Company bore the uniquely splendid motto: At Private Risk for Public Service.

The railway was to be a public highway, a turnpike road, open to anyone who wished to run a passenger or freight service on payment of toll – but it was not to be used during the hours of darkness. The general public seem to have been betrayed by the S&DR Committee in that they had been promised coal tolls at a maximum of 2d a ton locally, but in fact the 1821 Act permitted a maximum of 4d. On coal for export – 'sea coal' – the S&DR kept its promise and encouraged the trade by the very low toll of ½d a ton. The novelty of the undertaking is reflected in the wording of Section 2 of the Act which was at once ambiguous and naive. Where public roads crossed the iron way on the level Section 2 enacted that: 'the flanch [flange] of such railways or tramways for the purpose of guiding the wheels of carriages shall not exceed 3 inches above the level of such road'. The crossing gates were closed against the iron way – and the engine driver or horse leader, having opened the gate, was obliged to close it behind him on pain of a £2 fine, half of which would go to the informer and half to the poor of the parish.

Even before the Act was gained, Edward Pease, who had the largest stake of any individual in the venture, had grave doubts about the capabilities of the railway's Surveyor and would-be Engineer, George Overton. Pease felt sure a better route could be made. On 19 April, before he knew that the Bill had become law, he invited George Stephenson to meet him to discuss the Stockton & Darlington – not because he had built locomotives, but because he had also entered into civil engineering. He had rebuilt the Killingworth colliery to take steam-engines and he had designed and was in the process of successfully completing (by November 1822) a brand new, 8-mile-long railway for the Hetton colliery – his greatest work to date.

Stephenson interviewed Edward Pease on 19 April. They were two of a kind, rough-hewn and practical, and they got on well from the outset. Stephenson's principle, which seems an obvious one – that the best railway was a straight one – was the opposite of Overton's proposed meandering route for the S&DR. Of even greater importance was Stephenson's insistence that the route must be locomotive-hauled. Up to that time no one had given any thought to the matter; and indeed, the Act was vague on the matter of locomotion, stating merely that haulage would be by 'men, horses or otherwise'. The Committee still had even to decide whether to make the S&DR a tramway or a railway. There were 300 miles of tramway in South Wales and 225 miles of edge-rail railway in the Durham area, and of course Stephenson was an edge-rail protagonist. The broad running surface of the tramway would enable ordinary road carts to use the iron way, since they had only to be approximately to the gauge of the line. On the Surrey Iron Railway in 1805 one horse had once, for a wager, hauled 38¼ tons on slightly rising gradients, and on South Wales tramways 25 tons were regularly horse-hauled. But as has already been noted, the disadvantage of the flanged tramroad system was friction. On the edge-rail system there was no problem from debris, friction was reduced, permitting a horse to pull heavier loads. Obviously only wagons with flanged wheels could use the track; thus increased efficiency tended to make the edge-rail road an 'exclusive' rather than an 'open' right of way. The question of the source of motive power – animal or steam-engine, stationary and/or locomotive – was not even considered, the unspoken assumption being that, in either case, the wagons would be animal-hauled whatever the type of rail.

On 23 July the S&DR Committee took two historic decisions: to adopt the edge-rail railway and to employ George Stephenson to make a new survey to improve the route. The Minutes stated that they called in Stephenson because of the 'high character they had received of him from various quarters as an intelligent, active, experienced and practical man, assiduous in his attention to what he undertook – and moderate in his charges'. Stephenson estimated that his survey for the S&DR would take five weeks, and asked for £140 as payment for himself and his assistants – his eighteen-year-old son Robert and John Dixon, a young local man whose family had been associated with engineering canal projects in the area for many years. The survey was to begin on 15 October 1821; Pease gave Stephenson a Quaker's specification:

In making thy survey it must be borne in mind that this is for a great public way, to remain as long as there is any coal remains in the district. Its construction must be solid and as little machinery introduced as possible – in fact we remind thee to proceed in all thy level, estimates and calculations with that care and economy which would influence thee if the whole of the work was thy own.[6]

The injunction to have 'as little machinery as possible' indicates that Stephenson had not yet been able to convince Pease of the benefits of the steam-locomotive.

The route Stephenson devised was a new concept in railway planning. Where Overton's route was a succession of tight curves, around the hills and yet with steep gradients, Stephenson's had easier gradients and the now-familiar railway-line contour – long straights and sweeping curves. Stephenson's route reduced by 3 miles the distance to be constructed, and, by dispensing with the Darlington branch, also reduced the estimated cost to £74,300.

The Committee was delighted and, on 22 January 1822, Stephenson was formally engaged as Surveyor of the line. He took as his Principal Assistants his son Robert and John Dixon. On 23 May the building work began on the parts of the line not requiring to be re-routed. The first rails on the Stockton & Darlington Railway were laid by Thomas Meynell at St John's Well, Stockton, in the presence of the town's Mayor, Corporation and citizens.

A new Bill was required to sanction those parts of Stephenson's route that deviated from the path authorized by the 1821 Act. Stephenson was still very anxious that steam-locomotives should be used and took Pease to see the Killingworth engines at work. (His friend Nicholas Wood, the Manager of the mine, had accompanied Stephenson on his first visit to see Pease.) The latter was won over, and when the new Bill was presented to Parliament, early in 1823, it contained a Section specifically authorizing the use of 'loco-motive or moveable steam engines'. The Bill became an Act on 23 May.[7] Shortly after this, Stephenson persuaded the Quakers to invest in a locomotive factory which was then established at Forth Street, Newcastle, as 'Robert Stephenson & Co.' Overton, the superseded Engineer, commented that 'an engine on a public [rail] road would be a perpetual nuisance'. He assumed that the horse would always be the standard means of haulage and that the locomotive would remain a novelty.

Stephenson used wrought-iron rails instead of the usual cast-iron but the improvement stopped there. His rails were very short, about

15 ft, and were carried on heavy stone blocks, sunk to ground-level, which subsided under the weight of trains and were then very difficult to raise to the original level. This was a retrograde step, since timber cross-sleepers had been used by Outram in 1785. The rails were laid to the relatively wide gauge of 4 ft 8 in. A more usual gauge for wagonways was 4 ft. The 1805 Surrey Iron Railway had a 4-ft gauge, the South Wales tramways were around 4 ft 2 in., but the colliery wagonways of the north-east tended to be at the upper end of the 4-ft range; Kenton & Coxlode was 4 ft 7½ in. and Wylam was 5 ft. Since the Killingworth colliery railway, on which engines of Stephenson's design were running, was laid to 4 ft 8 in., it was natural that Stephenson, who was supplying the S&DR locomotives, should use his own gauge. Soon afterwards the extra half-inch was added to give a sure clearance between the rail and the flanges of the wagon's wheels, in order to avoid 'binding' and permit the freest running.

Engineers and promoters of proposed railways – in particular the Liverpool & Manchester, but also from Europe and America – came to view the S&DR and to ask the advice of its engineers and management. The 4 ft 8½ in.-gauge thus came to be exported abroad as well as becoming automatically accepted in Britain as the 'standard' gauge.[8]

The steady progress of the works on the S&DR coincided with a period of confidence in Britain, and in 1822 the first of several 'railway manias' took hold. Entrepreneurial spirits all over Britain proposed trunk railway schemes; one, with an estimated capital requirement of £2,500,000 was to link London to Birmingham, Derby, Nottingham and Leeds, and from Leeds, east and west to Manchester and Hull – the classic 'T'-shaped trunk system postulated by William James in 1808. Another scheme was mooted for a London to Edinburgh line, an 'absurd' notion, according to less adventurous spirits.

A rather less ambitious project involved the previously shelved Hagger Leases branch. On 18 August 1823 Prattman asked the S&DR to obtain powers to build a new branch line through Evenwood to his collieries. On 13 September 1823 the requisite Bill was lodged in Parliament, with Robert Stephenson and John Dixon named as the Engineers – George was too busy supervising the construction of the S&DR. This Bill was opposed by the widow and Trustees of the eighth Earl of Strathmore on the grounds that their business would be placed at a disadvantage if Prattman's coal was allowed to come out from Butterknowle and Copley by rail. So powerful were these people in relation to Luke Prattman that the normally punctilious Quakers felt forced to abandon the Hagger Leases branch. Prattman, however, persisted and warned the S&DR of his fiercest opposition to their Bill unless it included his branch line. Pease and company had to admit the justice of Prattman's case; the Hagger Leases branch clause was duly reinserted, and the third S&DR Bill became law on 17 May 1824.

3

'At Private Risk for Public Service'

THE CONSTRUCTION OF George Stephenson's improved route was extremely laborious: the road-bed had to be built wide enough for a 4 ft 8½ in.-gauge double track and included embankments 48 ft high. The works were carried out, over 26 miles of line, embankments, cuttings and bridges, by many small contractors, local building firms and local labourers, so Stephenson was fully engaged in their supervision. At the Myers Flat swamp hundreds of tons of hand-hewn rock were horse-hauled to the site and tipped – apparently, for several weeks, into oblivion. Stephenson persevered and eventually a firm road-bed was achieved across the waste.

The Brusselton and Etherley collieries were to be connected to the main trunk by rope-worked incline planes. Etherley, for instance, was situated in a valley with a 500-ft ridge between it and the railway, and so the coal wagons were hoisted up by a stationary engine. George Stephenson made the specifications for the engines, Robert designed them and Timothy Hackworth actually built them.

In May 1824 George Stephenson was appointed Surveyor of the proposed Liverpool & Manchester Railway, which obliged him to give even more responsibility for the S&DR to his two assistants. A month later Robert Stephenson had resigned. What had happened was that, in June, Timothy Hackworth had been offered a three-year contract as

Engineer with a British-owned company formed to mine the newly emergent countries of South America. He had declined it and had recommended Robert Stephenson for the post. Robert had taken it and departed forthwith.[1]

To have defected at such a critical time seems odd. Perhaps the twenty-year-old was irked by his father's domination of and dependence on him. (Robert was actually the Surveyor and Engineer of the Hagger Leases branch of the S&DR and was also in charge at Forth Street.) If Robert was discontented, the oppressive feeling could have been exacerbated by the imprisonment for bankruptcy of William James, the original Proposer and Surveyor of the L&MR. James had been a good friend to father and son, publicizing George's engines and giving Robert work when making his survey for the L&MR route. George Stephenson had given James no support in his time of need and now had his job as Surveyor of the Liverpool line.[2]

George Stephenson asked Hackworth to take Robert's place as Manager of the Forth Street locomotive factory in Newcastle. Hackworth was then employed by his good friend William Patter at Walbottle colliery as Foreman Blacksmith, and was reluctant to leave him. He might also have reflected that Robert Stephenson had gone half-way around the world to escape from working under his own father. Hackworth accepted the post only until George Stephenson returned from Liverpool. The Forth Street works had just received its first order: an engine for the S&DR, the specification of which Stephenson senior had prepared. When Stephenson returned to Newcastle at the end of 1824, Hackworth returned to Walbottle, not to his old job but to consider his future.

The most striking work on the line was the bridge over the River Skerne at Darlington (see Map 1). Stephenson intended to span the gap with an iron bridge on brick piers but the soft ground of the river bank made it difficult to create a suitable foundation and no progress was made in erecting the bridge for over a year. By April 1824 Pease had lost confidence in Stephenson's ability in the matter and ordered him to ask the advice of a Durham architect, Ignatius Bonomi, who had designed Lambton Hall and Durham Courthouse and Jail. Galled, Stephenson put off meeting Bonomi for five weeks; on 18 May the two men met and discussed the bridge and its foundations, but Stephenson seems not to have been moved to any action, since on 11 June the Committee went over his head and approached Bonomi directly for his professional assistance. Bonomi recommended various modifications, and the Committee ordered that the bridge be built to the revised plan. The foundation stone was laid on 2 July 1824. Because, however, no local ironmakers would quote a price for supplying the ironwork, Stephenson himself suggested on 19 October that the bridge be made in stone; this was done, but to Bonomi's designs. The central arch rose 30 ft above the river with a span of 39 ft 6 in.; there were piers 8 ft wide on each side of the arch and two side arches each of 8 ft span. Since the bridge was 22 ft wide at base and corbelled out at parapet level, it would appear to have been constructed for double track.[3]

George Stephenson's great strength, born largely of self-interest, lay in recognizing talent, recruiting first-class assistants, in his strong leadership, and his ability to propel a project forward. He wanted Timothy Hackworth's inventive and practical genius for the S&DR but the first meeting he arranged between Pease and Hackworth ended without agreement. Hackworth wanted to branch out into business on his own, and so his terms for going to work for the S&DR were steeper than the granite Quakers were prepared to pay. Then Stephenson discovered that Hackworth intended to open a loco-motive factory in Newcastle – and his desire to have Hackworth working for the S&DR acquired greater urgency. On 13 May 1825 Pease agreed to all Hackworth's demands and, four months before the railway was open, Hackworth was appointed its Superintendent of stationary and locomotive engines.[4] He was thus responsible for erect-ing and supervising the construction of the S&DR locomotive works at New Shildon.

The Stockton & Darlington Railway was opened on Tuesday 27 September 1825 to great rejoicing – although it was far from complete. It consisted of 33 miles of single track with passing loops, together with the ¾ mile of the Yarm branch and the ½ mile of the Evenwood branch. There were no engine-sheds, no coal staithes for direct dis-charge of coal from wagon to ships, and practically no siding space for wagon storage. The Black Boy, Coundon, Croft and Hagger Leases branches remained to be built. The entire capital of the Company had been spent: compensation to landowners had swallowed £18,000 more than anticipated,[5] and all the works had cost more than estimated, forcing the Committee to borrow £60,000 against their own promis-sory notes – and that had to be repaid in six months. In December 1825 the South American bubble burst and banking in Britain collapsed. Those who had loaned money to the S&DR urgently (and vainly) demanded to be paid. The following May, Pease paid the railway's employees out of his own pocket.[6]

When it opened, the S&DR Company owned a single locomotive (*Locomotion No. 1*), one passenger carriage and 150 coal wagons. The *Locomotion* had been designed by George Stephenson after the usual manner of all his engines since 1815, but Hackworth had invented an outside coupling-rod for the wheels as an improvement on Stephenson's chain coupling. The engine's boiler design had not, however, been improved in ten years; its steam-raising capacity, though possibly sufficient for a short, colliery railway, was very inadequate for constant steam along a railway 26 miles long.

The S&DR Directors intended to be the main carriers on the line while still maintaining the road as a public highway and earning a profit from the tolls they would charge the other users. On the turnpike roads, the Royal Mail was carried in a three-way contract: the coach, the horses and the road were all owned by different individuals, each trying to make his own profit, and this system was accepted without question as the way to organize the new railway. The maintenance of the road, the rolling stock required to move all the traffic, and the maintenance of all necessary warehouses, stationary and locomotive engines and coal staithes, were as far as possible contracted out – providing the Company with a known, fixed price for all their operations.

It was not merely a matter of the new railroad following the example of the turnpike road; there was also the relatively new philosophy of 'Free Trade', both nationally and internationally, which was opposed to the existing system of monopoly companies and the chartered monopolies of corporations and crafts. The new ideas were most eruditely postulated by Adam Smith (1723–1790) in 1774; William Pitt had even reduced or removed some import tariffs when in 1793 the first great European war broke out. In 1820 'free trade' and 'anti-monopoly' were again dynamic ideas. The S&DR was enacted as a free market in transport: demand would be met by enterprising suppliers; fares would be kept down by competition between carriers; operational costs would be kept down by competition between the aspiring contractors. On the other hand the same people, working for the lowest rates, would have to pay the interest on the capital they had raised to finance their own operations. All would be individualism and competition.

Applied to a railway, these principles created a mass of complications and conflicting interests. Timothy Hackworth and William Lister contracted with the S&DR to maintain and operate the winding engines at the Black Boy and Brusselton inclines at the rate of 5s 2d and 6s 4d, respectively, per 100 tons hoisted, – but the ropes around the winding drums, by which the wagons were raised and lowered over the inclines, were the responsibility of John Grimshaw who received a fixed sum annually from the S&DR. Grimshaw's income depended on the long life of the rope he supplied, but the health of the rope depended on the careful working of Hackworth's men – who had no interest in the longevity of Grimshaw's rope but a great deal of interest in moving as much tonnage as possible over the inclines. Grimshaw blamed Hackworth for damaging his rope and demanded compensation from the Committee which was not forthcoming; thus Grimshaw made a loss and the Committee had to find another optimist to supply and maintain the winding rope.

Matthew Stephenson, who had a contract with the S&DR for hauling coals and shunting the sidings at Stockton by horse-power, supplied his employees with horses and reported to the Committee on 21 June 1832:

> I have had the misfortune to lose one of my best horses on 16th which makes 9 horses I have lost since I came under the employ of the railway besides some that have gone lame at work. The horse I lost on 16th cost me £21 3 years ago. This misfortune occurred as I was coming over the suspension bridge.[7] When the wagons gets [sic] over the centre of the bridge they follow the horse quick. There was a horse before him that was rather slow which made the wagons come into contact with each other and before the man could bring them. He lay on the brake as soon as he saw the danger but the wagon end caught a hind leg and broke it. I hope the railway company will not take offence for me making application for a little of their assistance as my losses have been extremely heavy.[8]

He was paid £10 for the loss of this one horse. Matters had become so bad for him that he had been forced to ask for help, but he knew the futility of attempting to gain compensation for all the horses he had lost. Whatever the imagined advantages of the 'hands-off' system of railway management at the start, the reality of employing several small operators to run their trains at 'competitive' prices proved the fallacy of the theory. The small contractors, fixing their charges low to keep their jobs, did not make enough money, and were unable to recoup their losses when these occurred. There was also the problem of hauling passenger and freight trains up and down a single line of railway: people who had no loyalty to anyone but themselves would not willingly give way into a loop to allow an opposing train to pass.

For the first few months of the railway's operation the Committee conveyed passengers between Stockton and Darlington in their own, horse-drawn carriage named the *Express*. The business grossed just over £1 a day – before tax – and so the S&DR leased the service on 1 April 1826 to Richard Pickersgill, who paid £200 a year to run the *Express* coach and another, his own property. Soon other independent coach operators were in competition with him including some female innkeepers: Jane Scott, of the King's Head, Darlington (*Defiance*), Martha Howson, of the Black Lion Inn, Stockton (*Defence*), for instance. All these coaches, just a single stage-coach body on a spring-less, railway chassis, carried approximately sixteen passengers, (some of them on the roof in the old way), and parcels. On Stockton race days they arrived crammed and festooned with as many as forty-six people; at such times the coach would be hauled by a pair of horses.

Noting this enthusiasm for running coaches on the S&DR, the Committee decided to raise its charges, and imposed a toll of 3d per mile, rather than accepting a 'per annum' rent; at the end of his contract year, Pickersgill too came under this agreement.

By the end of 1826 there were seven coaches running over the 12 miles between Stockton and Darlington. The average speed was 10 mph with a maximum of 14 mph. A horse could canter at 12 mph, hauling sixteen people, without particular effort: it is recorded that on the level the traces hung loose. The coaches were brightly painted, in a manner similar to the road coaches, the guards carried the traditional horn which they blew as a warning of approach. Some passengers even said they enjoyed the experience as their springless coach clicked and bumped over the short rails. The main difficulty was that the horses became exhausted and lame from so much long-distance cantering – and of course they would get stuck following coal trains, which were supposed to give way to passenger coaches, but rarely did.

Though the turnpike railway system created operational chaos, the simple presence of the railway as a public facility for transport enabled 10,000 tons of coal to be delivered at Stockton in the first three months alone. Substantial quantities of good coal – much larger lumps than could be fitted into the pack-horse panniers – would arrive at Stockton and, because of the ease of transit, could be profitably sold for 8s 6d [42½p] per ton, rather than the pre-railway price of 18s [90p] a ton.

The S&DR, however, was not making a profit. By 30 June 1827 the Committee owned six locomotives, all built by Robert Stephenson & Co. at Newcastle, but these were unreliable in service and frequently under repair. To fill the gap the S&DR hired more horses. At this stage George Stephenson was hard-pressed to keep up with his engineering and surveying commitments to the S&DR and Liverpool & Manchester, let alone improve the design of engines at the Newcastle works – always supposing that he had the ability to do so: he had made no improvements to his design of 1815 in ten years.

Without Robert's engineering skill and with Hackworth's enormous talent employed merely in trying to maintain the primitive Stephenson engines in working order, the locomotive costs of the S&DR spiralled alarmingly upwards. Samuel Smiles, the Stephensons' sympathetic biographer, states that in 1827, 'the factory was by no means in a prosperous state';[9] both Edward Pease and Thomas Richardson, the principal shareholders in the works (and the S&DR) wrote to Robert begging him to come home. Pease wrote: 'I can assure thee that thy business at Newcastle, as well as thy father's engineering, have suffered very much from thy absence and unless thou soon return the former will be given up ... what is done is not done with credit to the house.'[10]

By the latter half of 1827 the S&DR Committee was 'on the point of abandoning locomotive haulage'.[11] George Stephenson now begged his son to return: 'The fate of the steam locomotive depends on it'. Robert returned in November 1827. Hackworth meanwhile asked the Committee's permission to build an engine at Shildon that he promised would fulfil all the requirements of the S&DR. The result was the *Royal George*, the world's first six-wheeled, all-wheels-coupled engine. It had the largest, most powerful boiler yet, whose 'U'-shaped flue provided the greatest area of heating surface of any boiler. Feed water to the boiler was pre-heated with exhaust steam to save fuel, and it was also fitted with the first spring safety-valve on the S&DR. The slide-valves were driven by eccentrics which could be reversed without stopping the engine, and which were designed with 'lap' to make use of the expansive property of steam. Exhaust steam was vented into the chimney through the first-ever specifically designed 'blast pipe', a coned exhaust jet mounted centrally at the base of the chimney. Never was there such a list of 'firsts' and positive improvements in a single engine: it was the greatest leap forward in locomotive design for twelve years. It might therefore have been forgiven for some 'teething troubles', but there were none; furthermore, the economy of its operation was such that the S&DR Directors, who were seriously considering abandoning lomotive haulage in favour of horses, regained their confidence in steam locomotion and voted to pay Hackworth a bonus of £20.[12]

Until more Hackworth engines could be put into service, large tonnages of coal were still mainly horse-hauled. The poor animals were made to haul four-wagon trains holding 12½ tons of coal; the only respite was on the downhill sections, when they trotted behind their free-wheeling train, or when they stood in the passing loops to allow steam-hauled trains by. A good horse hauling four chaldrons of coal could make three round trips in six days between Auckland and Stockton, but would not at that rate remain a 'good' horse for long.

In July 1828 George Stephenson introduced to the S&DR his 'dandy cart'. A four-wheeled trolley with railed-in sides and a manger full of hay was attached to the rear of the four wagons, and in this the horse would ride on the downhill stretches. Horses are intelligent creatures and quickly develop new skills. Having been uncoupled from their train, they stood aside to let the wagons by and then jumped into the moving cart. Some sat on their haunches, the better to rest, and all appeared to enjoy the ride. The horses came to expect to ride and, if the dandy cart was not at the rear, would try to climb on to the last coal truck of the train. With this system, a horse could make four round trips a week, carrying the same load, without going lame. The improvement in their health was noticeable.

Pease had hoped that the S&DR would be able to restrict the amount of rolling stock it owned, and that the collieries would supply wagons for their needs. This they did, but with no other power to influence them, the colliery owners short-sightedly put on to the rails the cheapest possible wagons, and skimped on their maintenance. It soon became obvious that regulations to ensure the standardized construction of 'private-owner' wagons were essential. For instance, the wagons would have to fit into the coal staithes' lifting and tipping mechanism, plans for which had been drawn up by the S&DR. There was no room in this area for individualism. Private-owner wagons that were cheaply made and not properly maintained would break down on the line.[13] Wagon buffers – such as they were – were not fixed at a standard height above the rail nor at a standard distance apart; furthermore, the type of coupling chains and draw-hooks should have been standard but were not.

These wagons also required storage space in sidings while waiting to be unloaded and again while awaiting the trip back to the colliery. The shortcomings of what had been provided quickly became apparent and Pease could see the 'urgent necessity' of providing additional accommodation, and controlling the trains – and even the ships that took the coal away. But this was difficult to achieve in the 'free market' situation of the turnpike railway. The existence of hundreds of privately owned wagons instead of S&DR-owned, 'common-user' wagons created yet more complications and expense because of the extra marshalling, extra sidings, extra engines and extra staff required to carry out the work. The need was obvious; the remedy was a very long time coming.

4

'Perfect Liberty'

O N 10 MARCH 1829, nearly four years after the main line had opened, the Revd Luke Prattman complained to the Committee about his loss of revenue owing to their failure to construct the promised Hagger Leases branch. Pease decided that 'he has a right to a line so it is now a matter to set the compensation. His loss is the lesser amount of coal vended from his colliery from 26.9.25 – 10.3.29 and I am of the opinion that proper compensation is £610.'[1] This sum was paid on 21 March 1829 and further compensation grudgingly followed on 31 December, though the S&DR was very short of funds. With his collieries nearer Barnard Castle than Auckland, Prattman seems to have been regarded as an interloper and not to have been fairly treated by the Committee, possibly because the owners of the large, Auckland district collieries were also Directors and/or major shareholders of the S&DR. When the Hagger Leases branch was finally opened on 1 October 1830, it was so lightly constructed that it could only be used by horses.

The Black Boy, Coundon and Croft branches had opened the previous year, and the congestion of the main trunk became severe. The service Prattman received from the S&DR was so poor, his coal wagons took so long to get to Stockton and return empty, that he decided to invoke his statutory right to haul his own trains over the line – and advertised for men to be 'horse leaders'. Of all those using the line, the horse men were the most pugnacious and least amenable to rules, and the Directors summoned Prattman to appear before them. In reply to this Prattman wrote to them:

> I conceived that coal owners were at perfect liberty to lead [haul] coals to the end of the line . . . [on] a public railway . . . everyone is at liberty to use the conveyance provided he conformed to the regulations and paid the tolls . . . I should never have thought of leading my own coals but for the overpowering influence of circumstances which have forced me into this measure. Out of our 114 wagons we have not been able, on average, to send more than 12 a day . . . every possible exertion has been in vain. The sale of 12 wagons per day will not pay the expenses of the railway . . . wagons have been grievously detained at Stockton and you will not draw half what we could send and so I am left with no alternative but to draw them myself.[2]

The S&DR engines of the period 1825–30 rumbled along at 5 mph on a good day. A driver would get off and walk beside the engine and if it could keep up with him he was pleased. The engines tended to throw hot cinders, and their effort might be eased as they passed a wood or cornfield, in the hope of not setting fire to the crops. Working normally they showered their passengers with red hot cinders that scorched or even burned holes in their clothing. There was no signalling, and brakes, where they existed, were very rudimentary; thus all the trains were in constant danger of collision on the single track. Railway Acts of Parliament did not concern themselves with safety matters for decades to come.

Travelling 'outside' on the stage-coach-like carriages was cheaper than going within and as a result it was common to have thirteen passengers squashed on to the outside seats. Not surprisingly people sometimes fell off the roof and sustained terrible injuries under the heavy, iron wheels. The contemporary answer to this was *not* to stop the deeply ingrained idea of riding on the roof of a carriage, but instead to place nets below door-level to prevent those who had fallen off from going under the wheels.

Train crews would scramble over the goods wagons to put out fires started by sparks from the engine, or walk over the roofs of carriages or squeeze along the footboards, to maintain order. At least as early as 1844 there were railway enthusiasts: people who simply could not resist putting their heads out of the window, risking red hot cinders in their eyes, to catch a glimpse of the engine at work. In October 1844 a passenger complained to the Directors about Guard Harbourne. 'I had my head out of the window', he wrote:

watching *the action of the engine* when he came along and in a very peremptory manner told me to 'take my head in'. I refused and he immediately attacked me by thrice thrusting at my breast. I still kept my position when he violently pushed me on the head so that he doubled-up my hat. I leave you to deal with this matter as you see fit.[3]

Merchandise trains carried a firewatcher whose job it was to put out fires on the train or lineside. In June 1840 a wagon carrying barrels of spirits – and a single barrel of gunpowder – was set on fire by cinders from the engine. A passer-by, full of (public) spirit, leaped into the blaze and extinguished it; only then did he discover that he had been standing beside a barrel of gunpowder which looked no different from the rest.

There was a real need for a police force on the S&DR: the Northumbrians were a hardy, independent breed to whom the concept of 'industrial discipline' was unknown and individual honour – or ego – was everything; and most disagreements had to be settled with fists. This was certainly the case on the roads, but occasions for offence were greater now that the coaches were running head-on at each other on a single line railway. The S&DR rule was that under these circumstances a coach had to reverse to the loop since it was lighter than a loaded coal train, although it is recorded not only that drivers of passenger coaches would fight drivers of approaching trains to settle the question of who was going to reverse, but that their passengers would also join in. Sometimes honour was satisfied when a coach was lifted off the track by its passengers to allow the other to pass and then re-railed: at least then they had not had to go backwards.

Because of a lack of understanding of the dangers involved (and doubtless also through exhaustion and exposure to the elements) there were several fatalities annually on the S&DR. Thomas Jackson, a brakesman or 'bank rider' at the Etherley incline, was killed as he applied handbrakes to wagons descending the hill; George English, another bank rider, was killed riding on wagons which became derailed at the foot of the incline. These bank riders were in constant danger, working long hours on the exposed moorland hillside in any weather. There was also the problem of trespassers: pedestrians who sometimes became entangled with passing wagons so that they were dragged under their wheels; others who hitched illicit rides and were killed or maimed when they fell under wagons on which they were riding.

In 1830, the S&DR established a railway police force. It consisted of one Superintendent (earning £1 a week), four Inspectors, 'and as many gate keepers' [constables?] as shall be necessary'. Their duties were as follows:

> Officers will be on duty from 6 a.m. to 8 p.m. with meal breaks and will spend 4 hours on the line on Sunday nights whenever told to do so. They will carefully watch the speed of trains and invariably report any engine-man stopping at a public house. They will prevent trespass and will notice all broken wagons on the line. They will watch for any irregularity in the Company's servants including track maintenance. They are strictly enjoined to effect a cheerful readiness to protect all the Company's inter-ests, extending that care over persons and property which cannot be defined in these regulations and on all occasions combining a manly firm-ness with great civility.[4]

The S&DR police did not always live up to these ideals. They would often adopt a high-handed, even bullying attitude, particularly towards those who were not employees of the S&DR. On 9 June 1838 the Revd Prattman wrote to the Committee to complain about the conduct of Constable Wilson on the Hagger Leases branch:

> The circumstances are these ... my Agent, William Forster, had gone from Butterknowle to St. Helen's Auckland to catch the railway coach. My servant Fenwick brought Forster's horse back whilst also leading another horse pulling empty wagons. He met Wilson who complained that he [Wilson] had twice complained about him going up and down the railway with a horse of ours which had been on a similar errand. Fenwick told Wilson that he was on colliery business and that instead of stopping him he had better bring him up before the Committee. Wilson did not bring Fenwick before the Committee but instead, he seized the horse's bit and forcibly backed him off the road. Fenwick then struck Wilson.[5]

At the start of the S&DR's operations the Company's horse leaders and locomotive enginemen were paid a weekly wage of 22s [£1.10] and the S&DR provided all horse-feed, locomotive fuel, oil and stores. The S&DR Committee soon decided that this was too much of a 'hands-on' approach to railway management, not in accordance with their view of themselves as 'track authority' taking the tolls with as little expensive responsibility as possible. From 17 February 1826 their drivers were obliged to become self-employed 'contractors', working S&DR locomotives or horses. The locomotivemen worked for ¼d a ton, horse leaders for ½d a ton. Out of this the men had to buy their own fuel (or oats), oil, grate bars and all other stores to keep the horse or engine running, and even the grease for the wagon bearings, as well as paying their fireman and engine cleaner. Inevitably the tendency was for the men to penny-pinch, which raised their pay but did no good to the S&DR's engines. The men did so well that the Quaker Directors became concerned that they would spend their high wages 'recklessly', to the detriment of their morals – and lowered their rates.[6] The men's response to lower pay was to become sinful where before they had been sinless: they stole fuel from the chaldron wagons they were hauling to burn in their engines. Various rates of pay were tried which either gave the men too much money (by the Committee's reckoning) or was insufficient for the health of the S&DR's *engines*; and so, on 1 March 1837, the Committee reverted to the simple expedient of paying the men wages. In 1833 locomotive power cost the S&DR one third of a penny per ton hauled; in 1839 this had been reduced to ¼d as the design of the engines improved and speed, power and reliability increased under Hackworth's locomotive management. In 1840 S&DR locomotivemen were once again paid according to the number of 'trips' they made, and out of their pay they had to find the locomotive's fuel, oil and maintenance.[7]

The enginemen were exceptionally tough. They worked in any weather without the slightest protection, they ran without any brakes until Stephenson's antique engines were replaced by those of Hackworth's with a 'lever-reversible' gear. Then they could stop by putting their engine into reverse. On a Stephenson engine they could only stop their train by the fireman jumping off and pinning down the wagons' handbrakes. The men worked in constant danger of death or mutilation or of falling foul of the searching, personal scrutiny of Edward Pease, who patrolled the line on the look-out for rule-breakers. Most of the S&DR Directors were Quakers, with strong religious scruples, and often felt the moral obligation to give financial assistance to a recently bereaved railway widow, or to donate money to a Wesleyan school; but with true Puritan thrift they ensured that such charitable grants were not a drain on the financial resources of their railway nor yet on their own pockets. Their piety was funded by discovering misdemeanours in their locomotivemen's or other contractors' behaviour and deducting a fine from their pay. Misdemeanours there were in abundance. The men were required to work very long hours and exhaustion was normal, but if Pease or a policeman caught a driver asleep while his engine was in motion he was fined. Many years passed before the Directors went to the expense of supplying signalling on the line: there was no timetable for the mineral trains, no means of knowing, on a single track, the state of the line ahead, no brakes worth mentioning. One signal was erected at the Croft branch junction in 1840, but it was several years before further signals were raised. The men themselves could improvise a 'Danger' signal at night by carrying fire in a brazier on the last wagon, or by throwing a shovelful of fire into the air. (Some care was needed when fire was used in this way, since the S&DR track was ballasted with slag containing coal.)

The points (or switches) to divert a train from one track to another took the form of a movable piece of rail, which was altered by the loco-motiveman. As the wagons passed over it he had to check carefully whether it gaped between one wagon's wheels and the next, and if so, give it a quick shove to keep it closed. Even if he used a stick or metal bar to do this, the danger to the man was great. On 3 September 1839 a passenger train was derailed twice between Shildon and Darlington because of this type of switch. The first modern type of point was installed on the S&DR in 1839 at Newport, near Middlesbrough.

There were understandably many collisions or derailments and correspondingly many opportunities for the Committee to swell their charitable fund by shifting the blame on to the hapless enginemen.

The affair of George Lisle of Aycliffe, injured on the line on 20 October 1840, gives an insight into several aspects of the line's oper-ation – and also demonstrates the remarkable, physical fortitude of the men, and their resignation to their fate. Lisle was coming from Shildon by gravity with his horse-drawn train of four loaded stone wagons. The horse was riding in the dandy behind. Near to the 'Wasser' (prob-ably 'Whessoe') curve, Ralph Coulson with the locomotive *Enterprise*, running tender first, came up behind. Lisle was pushing his wagons around the curve, the horse still in the dandy, and beckoned to Coulson to give him a shove. Coulson came on and Lisle got up in the dandy to hold the horse's head. The engine's tender struck the dandy and threw it off the railway; the horse was killed on the spot and the engine wheels ran over Lisle's legs. His head and back were also much injured.

At the subsequent Inquiry the Coroner seemed greatly concerned to establish that a leg actually could be broken by being struck by a wagon. Benjamin Croft, who had been horse-hauling a train ahead of Lisle, was called as witness and questioned specifically on this point. He testified to the fact that he himself had suffered a broken leg after it was struck by a dandy wagon.

As regards the accident to Lisle, Croft declared:

I seen [*sic*] Ralph Coulson shoving George Lisle['s] stone wagons with the 'Enterprise' on the Aycliffe levels. When I heard the noise and turned I see George Lisle sitting on the ground with his right leg near-but off, his left leg was injured and his back and his head was much cut about. I cannot say whether it was done by the engine.

William Witheral, a platelayer, stated that he saw the *Enterprise* go by at 4 mph. He heard the crash and, running to the spot, he found Lisle 'sitting with one leg off, the other badly injured and his head. *He was quite sensible and I helped him home*. I don't know if it was the engine or the dandy cart what done it [*sic*].'

George Lisle made a statement from his bed at home the following day. Suffering untold pain in those non-anaesthetic days, he corroborated all that had been said and forgave Ralph Coulson: 'There is no blame to Ralph Coulson the engineman; it was done with good intent. He was going very slow.' On 23 October Lisle's remaining leg was amputated and he died shortly afterwards.[8]

The S&DR records make no mention of what, if any, provision the Directors made for the widow and children of George Lisle. They were very rich, very hard men, deeply imbued with the harshly thrifty, Protestant work ethic. Their morals were defined in a puritanical way, and religion for them was more to do with maintaining an orderly society in which to make money than with the application of mercy. The balance between mercy and order was sharply defined. On 2 October 1846 the Revd Mainisty asked the S&DR Directors for support for the widow and children of one Atkinson who had been killed on the line. The Directors ordered 'two pounds to be placed in the hands of John Graham [the S&DR Engineer] to hand to her in such amounts as he may consider the case to require'.[9] They considered five pounds a fit sum to donate to the setting up of a Wesleyan Sunday School at Crook (the money being 'placed in the hands' of the owner of the Witton colliery, Henry Stobart, a Director of the S&DR), while another five pounds was spent 'to appoint a scripture reader to the men at Shildon who are in receipt of very large wages and who spend them recklessly'. All such charitable donations, it should be recalled, came from confiscations of the men's wages.

5

'To Unite the Disjointed Parts'

T HE COMMITTEE FREQUENTLY received complaints about bad
service on the railway and suggestions for improvement
from the coal owners. In response to such a letter, Pease
wrote on 22 February 1827 to Richard Otley, the Company Secretary,
musing on the problems of running a railway which was a paradox:
a privately owned public utility used by many self-interested, private
individuals who had no conception of the discipline and organization
required:

> Separate days for each colliery will not do. Can we learn anything from
> their letter? Except they have their just proportion of wagons marked for
> each and they keep their own wagons in repair. If they let them get out of
> repair they would be without wagons. Should [we] get quit of repairs or
> should we allow ⅛d if they find their own wagons? We must be quit of this
> unceasingly wasteful wagon establishment – let all be ¾ or 100% chaldron
> wagons.[1]

The railway's single track was crammed with traffic, and on 20
November 1830 Thomas Hall of Black Boy colliery wrote a lengthy
memorandum: 'The Better Management of the Stockton & Darlington
Railway':

> The present Committee consists of up to 20 of the principal proprietors as
> Directors of the Railway, assisted by as many Agents, all of these more or

less connected with other private interests adjoining the railway and these other interests will interfere with their operation of the railway. Therefore by adopting a Chief Manager, allowing him to choose his own assistants unconnected with any other parties he will transact business solely for the benefit of the public. I have no doubt [this] will be the means of putting away the unpleasant past of the business which the present Committee and their Engineers have now to contend with.[2]

The memorandum also referred to the constant complaints of favouritism where the Committee's staithes contractors would give preference to the loading of one colliery's coal by allowing certain wagons to 'jump the queue', the implications being that bribery was involved. Complaints were still being received on this score in 1844. An individual wagon's progress over the line was slow and most of its time was spent standing still. An S&DR investigation showed that the average journey time for one wagon over the 26¾ miles from Auckland to Stockton was 4½ days. The lack of track space gave rise to the ridiculous situation whereby trucks were stored on the main line, creating a blockage and a shortage of empty wagons at the colliery. This is also highlighted in the Hall memorandum:

In order to facilitate the work of the railway, one or two sidings should be provided at each colliery at Stockton and Shildon for a half or one third of the total wagons of each colliery and when no ships are in for such coals, the wagons belonging to that colliery, being put into their respective sidings, would not interfere with one another. It would also be necessary to have sidings or passing places intervening between Stockton and Darlington so wagons can stand all night without interfering with the main line. There is sufficient room at [the] north end of New Bridge to make up the deficiency of sidings and answer a much better purpose than stopping at Urlay Nook, 4 miles from Stockton as is now the case as it will suit the Stockton and the Middlesbrough Staithes. The same applies at Shildon – sidings are required. Each coal owner to know his own siding at each end and there would be no confusion. When the vessel for that colliery arrived a messenger to go to the siding to release those wagons. All this would have to be under the instructions of the Chief Manager.

Although Timothy Hackworth was at that time contracted only to supervise the S&DR's stationary and locomotive steam-engines he found himself increasingly drawn into carrying out the function of Manager of the whole line, and called on to bring under control eighteenth-century individualism and introduce nineteenth-century industrial discipline: to 'unite the disjointed parts and work out a beautiful and effectual system of public conveyance'.[3] In 1831 he 'implored' the Committee to double the line: 'I only wish you to know that it would make you cry to see how they [the users of the line] knock each other's brains out. The line must be doubled.'[4] The work was carried out from Brusselton to Stockton between 1831 and 1832.

In suggesting a 'Chief Manager', Hall's memorandum was asking for centralization of a sort. The number of individuals exercising their own wills on the line had to be reduced; to this end Hall had recommended that horses be banned in order that the locomotive-hauled railway could develop its full potential. But if horse-hauling were abolished, this would remove the means by which most people exercised their legal right to use the railway, an eventuality dimly perceived by George Overton. In fact the whole issue of public access to the railway was a difficult one. Although this was the railway's legal obligation, the principle was more or less unworkable from the start because of the inescapable fact that the wagons had to run on rails, one train behind another. There would have to be a central or 'monopolistic' control – an orderly *system*. Thus the Committee accepted that, for the sake of efficiency, they would have to get rid of these 'independents' and at once set about ridding the line of private (though legally entitled) individuals.

From the opening of the line in 1825 until the end of 1832 the S&DR had received an average of £460 per annum from the passenger contractors, a sum they felt was unsatisfactory since the annual cost of maintaining the track between Stockton and Darlington, through their contractors, was about £480. Competition between operators – and the Committee's edicts on fares in some cases – had kept fares down, a fact that pleased the users but was of little benefit to the person providing the service. The income was split between the haulier and the Committee, and neither side earned enough to make a decent living, while the smaller operators could not afford to build improved vehicles.

In 1833 the Directors determined to clear up the individualistic free-for-all of the railway in order to increase its efficiency. On 1 January they commuted its fluctuating annual tax obligations on ticket sales to a fixed payment, and entered a £400 Bond to the Government as a promise to pay ticket duty of £200 per annum. They placed Timothy Hackworth in charge of the entire railway by appointing him General Manager, Locomotive Superintendent and sole contractor, and set out to remove all the individual contractors. On 2 August 1833 the Directors decided that only locomotives would be used on the line,[5] a move tantamount to banning the small independents. The S&DR shareholders were in favour of this and gave the Directors their full support 'to induce' the independents to comply. The S&DR began negotiations with the independent coal and passenger hauliers to remove them from the railway. Horse-hauled passenger trains were abolished quite quickly, since the independents were making little money and were glad to sell their statutory rights, but freight haulage by horses continued for a few more years.

On 26 September 1833, Jane Scott agreed to sell her two railway coaches to the S&DR at a valuation supposedly taking into account the recent refurbishments she had carried out to the value of £51 7s 8d. Her coaches were valued independently at £25 each, with £10 for the horse harness. Additionally, she accepted from the S&DR £40 to cease her work on the line. Timothy Hackworth and William Lister sold out their (locomotive-hauled) coaching interest to the S&DR in 1834, accepting £1050 for 'coaches including water tank and tender'. In order to obtain their pay-offs everyone had to sign an undertaking 'not to re-establish any service without the consent of this company', although it seems unlikely that such an undertaking could actually divest them of their statutory rights under the Act.

A quarry owner wrote to complain to the Committee that the Company's policeman had turned back the quarry owner's wagons because they were on the line after dark:

> Surely you do not intend that the railway, which was built expressly for the use of the public, and which held out inducements to individuals having property adjoining, should not be equally open to all. On the same principle, Trustees of turnpike roads might close the gates at night except for their own carriages. All regulations as to lights must be adhered to but whilst the coal owners are allowed to carry their coals by night I certainly claim the same privilege for my wagons, for having invested nearly £3,000 in the quarry it is of some importance to me to endeavour to renumerate myself.[6]

The practice of running a free-market, turnpike railway was thus discouraged in the interests of a faster, more effective railway. The S&DR, being a Quaker railway, shut down on Sundays, but the Friends were willing to accept a toll from a privately owned horse-coach to run over the otherwise closed and locomotiveless section from Middlesbrough to Stockton on the Lord's Day. On the Hagger

Leases branch, horse-traction survived of necessity until 1858, when the line was rebuilt to permit locomotive working.

Contracting-out was relatively successful if the contractor had the high moral code of the Wesleyan Timothy Hackworth, but when lesser mortals were engaged the results could be disastrous. Messrs Mischamp and Harris, who were employed by the S&DR Permanent-Way department, took the contract to maintain the Weardale Extension Railway which was opened in November 1843 and leased to the S&DR. Later they contracted to operate the line as well. They agreed to maintain the Weardale line 'in perfect order' for £625 per annum but soon began to slip from their previously high standards – because of course they were using their own money, not the S&DR's. They used old materials and charged for new, charged for creosote having used none – and overcharged even for these fictitious items! They also went into business as a permanent-way contractor for other companies and did not give proper attention to the S&DR. In a long report to the Committee into the corruptions of Mischamp & Harris, delivered in December 1847, Dixon wrote: 'John [Harris] has tried to kill the goose that lays the golden egg and has overcharged for his work by £2,675 10s 9d.'[7]

Oswald Gilkes was, with William Bouch, contractor for the construction and repair of S&DR locomotives at Shildon works after Hackworth and, with the permission of the S&DR, they built locomotives for other companies (as Hackworth did before them). This was a complicated system financially, since they were using S&DR buildings and machinery; it was also inconvenient for the S&DR since the works' capacity was not wholly at the disposal of its owners, with the unfortunate result that the S&DR was, throughout its life, short of motive power – while the demands placed upon the locomotive fleet grew as the tide of coal rose. The result was expensive chaos. On 19 November 1852 Bouch and Gilkes warned that the railway was not only short of locomotives but had insufficient space on which to store them: 'There are 73 and we have not got room for 20, under cover, at Shildon. The locomotives are sent to distant parts of the line to stand them out of the way.'

A Minute of 20 March 1854 states:

This Committee has had the benefit of deliberate judgement of John Graham upon the general situation, location and efficiency of the locomotive and wagon department. The number of engines is 78 and 2 hired from L&NWR and 15 more are ordered =95. The number which the engine sheds now in use will house is 67. Engines must not be left outside and extra accommodation must be built.[8]

Even when the S&DR got the coal down to the river there was a shortage of ships into which to load it. Mr Pickering at Shildon wrote to Mr McNay at Darlington on 23 February 1854: 'The two L&NW locos have arrived. They are very powerful and will be a great help to us – if only we had some *ships* to get our wagons empty.'

The duties of S&DR senior officers were unclear – even to themselves. John Dixon, the Civil Engineer in charge of the track and bridges, was happy to give his opinion to the Directors on locomotive matters. On 22 January 1855 Dixon wrote to the Directors to warn them of the motive power shortage and the need to buy locomotives from outside because 'Shildon cannot build enough, nor even keep up with repairs'. Dixon's involvement in locomotive matters was constant enough to convince Oswald Gilkes that Dixon was responsible for the control of wagon movements. This vital function was not Dixon's responsibility, neither could he have said whose it was; but when Gilkes asked Dixon to investigate the whereabouts of lost wagons in December 1848, he did so most obligingly, and replied on 13 December 1848:

The wagons of R. Robinson were lost for months at a time and inquiry discovered that:

4 were empty at Eldon lime kilns 1 month

6 were laden at Eldon lime kilns and smelling so as to injure the wagons. Stanhope wagons Nos. 5140 and 4706 have been backed in amongst S&DR wagons at Auckland since 23 November. Stanhope wagon No. 778 laden with coke at Witton Iron Works and also others at Woodiford and Witton Park Collieries.

Walton's iron stone quarry is 10 wagons short of his daily requirement[;] this is why his costs in loco tons/miles is high. There are 20 coal wagons empty at Auckland, stood for 3 weeks.

There appears to be a screw loose [*sic*]. I have long thought so but until you handed me Robinson's complaint I did not think I had anything to do with this department – neither do I wish to but if either myself or an assistant can be useful I shall rejoice. I do not know whose duty it is to regulate wagons and therefore cannot be attacking any individual for neglect but I think the system capable of improvement.[9]

A fine example of the classic English understatement.

The 'turnpike' principle, with its divided responsibilities and divided loyalties, was not practical when applied to the operation of a railway. The S&DR became co-ordinated and grew. All around it, small companies sprang up, and the S&DR became embroiled in manoeuvres against them where the newcomers threatened competition. The Clarence Railway was the realization of the 'Northern line' of 1820 – a direct route to the Tees, cutting out the great southwards loop of the S&DR through Darlington. The Clarence was ruined by its fight with S&DR and the S&DR itself suffered from the competition. Gradually the later-built lines amalgamated to avoid competition and improve services, until the North Eastern Railway (NER) was formed in 1854. The S&DR expanded independently. In July 1861 its subsidiary Company, the South Durham & Lancashire Union, carried coal and coke west over the Pennines to the L&NWR west coast main line at Tebay and, through the Eden valley, via Kirkby Stephen, to Penrith in 1862, its trains travelling on as far west as Cockermouth (the purpose being to effect a transfer of iron and fuel between east and west). In the north-east the S&DR reached the steel town of Consett, 17 miles north of Bishop Auckland. Not until January 1861 did the S&DR condescend to co-operate with the NER, and it amalgamated with that great Company on 1 July 1863.[10]

6

The Liverpool & Manchester Railway

T HE GREAT WEALTH of Liverpool had come, initially, from that legalized form of piracy known as 'privateering', and from the slave trade. Carlson states that Liverpudlians were involved in the slave trade from 1709,[1] and in 1750 they received Royal approval in an Act of Parliament 'for extending and improving the trade to Africa for the Port of Liverpool'. Beads and saucepans, cutlasses, guns and gunpowder were taken to West Africa where the native chiefs accepted them in exchange for their own and other chiefs' people. These men and women were shipped and sold as slaves to the British-owned plantations in the West Indies and North America. Some plantations were owned by Liverpool merchants; Dale H. Porter states:

> In 1787 Liverpool sent out 78 slave ships to Bristol's 31. There were a total of 139 ships engaged in the trade in 1790, half of them owned by eight people. The slave trade was an integral part of the wider trading business undertaken by their owners who would also have business as insurers, bankers and merchants trading with Ireland, the Baltic, anywhere where there was a cargo.[2]

Many industries came into being to manufacture trade goods needed to barter for slaves in West Africa: the Birmingham small arms industry was supported in peacetime by making guns for the African trade.

Cotton burst into prominence only towards the end of the century, the first import – eight bags – arriving in 1787. In 1792, 503 bags were imported and, in 1822, 289,989.[3] Between 1723 and 1800 the number of ships using Liverpool increased from 131 to 4746, as the products of slave labour – sugar, cotton and rum – were brought back to Liverpool. The abolition of the slave trade in 1807 had no disadvantageous effect on Liverpool's prosperity, however, since the plantations were well established. In 1825, at the peak of the post-war 'boom', 10,837 ships docked, with a combined tonnage of 1,223,820.[4] The population of Liverpool grew from 55,732 in 1790 to 118,972 by 1821, and the River Mersey resembled a seemingly endless forest of masts, spars and rigging.

The men who became the great magnates of Liverpool and Manchester created a network of relationships through marriages, and thus there were many 'informal' connections along which investment money could flow. The first mention of a banker in Liverpool was in a gazetteer of 1774. This was William Clarke, 'banker and linen draper'.[5]

While there were rich and powerful persons who were opposed to slavery, they had no objections to financial partnerships with slavers.[6] Thomas Moss was the most important banker in Liverpool in 1824. The family fortune was derived in part from slavery; Moss was a timber merchant-shipowner who imported timber from the Baltic, a licensed 'privateer' who also owned several 'very large slave plantations in Demerara'. He was appointed a Justice of the Peace for Liverpool in 1816. The Moss family were related by marriage to the bankers Roscoe, who supported the campaign for the abolition of slavery. His son John was a leading figure in the drive to construct the Liverpool to Manchester railway.

Thomas Leyland (1752–1827) amassed a huge fortune directly from slavery and also from privateering during the American War of Independence and the Napoleonic War. In 1802 he became a senior partner in a bank owned by anti-slavers Messrs Clarke and Roscoe, where his capital was an enormous asset. Leyland dissolved his partnership with Roscoe in 1806, the year before the passing of the Act to prohibit the slave trade.[7] Leyland was popular with the ordinary people of Liverpool because of his reputation for defending them against the machinations of capitalists who tried to manipulate the food market to their own advantage. He was thrice elected Mayor of Liverpool from 1814, and in 1816 he became a partner with Bullins, a banker whose wealth was based on slavery.

The Heywood Bank, active from 1773 until 1883, was founded on the profits of slavery and the slave trade. The Gladstone family, whose son William Ewart became Prime Minister of England, were split between pro- and anti-slavers; they nevertheless married into the Heywood family and held partnerships in their bank.

The profits of the triangular trade to the Liverpudlian shipowners and Mancunian merchants were reinvested in their English-based enterprises and banks, and transformed Lancashire, which boasted coal and water power, into an important mining, industrial and cotton-producing area. Manchester became the centre of the cotton industry after the introduction of steam-powered machinery, and the population of the town and district grew from an estimated 57,000 in 1790 to 133,788 in 1821.

Transport facilities between Liverpool and Manchester and the hinterland of Lancashire were poor or non-existent until the last quarter of the eighteenth century. There was no turnpike road to Liverpool from the south until 1760, when a hard-surfaced road was extended from Warrington to permit the relatively fast stage-coaches to reach the town.[8] The tolls earned by the Liverpool–Manchester Turnpike Trust were insufficient to keep the road in good repair when tens of thousands of tons of freight passed over it every year. Though the rivers Mersey and Irwell provided another means of carrying goods, they were meandering, full of sandbanks and subject to winds and tides. The Mersey & Irwell Navigation Act was passed in 1720 to create a company with powers to dredge, make straight cuts across bends and generally make the two rivers properly navigable between Bank Quay, Warrington and Hunt's Bank, Manchester. The work was carried out between 1723 and 1734.

Later in the century the third Duke of Bridgewater (1736–1803) took an interest in the improvement of transport. He owned coal-mines at Worsley, north-west of Manchester, but the high cost of transporting the coal by road to its obvious market restricted the amount that could be sold. The Duke therefore obtained an Act of Parliament permitting him to construct a canal from his mines to the River Irwell at Barton. Realizing that his coal would be now at the mercy of the Mersey & Irwell (M&I) Commissioners' tolls, he obtained a new Act permitting him to extend his canal into Salford, Manchester, avoiding the M&I. It would instead cross the Irwell by an aqueduct 200 yards long, standing 39 ft above the river.

The Act of Parliament contained a clause obliging the Duke to show his commitment to the 'public service' aspect of the canal by selling his coal in Manchester for not more than 4d a ton, when the going rate, before the canal was built, was 7d. The canal was later extended 35 miles westwards along the Mersey, although rather circuitously, to join the river below the worst shallows, at Runcorn. This section was opened on 21 March 1776. The entire canal had cost the Duke no more than £250,000, probably because it passed through his own lands and thus there was no need to pay vast sums of compensation to supposedly aggrieved landowners.

The Duke then became a coal merchant, to the benefit of thousands of households and the growing number of factories. Worsley coal, canal-borne to Manchester, was sold there with true public spirit for 3½d per 120 lb. He also went into the general carrying business and, as early as 1780, had completed a 'no-competition' agreement with the Mersey & Irwell Navigation. The two transport concerns agreed all their charges, thereby guaranteeing the Duke and the shareholders of the M&I immense profits.

The Bridgewater Canal, which was the sole property of the Duke, passed on his death to his nephew, the Marquis of Stafford (1758–1833), who inherited an annual income from this source of between £100,000 and £120,000 a year. But the Marquis had no power over the running of the canal – this was bequeathed by the Duke to his Agent, the man who had run the canal for thirty-three years, Robert Haldane Bradshaw. The Duke's will made it clear that he intended this arrangement to be for the public good, but he appears to have misjudged his man. Bradshaw had a dictatorial turn of mind; he believed not only in taking as much money as he could from the users of the canal, but made himself lord (in all but name) of every other canal in the north-west. Whenever he felt his monopoly threatened, he found ways of interfering with any canal in Britain. At a national meeting of canal company delegates, Bradshaw expelled a delegate who owned £40,000-worth of canal capital because that man also owned five shares in a railway company.[9]

Neither the Bridgewater Canal nor the Mersey & Irwell Navigation provided a direct line between the towns. Goods could pass over the approximately 50 miles of meandering waterway between the two towns in 24 hrs in ideal conditions but two weeks was common and even six weeks in extreme cases. Sometimes cotton crossed the Atlantic faster than it progressed from Liverpool to Manchester. To guard against running out of supplies, manufacturers were forced to hold larger stocks of raw materials – tying up substantial capital sums – than would have been the case with a prompt and reliable delivery service.

Both the Bridgewater and the M&I canals suffered from shortage of water during droughts, and were sometimes frozen over or flooded in winter. At times of peak traffic a shortage of barges delayed goods and forced traders to queue for transport – or else to go to the even more circuitous Leeds & Liverpool. Bradshaw saw no reason to squander his large profits on accommodating his customers by building spare barges, which would lie idle outside the peak periods. Instead traders were obliged to queue, while he kept his operation working constantly at full capacity.

Bradshaw's policy in running the Bridgewater Canal was one of 'profit extraction to the utmost limit, regardless of the feelings and interests of the users of the canal'.[10] A railway was therefore seen as the way to break Bradshaw's monopoly. There had been several proposals for a Liverpool and Manchester railway. William Jessop and Benjamin Outram had surveyed likely routes around 1797 and William James had suggested a railway in 1808. Between 1801 and 1825, Lancashire industrialists had obtained 80 Acts of Parliament to improve transport: to convert roads to 'turnpike' status, to build canals or railways feeding canals. The first railway in Lancashire was built by the Leeds & Liverpool Canal Company, from their Wigan branch to Low Hall colliery. The Act for this was passed in 1819.

In 1821 William James was working on land surveys in the Manchester area and, having made a partnership agreement with George Stephenson whereby James would promote railways and Stephenson would supply the engines,[11] James approached Joseph Cowlinshaw, a corn merchant of Manchester, and suggested that a locomotive-hauled railway be constructed between there and Liverpool. Cowlinshaw liked the idea and introduced James to Joseph Sandars, a Liverpool corn merchant, underwriter and prominent Whig politician. Sandars was also the most outspoken critic of the Bridgewater Canal monopoly and became the prime mover for the railway project. He obtained promises of financial support from twenty-three of Liverpool's richest businessmen and manufacturers and from a smaller number of like-minded individuals in Manchester.

In April 1822 James began a survey for a route from Liverpool east to the outlying village of West Derby, south-east to Huyton and then eastwards through Rainhill, Newton-le-Willows, Newchurch and

Eccles, to Manchester. This route avoided aristocratic parks but would have to cross the swamp known as Chat Moss. James was confident that this 31-mile line could be built in 18 months for £100,000.

The promotion of the 'Liverpool & Manchester Railway Company' was in the hands of a 'Provisional Committee' of twenty-seven of the leading lights of Liverpool and Manchester. Charles Lawrence, the Whig Mayor of Liverpool was Chairman – although the Council generally was lukewarm in its support;[12] the Tory Member for Liverpool, William Huskisson (1770–1830), was actively in favour of the railway but not on the Committee; Thomas Booth, a Liverpool corn merchant, was Secretary to the Committee, and was succeeded by his son Henry; James Cropper, a Quaker businessman, John Gladstone, MP, John Moss the banker, William Rathbone and Charles Tayluer, who later set up his locomotive works at Warrington, were all Committee members.

The railway was most actively opposed, of course, by the powerful local landowners – the Earl of Sefton and Lord Derby – and the existing transport business of the district. Why should the stage-coach operator stand aside and admit a new means of transport which might remove his livelihood? As it turned out, after the Liverpool line was built, and indeed, as railways spread across Britain, horse transport was in greater demand than ever before, since people and goods had to be transported to and from thousands of railway stations. However, it would have required uncommon foresight to realize this; and Willam James faced frightening opposition during the making of his survey – so much so that he often had to work at night.

Robert Bradshaw, who himself owned land on the proposed route, ordered his tenants to fire their shotguns into the night to scare and distract James and his men. He also hired mobs of working people to stone and otherwise intimidate the railway surveyors. Coal-miners were duped into attacking the surveying party, yet the railway could only increase the amount of coal the miners could sell. Powerfully self-interested men exploited the fears of simple people.

James wrote to Sandars, early in 1822, in dramatic vein: 'The canal companies are alive to their danger. I have been the object of their persecution and hate; they would immolate me if they could but if I can die the death of Samson by pulling away the pillars I am content to die with these Philistines.'

Hiring professional pugilists to carry his theodolite, James pressed on with considerable bravery. He was hampered by violent opposition and foul weather, but was also having to spend money on wages and expenses with little to show for it. At the same time, he was pursuing the construction of his Stratford & Moreton line, and he also completed his survey for the Canterbury & Whitstable Railway early in 1823. The Liverpool survey fell further behind schedule. In mid-1823 the value of James's shares, which underpinned his borrowings, fell. His brother-in-law filed a suit against him in Chancery to recover a loan, and in November 1823 James admitted to Sandars that 'the surveys and plans can't be completed till the end of the week. With illness, anguish of mind and inexpressible distress I perceive I must sink if I wait any longer. I have so neglected the suit in Chancery that if I do not put in an answer I shall be outlawed.' Shortly after this James was imprisoned for debt. In April or May 1824 the Provisional Committee appointed James's partner, George Stephenson, as their Engineer; Stephenson also subsequently took over as Engineer of the Canterbury & Whitstable and soon sent his bright young men, Dixon and then Locke, to Kent to complete the job. James was released after some months but his health had failed, he was never again fully solvent, and his days in the railway business were over.

William James's place in railway history is important, not for what he actually achieved in terms of rails laid, but because he had the unique foresight, as early as 1804, to realize what *could* be done with railways. Trevithick had lost interest when the entrepreneurs scorned his engines, but James never lost an opportunity to advocate high-speed, locomotive, passenger and freight railways, at a time when all other engineers conceived of railways as horse-drawn or, if loco-hauled, then as slow, freight-carrying facilities. It was this belief that led James to befriend and encourage George Stephenson; indeed, James was ahead of Stephenson who, paradoxically, never fully realized the potential of the steam-locomotive because he doubted its ability to surmount gradients. George Stephenson is now, with some justification, known as 'The Father of Railways', but in the 1820s Robert Stephenson – who was admittedly very sympathetic towards James and perhaps not on the best of terms with his father – awarded the title to William James.

George Stephenson embarked on a new survey of the Liverpool line, and suffered the same hostility experienced by James. Stephenson's line went north out of Liverpool and turned east near Bootle, thereafter crossing lands owned by their Lordships Sefton and Derby. The Provisional Committee and George Stephenson maintained that these owners had no legal power to prevent the survey: 'it is the [tenant] farmers only who have the right to complain; and by charging damages for trespass, it is all they can do'.

Sometimes Stephenson hired men to create a noisy diversion at a place away from the field he wished to enter. Frequently the survey- ing party was stoned or otherwise attacked, always they had to be vigilant. Since Stephenson was also much occupied with the S&DR, and with his locomotive works in Newcastle, and could not therefore adequately supervise everyone, errors were made in the surveys. Whether the semi-literate George could actually have carried out the surveys on his own is debatable, but when mistakes were discovered they were conveniently blamed on Stephenson's 'busyness'. Two of his surveyors, Elijah Galloway and Hugh Steele, made errors so grave that, when these were discovered in Parliament, Stephenson claimed the men must have been planted on him as saboteurs by Robert Bradshaw.

While Stephenson was engaged on the survey, Charles Sylvester, a well-known civil engineer of the time, was commissioned to investi- gate the possible utility of locomotive steam-engines on the L&MR. He took himself off to the colliery railways of the north-east and, after months of careful research, issued his Report, crammed with mathematics, to the L&MR Chairman Charles Lawrence, on 15 December 1824. Significantly, on p. 16 Sylvester notes that, in theory,

> it would be practical for a locomotive to go at any speed, limited by the means of creating steam, the size of the wheels and the number of strokes in the engine. If the number of double [piston] strokes could be as great [as] 60 per minute and the [driving] wheels were the enormous size of 6 feet diameter the speed would be not quite 13 m.p.h.

He also warned that, in the case of a derailment, 'a greater speed than that recommended above would be attended with proportionate danger'.

His report, which was very optimistic about the future of steam locomotion, was written when there was a craze for speculative invest- ment in South America, and so he concluded his report, with a timely and prophetic warning against

> a rage for proposing new rail-roads. The delusion that, because rail-roads are better than canals or high-roads they will answer everywhere. The pre- tensions held out by some of the projectors do appear to me unwarranted

– and I have no doubt that when the public mind becomes more sober on the subject the real importance of [the] rail-road system, great as it undoubtedly is, will be more correctly estimated. This new application of locomotive power is of infinite importance to the country and I should regret to see it abused.

There spoke a true engineer, not a sharp solicitor or manipulator of the money market. What a pity engineers did not have full control of the country!

In summing up Sylvester's very technical treatise Charles Lawrence wrote:

Upon the whole, the advantages of a rail-road, on which locomotive power is used, are so striking that it is a matter of surprise this mode of conveyance has not been resorted to earlier. Its adoption is now inevitable and under judicious management cannot fail of becoming highly beneficial to the proprietors and public.

The Liverpool & Manchester Railway Bill, together with its plans and surveys, were deposited in Parliament in November 1824 for consideration the following year. With the L&MR Bill went another, for the Bolton & Leigh Railway, whose principal promoter was William Hulton, owner of the Chequerbent collieries, about 2½ miles north of the proposed L&MR and about 8 miles south of Bolton. Its Engineer was George Stephenson. This line ended several feet above the canal at Leigh so that coal could be dropped into barges, but the great hope of the promoters was that the L&MR would be constructed so that they could extend their own railway over the waterway to a junction with the L&MR. The Bolton & Leigh Act was obtained without any difficulty in March 1825. It was a very different matter for the promoters of the Liverpool & Manchester Railway.

7

The Triumph of George Stephenson – and his Assistants

THE LIVERPOOL & MANCHESTER Railway Bill came before Parliament in February 1825 and was supported by petitions from trading associations and the Chambers of Commerce of Liverpool, Leeds and Manchester, and from across the water in Belfast, Galway and Waterford. The canals, they claimed, were slow, unreliable and unresponsive to the rapidly growing volume of goods and materials which had to be moved.

Those who opposed the Bill did so on many grounds. The Bill had a clause excusing the locomotive engines from having to 'consume their own smoke', and Mr Smith, Editor of the *Liverpool Mercury*, correctly prophesied a sooty future for those living close to 'the places of rendezvous for the engines'. Mr Creevey, MP, the illegitimate son of the first Lord Sefton, represented Lords Derby and Sefton in Parliament, and on 16 March 1825 wrote to a friend about 'this infernal nuisance, the locomotive monster carrying eighty tons of goods, navigated by a tail of smoke and sulphur, coming through every man's grounds between Liverpool and Manchester'. There was also great concern about the safety of high-pressure boilers – 50 lb psi – and for many years to come, exploding steam-boilers gave satisfaction to the 'I told you so' brigade. Even some who ought to have known better contradicted the railway's claim to high speed. Nicholas Wood,

Manager of Killingworth colliery, George Stephenson's friend and one of the leading technical writers of the day, declared that 12 mph was 'too fast' and that it was 'nonsense' to suggest that locomotives might even attain 18 mph. Liverpool City Council swung from lukewarm support to active opposition, as those members with interests in the canals combined with those who simply did not want a sooty future with steam-engines.[1] Stephenson's survey was examined minutely and found to be flawed, giving the opposition plenty of ammunition to throw. The plight of 'the inarticulate genius' before the Committee of Parliament was a sorry one. Cross-examined by a highly trained barrister, Stephenson's credibility was completely undermined by the errors of levels in his surveys. He also admitted to indecision over certain details of how he was going to construct the line. His Northumbrian vocabulary was no match for the powerful legal men ranged against him. For instance, when explaining how he would cross Chat Moss swamp, he spoke of 'floating' the railway, a term mockingly seized on by the lawyers. Chat Moss was the greatest physical obstacle to the line's construction and was one of the trump cards of those opposed to the railway. It was, claimed the opposition, impassable except at prohibitive expense. Its surface was long grass and rushes, floating on watery, pulpy vegetable matter and sand to a depth of 34 ft, with hard clay at the bottom. Stephenson's phrase was unfortunate because that was *not* what he intended.

He planned to dig two drains, one on each side of the proposed embankment, and when the area between became less waterlogged he intended to place woven hazelwood hurdles on the ground, overlaid with faggots of brushwood, and gravel on this foundation. It would sink slowly and squeeze the water into the drain; as it sank further, more earth and gravel could be piled on top until the embankment rested on the hard, bottom clay. It was a perfectly feasible solution, long known to engineers; indeed, in 1826 there were districts along the Thames, not so far from the Houses of Parliament, where houses had been built on marshy ground, 'floating' on rafts of wood.

Stephenson estimated the cost of such a venture at a mere £40,000, but because he had not been able to explain himself properly (and because of the awe in which the Moss was held) the capable but roughly spoken North-countryman – who had already conquered the swamp at Myers Flat on the S&DR – was ridiculed. His evidence was a liability rather than an asset to the promoters of the Bill.

Francis Giles was the 'expert' witness called to dismiss Stephenson's plans for Chat Moss. Since he had worked for twenty years on canals under Sir John Rennie and was, at the time of giving evidence, the promoter of a canal from Liverpool to Warrington, he had an axe to grind. His lack of impartiality did not, unfortunately, affect the value placed on his evidence and, furthermore, he spoke with that accent associated with education and authority.

Giles told the Parliamentary Committee of the 'utter futility' of trying to cross the Moss by the means planned, and that it would have to be excavated to rock bottom at a cost of at least £200,000. Further, the entire Liverpool to Manchester line, its construction, warehousing, stations and rolling stock would cost not £400,000, as Stephenson had estimated, but nearly £1.5 million.

Giles's evidence carried great weight with the Parliamentary Committee – as did Stephenson's self-confessed lack of knowledge of the details of his plan and the many errors in his drawings. The evidence, given by independent carriers, of unnecessarily high rates on the canals was cancelled by the witnesses brought (or bought) by the Bridgewater Canal to state their entire satisfaction with water transport. The preamble of the Bill, stating that the construction of the railway between Liverpool and Manchester would be to the benefit of the public, was thus considered 'Not Proven' and the Bill was thrown out.

Ironically, the canal companies had taken such fright at the simple presence of such a Bill that they had reduced their tolls and embarked on engineering projects to improve their waterways, build new locks and provide more warehousing, thus confirming in bricks and mortar what had been asserted by witnesses *for* the railway in the Parliamentary Committees.

After their defeat the L&MR Directors reluctantly sacked George Stephenson, appointing George and John Rennie as Engineers and the brilliant Charles Vignoles as Surveyor, on a brief to find a route which would remove the objections of Lord Derby and the Earl of Sefton. Apart from the enormous, combined engineering skill of this trio they possessed the added advantage of a proven skill at Parliamentary duelling with sharp-tongued barristers. In spite of receiving Bradshaw's and the noble Lords' best attentions, Vignoles made a new and more accurate survey of a less offensive route 2 miles shorter than hitherto. It ran east out of Liverpool through a long tunnel followed by a deep cutting, and went south of Stephenson's line, avoiding the Liverpool–Manchester turnpike, crossing none of Lord Sefton's land and only a few fields belonging to Lord Derby.

The disadvantage of the Rennie/Vignoles line was that the tunnel and cutting required an extra £100,000 of capital. In 1825 such large sums were hard to find: the booming speculations of 1820–23 had resulted in a restriction on the issue of credit and the subsequent bankruptcy of thousands. The famous bankers of the time, Barings, Rothschild and Labouchere, all refused to become involved, and funds for the railway had to be raised by interested merchants and small, provincial banks.

One man with a solid income was the Marquis of Stafford, the owner of the Bridgewater Canal. An unlikely source of railway capital, he was brought into the L&MR camp in one of the great *coups* of railway history. Stafford disapproved of Bradshaw's arrogance and the autocratic monopoly he had created. He felt that if Bradshaw was not curbed, his policies could ruin the canal altogether. The L&MR Committee knew of Stafford's attitude in this respect and also knew that he was already a shareholder in the proposed Liverpool & Birmingham Railway. After some delicate negotiations Stafford purchased 1000 shares in the L&MR in return for the right to appoint three Directors to the L&MR Board. The railway Committee had checked their fiercest opponent – Bradshaw and 'his' Bridgewater canal – *and* found the £100,000 they needed to complete the new line of railway.

A second Prospectus was issued to broadcast the advantages to the district of having the railway and of the new route. Readers were reminded that before the first Bill went to Parliament, the Bridgewater Canal had reduced its rates for the carriage of coal by 18d [7½p] per ton, and that immediately after the defeat of that Bill the old rates were restored. If the railway got its Act, the L&MR promised to reduce the price of coal by 2s [10p] a ton – a move which would benefit every poor family in Liverpool and Manchester.

The opposition of Liverpool City Council was won over, without bribery, after some members of the Council suggested that the railway Committee might like to offer them the same sort of 'bribe' which they had given Stafford. The L&MR Committee indignantly replied that the Marquis had purchased his shares in a proper manner, and insisted that they wished to proceed properly at every step because they were bent on achieving 'a great National end'. Again, there is an emphasis on the idea of the idea of public service: the railway, built with private money but for the national good.

The second L&MR Bill went before Parliament early in 1826.

Vignoles and John Rennie explained the engineering case well; and since Bradshaw, for the Bridgewater Canal, had spent large sums of money opposing the 1825 Bill, he was unable to oppose it with the same vigour in 1826. In the House of Commons the assertion was made that the Mersey & Irwell and the Bridgewater canals could provide all necessary transport and could carry goods almost as fast as the horses on the L&MR. (The petitioners, remembering the hostility to smoky engines during the fight for the first Bill, spoke only of their intention to work the line with horses – although the Bill included a clause to work the line with steam-engines.)

Sir Isaac Coffin waxed indignant on the subject of that perennial favourite of outraged politicians – widows and old ladies living alone – and stoutly objected to the invasion of their premises by railways, or to the smoking-out of anyone's parlour. He considered railways 'one of the most flagrant impositions ever known'. After this bluster, William Huskisson's speech struck as so sincere and sensible, emphasizing the great, national benefit of the line, that it restored the balance in the collective mind of the Select Committee. He agreed that there would be some upset for individuals but that there was a need for an alternative transport system between Liverpool and Manchester. The Bridgewater Canal charged so much that it enabled them to pay investors 100 per cent of their investment annually. Obviously, there was a crying need to break the canals' arrogant monopoly. Huskisson pointed out that the railway Bill contained a clause binding the Company to reduce its charges, should it pay a dividend in excess of 10 per cent. The Bill passed the Commons – in spite of opposition from two Lancashire MPs – and went to the Lords.

Here Lord Derby was its most bitter opponent. The Rennie brothers, George and John, were quite unshaken by the searching inquisition and made a very good impression on the Select Committee, while other engineers testified to the efficacy of the method proposed for crossing Chat Moss. All the old, threadbare objections were raised and countered, and on 2 May 1830 the Lords passed the Bill by 30 votes to 2, Lords Derby and Wilton against. The Bill received the Royal Assent and became an Act on 5 May 1826.

The Liverpool & Manchester Railway Act had cost the Company £27,000. It forbade the Company to use locomotive steam-engines in Liverpool, and any locomotive used elsewhere had to be capable of 'consuming its own smoke'. At level-crossings the gates were to be kept closed across the railway unless a train had to pass. It gave the

Company rights of compulsory purchase but ordered that compensation be paid to landowners. If the dividend exceeded 10 per cent in any year the fares had to be reduced. Conversely, 10 per cent of profits were to go to a reserve fund for the purpose of maintaining the dividend at that level in any year where it would otherwise have fallen. The Company was obliged to wait until it had obtained all the required capital – £510,000 – before starting to build the line. If this was not enough for the purpose, the sum that could be borrowed by mortgaging the assets of the railway was not to exceed £127,000. Shareholders were given the power to vote on company policy, one vote per 20 shares held.

The Act *permitted* the Liverpool & Manchester Railway Company to act as a common carrier on its own road, but at the same time *obliged* the Company to maintain the railway as a public highway: 'All persons shall have free liberty to use with carriages all Roads, Ways and Passages for the purposes of conveying goods, wares, merchandise or other things, passengers or cattle . . . and to pass along the said railway with carts or waggons properly constructed'. The maximum charges for carriage were laid down by the Act; it also stated that these charges should be displayed on large notice-boards at all stations and toll gates (it actually envisaged toll gates across the rails in exactly the same way as on a turnpike road).

Several of the Directors of the new Company, Benson, Ellis, Moss, Rathbone, Rotherham and Sandars for instance, became well-known names as 'the Liverpool Party' in later railway promotions. Henry Booth was the Company Treasurer. He was not merely a good accountant and an able organizer; he also had an appreciative eye for good engineering and was thus a double asset to the Directors.

On 29 May the Company held its first meeting and announced that it would feel free to pay any dividend over 10 per cent provided that, if it did so, it reduced its tolls and charges the following year. This reading of the Act increased the value of the shares, encouraging investors not only to invest but to pay their 'calls' promptly – a masterstroke in 1826, when the money-lending business was in the doldrums, following the wild borrowing to speculate in loans to unstable South American governments or in the shares of over-optimistic mining ventures in that part of the globe.

The L&MR Board met to appoint their Officers on 30 May 1826 and invited George and John Rennie to state the terms on which they would act as Engineers, in conjunction with George Stephenson or

John Rastrick, to build the line. On 9 June George Rennie attended the Board and stated that, for 6 guineas a day [£6.30] each plus travelling expenses – or for a fixed salary of £600 a year – they would give the Company sixty days a year maximum. They also wanted the right to appoint their Resident Engineer, who would work full time on the line, and they wanted complete control over all aspects of the construction of the line. They said they would not mind working with any Member of the Society of Engineers but on no account would they work with Rastrick or Stephenson.

The Directors refused the Rennies' terms. Neither did they go back to Charles Vignoles, since it was well known that he disliked George Stephenson. Perhaps there was some snobbery or jealousy in Vignoles' attitude towards Stephenson, whom he perceived as a mean, parochial individual. In a letter to Edward Riddle, Vignoles said of Stephenson: 'He did not look on the concern with a liberal and expanded view but with a microscopic eye, magnifying details and pursuing a petty system of parsimony very proper in a colliery but wholly inapplicable to this National work'. Vignoles was paid for his Parliamentary work, plus a month's salary and the Company's thanks for his 'zeal' on their behalf.

The Directors then offered the job of Engineer to George Stephenson. This course was urged on the Board by Henry Booth, who recognized Stephenson's great ability and determination as a manager and engineer. Stephenson offered to give the L&MR nine months of each year of his time in return for only £800 a year, which would include his expenses. This was gladly accepted and thus Stephenson combined the dual roles of Civil Engineer and Locomotive Engineer. It may be recalled that he was also similarly responsible for the S&DR at this time. He had taken on the responsibility for making designs and specifications, dealing with the contractors, and visiting rail-rolling mills and brickworks to ensure he was getting what he wanted. As for stationary pumping engines, deep cuttings, long tunnels, stations, earth-moving wagons, the track and point-work, and the locomotives, he either designed these things himself or got others to submit designs, which he would accept or reject, according to his judgement of their suitability.

This was a vast field for a man who had dragged himself up by his bootstraps and who had not learned to read until he was eighteen. Stephenson's practical genius is not questioned, but the task of constructing the Liverpool & Manchester Railway was far more complicated than building the Stockton & Darlington. His lack of a formal scientific education was a drawback, but he was adept at finding talented young men to help him carry out the more scientific parts of railway engineering and the detailed work of design and specifications. Having spotted ability, Stephenson did not waste it. All his protégés worked for very small reward, or none, in the hope of learning the business and that one day they would be engineers in their own right. Stephenson meanwhile took the credit and increased his bank balance.

The first of these assistants was his son Robert, for whom he had mended shoes so that he, Robert, should have a first-class education culminating in 1822 in six months at Edinburgh University. Together they had established a locomotive factory in Forth Street, Newcastle, in June 1823 under the title 'Robert Stephenson & Co.' George supplied £500 of the capital but most came from the S&DR Quaker Committee; Edward Pease put in £1500 and loaned Robert £500 so that he too could buy shares and be a partner. Most of the brain-power came from Robert, designated 'Managing Partner'. The tension between father and son has been noted in an earlier chapter (p. 22), and in June 1824 Robert left his father to become the mechanical engineer of the Colombian Mining Company. Without Robert, George was out of his depth in design.

George Stephenson's team of bright young men included John Dixon from Durham, Joseph Locke, born in Barnsley in 1805, and William Allcard, a Londoner born in 1809. They had all begun their careers in the Stephenson locomotive works in Newcastle. John Dixon was appointed the Resident Engineer of the central and eastern sections of the L&MR (including the works at Chat Moss), with the seventeen-year-old Allcard to help him. At the beginning of 1828, with Dixon heavily engaged on the S&DR, Allcard took over Dixon's role on the L&MR. This involved the construction of the Sankey viaduct, which consisted of nine, 50-ft-span arches rising to a height of 70 ft, and the Kenyon cutting, from which 400,000 cubic yards of soil was excavated.

Joseph Locke became a pupil of Stephenson's in 1823, and in 1824 Stephenson put him in charge of the construction of the Black Fell colliery railway. Aged twenty, Locke became Resident Engineer of the western end of the L&MR, which made him responsible for the Olive Mount cutting, 2 miles long and 70 ft deep, the passenger terminal station at Crown Street near the top of the Edgehill incline and the problem of making the 1¼-mile tunnel, from Edgehill, to the Wapping terminus, close to Queen's Dock. Stephenson was the Engineer-in-Chief but it was these young men who directed the work on a day-to-day basis. It was Locke who rescued the Edgehill tunnel from Stephenson's survey errors. In 1828 Stephenson, who had made the general survey for the Manchester–Stockport branch, sent Locke to make the detailed plans for the line. The L&MR Directors protested at the loss of Locke – since they were paying his wages – but Stephenson insisted that Locke was his property. A row was imminent and, to save Stephenson embarrassment, Locke resigned from the L&MR.

These errors and arguments were not public knowledge and George Stephenson's engineering reputation remained unassailable. Indeed, it was his supreme confidence and granite determination which conquered Chat Moss. He brought the same determination to his support for the locomotive steam-engine when others would have had rope – or even animal – haulage. His recommendations, even when these were expensive, were accepted by the Directors without question. On the subject of the gauge of the line, which was not mentioned in the enabling Act, the Company's Minutes stated simply: 'Resolved that the width of the waggon-way between the rails be the same as on the Darlington road, namely 4 ft 8 in. clear inside the rails.'[2] It was this lack of thought on so important a matter which later offended Isambard Kingdom Brunel – although he overreacted somewhat – but with George Stephenson as your Engineer-in-Chief *and* supplier of your locomotives, the gauge of your railway could only be 'Stephenson's own'.

8

The Battle for the Locomotive

CHAT MOSS WAS, very approximately, triangular in shape, its apex to the south, its eastern extremity within 5 miles of Manchester. It was perhaps once a lake that had silted and become overgrown to form a quaking, watery swamp of peat and grasses. The railway was to cross four miles of this on the northern side.

The work began in July 1826. George Stephenson's plan, supervised by Dixon, involved a considerable amount of faith on the part of everyone prepared to pour money and toil into what was, according to legend, a bottomless pit. Stephenson describes this period:

> After working for weeks and weeks, filling in materials to form the road, there did not appear to be the least sign of our being able to raise the solid embankment an inch. We went on filling without the slightest, apparent, effect. My Assistants began to be uneasy and to doubt the success of the scheme. The Directors spoke of a hopeless task and became seriously alarmed. An immense outlay had been made and there would have been great loss had the scheme been abandoned. The Directors were compelled to allow me to proceed with the plan.[1]

It was not until July 1827 that the first part of a solid embankment appeared above the swamp. A temporary railway track was laid on it and the work of filling continued to creep forward, with increasing confidence. The 'impossible' task was finally completed in December 1829 and was, in fact, the cheapest part of the line. The 4 miles cost only

£28,000. It would be interesting to know what Francis Giles had to say about that.

At the Liverpool end, Crown Street station was on a short spur, while the railway swung north-west, to tunnel below the City from Edgehill to Wapping, close to Queen's Dock. The task of marking out the precise centre-line of the tunnel on the surface of the ground was exceptionally difficult, because scores of houses stood in the way. Shafts would be sunk from a point on the surface measured from the essential centre-line to the proposed rail level, and tunnelling would begin on a compass-bearing from the bottom of each shaft. If the centre-line between the houses was not true, the shafts would not be in line and the individual sections of the tunnel, working outwards from the bottom of each shift, would not meet. To lay out the line, through the houses, would have been a puzzle even for a first-class Surveyor and, under George Stephenson, the survey was prone to errors which translated into misaligned tunnels below ground.

The job of excavating the tunnel commenced around 1st October 1826 under the immediate supervision of Joseph Locke. Shafts were sunk 200 yds apart, 20 ft south of the tunnel's centre-line, their depth varying between 20 ft and 90 ft. The work was carried out by men using picks and shovels, while the buckets of spoil were raised to the surface by ropes, running over pulleys then wound around drums turned by horses.

From the bottom of each shaft the men dug through stone into the line of the tunnel by candle-light. Sometimes the rock was loosened by blasting with gunpowder, which created a great deal of acrid, white smoke. Several men were killed in the explosions and many more were drowned when they dug into underground streams. Until two vertical shafts could be connected by at least a small-bore heading there could be no ventilation and in a choking, smoking, candle-flickering twilight the men hacked away below the streets of Liverpool. It was June 1827 before a heading was cut throughout the whole length of the tunnel, and it was seen that, because of the inaccuracies in the laying-out of the centre-line above ground the eighteen or so separate excavations did not meet perfectly. Locke was able to correct the errors and the tunnel was completed to its full size on 7 June 1828. It was 22 ft wide and 16 ft high and passed for 2250 yds through solid rock.

The Company had hoped that it would remain dry and would not require a brick lining, but water soon percolated the sandstone rock so that a coating of very hard cement had to be applied, together with a brick lining. The tunnel was whitewashed and pendant gas lamps were installed at 50-yd intervals. In the summer of 1829 it was opened as a tourist attraction; for the price of one shilling a visitor was allowed to walk through the 1¼ mile-long hole under Liverpool.

The tunnel, the Olive Mount rock cutting, the Sankey viaduct and Chat Moss were gobbling money, and by March 1827 the Directors realized that the authorized capital would be insufficient to complete the line. In April, they borrowed £100,000 for twenty years from the Government, or rather, the Exchequer Loan Commissioners.[2]

The loan carried 3½ per cent interest which the Company convinced themselves would become feasible once the railway was opened. In fact the Government was not prepared to wait until the line was working, but demanded that its 3½ per cent be paid annually, starting the following June. The Directors tried to pay back the loan at once by attempting to borrow from some more understanding institution which would be prepared to wait for their interest until the railway was earning money, but they were unable to do this, given the state of the money market late in 1825. The 3½ per cent would have to be paid, even though the Company had no revenue. Late in 1827 the Directors realized that the line could be built more cheaply if the central section was straightened. The required Bill received the Royal Assent on 25 March 1828.

The railway was by now proceeding so well under Stephenson's direction that on 21 April 1828 his salary was almost doubled to £1500 per annum, an unprecedentedly large sum for any employee to earn. At the same time the Company was faced with three strategic questions, answers to which were essential:

1. Should the railway company become a common carrier?
2. Should the railway be taken across the Irwell and into Manchester proper?
3. What sort of motive power should be used?

In February 1828 a Committee of Directors was formed to look at the pros and cons. The Deputy Chairman, John Moss, was very keen that the railway should become the sole carrier of goods and passengers, rather than operate as a 'track authority' for independent carriers who would run trains over their line. To become a carrier would require the ownership of locomotives and wagons, horses and carts, warehousing, hydraulic lifts and wagon-moving equipment, and direct employment of a large staff. By June, most of the Committee were rather in favour of remaining as the 'track authority' and allowing others to undertake the expense of acting as carriers. The chaotic situation of the 'public-highway' railway had to be rationalized, but many on the Committee doubted whether it would really be profitable to become involved in the fiddling business of collection and delivery, the packing, sheeting and invoicing of wagons full of small packages, when there were long-established and experienced carriers, such as Pickfords, Paterson, Chaplin & Horne, Parker, Robins, Hargreaves and many more, eager to carry out this work. This was a matter of intense debate in the railway world for many years to come. If some co-operative arrangement between all parties could have been arranged, all would have been well; but in those days the spirit of competition was too powerful. Co-operation would have to be learned through bitter experience.

Moss admitted the additional expense involved in being a carrier but he pointed out that the Company would in any case be obliged to provide some warehousing, cranes and other facilities for the independent carriers. It would also be obliged to own at least some locomotives to haul trains of goods for the independent carriers, and so it might as well be a carrier, or *the* carrier, and take the whole of the money for carrying, not just the toll received from the independents. Moss was aware of the difficulties of the S&DR management and decided that if his Company acted as sole carrier and organizer of operations there would be greater efficiency and cheaper operating costs. The L&MR Committee of Directors allowed itself to be swayed by Moss and at a Special General Meeting, held on 3 November 1828, the shareholders were persuaded to give their permission for the Railway Company to become sole carrier and to cross the Irwell. A new Act was required, and this was obtained on 14 May 1829.

The Board began their serious investigation into Item 3, the sort of motive power they required, at a meeting held on 29 September 1828. Some Directors wanted horse haulage, believing (wrongly) that it was the cheapest system and (rightly) that it was the only one which would ensure the line remained a public highway. Another group, led by James Cropper, was impressed with Benjamin Thompson's patent 'reciprocating' rope-haulage system, in use on the Brunton & Shields Railway, a mineral line in County Durham. This managed reliably to haul wagons at 7 mph over an undulating track. Because of the poor performance of the Stephenson engines at that time, rope haulage was attractive because it used the tried and trusted technology of the stationary steam-engine. The third group of Directors, including Rathbone and Sandars, supported by the Company Secretary Henry Booth and George Stephenson, backed the only really practical system: locomotive haulage.

Over a 5-mile section of the Brunton & Shields Railway, stationary winding engines were placed at about one-mile intervals. Each engine had two winding drums. The rope extended from one drum of engine 'A', on rollers along the centre of the track, beneath the train, to a pulley very close to winding engine 'B'. The rope passed around this pulley and back to the second winding drum of engine 'A'. When the latter drum was made to revolve, the trucks were pulled along, while the other drum simply paid out the slack rope attached to the rear of the train. When the wagons arrived at the next engine they could be attached to the next rope for onward haulage while, at the same time, the rope for the first engine was waiting to haul another set of wagons back.[3]

Cropper was adamant on the subject of stationary engines, believing they would be cheaper than locomotive power. Stephenson was equally adamant that they would not be practical for a double-track, locomotive-hauled main line railway where speeds and weights hauled would increase annually as traffic developed.[4] Cropper's obsession with what he thought was the cheapest system blinded him to the practicalities of the case. Brunel was to be similarly blinded, twenty years later, over a similarly 'cheap' but entirely impractical 'atmospheric' system which also depended on stationary engines. Even learned individuals can be misled by concentrating on a single aspect of a business to the detriment of the whole. The railway, being a means of transport, must be practical, and mere 'cheapness' does not necessarily produce practicality.

The L&MR commissioned two eminent engineers, James Walker (who later became President of the Institution of Civil Engineers) and John Rastrick, to undertake a comparative study of the merits of locomotive and stationary engines. The two men went to see Blenkinsop's engines at Middleton colliery, George Stephenson's *Lancashire Witch* at work on the Bolton & Leigh Railway, to the Brunton & Shields line, and to the S&DR to talk to Timothy Hackworth, whose inventiveness and practical experience of stationary and movable engines was unrivalled. At the insistence of Robert Stephenson, they made a special trial of the capabilities of Hackworth's *Royal George* as the representative of the very best of locomotive practice.

Walker and Rastrick reported on 9 March 1829 that the *Royal George* was 'the most powerful that has yet been made'; but yet the report as a whole was a classic example of the 'on the one hand – on the other hand' school. They stated that stationary engines cost far more to build than locomotive engines but stationary engines could haul one ton 30 miles for 6.4d against 8.4d for locomotives; nevertheless, there had been improvements to locomotives which would make them cheaper to operate and there might be further improvements in the future. The economy, safety, convenience and dispatch of the reciprocating rope-haulage system was best if the Directors wished to open the railway at its fullest capacity at once, but if they wished to open business cautiously, so as to see how traffic developed, then it would be best to start with locomotives, which could be purchased in quantities appropriate to the traffic.

Walker's and Rastrick's report was of little use either to the 'reciprocating rope' or the 'locomotive' lobby of Directors. In response, George Stephenson – heavily engaged with the supervision of works on the L&MR and other lines – delegated the job of promoting the steam-locomotive to his son Robert and Joseph Locke. On 11 March Robert wrote to a friend: 'We are preparing for a counter-report in favour of locomotives . . . rely on it, locomotives shall not be cowardly given up. I will fight for them until the last. They are worthy of a conflict.' He wrote to Hackworth on the 17th: 'They [Walker and Rastrick] have increased the performance of fixed engines beyond what practice will bear out and depreciated the locomotive below what experience has taught us.'[5] Timothy Hackworth's reply contained the following declaration of faith:

> I am verily convinced that a swift engine upon a well conditioned railway will combine profit and simplicity and will afford such facility as has not hitherto been known . . . and if it happens that the Liverpool & Manchester Railway has been strangled by ropes we shall not accuse you of guilt in being accessory either before or after the fact.[6]

Robert Stephenson and Joseph Locke studied the problem thoroughly and on 20 April 1829 issued to the Directors of the L&MR their 'Observations on the Comparative Merits of Locomotives and Fixed Engines'. Where Walker and Rastrick had been lukewarm or equivocal on the merits of stationary engines, Stephenson and Locke were adamantly in favour of locomotives. Stationary engines were useful on steep inclines, they said, but they were not flexible enough for day-to-day operations. The breakdown of a stationary winding engine would bring all traffic to a halt until it was repaired whereas a broken locomotive could be shunted out of the way. If a train was extra heavy, two locomotives could be used, but the stationary engine had a fixed horsepower, calculated for certain conditions, and could not cope with overloading. Speeds 'on the rope' would always be low, and loads would be restricted by the fixed power of the winding engine. Comparative haulage cost, per ton, for stationary engines and locomotives was 7.86d and 4.43d respectively, and as locomotive design continued to improve, so the differential would increase.

The Report was without doubt the work of Joseph Locke and Robert Stephenson equally, but George Stephenson insisted that only his name should appear as the author. When Locke, hitherto devoted to his master, protested at this piracy, Stephenson allowed his name and that of Robert to appear as the authors but, with the addition of the entirely untruthful statement, 'Compiled from the reports of George Stephenson', claimed authorship. The real authors were his assistants so, as far as he was concerned, it was his property. This was the first of several incidents which opened Locke's eyes to the grasping and ungrateful character of his mentor.

The protagonists of the stationary engine would not accept the obvious. As a result of this a trial of locomotive performance was organized during October 1829, on the L&MR, at Rainhill, where there was 1¾ miles of straight and level track. Specifications for 'an improved moving power' were set down:

1. The said engine must effectually consume its own smoke.

2. The engine, if it weighs 6 tons, must be capable of drawing after it, day by day, on a well constructed railway, on a level plane, a train of carriages of 20 tons at a rate of 10 mph with a boiler pressure not exceeding 50 lb psi.

3. There must be two safety valves, one of which must be out of control of the engineman and neither of which must be fastened down while the engine is working.

4. The engine and boiler must be supported on springs and rest on six wheels and the height from the ground to the top of the chimney must not exceed 15 feet.

5. The weight of the machine, with water in the boiler, must not exceed six tons and if the gross weight does not exceed five tons then the gross weight to be drawn need not exceed 15 tons, and that in pro-

portion for machines of still smaller weight provided that the engine be on six wheels . . . an engine reduced to 4½ tons may be placed on four wheels. The company shall be at liberty to test the boilers to 150 lb psi and shall not be liable for any damage caused.

6.   The engine's boiler must be fitted with a pressure gauge.

7.   The engine to be delivered complete for trial at the Liverpool end of the railway not later than 1 October next.

8.   The price of the engine not to exceed £550.

The rules were curious in so far as no standard was set for fuel economy, and competitors were encouraged to build a lightweight engine pulling a small load. The designer of the winning engine was to be awarded £500 and, of course, his design would become that used on the L&MR – and probably in Europe and America, since the trials were witnessed by engineers and railway promoters from both continents.

Five machines arrived for the trials: the *Rocket*, *Sans Pareil*, *Perseverance*, *Novelty* and *Cycloped*. The last-named was entered by Thomas Brandreth, a leading figure in the L&MR and a friend of George Stephenson, though how Brandreth came to enter his contraption in a trial of locomotive power is a mystery: it was merely a horse-driven treadmill on wheels and was disqualified on that ground when the time came. The *Novelty* was designed by a then unknown Swedish engineer, John Ericsson and built at John Braythwaite's works in London. It was a four-wheeled trolley on which coal, water, boiler and cylinders were carried. The boiler was vertical and supplied two 6 × 12 in.-vertical cylinders. It had been built in a hurry to meet the deadline of the trials and was in trouble even before it ran. These pre-trial faults were rectified by Timothy Hackworth, whose sense of sportsmanship was greater than his competitive instinct. On trial, *Novelty* propelled itself, without a load, at the entirely novel speed of 28 mph but in spite of Hackworth's and Ericsson's best efforts, the haste with which the machine had been constructed caused its boiler to leak, and it was disqualified.

The *Perseverance*, designed by Timothy Burstall of Edinburgh, was not a locomotive but a rail-borne variant of his steam-powered road carriage and therefore disqualified from the trials. It was allowed to run, but was unable to exceed 6 mph.

Being a man of small salary and large family, Timothy Hackworth had little money available to build a locomotive. What he achieved was a small but potent machine, the *Sans Pareil* – the only engine which Robert Stephenson regarded as a serious threat to his own machine. It was very important to the future of the business of Robert Stephenson & Co. that their engine won the competition.

The *Sans Pareil* had four driving wheels of 4 ft 6 in. diameter, with a powerful boiler having a return-flue, while the fire was drawn up fiercely by a coned blast pipe. The cylinders (which had been cast and bored at Robert Stephenson's factory) were mounted vertically, Hackworth-style, at the trailing end of the boiler, driving directly on to the rear wheels. The drive was taken to the leading wheels by a coupling-rod. The engine had, however, no springs, which disqualified it from the trials and, according to the trial judges, it was overweight for an engine on four wheels by ¼ ton. Hackworth asked to see the engine weighed but was refused.[7] Having removed *Sans Pareil* from the competition the judges were understandably keen to see how it would run, 'to ascertain if the performance was such as would enable them to recommend the point to the Directors'.[8] Its Hackworth excellence was required but the prize was, perhaps, already destined for someone else.

The *Sans Pareil* began its demonstration with a load of 25 tons and had just commenced running when the metal wall of one of the Stephenson-cast cylinders burst, opening a passage direct to exhaust for live steam entering the cylinder. In spite of this the engine ran for two hours, hauling its 25 tons at nearly 15 mph. Afterwards the cylinder was cut open and it was revealed that the metal in the area of the lesion was not more than ⅟₁₆ in. thick where it ought to have been ⅞ in.[9]

Robert Stephenson's *Rocket* was a development of his 1828-built *Lancashire Witch*. The latter was a four-wheeled engine with steeply inclined, rear-mounted cylinders, driving only the leading pair of wheels. Its boiler was of the return-flue type. Robert Stephenson's *Rocket* looked similar to the *Witch* with the important difference that it was fitted with slide-valves, a multi-tubular boiler and a 'firebox'. Such a device had been patented by Marc Seguin in France in 1828, but it seems that Henry Booth thought of the same idea, without knowledge of Seguin's patent, and suggested it to Robert Stephenson. The concept was excellent, but time was short in which to realize a working example properly. As a result the firebox was crudely applied to the boiler; it stood in the open air, uninsulated, circulating water between itself and the boiler through two copper pipes. From the firebox's inner wall, twenty-five brass tubes, of 3 in. external diameter, passed through the boiler, surrounded by water, to the 'smoke box', on which stood the chimney. The *Rocket*'s driving wheels were 4 ft 8½ in. in diameter. Its boiler was 6 ft long and 3 ft 8 in. in diameter, slightly smaller than that on the *Sans Pareil*, but thanks to the new technique of multi-tubes, the heating surface presented to the water was 117¾ sq. ft, while the firebox added another 20 sq. ft of heating surface. The engine's two cylinders, 8 in. by 16½ in., were fixed to the boiler at the firebox end and were inclined at 45 degrees, the pistons driving connecting rods direct to the leading wheels.

Each cylinder's exhaust steam was discharged through its own, separate nozzle within the chimney. They were not blast pipes, placed centrally within the chimney, but they did create some sort of suction through the boiler tubes and thus drew air through the fire to make it burn more fiercely. The *Rocket* ran 'light engine' at 24 mph and hauled its test load of people and rocks weighing 13 tons at 15 mph on level track; it then went on to astonish everyone by hauling its train up the Rainhill incline – for which stationary winding engines had been deemed necessary – at 12 mph. The L&MR Directors were impressed with all they had seen, the doubters were won over to the utility of the steam-locomotive, while the *Rocket* and Robert Stephenson carried off the prize – plus construction orders for engines on the L&MR, in Europe and America.

Hackworth's powerful *Sans Pareil* was repaired and sold to the L&MR, for whom it hauled trains successfully until 1844, when it was no longer heavy enough to haul the increasing weight of traffic. Hackworth may well have been beaten by skulduggery but it must be said that his system, excellent though it was (as represented by the *Sans Pareil* or *Royal George*) was not in the evolutionary line, whereas the *Rocket* was. This is not to deny Hackworth's credit as a vital link in the development of express steam locomotion. In 1829 he designed the *Globe*, the first locomotive to have a crankshaft below the boiler, driven by horizontal pistons (although these were placed at the rear, beneath the furnace). The boiler was of the return-flue type.[10] Hackworth had to send the designs to Robert Stephenson & Co. for construction, and before the firm completed the *Globe* they used the idea, coupled with a multi-tubular boiler, to build their own version. This had the cylinders below the smoke box and a multi-tubular boiler with separate firebox: the first of the 'modern' engines. It left the works in October 1830 and was called – with a degree of one-upmanship – the *Planet*. The *Globe* locomotive came out two months later.

Hackworth continued to develop his rear-mounted cylinder engines with return-flue boilers on the S&DR, adding many refinements which were vital to all locomotive design.[11] His invention for loco-motive use of a combined large flue and multi-tube boiler was later used to power ships. His first engine in the 'modern' style was a 2–2–2 for Russia, built in 1836. Thereafter his modern designs were excep-tionally good but now forgotten, overshadowed by the more famous name, but less inventive personality, of Robert Stephenson.

9

Inter-city Turnpike Railway

THE LIVERPOOL & MANCHESTER Railway was to be officially opened on Wednesday 15 September 1830 but the celebrations began on the previous Monday. Every hotel, pub and boarding house was full of paying guests; people living within sight of the line hired their rooms as observation posts and sold food and drink as well. The special trains were assembled at the Crown Street depot and would start from there, thus avoiding the necessity of rope-hauling them through the tunnel up the Edgehill incline. By dawn on the 15th all Lancashire seemed to have come to the railway. Lineside grandstands had been erected and dense crowds lined the route for miles out into the countryside.

At 9 a.m. the Prime Minister – the Duke of Wellington – arrived at the Liverpool station with a large party of dignitaries including Prince Esterhazy, the Home Secretary Sir Robert Peel, and William Huskisson, MP for Liverpool, accompanied by his wife. There were eight trains: one, for the Duke of Wellington and the most important English and foreign visitors, ran on the southernmost track of the double line of rails, the other seven moved along in procession on the north line. The engines were driven by the engineers of the Company. George Stephenson drove the *Northumbrian*, hauling the Ducal train consisting of three carriages: the first was for the band; the second (at 32 ft long by 8 ft wide, the most sumptuous vehicle yet put on rails) carried the Prime Minister and his party; the third was for the

Directors and their friends. Joseph Locke drove the *Rocket*, Allcard the *Comet*. About 9.45 a.m. a gun was fired. The wadding which had tamped down the gunpowder charge tore out a labourer's eye, and the trains steamed out into the dawn of the truly inter-city, passenger carrying Railway Age.

Political relations were very strained between the Prime Minister and the MP for Liverpool. Huskisson sat as a Tory but his politics were so Whiggish on the vital issues of electoral reform and the repeal of the Corn Laws that, when he had been in the Cabinet, some Tories reproached the Duke for including him. Wellington is said to have justified his inclusion by saying: 'He is a good bridge for rats to run over.'[1] In 1828 Huskisson, then Colonial Secretary, had voted against his Prime Minister over the Penrhyn borough Voting Reform Bill. He then offered to resign, wrote to retract his resignation but then resigned anyway. Wellington's premiership had been jeopardized for a few days and so the whole matter had been threatening to the Party. Now, on this auspicious day on the railway, Wellington was enjoying himself. Stephenson took the train up to 30 mph and the Duke was exclaiming 'Magnificent!', 'Stupendous!', 'Like the whizzing of a cannon ball!', while the cheers of the crowd on the lineside – although not necessarily for him in particular – were a pleasant change from the baying of pro-reform mobs.

All the trains were booked to stop at Parkside, 17 miles out, to take on coal and water, and all passengers had been told that they were to remain within their carriages during the stop. The Ducal train was at a stand at Parkside (the modern Newton-le-Willows), with the *North Star* and its train alongside on the north line. This train moved away, whereupon the noble personages in the Duke's train disobeyed orders, got down on to the track and milled about in the way that people do on railway lines. Only the disciplined Duke of Wellington remained in his carriage. While the Duke was in a good mood, Huskisson's friends thought the moment was right to bring about a reconciliation between the two men. Huskisson was escorted through the milling throng to the Duke's carriage. Wellington was leaning out to shake hands with Huskisson when the cry went up that the *Rocket* was approaching on the north line.

Something close to panic ensued in the narrow space between the rails; princely dignity was forgotten and coat tails flapped as Prince Esterhazy, who was among those on the ground, half-leaped, was half-pulled, up into the carriage, others pressed themselves against the

Ducal train. The Duke's carriage overhung the rails by two feet and the approaching *Rocket* had a six-inch overhang, leaving only eighteen inches of clear space, so only slim people would have been safe. North of the north line were large puddles and a steep, earth bank, uncomfortable but safe. Several people, including William Huskisson, ran across the track to stand in the water, and lean back against the mud; but, having reached safety, Huskisson responded to a call to get into a carriage on the Ducal train. He dashed back across the north line to the open door. The door of the carriage was 3 ft wide and was thus 'foul' of the approaching train. Huskisson was trying to scramble up into the carriage when the *Rocket* went past and slammed the door against him, throwing him on to the track. His left leg fell across the rail and the rear wheel of the engine and all the wheels of the train passed over it from thigh to ankle. The crunching of broken bones was clearly heard in the trains and pandemonium reigned. Lord Wilton tried to stem the flow of blood with a tourniquet; Huskisson was heard to say, 'It's all over. Bring me my wife and let me die.' Mrs Huskisson was screaming.[2] He was rushed away by the *Northumbrian* engine to Eccles, to the home of an Anglican clergyman.

With vast crowds waiting for the train in Manchester it was thought best to continue, rather than risk a riot, but with silenced bandsmen and without responding to the crowd. That was, of course, impossible. At Manchester the train was brought to a halt by the crowd; thousands hissed and booed the Duke and waved their revolutionary tricolour cockades (reform was all the rage), but others pressed babies into the Duke's arms and insisted he kiss them – which he did.

William Huskisson meanwhile received the Sacrament from the clergyman and lingered on in terrible pain until the evening, when he died. He had seen railways as a positive force for good, and had been of great assistance to the Liverpool & Manchester, playing a large part in getting its various Bills through Parliament. At his funeral in Liverpool on 24 September, 15–20,000 people lined the route. The Liverpool & Manchester Railway Company erected a monument at the Parkside in his memory.[3]

Huskisson has been awarded the dubious and perhaps undeserved honour of being 'the first casualty of the Railway Age'. George Lisle, the horse leader crushed to death on the S&DR, was denied the privilege, as were those accidentally blasted to death with gunpowder – or drowned – while digging the Edgehill tunnel in 1828. Even the man who lost his eye to the cannon which set the trains in motion that very day was not 'the first casualty of the Railway Age'. One might split hairs and say that, with the S&DR, the true railway age had not yet begun; or that the anonymous workmen building the L&MR died before it began. But clearly, no one less than a member of the ruling class could be accorded the curious distinction of this tragic title.

On Friday 17 September, having been running for free or at half-fare since the 13th, the Liverpool & Manchester Railway took up its normal, daily working, to published timetables (which gave departure but not arrival times). Smoking was not allowed on the trains. The horse coach fare from Liverpool to Manchester was 12s [60p] inside and 7s [35p] outside for a journey which took 4½ hrs. The railway did the run in 2 hrs for 7s in a 1st-class (covered and glazed) carriage and 4s in a roofed but open-sided 2nd-class carriage. Between 17 and 25 September an average of 763 passengers a day were carried, and during October the number rose to 1000 – all at relatively high speed and without injury. The public mails were carried on the line from 15 November. On Sundays, excursions were run. The people who travelled in the trains were called 'passengers', rather than 'customers', and at every station a 'passengers' diary' was kept, so that passengers could write complaints or praise.

George and Robert Stephenson's locomotive works had difficulty in meeting the demand for locomotives, and not until 4 December 1830 did the railway commence its dedicated goods service – as opposed to occasionally attaching a goods truck to a passenger train. The first freight train conveyed 50 tons of imported cotton, oatmeal and malt to Manchester, and was 'double-headed' on the Rainhill incline. By the end of the month, 1432 tons of freight had been carried, in January this rose to 3848 tons, in February, 4818 tons and in March, 5500 tons.

The locomotives performed feats beyond the wildest dreams of their owners. On 25 March 1831 *Samson* hauled 151 tons from Liverpool to Manchester in 2 hrs 34 mins, with 'triple heading' (*Mars, Mercury* and *North Star*) on the Rainhill incline. This tonnage was insignificant in relation to the tens of thousands of tons to be moved, but such was the income from freight that passenger fares were cross-subsidized and reduced to 5s (return) and 3s 6d (single), Liverpool to Manchester or vice versa, and especially luxurious, 'extra-1st-class' carriages, costing the passenger an additional 2s, were introduced on the express trains.

It was in passenger carrying that the L&MR gained most of its revenue in those early days.[4] Before 1830 the Liverpool–Manchester Turnpike Trust had leased the tolls of the road to contractors. The

Eccles gates, worth £1500 in 1829, and the Irlam gates, worth £1335, could not now be leased to anyone at any price. The turnpike emptied of traffic, and all but one of the regular stage-coaches had disappeared by 1832 – the sole survivor carrying only parcels. The Bridgewater and Mersey & Irwell canals at once reduced their rates by 30 per cent and continued to carry large quantities of freight. The competition with the local railways was severe, and in 1844 these two canals amalgamated in all but name by making a 'no-competition' treaty between themselves and agreeing standard charges for both systems. This was the shape of things to come in all transport.

In 1830 such railways as existed were still operating according to eighteenth-century notions developed for turnpike roads. Early in 1831 the L&MR, in accordance with its Parliamentary obligations, invited independent operators to put their own trains on the line. Such trains had to be licensed by the 'track authority' (the L&MR), and drawings and specifications of locomotives, carriages and wagons, approved by the Company, were displayed for the benefit of would-be operators. Rolling stock built to these specifications was, of course, expensive, especially as they were only to be used for the independent operator's relatively few trains: the cost of wagons, in relation to the tons per day they would carry, was high. There was also the problem, already experienced by the S&DR, of forcing the independent oper-ator to maintain his rolling stock in a safe and proper condition, since any additional expense would reduce his profits. Furthermore, he would have to fit his services into a timetable drawn up by the L&MR – and face the severity of competition from the L&MR and any other independents who might decide to enter the field. The L&MR was opened to independent operators, subject to the above conditions, from 1 May 1831.

The Bolton & Leigh Railway (B&LR), mentioned in chapter 6, was opened from Bolton to William Hulton's colliery at Chequerbent on 1 August 1828. The event was marked by a day of free rides in wagons hauled by the *Lancashire Witch* and the distribution among the poor of eight wagon-loads of free coal. In 1829, the 2½-mile link from the L&MR at Kenyon Junction to Leigh was authorized as yet another discrete company. On 6 April 1830, the *Sans Pareil* hauled a coachload of Directors from Kenyon to Bolton and the line was declared open for freight. It was opened to passengers on 11 June 1831.

After several unsuccessful attempts at incorporation, dating back to 1823, the promoters[5] of the Warrington & Newton Railway (W&NR)

were finally successful in obtaining an Act on 6 May 1829. This 5-mile line, engineered by Robert Stephenson and supported by the L&MR, must have been intended as the start of a line to Birmingham and London, and yet, when opened, on 25 July 1831, the W&NR was built lightly and laid with light track suitable only for branch working.

After the manner of the times, the Directors of the W&NR, the Bolton & Leigh and the Leigh & Kenyon Junction Railway leased the working of their lines to a local carrier, John Hargreaves Jnr, of Bolton, one of their co-Directors, a man whose father was a well-established carrier on the turnpike roads and canals. Hargreaves's rent gave the Company a guaranteed minimum dividend, but he then had to make a profit for himself out of his remaining income, while being unable to prevent any other operator from hauling goods and passengers over the lines and taking away traffic he might otherwise have carried.

Thus there were four connected turnpike railway companies, with each independent operator having made his own arrangements to run over the tracks of all four companies. That these arrangements would become complicated is obvious. The track-owning Company had made expensive capital outlays on cuttings, embankments, stations, water columns, turntables, engine-sheds and goods-sheds, and would be rather jealous about letting independent competitors have the use of that equipment. The scale of charges to Hargreaves by the L&MR, for instance, were such as to prevent him competing with the L&MR. Even then, Hargreaves was taking traffic which could have been carried by the owning Company, so the owning Company still lost.

The L&MR was obliged to allow Hargreaves on to their track but banned his engines as unsuitable and made him hire locomotives from themselves. It constructed at its own expense, specifically for Hargreaves's use, a wharf, goods-shed and cranes at Wapping, on the docks at Liverpool, for which he was charged £150 a year. He also rented a warehouse on the Company's property in Manchester, and shared some coal staithes there. Presumably every independent carrier who decided to try his luck on the railway would have required warehousing to be provided.

When Hargreaves began carrying freight on the Bolton & Leigh and Liverpool & Manchester railways, the highly circuitous Leeds & Liverpool Canal reduced the cost of carrying to half the Parliamentary rate, or so Hargreaves alleged, and a great legal battle then commenced, between Hargreaves Jnr and the canal, extending over several years.

This was an interesting situation, since Hargreaves Snr owned a long-established carrying business over the Leeds & Liverpool and Bridgewater canals and would have benefited enormously from the reduced rates. His son constantly complained to the L&MR that his carrying business was being squeezed between his obligations to pay the railway tolls and the very cheap rates charged for freight on the canals. The L&MR accordingly reduced their charges to Hargreaves as far as they could, in a series of complicated agreements over tolls.

By 1840 John Hargreaves operated six 1st-class and eight 2nd-class carriages, several dozen coal wagons and fourteen locomotives (these from eight different manufacturers). The L&MR had frequent cause to reprimand him for the poor condition of his fleet – lack of brakes was the commonest complaint – and more than once he was threatened with exclusion from L&MR metals if he did not improve matters. He obviously had a problem with costs, and skimped wherever possible. Similar complications existed on the Warrington & Newton Railway where Hargreaves was trying to run his trains in competition with those of the colliery owners.

The Wigan Branch Railway, north from the L&MR at Parkside and ¼-mile east of Newton, opened on 3 September 1832. A separate company formed to extend this line northwards: the Preston & Wigan Railway got its Act in April 1831. Before construction began, these two amalgamated to form the Northern Union Railway (NUR). This opened from Parkside to Preston on 31 October 1838.

John Hargreaves Snr became the contractor for this railway, making agreements with the L&MR and the NUR to carry all traffic to and from Liverpool and Manchester for Wigan, Preston and Yorkshire, using the L&MR, the NUR and the Leeds & Liverpool Canal. He had six locomotives at work over these railways, had leased seven more to colliery owners, and others again to the L&MR; a further seventeen were owned by the NUR. The Wigan branch was also used by the private trains of colliery owners.

These wheels within wheels created confusion and complications in management and operation. The many and varied machines with their individualistic drivers, owing allegiance to a variety of employers, plied to and fro without much regard for safety: and collisions were common. Evidence given to the 1839 Select Committee of Parliament speaks of the dangerous rivalries between drivers of different companies. Safety required a standard set of rules and one authority to apply them. When damage occurred there would then be a row between the various parties as to who was to blame and who was to pay. Sometimes when damage was done to the fittings of the railway the culprit would slip away, so that the 'track authority' knew not to whom the bill for repairs should be sent.

10

The Grand Junction Railway: Stephenson versus Locke

A RAILWAY SOUTHWARDS FROM a Liverpool–Manchester line to Birmingham and London had been suggested by William James in 1808 and again in 1823. By then he was not alone: several different committees were exploring ways and means of making such trunk railways. Among these were George Stephenson, backed by various Liverpudlian and Mancunian business people. A Bill for a Liverpool and Birmingham railway was presented to Parliament in 1831 but failed because Parliament itself collapsed after the rejection of the Reform Bill. With the great success of the Liverpool & Manchester Railway the southward extension was inevitable. New prospectuses for a 'Grand Junction Railway Company' (GJR) and for a 'London & Birmingham Railway Company' (L&BR) were issued in January 1832 when public meetings were held in Liverpool and Birmingham.

George Stephenson was to be Chief Engineer of both railways but with his son Robert as his Resident Engineer on the L&BR and John Urpeth Rastrick and Joseph Locke on the GJR. The Grand Junction was to be a 78-mile-long trunk line, from Warrington to Stafford and into the centre of Birmingham, where it would meet the 112-mile-long London & Birmingham Railway end-on. The total of 190 miles of railway was expected to take only four years to build.

The GJR was a Liverpool and Lancashire venture and no important Birmingham businessman subscribed to the shares. The Chairman was the Liverpudlian banker John Moss, and other Directors included Charles Lawrence, Joseph Sandars, Hardman Earle, John Cropper and Robert Gladstone, brother to the future Prime Minister. The GJR Directors wanted a workmanlike job, without unnecessary frills, which would pay a good dividend. In this the Directors were served best, not by their Chief Engineer, George Stephenson, nor by John Rastrick, but by the young Joseph Locke. They were also fortunate to have as contractors the old-established, solvent and very experienced Hugh and David McIntosh and the brilliant young Thomas Brassey. The GJR and the L&BR were most fortunate railways: sound, commercial propositions. There was already a heavy traffic flow to and from London–Birmingham–Liverpool/Manchester and the two companies would provide a fast trunk route, relatively unaffected by weather conditions, which was bound to encourage travel and industrial expansion. Its Directors were not looking for 'a quick killing', nor for personal glory; they believed they were embarked on a profitable investment which was also a great public work.

In Stephenson's original plan, the end-on junction in Birmingham would have been on the site of Nova Scotia Gardens, Curzon Street, about three-quarters of a mile east of the Bull Ring and St Chad's Cathedral. The GJR was to have turned south near Perry Bar and cut into the rising ground of Aston Park, on which was built Aston Hall, the home of James Watt. He was the son of the great pioneer of the steam-engine and himself a leading figure in the Birmingham canal industry. Having climbed through the park, the railway would have tunnelled the ridge for perhaps half a mile and emerged to meet the L&BR at Nova Scotia Gardens (see Map 2).

George Stephenson was in 1832 the country's most widely sought-after engineer. He was regarded as the man who had made railways possible – the champion of the steam-locomotive, the conqueror of Chat Moss. Some time in 1831 or early 1832 Stephenson transferred Locke from the L&MR to work on the preliminaries of the Grand Junction Railway. Locke earned a pupil-assistant's pay of £100 per annum; George Stephenson as Engineer-in-Chief received £1500 per annum, while relying on Locke's skill to produce answers to difficult questions. Joseph Locke turned out to be a truly commercial engineer: unegotistical, enormously energetic, clever and practical. He developed a 'Theory of Gradients'[1] which, coupled to his belief in the developing power of steam-locomotives, enabled him to construct relatively cheap trunk lines over the shortest practical route. Locke did not ill-treat his contractors, nor did he use his shareholders' money to indulge in expensive experiments. There would be no tensions over extravagance between Locke and his Directors as there would be, later, between Brunel and his employers on the Great Western Railway.

At twenty-eight, Locke had a reputation to make and threw himself into the work. Stephenson and Rastrick were already established and, with a great many irons in the fire,[2] neither man spent as much time on the GJR as he ought to have done. Rastrick prepared a detailed survey of his southern section of the line, together with plans for stations, bridges and so forth. He estimated that the section would require £1 million to build, which would cover the cost of a branch to Wolverhampton, and all earthworks, locomotives, rolling stock and 'contingencies'. He also estimated that the opening would take place in June 1837. After this great surveying work, Rastrick appears to have lost interest in the railway and to have given it less of his time.

Prior to going to Parliament with its Bill, the GJR Committee had to placate not only the usual land-owning and canal interests, but also the Staffordshire iron and pottery masters who could only gain from the railway. These latter, opportunistic 'captains of industry' would benefit from cheap transport for their products and yet they felt the need to demand both extortionate prices for land and high compensation. James Watt refused to co-operate with the GJR at any price, and since the cost of houses and land in the Birmingham central area was too high, the GJR cut their line short to a terminal at New John Street, still on the north side of the ridge and half a mile from the proposed L&BR terminus. The GJR's Parliamentary legal fees amounted to a mere £18,596 but the cost of land and compensation to the landowners over the 78 miles totalled, £211,862 – and not a brick had been purchased for that expense. The Grand Junction Railway Act was obtained, simultaneously with that for the London & Birmingham Railway, on 6 May 1833.

Stephenson did a similar survey for the northern half of the line and planned, in a general way, the great viaduct at Dutton and lesser works elsewhere. Subsequently Stephenson distanced himself more and more from the work and, had it not been for Locke's planning of the fine detail for the whole line, the works would not have been realized. On 25 September 1833, Stephenson submitted to the Directors some improvements between Madeley and Aston and for the extension of the line through the ridge to meet the L&BR in Nova Scotia Gardens. The Directors were so impressed with these alterations that they increased Stephenson's pay from £1500 to £2000 per annum and ordered Joseph Locke – then embroiled in the detailed planning of 10 miles of the heaviest engineering works from Warrington to the River Weaver – to make working plans of Stephenson's general ideas without any increase in *his* pay. Locke began to feel the injustice of the situation and raised the matter with the Directors. On 22 October 1833, they minuted that: 'Mr. Locke be appointed Engineer under Mr. Stephenson with special care of the Liverpool end but with the superintendence of the whole in the absence of, or when required by, the principal Engineer and that he be allowed a salary of £800 p.a.' He was also awarded £200 a year for his expenses. Locke, who had long been engaged to Phoebe McCreery, now fixed the date for the wedding.[3]

On 12 December 1833 Rastrick formally resigned from the GJR to become Engineer of the Manchester & Cheshire Junction Railway. This was to form a short-cut between Manchester and the GJR at a point in the fields which became known as 'Crewe', and, when completed, would siphon away from the GJR the entire Manchester traffic and the accompanying revenue. Rastrick was replaced by William Allcard – who was at that time supervising the construction of the Lime Street tunnel of the L&MR. Allcard was placed under Locke's supervision rather than Stephenson's, an indication of the declining reliance being placed on the latter by the GJR Directors.

Stephenson now regarded Locke as a treacherous usurper of his glory. It is impossible to know how much of the railway's design really was Stephenson's and how much was Rastrick's or Locke's. As Engineer-in-Chief, Stephenson, must have sketched all the large works (from south to north): the Handsworth/Aston tunnel, the Darlaston aqueduct, the Penkridge viaduct, the Preston Brook cutting and aqueduct, and the Dutton, Vale Royal and Warrington (Acton Grange) viaducts, as well as station architecture. Rastrick's notebooks show he sketched many details even down to wheelbarrows, lampposts and locomotive turntables but someone had to translate these sketches into precise working drawings and it was at this point that Locke could influence, correct or improve the sketches. Locke staked out the Whitmore–Warrington section, drew up the contract specifications, found contractors and then supervised all construction. He had signed up the last contractor needed for the northern section by September 1834. His energy was in marked contrast to the dilatoriness of George

Stephenson, who, busy sweeping up engineerships for various railways, had by then only signed up his first contractor for the southern section of the GJR.

The Preston Brook Canal underpass was set in a 45-ft-deep cutting, 1¾ miles long. It was Locke who, on 19 June 1833, urged an immediate start here, because he knew that the canal was about to have its annual maintenance, for which the water would be removed, and that this would be the golden opportunity to erect the aqueduct across the railway simply and cheaply.[4] The Dutton viaduct, the more northerly of the pair which cut across the loop of the River Weaver, also crossed the Weaver Canal. It is 466 yds long,[5] and consists of twenty red sandstone arches each of 60-ft span, the rails 65 ft above the river. The arches have the stamp of George Stephenson's style about them and he claimed their design for his own but it was Locke who laboriously worked out the details and supervised its construction throughout. The contractor was the father-and-son partnership of Hugh and David McIntosh, later to be so ill-used by Brunel. The combination of McIntosh and Locke produced the great viaduct on time, within the £54,440 estimate and, although over 700 men had been employed for two years, not a single life was lost.[6] The southernmost Weaver viaduct, Vale Royal, was 150 yds long, with five arches of 63-ft span, 65 ft above the river, and had also employed 700 men for two years.[7]

The Warrington or Acton Grange viaduct was designed by Locke.[8] The most difficult work it involved was the crossing of the River Mersey and the Mersey & Irwell Canal. Locke designed a very fine series of twelve masonry arches here, several approach spans, a larger span over the canal, and two 75-ft spans across the river. The contract to build the viaduct was taken by James Crompton, James Dalziel and William MacKenzie in June 1835 and Locke appointed the nineteen-year-old Alfred Stanistreet Jee (1816–1858) to supervise its construction[9] – and indeed all construction in the Warrington area.

The Penkridge viaduct and 10 miles of associated earthworks, south of Stafford, were constructed by Thomas Brassey (1805–1870). This was his first railway contract. Brassey, who became the greatest of all the railway contractors, was born into a family of prosperous yeoman farmers who had worked the land at Bulkeley, Cheshire, for 600 years. In 1826 he was managing (or perhaps owned) a stone quarry at Stourton. George Stephenson had gone to view the stone there, for use in the Sankey viaduct of the L&MR, met Brassey and was immediately impressed with his remarkable character – as, apparently, was everyone else who came into contact with him. Stephenson wanted Brassey to come to work for him on the railway but Brassey, as good a judge of character as old George, declined the offer and instead, became his own master.[10]

In 1834, at the suggestion of Stephenson – and also, it must in fairness be said, with the enthusiastic encouragement of the very businesslike Mrs Brassey – Thomas tendered for the contract to build the Dutton viaduct. In this he was beaten by the long-established McIntoshes, but on 25 February 1835 his tender of £26,500 to build the Penkridge viaduct was accepted by Stephenson on behalf of the GJR.[11] Brassey's bankers, Dixons of Chester, unhesitatingly advanced the capital he required for the work – probably the most profitable decision they ever made, for Brassey retained them as his personal bankers for the rest of his exceedingly wealthy life.

When Locke later took over responsibility for the southern part of the GJR he examined the Penkridge contract. The viaduct, which was to comprise seven spans of 30 ft each, 77 ft high[12] and approximately 110 yds long, was only a quarter the length of the Dutton, but was to cost half as much. He saw that Stephenson's specification was not clear, and had caused Brassey to charge more than was required. Locke went at once to Brassey's house in Birkenhead and, over breakfast, showed him that an error had been made and that, in fact, the job could be done for £6000 less. Brassey at once agreed to the lower price.[13]

The Penkridge contract was completed on time and within the lower price, and so began Brassey's long and very profitable career, worldwide, in railway building – much of it working with Locke in England, Scotland and France. Brassey's word was his bond and he became a legend in his own lifetime for honesty[14] and efficiency – his working principle in business being: 'A hard bargain is a bad bargain.'

Relations between Stephenson and Locke were finally poisoned in mid-1834. At Liverpool, the Lime Street tunnel, inexpertly surveyed by Allcard or Stephenson or both, was driven under Allcard's supervision. It was intended to be 2230 yds long, 17 ft high and 25 ft wide. Stephenson, whose earlier tunnelling experience had not been altogether successful, left Allcard – with no tunnelling experience – in charge of building the Lime Street tunnel, and, after December 1833, gave the young man the additional responsibility of the southern half of the GJR. Allcard was not incompetent: he and Locke went on to build railways together in Britain and Europe.[15] He did his best with the tunnel but in mid-1834 he reported to the L&MR Directors that the headings from the bottom of the various shafts were 'off line' to such an extent as to be in danger of missing each other underground.[16]

Locke, who had corrected and then guided Stephenson's first tunnel to a successful conclusion, was recalled by the L&MR Directors to sort out this much greater mess. His corrections, faithfully followed by Allcard, produced a satisfactory conclusion. George Stephenson, however, was not at all pleased. He sulked and either refused to answer written requests for guidance from the Directors of the GJR (who were, after all, his employers), or else gave his advice grudgingly after months of delay.

The plans which George Stephenson had drawn up in September 1833 for the extension of the GJR to the L&BR at Curzon Street, tunnelling under Handsworth, were submitted to Parliament in November 1833. Among the clauses in this Bill was one of unique naivety. The GJR had, by virtue of their Act of Incorporation, the legal right to take their railway through Watt's Aston Park, but now the Company inserted a clause binding them not to enter Watt's lands without his written permission. This they did in the hope of winning him over to their cause and thus avoiding the punitive land costs and compensation he would undoubtedly demand. The Bill for the extension became law on 16 June 1834.[17]

James Watt remained unmoved by the GJR's throwing itself upon his mercy, and as early as March 1834 George Stephenson presented the Directors with his plans for a line, circling around the east and south of Birmingham from Aston to Curzon Street, about ¼ mile south of the city centre. Locke was told to examine Stephenson's plans so that he could defend them in Parliament – and Stephenson was ordered to co-operate with Locke on this.[18] It is easy to imagine Stephenson's disgust at having his designs raked over by his erstwhile pupil but the GJR Directors were well aware of the dangers of allowing Stephenson to defend his proposals in front of Parliamentary inquiries. Locke reported that the new route was an excellent improvement on the original, in so far as it was cheaper (£264,600 against £414,000) because it avoided a tunnel, and had better gradients; however, there was the enormous disadvantage that it would not meet the L&BR end-on but could only run into a parallel terminus alongside. Locke was then saddled with the additional work of making the detailed survey for the Parliamentary Bill, negotiating with landowners, designing the many bridges and several large embankments and viaducts, making specifications and signing up contractors – this on top of his heavy responsibilities for the rest of the line to Warrington.

The Act for the new line into Birmingham was obtained on 12 June 1835. It was fortunate that Locke had Hugh McIntosh to do the lion's share of the construction work – there were just two years in which to build this heavily engineered line. Simultaneously with the new survey at the southern end Locke was also called upon to plan a new route at the northern end of the GJR, owing to a magnificent example of free enterprise by the Directorate of the lightly engineered Warrington & Newton Railway, which included among its shareholders George Stephenson and Joseph Sandars. The W&NR Directors saw that as the GJR had to use their route to reach the L&MR and beyond, they were in a strongly piratical position, and could extort large sums of money from the GJR by over-valuing their £100 shares at £125 when approached with a view to purchase.

The GJR responded by ordering Locke to plan another route to the L&MR: the 'Fiddlers Ferry' line, which would involve Locke in the design of a new crossing of the Mersey & Irwell Canal, west of the original site, and a new, large bridge to cross the (wider) Mersey and the Sankey Canal at Fiddlers Ferry. George Stephenson's part in this proposed railway, as Engineer-in-Chief, was to agree, on 28 May 1834, that Locke and Allcard could design all bridges and slopes, make all specifications, drawings and contracts, all of which were to be presented to him for his approval.[19] In view of the GJR's evident determination to do without the W&NR, the latter Company agreed, late in 1834, to accept the ordinary market price of their shares. Only then could Locke go ahead and plan in detail the reconstruction of the 4¼ miles of the Warrington & Newton line. The Warrington & Newton was absorbed into the GJR by Act of Parliament on 18 June 1835.

Throughout 1834 the GJR Directors were waiting for Stephenson's advice on the sort of track they should use and his specifications for the engines. They waited in vain and came to depend ever more on Locke. On 26 November 1834 Joseph Locke was promoted to 'Engineer', equal in status to George Stephenson: 'Mr. Locke to have the general superintendence of the entire line but that Mr. Stephenson shall be required [up] to ten days of every second month in surveying the works and making report on them.' Stephenson's salary was to be halved from 30 June 1835 and 'Mr. Locke to be understood to be the Engineer referred to in the contracts'.[20]

Stephenson refused to have anything more to do with the GJR (while still drawing his pay, of course). Repeated requests for help were ignored, and in May 1835 Locke prepared his own recommendations for the kind of track required. On 10 June Stephenson ignored an urgent request to attend the Board to discuss Locke's proposals. Another request for Stephenson's proposals was made on 2 September. Stephenson answered by letter in which he said he had not thought it necessary to prepare a report, and then tendered his resignation, which was accepted on 16 September, when Locke's proposals were adopted. This was a blessing, because Stephenson's track was archaic and not in the evolutionary line, whereas Locke's track was definitive.[21] Thereafter, whenever Stephenson could say something to the detriment of Locke, he did. Locke suffered a nervous breakdown because of the bitterness of his old mentor and benefactor, but Mrs Locke was strong as well as gentle and, with her support, Joseph recovered and continued his work on the line.

The Grand Junction Railway was opened on time and within its budget on 4 July 1837, although the navvies were still working on some earthworks and the Birmingham terminus, at Vauxhall Gardens, was a temporary one. Estimates of its final cost vary; Locke himself gave the figure of £25,000 per mile while other sources give much lower figures. The London & Birmingham opened throughout on 24 June 1838, at a cost of £53,000 per mile: £500,000 had been spent in buying-off its opponents.[22] The route had nine tunnels and three particularly long, deep cuttings: Tring, Blisworth and Weedon. The Kilsby tunnel, 2400 yds long and lined with an estimated 36 million bricks, cost £300,000 against an estimate of £99,000: trial borings into the hill had failed to discover a large pocket of quicksand enveloped in the clays. The Primrose Hill tunnel on the outskirts of London had been lined with brick when the clay moved and crushed the ring; Watford tunnel killed many of its crew of navvies when the gravelly ground gave way. The L&BR was, nevertheless, a stupendous feat of engineering, creating good gradients through a difficult terrain – with the exception of the steep incline which rose at 1 in 68–77, almost from the platform ends at Euston for a mile to Camden. Trains were cable-hauled up the incline until 1844 and it remained an operational nuisance until the advent of electric traction at Euston in 1966. In respect of its track the GJR was, at opening, more technically advanced than the L&BR and this was a direct result of Locke's growing dominance over its engineering. The Stephensons remained in charge of the L&BR,

where Robert Stephenson adopted the archaic system of track laying employed on the Surrey Iron Railway in 1805 and the Liverpool & Manchester in 1830: stone blocks and short, wrought-iron rails. Soon, and obviously at great expense, it all had to be relaid in the modern manner devised by Locke.

The GJR trains were able to run into their permanent terminus at Birmingham, Curzon Street, alongside the L&BR, in the autumn of 1838.

11

A Natural Monopoly

THE FIRST GREAT field of British investment after the conclusion
of the Napoleonic wars was South America. Several territories
here won their independence from Spain after 1820, using
British loans for arms, and British companies were subsequently established in those countries to exploit their mineral wealth. £10 shares in
the Real del Monte Mining Company were sold for £158 in 1822,[1] as
British investors scrambled on to the speculation. The South American
bubble collapsed into bankruptcy in December 1825 when the returns
on investments failed to materialize and when the newly formed
governments were unable to repay their debts to the City of London.
The British banking system could no longer sustain the credit it had
issued. There followed a financial depression accompanied by the
unfortunate coincidence of successive bad harvests. Civil unrest
became widespread, together with a growing demand for a reform of
the voting system.

First to be reformed, however, was the banking system. The Bank of
England had the monopoly of joint-stock status, and all other British
banks' capital was restricted to the amount which could be raised by a
partnership of six people. In 1826 an Act was passed permitting joint-
stock banks, but their notes would not be legal tender within a 65-mile
radius of London.

The first Reform Act was passed in 1832, enfranchising an additional
250,000 males, 'persons of the better sort'. In 1833 there was a good

harvest, the great political uncertainties and agitations were over and the country felt confident once more. By 1833 the Liverpool & Manchester Railway had proved the utility of the steam-locomotive for fast passenger and freight haulage and some huge new railway projects had just been incorporated or were planned. Nine joint-stock banks were formed in 1833 and forty-five in 1836.

Railways appeared as a bright new prospect in a bright new age: a visible investment at home, not an invisible one, thousands of miles away. However, the arrival of railways was also likely to be a source of disaster, if speculation was allowed to run riot, as had happened ten years before. A rational, national, trunk network to distribute food, minerals, manufactured goods and to transport passengers between the greatest cities and the ports of England: this was the way the earliest prophets of the railway, Thomas Gray, William James and Charles Sylvester, wanted the invention to go. Sylvester had warned, in 1827, against 'the abuse' of the railway system – by which he meant not allowing it to become a free-market football, a financiers' opportunity to lend money. But in Britain the mood was as individualistic as ever: railways were to be developed by the free market; 'control' would hamper individuals in their pursuit of 'wealth and happiness', which were assumed to come together in the same package. All that was required was unrestricted self-interest, and railways would be controlled by the very mysterious 'invisible hand'[2] of The Market, thus ensuring competition, low fares, high profits, lots of trains and fair play all round.

No important figure within the railway industry believed this. Men who would otherwise have been ardent supporters of *laissez-faire* were at best uneasy at the prospects when ubridled competition was applied to railways. A railway company was a very large investment of funds, which would not produce a proper return if subjected to competition. Among politicians there was a small group who were more or less opposed to a speculative free-for-all. James Morrison[3] (1790–1857) urged a state-controlled system along French lines, whereby government decided on a route and then invited capitalists to invest for a certain period, after which the line would become state property. The capitalists' investment would be protected because there would be no competition, but a top limit would be imposed on their profits. Even such a high Tory as Lord Londonderry suggested that a railway should be purchased by the state once the Company that built it had received its just return on the investment.

In 1833, the London financial newspaper *Circular to Bankers* had warned that the new laws permitting joint-stock banking would lead inevitably to another explosion of credit as people speculated in railway projects, among other things, and this would be followed by the inevitable crash. The second investment boom and railway 'mania' duly developed in 1834 as Lancashire cotton made extra large profits, harvests were good and optimism soared. In an attempt to restrict the number of railway Bills coming to Parliament, Parliamentary Standing Orders were introduced to apply exclusively to railways: these Orders demanded high standards of planning accuracy and a cash deposit equal to 10 per cent of the total capital required, before the House would read a Bill. Running a railway had become, even by 1835, a surprisingly complicated affair, the convolutions of which were to strain to the limit laissez-faire ideas on non-interference by government.

The frenetic activity in the money market created inflation; during 1835 the Bank Rate doubled to 5 per cent, the harvest failed, the price of raw cotton rose, gold poured out of Britain to buy food and cotton and, in the financial collapse that September, the second railway mania died. The deadening effect this had on confidence lasted for about seven years. A Select Committee was established in 1839, chaired by Sir Robert Peel, to investigate all aspects of railways: their financial difficulties; labour problems; the inconvenience to passengers and freight when what appeared (on a map) to be a continuous route was actually owned by two or more companies in separate sections; and the problem of competition and of a railway company's monopoly of its route.

The Second Report gave the Committee's view on railway companies as monopolies:

It does not appear to have been the intention of Parliament to give a railway company the complete monopoly of their line [but] the intention of Parliament cannot be carried out in the way contemplated for it is obvious that the payment of tolls is only a small part of the arrangement which is necessary to open a rail-road to public competition. The safety of the public requires one supervising authority which should have the power of making and enforcing all regulations necessary. On this account it is necessary that the Company should possess complete control over their road although they acquire an entire monopoly of the means of communication. But if these extensive powers are granted to private companies it becomes most important that they should be controlled so as to secure the Public as far as possible from any abuse which might arise from irresponsible authority.[4]

The result of the lengthy deliberations of 1839–40 was the Railway Regulation Act of 1840. This inaugurated the Railway Department of the Board of Trade under G.R. Porter, Lt.-Col. Sir Frederick Smith, RE, and Samuel Laing. The Act empowered these gentlemen to order all new railways, prior to their opening, to present themselves for inspection to an Officer of the Royal Engineers – initially, Sir Frederick – in order to ensure that they had been constructed according to their Act. Sir Frederick very soon became concerned about the lack of safety procedures in the operating of railways, but had no power to forbid the opening of an unsafe line. The following year, Gladstone became President of the Board of Trade and obtained an Act to give such powers to the Board's Inspector.

Admirable though this was, it was merely tinkering at the edges and had no effect on the central question of planning railways on a rational system. Planning might have been difficult, even for such a powerful Cabinet as existed between 1841 and 1845 under Sir Robert Peel, given that there were also many great political problems during this period – and that there was, in any case, much confusion in the minds of the railway Directors. The representatives of the existing companies said they did not want 'dangerous meddling' from the Government – and then complained bitterly that the Government did not prevent the construction of competitive lines which 'destroyed' the capital of the original lines. Then again, when railway companies amalgamated to reduce competition and improve their efficiency, they were accused of 'monopoly' by Parliament and public.

The principle of 'open access' was intended to prevent a rail monopoly, and this was enshrined in the Acts of Incorporation of all British railways, but only the first, the Surrey Iron Railway (which was more like a tramway) worked entirely under the 'turnpike' principle. The S&DR and the other north-eastern lines incorporated between 1825 and 1830 were to a significant extent used by individual hauliers, but only for a few years. The same was true of other railways incorporated as late as 1833, but the practice soon lapsed. Lines incorporated after 1833 were seldom, if ever, used by independent hauliers – with the exception of the Northumberland & Durham Coal Company, which hauled its own trains on the North London Railway from 1850 to 1859.[5] It could be said that the individualistic 'turnpike railway' concept, born out of the eighteenth century and the age of the horse, died in collision with the power of steam locomotion – and the need for streamlined management.

But would the independent carriers of freight expect to use the railway as a conduit for their business as they were using the canals and roads? It might appear advantageous for the railway companies to leave freight to the carriers and concentrate solely on passenger carrying. Passengers have the means of self-locomotion: they arrive at a station, board a train and remove themselves from the premises at the end of the journey, whereas freight and parcels have to be carried every inch of the way. The carriers already had the traffic, an experienced staff, plus a nationwide system of depots and accountancy. When the London & Birmingham Railway opened, Pickford & Co. had been in business for nearly a hundred years, and were running a scheduled service over a network of regular routes, by road and canal, covering 340 towns in England and Scotland.

In the early 1840s, when the railway companies were relatively small and unaccommodating towards each other, the idea of a carrier using the railway was attractive. In a letter to *The Times* of 19 September 1840, the owner of a horse sent from London to Barnsley complained that the Midland Counties and the North Midland at Derby were so uncooperative that, in order to get the horse out of the Midland Counties train, re-booked, and into the North Midland train, he had been obliged to send a servant from London to Derby just to pay the second fare and lead the horse from one wagon to another.[6] Unity was required, and by making a single carrier responsible for a wagon-load of merchandise throughout its journey over different companies' tracks, that unity of responsibility was introduced. Furthermore, the railway companies would be saved the expense of maintaining the necessary staff, horses and vehicles to collect freight, load and sheet the wagons, deliver the goods and carry out all the paper work, and would receive a toll from the carriers simply for hauling their block trains or single wagons.

Joseph Baxendale, for twenty years head of Pickford & Co., told the 1840 Select Committee that the railways ought NOT to act as carriers: 'so as to give small capitalists an opportunity to enter the carrying business'. He was sure that the road carriers were both cheaper and more sensitive to the needs of their customers. Railways gave customers only one month's credit whereas the carriers gave three or even six months, and would also store consignments for nothing, while the railways charged demurrage after three days. Edward Bury, Locomotive Superintendent of the London & Birmingham, told the same Committee that he saw 'endless confusion' if the railway companies had to negotiate with each other for the carriage of goods.[7]

The L&BR then engaged Baxendale as their Superintendent of

Traffic, to set up the organization of their goods department. They nearly gave Pickford the monopoly of freight carrying on the railway, but then decided to allow any carrier to use the trains. Robert Stephenson told the Parliamentary Committee of 1844 that the carriers were allowed to use the London & Birmingham Railway because the L&BR was anxious to avoid the charge of 'monopoly'; even so, the Company remained convinced that they could carry goods cheaper than the carriers, who were no more than 'middle men' in the transport system, since the L&BR provided the wagons, locomotives and warehousing. The warehouses at London (Camden) and Birmingham were large and very modern, with powered lifts and cranes. The wagons hired to the carriers were held in the warehouse until they were full for a particular destination – which meant those wagons were out of circulation, more wagons would be required, and thus, costs would be increased. The carrier brought his traffic to and from the warehouses and the L&BR charged 30s per ton to cover locomotive, wagon, crane and warehouse costs; the carriers then charged their customers 60s a ton.[8] The average 'per-ton' cost to the customer of carrying merchandise by the L&BR in 1844 was £2 10s, while on the GWR – which did its own goods work – it was £1 10s 6d.[9]

But there was yet another side to the story. While the companies might have spent much time in making agreements on their charges for carrying through-freight over each other's lines, the problem of litigation between themselves and the carriers was real and expensive. Captain Laws, of the carrier-friendly Manchester & Leeds, complained to the Board of Trade of 'the numerous frauds' committed by the carriers at Leeds[10] – who falsified tonnages on their invoices, for instance. David Stevenson in his memoirs, *Fifty Years on the London & North Western Railway*, wrote of 'false invoices', and 'pitched battles' among the carriers' men for the use of scarce wagons.[11]

Each railway company had to be in control of what took place on its premises, and they had to work together in order to carry freight across company boundaries without delay. For this reason the Railway Clearing House was founded in 1842, to emulate the big carriers' unified and nationwide system. The Liverpool & Manchester Railway was permitted by its Act to engage in the carrying trade, and its management set out to become the sole carriers on their line. The Grand Junction was used by Pickford and Chaplin & Horne among others, but like the L&MR, the GJR management wanted complete control of their railway. When Mark Huish became General

Manager of the GJR in July 1841 he opened a vigorous attack on the carriers.

In October he ordered that all carriers' traffic arriving in L&BR wagons had to be transshipped into GJR wagons. He also attacked the carriers on the matter of 'packed parcels'. The carrier would pack parcels into a single container and expected the container to be charged at a 'per-ton' rate but the GJR wanted to charge each parcel separately at a penny a pound. This matter was referred to the court – GJR v. Pickford in July 1842. The judge ruled that the railway was acting illegally and could not make discriminatory charges so as to create a monopoly for itself or to favour one firm against another. Huish nevertheless continued to harass the carriers as best he could.

In 1844 the Midland Railway (MR) had been formed through amalgamations; in 1846 the GJR, L&MR and L&BR amalgamated to form the London & North Western Railway (L&NWR), the largest Company in the world, with Huish as General Manager. Huish's co-operation with the Railway Clearing House to set up a Goods Managers' Conference was decisive. These large groupings, their share of 'through working' revenue apportioned by the RCH, meant that independent road carriers would no longer be able to use the railways. Huish negotiated with Pickford and Chaplin & Horne and from 1 September 1847 they agreed to become cartage and delivery agents, feeding the railway, which was to be the sole carrier. Railway freight cartage rates were at once reduced by 25 per cent and more.[12]

The removal of the independent carriers from the railway system was dogmatically condemned by certain people as an extension of railway company monopoly when, practically, they ought to have welcomed it as an improvement in transport efficiency. In 1844, Joseph Baxendale, now Chairman of the South Eastern Railway (SER), had altered his view, and told the 1844 Parliamentary Committee on Railways: 'the powers which Parliament conferred on railway companies would never have been given if Parliament thought that the companies would become monopolies. This monopoly could not have been foreseen but it has arisen out of the nature and imperatives of railway operating and experience.'[13] The railways were 'a natural monopoly', and the 'turn-pike' or 'open access' principle was, and remains, incompatible with standardization of operating practice, essential in a public utility. The sole remnant of the original idea – the 'private-owner' wagon – remained in use until 1948, a poorly maintained nuisance, causing extra costs in marshalling then, just as it had in 1825.

Between 1838 and 1841 only 10 miles of new railway was authorized. During 1843 only ten Acts for 41 miles of new railways were
granted,[14] although most of the established railways were making good
returns.[15] The commercial gentlemen of London and Liverpool were
dissatisfied. New capital formation for railways had peaked at £11.1
million in 1839 and in 1843 only £4.7 million was required.[16] The
money lending industry felt the need to encourage railway building.
Parliament's Standing Order on the cash deposit for proposed railways was seen as holding back entrepreneurs. On 5 February 1844
Gladstone, in moving for a Select Committee to investigate ways of
making railways more advantageous to the public, suggested that the
deposit should be reduced.[17] The Committee was set up, its members
including Gladstone, Henry Labouchere,[18] Lord Granville Somerset[19]
and Beckett Denison.[20]

Gladstone, Lord Dalhousie,[21] Samuel Laing[22] and Thomas Brassey
were among those who saw railways as a government department, like
the General Post Office; Gladstone's intention was to allow private
capital to build routes selected by Parliament, subject their fares and
profits to state control and, eventually, to nationalize them. Few
beyond this group advocated outright state ownership, but many
agreed that, since railways must be monopolies, they should be controlled. Francis Mewburn, veteran Solicitor of the Stockton &
Darlington; Joseph Baxendale, Secretary of the GWR; Charles
Saunders; Carr Glyn, Chairman of the L&NWR; Robert Stephenson;
Joseph Locke; Captain Laws, General Manager of the Manchester &
Leeds: all supported the idea of state control 'to discourage railway
schemes got up for the mere purpose of speculation', since this
destroyed or reduced the profits of an existing investment. Even
Isambard Kingdom Brunel, an extreme 'free-marketeer', wrote privately of 'the present extraordinary state of railway matters when
everybody around seems stark, staring, wildly mad' and in 1845 went
so far against his *laissez-faire* principles as to wish that government
would forbid all railway Bills for a year until some control could be
established. Publicly, however, he would not support a campaign for
legal controls. Robert Stephenson offered the Government the control
of railway fares and dividends, if in return Parliament would refuse to
incorporate competitive lines and leave the expansion of the network
to the existing companies.

Samuel Laing, Secretary to the Board of Trade and one of the greatest administrative and financial talents of the period, told the 1844

Committee that only £17 million of railway capital returned more than 5 per cent, and also that 'competition is more efficient as an instrument of injury to existing companies than a means of guaranteeing cheapness of travelling'. Laing believed it to be inevitable that, eventually, there would be '6 or 8 companies',[23] and that they would therefore have to come under state control to protect the public interest.

The freedom of the situation in those days is illustrated by Charles Saunders' suggestion to the 1844 Committee that reckless speculation could be stopped by obliging those who received share allocations to hold them at least until the Company obtained its Act and, when being allocated shares, to pay at least something of their face value to the Company.

The great problem for those wishing to restrict railway promotion was the fact that, as a result of *laissez-faire* principles, a huge and stimulating investment was being made in Britain. An effort was made to accelerate the passage of Irish railway Bills through Parliament for this very reason. On 15 May 1844, Gladstone asked Parliament to approve the recommendation of the Select Committee's Fourth Report: to halve the 10 per cent deposit and abolish the requirement that three-quarters of shareholders contribute to raising the deposit. This was necessary because the Standing Order 'effected a restriction on speculation at a time when anything promising to stimulate the demand for labour would tend most materially to revive public confidence'.[24]

The third railway mania began from that May. During 1844 hundreds of Bills came crowding into Parliament for consideration in 1845, and the majority of MPs, the legal profession and the general public were looking forward to a profitable speculation, which was, after all, why Gladstone wanted the deposit reduced. The 'controllers' grumbled but John Bright defended the *laissez-faire* principle in Parliament with this wonderful piece of wishful thinking: 'There is a wholesome absence of interference in this country in all those matters which experience has shown might wisely be left to private individuals stimulated by the love of gain and the desire to administer to the wants and comforts of their fellow men.'[25] Anything less 'wholesome' and 'wise' than the frantic speculations of individuals in 1826, 1835 and 1844–7 could hardly be imagined, while the 2nd- and 3rd-class carriages provided by the railway companies were noticeably lacking in a 'desire to administer to the wants of their fellow men'.

Meanwhile Gladstone was trying to steer through Parliament his Bill for a 'Regulation of Railways' Act, its 48 clauses based on the Third

Report of the Select Committee. Parliament was much less enthusiastic about this, since it intended to restrict individual self-interest. It set out to give the Government powers to revise the charges of any railway which paid an average dividend of 10 per cent over a three-year period and to purchase *any* railway after fifteen years had elapsed from its incorporation. It also provided for the cheap transport of troops, the poor and the insane. The Bill was bound to be immensely unpopular: a deputation of railway Directors, led by George Hudson, came to 10 Downing Street, to dispute with Sir Robert Peel and Gladstone. In his speech in the House on 8 July, Gladstone described the group as 'a most lugubrious body. In the front were Directors, in the rear great multitudes of railway solicitors.' The railway companies produced a pamphlet in defence of their liberties and circulated it widely. To the charge of monopoly the companies pointed out, rather paradoxically, that Parliament could always sanction the construction of a competing railway – which was the very thing they, the railway companies, did not want! Rather more sensibly, the pamphlet pointed out that no railway company had ever paid dividends of the sort associated with a monopoly – unlike some canal companies. The cost to railways of building and operating was too high to allow 'monopoly' profits – indeed only a 'monopoly' situation could ensure a half-decent return.

Gladstone's Bill was diametrically opposed to the spirit of the times. The nation clamoured to invest freely in the hope of a 'quick killing' or long-term security. Railways were to be built into every nook and corner of Britain in the expectation that they would provide large dividends for shareholders, fast and comfortable trains for the travellers – and all at competitively low fares! It was very much in the interest of the insider-dealing MPs, lawyers, bankers, engineers and contractors to encourage such a delusion. In the heat of debate, and opposed by the most powerful interests in Britain, Gladstone's Bill melted from 48 clauses to 24 and as such received the Royal Assent on 9 August 1844.

The Act gave Parliament powers to reduce fares and charges and of purchase but only for those railways incorporated after 31 December 1844, and then only after a 21-year period of private ownership. The powers of fare revision and purchase would also only apply if, for a period of three years, the company had paid a dividend of 10 per cent or more:

> It shall be lawful for the said Lords Commissioners, if they think fit, at any time after the said term of 21 years (from date of incorporation) to purchase

any such railway in the name and on behalf of Her Majesty . . . upon payment of a sum equal to 25 years' purchase of the said annual divisible profits estimated on the average of the three preceeding years.[26]

The clause was useful for practical reasons, not least because, after the third railway mania, there was almost no railway which paid its shareholders a dividend in double figures.

The Act's most famous achievement was the 'Parliamentary' train. Each railway had to run at least one train in each direction from end to end of its line, stopping at every station, and running at an average of 12 mph inclusive of stops. The passengers were to be accommodated in carriages with seats and all-weather protection, they were to be charged a maximum of one penny a mile and each person could carry 56 lb of luggage free. The 5 per cent ticket tax, which was due to the Government on every ticket sold, was waived for these 'Parliamentary' trains. Their specification does not look promising, but in the first full year of operation, four million people travelled by 'Parliamentary' train, and by 1850, 55.2 per cent of all railway journeys were made at the fare of 1d per mile.[27]

12

George Hudson and the
Great Railway Mania

I N THEIR EARLY period, between 1821 and 1840, the railways' greatest success was in taking passenger traffic from roads and forcing
the canal companies to reduce their freight charges. Parliamentary
Returns for railways published in 1842 show that in 1841, 5 million
tons of merchandise was carried on British railways and of that, 4
million tons was coal – but no coal came rail-borne to London until
1845. Of the total income of £4.5 million, £3.1 million came from passenger traffic.[1] A number of new industries were directly related to
railways: locomotive, carriage and wagon building; rail rolling and
iron-bridge building. Even by 1840, railways had also given rise to a
tremendous expansion of banking and financial services, earthwork
contracting and enormously increased opportunities for employment
and careers, not only on the railways, but also in the related industries
and in the expanding financial world.

Locomotives of 1840 were usually six-wheeled with one or two
driven axles; six-wheeled coupled locomotives were comparatively
rare. The track of the L&MR, built in 1830, followed Stephenson's
practice on the S&DR of supporting the wrought-iron rails on sunken,
stone blocks. Robert Stephenson opened the L&BR with timber cross-
sleepered track but this was considered a temporary measure, and the
archaic system was soon installed. On the Great Western, from 1837,

Brunel used a 'bridge' rail nailed to a continuous wooden support, which was supposed to be held firmly to the ground by attachment to massive wooden piles driven deep into the soil. This system was useless so long as the piles remained. Wooden cross-sleepers, to which were spiked cast-iron 'chairs' holding doubled-headed rails, had first been used by George Stephenson as a special expedient over Chat Moss, but it was Joseph Locke, on the Grand Junction, who first appreciated the true utility of the method – which indeed became the basic system for the world's railways for a hundred years.

In 1836, there were 400 miles of public railways working in the United Kingdom, most of that in the north of England and southern Scotland. South of the Wash there were only the Leicester & Swannington, the London & Greenwich, the Canterbury & Whitstable and the Bodmin & Wadebridge. By 1840, 1500 miles had been opened; with the exception of a London–York direct line, which was entirely lacking, the great trunk routes were open throughout, or in part, or were under construction. What was required to ensure the financial success of these routes and their owning companies was stability in the money markets and a lack of competition from other projects. One man in particular attempted to create some co-ordination among warring factions but, because he was working within the system at his disposal, he only made matters worse. This man was George Hudson.

Hudson was born the fifth son of a farmer at Howsam, between York and Malton, in 1800. After only a cursory education he was apprenticed at fifteen to Bell & Nicholson, a York drapery business. Hudson finished his time in 1820 and was taken on as a tradesman. The next year he married Nicholson's daughter. After this, Bell retired, and Nicholson, the 'sleeping' partner, took Hudson as his 'working' partner. By 1827, Hudson's was the largest drapery business in York and one of the largest businesses of any kind in the city, turning over (to quote Hudson) '£30,000 a year and 25 per cent of that was profit'. During this time he was a loyal attender at a Methodist chapel in York and a lay-preacher.

In 1827 his rich great-uncle Matthew Bottrill became ill. Hudson rushed to the old man's bedside and was most attentive to the old man's comfort. So moved was old Matthew by this that he made a will bequeathing everything to his great-nephew. A few days later he died and young George was £30,000 better off. Some contemporary scandalmongers remarked on these coincidences but no one in Bottrill's family seemed to mind, so the rumours died away. With this sudden acquisition of great wealth, Hudson decided he could no longer remain a Dissenter and instead became an anti-Free Trade, High Church Tory. He also began to involve himself in local politics, and volunteered to work on the York Board of Health, a Tory enclave in a Whig-run city. In his self-appointed role as a Whig-baiter Hudson hoped to establish his position among the old-Tory heirarchy. A cholera epidemic was ravaging the slums at that time, but the Board did little to improve living conditions there. A wonderful political row developed, over the site of the burial ground for the cholera victims, during which Hudson was able to demonstrate his new-found loyalties to the full, using what was to become his famous, bullying invective.

In 1832, after the passage of the Reform Act, a General Election was held. Hudson supported the Tory effort by putting his money at the service of his party for the illegal practice of buying votes. The Whigs were not in favour of bribery but instead used gangs of thugs to intimidate any would-be Tory voter – in those days, a vote was given orally and in public, surrounded by the crowd. The outcome was the return of a Whig member for York to Parliament.

In 1833 when an Act of Parliament permitted the joint-stock 'country banks' to set up in the City of London, Hudson and his friends were quick off the mark. That same year they clubbed together to form a capital of £500,000 with which they founded the York Union Bank. Their agent in London was the banker George Carr Glyn (1797–1873), later to become Chairman of the London & Birmingham Railway. Having founded their bank, towards the end of 1833 the York Tories formed a Committee to promote a railway line to Leeds, with Hudson at Treasurer. John Rennie was employed as Surveyor and Hudson went everywhere with him, learning a great deal about the practical side of railway promotion – including the job of pacifying irate landowners. Early in 1834, despite four successful years of the L&MR, Rennie recommended a horse-drawn tramway rather than a railway. This was an uninspiring prospect, deemed unworthy of the City of York, and the project was shelved. But Hudson was now a convinced railwayman.

That same year, Hudson's career was accelerated by two events: he was elected to the York City Council, and he met George Stephenson, quite by chance, in Whitby. Hudson and Stephenson liked each other and were to make a powerful combination. Both were farm boys who had 'made good', both were hard, jealous, ambitious men. In business they complemented each other. Stephenson's great strategic plan for railways was flawed inasmuch as he distrusted locomotive power on any but very moderate gradients, but this was a minor detail: any project to which he put his name would attract investors. Hudson was a most able – and indeed, unscrupulous – manipulator of the financial system, who conjured money out of the proverbial hat. Together they could and would pull in the eager investors for Stephenson's grand design: the speculators would come uninvited.

Stephenson's vision was for strategic trunk lines which would link the large populations of manufacturing and coal-mining areas with residential areas, ports and food supplies. Hudson learned from Stephenson that he was proposing a line north from the London & Birmingham line at Rugby, through Derby to Leeds, and onwards to Newcastle. Hudson's excitement at the prospect of the gigantic capital to be raised was tempered by the fact that Stephenson intended to bypass York, which lay on low ground to the north-east of Leeds; in Stephenson's opinion, a railway between the two places would require gradients too steep for locomotive haulage.[2] Hudson was aghast that the City of York should not be included in the great design and determined that he should 'mek al't railways cum t' York', and so entered the railway promotion and production business. In 1833 three important lines were proposed: the Midland Counties, engineered by Charles Vignoles, from Rugby on the L&BR to Derby and Nottingham; the North Midland, engineered by George Stephenson, from Derby to Leeds; and, also engineered by George Stephenson, the Birmingham & Derby Junction, connecting Derby to the L&BR main line at Hampton-in-Arden, west of Coventry. In York, Hudson formed – and chaired – a Committee to promote the 'York & North Midland Railway' (Y&NMR) on 13 October 1835. The line would link York with the NMR at Normanton, a few miles east of Leeds.

He needed to carry a very substantial mass of opinion with him if he was to raise money in large quantities and defeat opposing projects. He had to create trust and optimism on a scale as vast as the sums of money involved, a miracle he achieved through an outrageous daring, a bullying boorishness combined with vast stamina, and tremendous powers of organization. He understood how to make himself vulgarly popular in order to drive his particular will onwards. Luck decided that he should become Lord Mayor of York in the Coronation year of 1837 and he used this auspicious year to reinforce his standing in the public mind. As Mayor he could give banquets for large gatherings of would-be supporters, and did so: sumptuous gas-lit banquets. So much gas was burnt at these various functions that the York Gas Company elected him a Director out of sheer gratitude. He also organized Coronation feasts for the working people of York, and for the paupers in the workhouse.

These civic extravagances were paid for in large part out of local taxation. (It was always part of Hudson's winning technique to 'feed the donkey its tail'.) When subsequently the City became short of money he reduced the council workers' wages and the rations of the workhouse inmates – and was then the first and largest contributor in a public appeal for donations to relieve distress among the poor of York. The public, with little insight and short memories, found his rough speech and roguish ways endearing.

He could make a company show a profit where no profit had been before, and his utterance or mere presence as the Chairman of a company could dramatically increase the value of shares on the market. Who could object to such a wonderful man? Very few. Occasionally a Director of a company he had taken over might resign. The York solicitor George Leeman, a Whig, was never taken in by him and never ceased in his attempts to expose his corruption but Leeman was pilloried mercilessly in the local press – which was, of course, owned by Hudson. Once, in 1844, the Board of Directors of a railway company of which he was Chairman, plucked up courage to ask him: 'As we are equally responsible with yourself for what this Company does, we would like to know what you have in mind for the future of the Company'. Hudson soon disposed of this impertinence: 'Oh, you want to know, do you? Well, you will not.'[3]

Hudson's antipathy to keeping accounts was well known. When he became Chairman of the North Midland, he dispensed with the meticulous accounting system and carried the figures in his head. The scrapping of accountancy on the NMR was notorious; to quote from D. Morier Evans: 'Good accounts are troublesome things to keep and occasionally they cause trouble to the parties of whose affairs they are registers. The true chandler's shop system, is to keep no books at all.' A celebrated wit of the period, Bernal Osborne, said of Hudson: 'He became rich by keeping everything but his accounts.' But Joseph Rowntree, the great York Quaker, factory-owner, philanthropist (and a Director of the York & North Midland) defended Hudson's refusal to allow an independent auditor to examine the Company's accounts, using Hudson's slogan 'every shareholder his own auditor'.[4] The chaos of the Y&NMR accounts being beyond the wits even of an accountant, Hudson was on safe ground in making this seemingly democratic promise.

Having dispensed with accountancy, Hudson substituted a fantasy world where high dividends were paid on request, whatever might be the true situation. Both the 'good and great' and the small investors were eager to believe in him. Hudson would *guarantee* a high dividend on any line which he intended to build or lease or of which he became Chairman. If Hudson was indeed a dishonest railway speculator and financier, it is worth remembering that many worthy Victorians, George and Robert Stephenson, George Carr Glyn included, were his close supporters for many years. There was more to Hudson than mere speculation. He could see the need for a unified railway nationwide, and this belief he shared with a very select and powerful group of reputable men. Hudson's reckless and sometimes even illegal manoeuvrings were also his attempt, within a totally free-market system, to bring about a co-ordinated railway system.

Without his co-operation the Railway Clearing House would not have been possible. Rail passengers in 1840 from, say, London to Manchester had to re-book at each company's boundary, yet a stage-coach passenger from London to York would be conveyed by several different companies on one ticket and the coach companies were allocated their proportion of the fare through a 'Clearing House'. On 2 January 1842 the Railway Clearing House began its pioneering work to simplify the use of the railway for the benefit of the traveller and for ease of trade. Nine companies were originally party to the RCH: the London & Birmingham, Midland Counties, Birmingham & Derby Junction, North Midland, York & North Midland, Great North of England, Manchester & Leeds, Leeds & Selby and Hull & Selby. Of these, six were controlled by George Hudson. The Grand Junction Railway (GJR) is notable by its absence. Its Directors objected[5] to spending £300 per annum on the pre-printed, consecutively numbered, robust, paste-board 'Edmonson' tickets – the essential, standard feature common to all RCH companies. The system was the invention of Thomas Edmonson, a Quaker who, though trained as a cabinet-maker in Lancaster between 1836 and 1842, made his career as a railway clerk and station-master. He found that tickets were hand-written by the clerk in the booking-office, a time-wasting procedure and wide open to fraud. His Quaker feelings were revolted, and his ticket system, which greatly reduced fraud,[6] was the result. Without the co-operation of the GJR, the Liverpool & Manchester was cut off from the L&BR and saw no point in joining, though both joined in 1844.

Hudson's York & North Midland opened simultaneously with the North Midland on 1 July 1840. The Midland Counties had opened the day before. There now existed, over four independent companies' metals (the L&BR, MCR, NMR and Y&NMR), a through-route from London to York. The next step was to make the route to Newcastle and Edinburgh. Several companies would be required to build it, yet if the route was to give satisfaction to the public it would have to be under one management. It would be Hudson's task to promote them, to amalgamate them, and to fight off competitors who would reduce profits on the investment.

The main competitors were the London & York Railway group, led by the Doncaster businessman Edmund Denison, MP, and yet another group – the Direct Northern. Denison's proposals was for a line from King's Cross, through Hitchin, Peterborough and Doncaster, to York, which would shorten the distance from London to York relative to Hudson's route by 29 miles, and would certainly damage the huge investment that represented. All these proposals had to be argued in Parliament and the competing railways destroyed. Parliamentary legal fees would be richly rewarding for the lawyers.

Hudson manoeuvred expensively, promoting new railways, buying out existing companies in amalgamation deals, opposing his rivals in Parliament. In bringing about the amalgamation of the ruinously antagonistic Birmingham & Derby Junction, Midland Counties and North Midland to form the Midland Railway (MR) on 10 May 1844, he worked a miracle of sorts. This was then the largest Company in the world, with 397½ miles of route under one management and the enormous capital of £17,344,823. The first regular through-service from London to Derby and Nottingham commenced on 27 May. Thanks to the co-operation of the London & Birmingham, and with the co-ordination of the Railway Clearing House, passengers could travel without stopping to re-book their ticket or waste time changing trains. MR carriages were hauled by L&BR engines to and from Euston to Rugby where the Midland engine took over (see Map 3).

On 6 June 1844 an Act was obtained for the Lancaster & Carlisle Railway (L&CR), to be engineered by Locke. A vital link in the west coast route to Scotland, it was subscribed to by the L&BR and GJR. On 18 June Hudson's Newcastle & Darlington Junction Railway opened with a celebratory MR train which left Euston at 5.30 a.m. for Newcastle. It astonished the nation by covering the 303 miles in 9 hrs 32 mins, inclusive of engine changing and passenger refreshment-stops. Even in good weather, the stage-coach required 36 hrs for the journey.[7] In May 1845 Hudson's Midland Railway purchased the Bristol & Gloucester and the Birmingham & Bristol so that there was a route under one management from Newcastle to Bristol. Unified command enabled through-running on one ticket, without having to wait for connections at the frontiers of rival companies; but instead of congratulations there was much bitter talk about 'monopoly' from writers of letters to *The Times* and from certain Members of Parliament who would also be the first to complain about a lack of convenience.

The first 'Race to the North' was undoubtedly that to build the necessary railways. On 31 July 1845 the Royal Assent was given simultaneously to the Bill for the Caledonian Railway, from Carlisle to Glasgow, and to Hudson's Newcastle & Berwick. Once the Tweed was bridged it would join with the Edinburgh & Berwick, authorized the previous July to produce a Midlands and north-east coast route between the two capitals.

In 1845 Edmund Denison and the promoters of the London–York Direct Railway felt that Parliament was looking favourably on their proposals, which encouraged them to propose another railway, from their yet-to-be-built main line at Hitchin to Hudson's MR at Leicester. This spawned a counter-proposal from Hudson. Tens of thousands of shares were created; these rose and fell dramatically as proposal and counter-proposal marched across the scene. In Parliament hundreds of thousands of pounds were paid to the lawyers as the cases for the York Direct line and the Hitchin–Leicester line were argued. In the end the Bills were talked out of the Session and were lost, along with the shareholders' money.

In October 1845, hoping to repair their shattered fortunes, the shareholders of the impoverished Eastern Counties Railway (ECR) invited Hudson to become a Director. The Chairman of the ECR, Henry Bosanquet – also a Director of the London & Westminster Bank, which had invested heavily in the line and whose poor management had contributed to the perilous state of the Company – fastidiously resigned, along with the Secretary and the General Manager. Hudson went direct to the Chair. The ECR was incorporated in 1836 to build a railway from London, Bishopsgate, to

Norwich and Yarmouth via Ipswich, but by October 1845 had advanced their main line no nearer Norwich than Colchester. It should be mentioned, however, that ECR trains had just at that time reached Norwich via Bishop's Stortford, Cambridge, Ely and Thetford, by means of the extension of the Northern & Eastern Railway which the ECR had leased. The ECR shareholders, many of whom had never seen a dividend, are said to have gone 'wild with joy' when the great magician was elected to the Chair and informed them that their railway would shortly become 'a 10 per cent line'.

Hudson had become Chairman of the ECR in order to use the Company in his war with the York Direct group. He wanted to resurrect the original purpose of the Northern & Eastern: a railway from London, through Ely, to Lincoln and York. He intended to persuade his MR and his newly acquired ECR to agree to finance railways in opposition to Denison, to occupy the territory Denison required, in which cause he spent ECR money like water. But he paid the shareholders their 9 per cent dividend that year – without the formality of waiting until the Company's annual accounts had been calculated.

On 5 May 1846 Denison took the sensible course and merged his London & York Direct project with the Direct Northern. They could now present a united front to Hudson and to Parliament, no longer making laboured objections to each other's proposals, and on 26 June 1846 duly obtained their Act for the 'Great Northern Railway' (GNR). This authorized a railway from King's Cross to York, through Peterborough and Doncaster, with a great loop eastwards from Peterborough to Boston, back to Lincoln and out to the main line at Bawtry, 7 miles south of Doncaster. The £5.6 million capital authorized to be raised was a record; the legal expenses incurred through the long-drawn-out competition between the rival factions were also a record – £630,000.[8] Not a shovelful of earth had been dug for the outlay and now the GNR had millions of pounds to raise.

Hudson's MR had meanwhile cut across GNR territory with the opening, on 3 August 1846, of the Nottingham–Lincoln line. The MR line from Leicester to Melton Mowbray, Stamford and Peterborough was opened on 1 May 1848. Buying out various small companies in the north-east Hudson finally formed the York, Newcastle & Berwick Railway (YN&BR) in 1848. On 19 July 1844 the Edinburgh & Berwick Railway was incorporated. Hudson offered to take a lease on it so that as much as possible of the route from Rugby should be under one management but the E&BR rejected him. The E&BR opened on

11 June 1846. Hudson's railway reached the south bank of the Tweed on 1 July 1847, leaving passengers to de-train and cross the windy Tweed by ferry. The L&BR Anglo-Scottish service to Glasgow and Edinburgh had been running for two years and so there were few passengers for the new and inconvenient route.

The GNR, impoverished by the enormous cost of its Act, was struggling to complete its line, and by 17 October 1848 had only managed to open a piecemeal route across easy country, from Peterborough to Boston and Lincoln. On 9 April 1849 it opened from Lincoln to Gainsborough – 20 miles from Doncaster. Meanwhile the Company was still in the process of constructing the line from King's Cross to Peterborough and from thence direct to Grantham and Doncaster.

Immediately the GNR had obtained its Act Hudson began to scheme a way to get some control over it. He put a Bill into Parliament in 1846 for a 3-mile-long railway from Burton Salmon on his Y&NM to Knottingley, where it would join a branch of the Wakefield & Goole Railway which was to run down to Doncaster. He obtained this Act in 1847. The Wakefield Company had already offered the GNR running powers over their branch to Leeds in return for similar powers into Doncaster, which created an alternative route to London to that offered by the MR (see Map 4). Without consulting his shareholders, Hudson offered the GNR running powers over his line from Knottingley into York if the GNR would give up their powers for a line from Doncaster to York. Although the GNR was very short of money, it did not at once agree, and this lengthy delay enabled the secret to leak out during 1848. By that time the great railway financial boom of 1845–7 had collapsed, millions of pounds had been lost and George Hudson was a convenient Aunt Sally at whom the press could throw its abuse. Within this general feeling of anguish, there was actual discontent among Hudson's shareholders about unusually low dividends; and those rare few who had always opposed Hudson's Machiavellian accountancy now had a more amenable audience, and were able to institute the inquiries which led to his downfall. Coincidentally, Hudson's great friend and staunch supporter George Stephenson died in August 1848, removing from Hudson a strong ally.

The MR shareholders were, in addition, furious that Hudson should have given the GNR a free route into York. Their anger was vented publicly at their AGM on 15 February 1849, when they forced Hudson to concede that he had cooked the books. Those erstwhile Hudson enthusiasts on the ECR held their reckoning on 28 February, at a meeting which Hudson did not attend, where it was 'discovered' that Hudson had not so much been 'cooking the books' as dispensing with the books altogether, and that he had been paying them out of their own capital – as if they could not have guessed as much when their poverty-stricken Company suddenly began to pay them 9 per cent.

Hudson's rip-roaring confidence was the most remarkable single aspect of the third and greatest 'railway mania' to have gripped the nation. To blame him for the speculative system which this brought about is unfair: there was no other way to create the necessarily large amalgamations of companies than by battling through the competitive jungle; Parliament might have exercised some control but preferred the quick profits. Hudson created the MR, one of the four greatest British railway companies, and laid the basis for the NER. His scheme of amalgamation and the use of the Railway Clearing House were antidotes to Parliament's refusal to legislate for railways on a strategic plan. His payment of dividends out of capital and lack of accountancy were reprehensible, but they were not methods unique to himself; the financial affairs of the Caledonian Railway, for instance, were in 1849 reported by *The Times* to be 'in just such a tangle as one might dream of after supping on lobster salad and champagne'.[9]

Hudson was simply a large player within the system. The mania occurred because Parliament actually encouraged it because of the vast fortunes which were to be made – not out of running railways, but out of legal fees and share dealing, and for the employment it created at a time of crisis. It happened because the right conditions existed in people's minds and in the money markets. Few wanted to question where their 9 per cent came from while they were receiving it, but on losing it they became moralists. The Duke of Wellington, censorious on the subject of speculation, sought Hudson's advice on how to double his money at the stroke of a pen. The nation had a guilty conscience and someone had to be the scapegoat: better that it be the upstart draper's lad than the Duke of Wellington. Hudson and his wife were ostracized by 'polite society' and obliged to go into exile in Paris.

13

'An Exaggeration of Enterprise'

BY THE END of 1844, 2148 miles of railway had been built. At the start of 1845 hundreds of Bills for new railways were lodged in Parliament, representing a mileage more than double that constructed in the previous twenty-five years. There was about to commence another orgy of what Mr Brotherton (1783–1857), Liberal MP for Salford, described as 'more fraud and felony than I have ever seen in public works'.[1] Gladstone established an Advisory Committee – the Five Kings – under the chairmanship of that most industrious and capable administrator, Lord Dalhousie. Its function was to examine all railway Bills, to recommend to Parliament those which were truly of public benefit and reject the rest. Dalhousie's criteria of suitability included the ability and honesty of the line's promoters and its Engineer, and the likely profits of the line relative to its cost of building. He worked at the task with such energy and for such long hours, that he is said to have shortened his life thereby. He was swamped with Bills, representing in total over £100 million of investment. Such a juggernaut could not wait while the earnest Lord weighed the utility of each proposal, and Bills went to the House without his scrutiny. His Committee was in any case only advisory, and in July it was abolished.

Parliament did throw out a lot of Bills. Often there were several companies all trying to build the same line, so that, in selecting one Bill for that route, the others were lost. During 1845, 121 railway Acts of

Parliament were obtained, 94 of these for new railways, while out in the countryside manic canvassing, planning and surveying went on for yet more railways. In the final 30 days leading up to the November 1845 deadline, 412 railway Bills were deposited in Parliament, many of them concocted with such haste that they contained inaccuracies in the drafting and thus failed to pass Standing Orders.

In 1846 several proposals were lodged in Parliament for railways across central London to a central railway terminus, and a Royal Commission was established to ascertain 'whether the extension of railways into the centre of the metropolis is calculated to afford such additional convenience as will compensate for the sacrifice of property, the interruption of important thoroughfares and interference with plans of improvement already suggested'.[2] The precise brief of the five-man Commission – whose members included Lord Dalhousie, George Canning and the Lord Mayor of London – was to assess the effect of railways on a district lying within a 'quadrilateral' around central London. They advised that there had been no significant increase in the value of residential property close to railways in London, and that those railways which had been built close to the city limits, Bishopsgate and Fenchurch Street, had impeded street improvements while throwing out of their homes thousands of very poor people. No new railways should, therefore, penetrate the specified area, whose northern boundary was the 'New Road' (now known as Marylebone) and the Euston Road, from Paddington to King's Cross, and whose southern limit was the north bank of the Thames.

The establishment of the Quadrilateral was a rare example of planning control on railways. Its boundaries were, for the most part, respected and thus shaped all future London railways. The present day 'Circle Line' of the London Underground, connecting all main line termini, was conceived as an alternative to a central terminus, and runs around its perimeter. Only the London, Chatham & Dover Railway seriously breached it when, in 1864, it broke into the City of London at Ludgate Hill, Holborn Viaduct and Blackfriars, all stations within a quarter of a mile of each other.[3]

By the end of the 1846 Session, 272 railway Bills had received the Royal Assent: 219 for new lines. In the three years 1845-7, 425 new railway companies were incorporated,[4] with a total proposed capital, to be raised by share subscription and loans, of £231,556,000. D. Morier Evans, a contemporary economic historian, calculated that this was equal to 6.7 per cent of national income, equal to two-thirds of the value of all exports for 1846. The value of gold held by the Bank of England in June 1846 was £16.6 million.[5].

The prospect of raising so much credit – unsecured by gold – was very alarming to the thoughtful, but a source of delight to the innocent and the cunning. Railway promotions brought into being a vastly enlarged share-owning class, people who had hitherto been considered 'uncommercial' (to use the contemporary description), whose investments had been in Government Stocks. Duchesses, widows, spinsters, clergymen, army officers, tailors and gentlemen now purchased railway shares as a safe and profitable depository for savings and a source of regular income. The difficulty was that expectations ran far beyond the financial machinery of the day – even honest railway companies found that their accountancy systems were unable to keep up with events, while dishonest or merely inefficient companies played havoc with their shareholders. Parliamentary Standing Orders demanded that companies compiled share subscription contracts, to prove that they had the required shareholders, and these lists frequently included fictitious names or those of people without resources: 'men of straw'. Errand boys and porters were paid 10s to put their signatures to the list, thus claiming to have subscribed £40,000-worth of shares. The Company Prospectus made glowing promises, and the beautifully engraved share certificates were at once endowed with a value by the hysteria of the market.

Stock exchanges mushroomed across the land in large towns and small. In 1844 a Yarmouth coal merchant placed an advert in the *Norwich Mercury* offering his services as a stockbroker and share-dealer, and clamouring to give cash now in return for shares of yet-to-be-built railways. Morgan & Co. of Norwich placed another. The shares on offer varied, from the reasonable Norwich to Ipswich, via Stowmarket, to the decidedly unsafe, such as the Blakeney, Wells & Thetford or the Diss, Thetford & Wells. Often there were several rival schemes along the same course and, at best, only one could be successful, yet cash would be advanced on the shares of them all. Loans to buy yet more shares were based on future harvests, future cargoes, the future rise in the value of an already-held share certificate: all dependent utterly on something that might not happen. And the greatest stupidity was that the ever-increasing value of shares depended on the continuing hysteria for buying them. The individual pursued his own best interest in a free market which, far from being the panacea for all economic ills, actually created serious economic problems.

The *Illustrated London News* of 11 October 1845 encapsulated the craze:

> Railway Shares! Railway Shares!
> Hunted by Stags and Bulls and Bears.
> Hunted by women – hounded by men –
> Speaking and writing – voice and pen.
> Claiming and coaxing – prayers and snares –
> See the world made about Railway Shares!

The Times was full of 'bubble' railway projects, their prospects portrayed in the most glowing and misleading terms. Take, for instance the advertisement placed on 23 July 1845 for the 'Somersetshire Midland', from Frome to Shepton Mallet, Glastonbury and Highbridge on the Bristol & Exeter. This stated that the 'peculiar advantage of this line is that the greater portion of it will be perfectly level'. Perhaps one third of this line could have been level, but the rest would have been very steep as it climbed on to and through the Mendips. On 1 August a competing company appeared – the 'Bridgwater, Frome and Central Somerset Railway', engineered by William Gravatt, Brunel's Resident Engineer on the Bristol & Exeter line. The proposed route was intended to be 32 miles long, over country which was said to possess 'every facility for railway construction'. One supposes this to mean that there was plenty of rock for hacking through and plenty of marshes for filling-in. The previous fib about level track was repeated and embroidered with a breathtaking lie: 'There will be no tunnels and only two short cuttings including one at Doulting where the stone recovered would be sufficiently valuable to be sold and defray the costs of building.' In so 'short' a cutting the stone must have been worth its weight gold to pay for the whole railway.

In 1845 Parliament was considering the need to organize railways on some 'plan', such as making them 'direct'. The simple-mindedness of politicians and the public knew no bounds, and the routes of 'Direct' railways grew ever more fantastic. In September 1845, cash subscriptions were invited for 'The Direct Great Western. From the GWR at Reading in as near as possible a straight line to Lands End.' There was a 'Harwich, Oxford and Bristol Direct', a 'Cheltenham, Oxford, Brighton Direct', and a 'Gloucester, Aberystwyth & Central Wales Direct'. Besides these there was the Bridgwater & Minehead, with its proposal for making Minehead the port for Ireland.

An editorial in *The Times* for 1 September 1845 thundered:

Reckless speculators, when their bills are about to fall due, have been known to draw other bills for larger sums and sell these at a discount to get the money to pay the first bills. Financial operations of this sort have generally been understood to indicate that a man's career is close to its end. If this is so then there are good grounds to believe that the general railway crash – predicted by many – cannot be far off.

The same issue published a rumour that the Stock Exchange was trying to reduce the frantic speculation by the excellent means of only accepting cash in share transactions, an indication that even the High Priests of The Market were beginning to have some doubts about 'Perfect Liberty'. On 27 January 1846 a leading article in *The Times* was entitled 'An Exaggeration of Enterprise'. The figures it quotes are at variance with those shown by Professor Simmons on p. 42 of his *The Railway in England and Wales, 1830–1914*; however, the article usefully summarized a contemporary view of the mania, and expressed the concerns of the thoughtful section of the community:

The Parliamentary Acts of 1835/37 permitted 1000 miles of railway, the accomplishment of which proved to be too great for the resources of the country . . . In 1844 Acts for 800 miles were passed as business revived and in 1845 Acts for 2766 miles were passed – and this before those of 1844 had begun to be built – in some cases. The 1845 lines are estimated to require £43 million. Reckoning 3 years for the completion of a railway it follows that, of this total of £64.75 million, £23.5 million would be required for 1846, a like sum in 1847 and £18 million in 1848. Besides these sums a further sum of £350 million is contemplated for the 815 schemes which this year [1846] have been deposited – an exaggeration of enterprise which may not be lightly entered into and to which Parliament, even if it ought not to interfere to check it, at least ought not to lend any assistance.

The Times followed this three days later with a sorrowful comment on the Adam Smith method: 'This *laissez-faire* system, excellent though it is in principle and beneficial as it has proved to be in practice, may be adhered to with a rigorous pedantry until it produces evils as great – in the contrary direction – as vexatious interference.' The Editor's worries were discounted by an optimistic speculator who, two days later, as the storm gathered force, wrote to ask 'what storm?':

With regard to a monetary crisis. Will you explain to your readers how this is to happen with a currency founded on gold? I submit that money cannot be scarce whilst it remains in Britain whatever may be the losses or gains of individuals – 'A' may be poorer but 'B' is richer. Permit me to doubt the propriety of your recommendation for Parliament to control railway expenditure.

On 8 May 1845 the Railway Clauses (Consolidation) Act became law. The Act brought together many often-used clauses, and laid it down that these clauses were henceforward to be 'taken as read', and not required to be included in any new Act, making easier the process of drafting a Bill. Section 42 enshrined the unworkable principle of the 'turnpike' railway: 'All companies and persons shall be entitled to use the railway with carriages and engines properly constructed.' Having reiterated pure *laissez-faire*, and made it easier to get a railway Bill into the House, a year later Parliament established a Select Committee to look into ways of 'securing a uniform system of management and into the practicality of restraining speculation'.[6]

The free-for-all of 1845–7 had created tremendous inflation. On 7 July 1846 Brunel testified to a Parliamentary Select Committee: 'Since the Act for the Oxford and Worcester line (obtained August 1845) prices have risen 50 per cent.' Before the same Committee, Lord Dalhousie stated that: 'Every description of trade has been injured in the increase in price of labour and materials and also, the great demand for money reduces the amount available for lending, increases the cost of borrowing and prevents undertakings taking place.'

Robert Stephenson[7] told the Committee that rival lines to the existing companies should not be permitted:

Q. Are you against any new Company being formed independent of those existing?

A. If the present Companies are placed under stringent control – I care not how stringent – the advantage of co-operation and uniting the managements are so great that I believe that if you allow existing Companies to expand until they meet, that the country would be better occupied than by rival, independent schemes.

Q. Is it not desirable to have a strong competition between parallel lines?

A. I think that this is the most injudicious expenditure of capital possible.

Q. Do you think that cheapness of fares would not best be obtained by competition?

A. Certainly not.

Q. Would not competition lead to Amalgamation?

A. It has invariably done so.

Q. And may it not lead to a desire on the part of the competing parties to so manage their concerns, to economise so much as to be incompatible with the well serving of the public?

A. Certainly. Such would be the result of bringing on a violent competition between two railways. I could quote a number of cases where the public is now taxed for an illegitimate expenditure of Capital for the purpose of competition and now that Amalgamation has taken place the Companies are aiming at giving interest to both sets of share holders and they have to tax the public for both.

At the end of a lengthy investigation the Committee reported:

Your Committee have considered the very serious extent to which the projection of new lines has been carried out without any well defined system for the accommodation of the Country. Schemes have frequently been got up and Acts obtained for the mere purpose of speculation without any definite object beyond selling them to the Companies with which they might compete. Existing Cos have been compelled to project new lines before their own means would warrant their undertaking them or the necessities of the district called for them – in order to protect themselves from rival schemes.

Your Committee have had their attention directed to the fearful amount of gambling consequent upon the existing state of things by which many persons have been entirely ruined and a demoralising effect extensively produced upon the humblest as well as the highest classes of Society while the trade of the Country has been injured owing to capital being diverted from its ordinary channels.

After mature consideration your Committee have come to the conclusion that it is absolutely necessary that some Department of the Executive, so constituted to command general respect and confidence, should be charged with the supervision of railways and canals with full power to enforce such regulations as may be made. This is indispensible for the general interest of the public.[8]

Parliament was divided on what to do. The vulgarity of the mania was repugnant to some. Lord Brougham remarked in the House of Lords on 23 April 1846: 'My Lords, you have enabled persons who were not makers of railways but of railway plans and attorneys' bills to go on without the least check on their proceedings. I want to know what was paid to Members of Parliament in passing Bills.'[9] In

Parliament in October 1846,[10] George Hudson, the epitome of vulgarity in the mind of Lord Brougham, said with perfect truth: 'Unless we have a monetary drain, not arising from railways but from any drain to which the country may be liable, I am satisfied that we need not be alarmed as to the amount which we are to sanction in these great works.'

Robert Stephenson, begged Parliament to legislate against 'violent competition', but in those *laissez-faire* days that was like asking for legislation against breathing. The majority were convinced that enterprising individuals should be left alone to follow their best interests. Such vast financial enterprise and activity created work for an army of labouring folk but tended to hurt the middling sort of investors and, because of the inflation of costs in wages and materials, was also hard on railway construction and other industries.

Hudson was right in his assertion that not even manic investment in railways could bring down the British economy. It would play its part undoubtedly but there were far greater movements afoot. In late 1845 or early 1846 Parliament decreed that the 5 per cent deposit of a prospective railway company's capital must be paid in bank notes.[11] At the time it was believed that the total of all deposits would amount to £59 million and that there would consequently not be enough notes in Britain for the purpose. In the event, only £11 or £12 million was deposited but that was not noticed. It was also believed by some economists that investing such large sums in railways 'must be fraught with ruinous consequences [for the rest of industry], for it is utterly impossible that a diversion of such immense sums from the industrial pursuits of the country should not deprive them of their life blood'.[12] The idea that the railways were *the* cause of the country's financial problems stems from the fact that such big figures were earmarked by Acts of Parliament for the one industry.

The machinations of the railway speculators were 'high-profile' news, but there were other, larger markets where money was being 'locked up' without making headlines. Referring to the Royal Bank of Liverpool, Sir Robert Peel observed that there were 'banks with a paid-up capital of £600,000 lending £500,000 to one house'.[13] Money was locked up by advances on harvests, imports and every possible commodity, and when the high prices fell and matters began to look shaky, people withdrew their money from their bank, thus locking up more money simply by hoarding it.

Early in 1847 the price of corn began to rise. In May it peaked at 115s a quarter, and then fell to 64s in ten days. Banks who had advanced money to home farmers and importers on the basis of these high prices were now in serious trouble. The largest corn-dealers in the land, Robinson & Co., whose Chairman was a Governor of the Bank of England, went bankrupt, and they were followed by other highly respected corn-dealers – and their bankers. Thus by July 1847 there was a great unease in the markets. Ireland was suffering the second year of severe famine and in September 1847 there were poor harvests in the rest of Britain, so that gold was sent abroad to buy food. There was also a sharp rise in the price of raw cotton and other raw materials, which carried to Egypt and America yet more gold and silver. The banker Francis Baring estimated that £7 million in gold left the country within a few months, while the amount of paper notes in circulation increased.[14] To pay debts, shares were sold in large numbers, and as the market became glutted their value fell, so that earlier borrowings were no longer covered by existing share values.

Inevitably railways were saddled with the entire blame. On 1 October 300 mill-owners and other businessmen presented a petition to the Mayor of Manchester stating that 'the mercantile affairs of the country have been seriously damaged by railway investment', and asking what steps could be taken to control railway promotions – this from Manchester, the home of *laissez-faire*. That same day the Bank of England announced that it would no longer advance money on public securities.[15] Only £3 million of gold remained in the Bank, while the amount of banknotes in circulation had a face value of £7 million. This contravened the 1844 Bank Act. On 25 October 1847 the Bank of England stopped trading and there was an actual riot of City gents in Lombard Street. The supposedly self-balancing system of market forces had been overcome by uncontrolled self-interest. The Prime Minister, Lord John Russell, suspended the Bank Act on 25 October and permitted the issue of paper money at 8 per cent interest, promising to indemnify the Bank should this lead to 'any infringement of existing law'.[16] The knowledge that paper notes were guaranteed by the Government calmed the panic.

Railways became a popular scapegoat once they ceased to be a popular speculation. By blaming the crisis on railway speculation others, more culpable, were ignored. While those outside the railway industry blamed railways those most closely connected with railways blamed Parliament. Samuel Smiles, author of the famous book *Self Help* and Secretary of South Eastern Railway, wrote:

The result of the labours of Parliament was a tissue of legislative bungling involving enormous loss to the Nation. Railway Bills were granted in heaps ... Committees decided without judgement and without discrimination; and in the scramble for Bills, the most unscrupulous were usually the most successful. The course adopted by Parliament was as irrational as it proved unfortunate. The want of foresight displayed by both Houses in obstructing the railway system so long as it was based on sound commercial principles was only equalled by the fatal facility with which they granted railway projects based on the wildest speculation.[17]

Lord Dalhousie, in establishing the Indian State railways, adopted the French system of combining state direction with private enterprise to avoid the competitive expense inflicted on British railways. On 20 April 1853 he wrote a Minute on his policy regarding Indian railways in which he observed that 'railway construction [in India] was directly but not vexatiously controlled by the Government and had this principle been adopted in England it would have placed the proprietors of railway property and the suffering public in a better position'.[18]

In January 1856 Robert Stephenson used the occasion of his inaugural Presidential Address to the Institution of Civil Engineers to express his disgust at Parliament's lack of control of the market in railways:

Legislative sanction having been given to a line, it might be supposed that Parliament would grant adequate protection, [from competing lines] exacting from the railway company certain public advantages in return. But instead the Legislature has exacted facilities [for the public] ... but so far from protecting the interests of those to whom they have conceded the right of making the line, they have encouraged every description of competition!

He attacked 'Parliamentary incompetence', giving as an example the occasion when, in 1845, Standing Orders did not constitute any obstacle to nineteen competing proposals for one (unnamed) route:

Judged by such a case the policy of Parliament really would seem to be to put the public to expense to make costs for lawyers and fees for Officers [of Parliament]. Is it possible to conceive anything more monstrous than to condemn nineteen parties to the same contentious litigation? They each and all had to bear the costs of opposing all the other Bills. Of the £286 million expended on railways it is believed that nearly one fourth has been paid for land and for conveyancing . . . blame for this waste had been put at the door of the railway Directors. 'See how the shareholders have been plundered by the railway companies.' But never do those who make these bitter comments attribute the monstrous result to the proper cause, which is exclusively the fault of Parliament. What interest can Directors have in feeing Counsel and paying the expenses of crowds of witnesses to await the pleasure of a Committee? The ingenuity of man could scarcely devise a system more costly than that of getting a railway Bill.

He gave the example of the Trent Valley Railway Bill of 1836, introduced as a measure to straighten the main line between Rugby and Stafford and by thus avoiding the detour into and out of Birmingham expedite the journey between London, Liverpool, Manchester, Ireland and Scotland. Stephenson stated that this important, national measure was thrown out by the Standing Orders Committee because a barn, shown on the general plan, was not included on a more detailed plan. Hence all the legal fees paid up until that moment were wasted. When the Bill was returned in 1840 the Grand Junction Railway was able to make 450 objections on grounds arising from Standing Orders. Arguments for and against those objections took two teams of expensive barristers twenty-two days to prove or disprove before the Standing Orders Committee – leaving only five of the objections sustained. The Bill had therefore failed the test of Standing Orders – whereupon the Committee decided they would, after all, let it go forward! During its passage through Parliament it was supported by the Prime Minister Sir Robert Peel and a majority in the House, but still it was argued before the Parliamentary Committee for sixty-three days. Before all the evidence could be heard Parliament was prorogued and the entire cost of the Bill to date, running into tens of thousands, was lost.

The Trent Valley Railway Bill finally became law on 21 July 1845 and it was Stephenson's opinion that the cost of building the line was 'not much greater than the Parliamentary legal costs of obtaining the enabling Act'.[19]

The final effect of the unhindered activity of individuals following their own best interest was the collapse of the country's financial markets. Lacking fresh sources of credit, new railway building practically ceased. In 1847 the mileage of new railway authorized was 1295; in 1850, the figure was 6¾ miles. The dividend of the MR and GWR fell steadily from 7 and 8 per cent respectively in 1846 to 2 and 4 per cent in 1850. In the Exhibition year of 1851, shares of 34 out of 40 leading railway companies were still selling at a discount,[20] and in 1852 Gladstone was of the opinion that 'enormous evils' had resulted from 'the incapacity of, or the cowardice of, Parliament in failing to deal with speculative and competitive railway building'. The 'free-for-all' had indeed resulted in 'A' being richer and 'B' poorer. The Ipswich lawyer Charles Austin, QC, earned more working for George Hudson between 1844 and 1847 than in the previous seventeen years.[21] He reinvested his fees from his Parliamentary work of opposing or advocating railways in the purchase and rebuilding of the run-down farms and villages of the Brandeston estate in Suffolk, to the great advantage of the inhabitants but to the detriment of the shareholders, who thought they were subscribing to the construction of a railway.

14

Repentance, Competition and Alliances

A FTER THE SPECULATIVE fantasies came the dead calm of reality. For railway workers, quite innocent of any guilt in the preceeding financial abuses, this was a grim catalogue of wage cuts, dismissals and loss of housing as the companies economized to reduce their losses. At Swindon, workers' housing projects were suspended and medical help became unavailable to those injured at work.[1] Share values of even the greatest companies were severely reduced while others had utterly collapsed. It was a time of reckoning especially for those shareholders of the Eastern Counties (ECR) and North British Railway (NBR) who discovered that their Directors had been paying them for years out of their own capital. The voices of railway company chairmen were heard at shareholders' meetings making Acts of Contrition for past extravagance and promising never to build another branch line without shareholders' consent.

George Carr Glyn, Chairman of the L&NWR, said on 18 February 1848: 'If, instead of destroying each other's interests, railway companies can be brought to unite, if, instead of encouraging competition, Parliament will impose on all railway companies a proper system of fares and charges so as to secure the public welfare . . . the railways will continue to be a safe investment.'[2] Glyn even engaged in talks with the L&SWR and GWR to explore the possibility of an amalgamation, but Parliament would never have agreed, and the matter dropped. In 1849 Parliament set up yet another Select Commitee[3] to inquire into all the well-known abuses and, uniquely the fact that Parliament had encouraged the Gadarene rush for shares by authorizing the raising of £173,797,447 of capital. The Committee's Report roundly condemned all the abuses, and a Government Bill to establish some controls on speculation in railways was put before the House. It was abandoned within the year. Thus the chaotic state of railways continued: existing companies felt threatened by each other New lines, defensive, aggressive and investment-speculative, would be built; few would be profitable and they would detract from the profits of others. There would be simultaneous inter-company co-operation and treachery.

The Great British Public had burnt its fingers and never again would they, with such naive enthusiasm, trust their money to British railway promoters. Many were the injured companies trying to raise fresh money to complete what they had started or to pay off old debts, but the Bank Rate was high and they were forced to issue new shares at a relatively high rate of *guaranteed* interest. These took preference for payment over earlier shares, so the original investors had to buy the new shares if they could, or lose everything.

If all else failed, the shareholders attempted to get rid of their expensively won, statutory obligations. To abandon a railway required another Act of Parliament; this frequently used up the Company's remaining cash. Such was the demand to abandon 'mania' railway companies that a general 'Act to Facilitate the Abandonment of Railways' was passed on 14 August 1850: 'Whereas divers joint-stock companies have been Incorporated by Act of Parliament and it has been found that such railways . . . cannot be made . . . with advantage to the public . . . it is expedient therefore that facilities should be given for abandonment of such railways'. Under this Act, 2000 miles of proposed or partially constructed route were abandoned.

Freedom was soon to reassert itself. Gold was discovered in California in 1849, and American expansion boomed. British money began to be invested in America, and by April of 1851, the returns were boosting the gold reserves of the Bank of England. On 5 April 1851, Herapath wrote optimistically in his *Railway Journal*: 'If no more follies of 1844–46 are committed we can expect the system to come around to a fitting state of prosperity because the traffic using the existing lines has increased by an average of 19 per cent this year over

1849.' It was vital to the railways' prosperity that no more lines were built. The article showed how profits per mile decreased as more mileage was built. This was because mileage built since 1846 had tended to serve either less profitable areas or to be competitive, duplicating existing routes, and of course it all increased the owning company's working expenses. The orgy of investing during the mania period had produced its hangover. The stock-market value of all railway capital in June 1847 was £54 million; by 1853 the same capital was worth £18 million (see Appendix 1).[4]

The largest railway company in Britain 1850, in terms of route miles, was the MR, with 434 straggling miles and a capital of £16,794,366, but the dominant company was the L&NWR, with 385 miles of mostly strategically placed route and a total capital of £25,161,150. The GWR was the third-largest, with 231 miles and almost £14 million of capital but, of the 'big three', was paying the smallest dividends. The L&NWR's superiority was due to its absolutely vital trunk, London, Birmingham, Liverpool/Manchester and, with closely tied allies, the Lancaster & Carlisle and Caledonian Railways, to Glasgow and Edinburgh. But its dominance was also due to the very strong character and most able General Manager, Mark Huish, the pioneer of 'corporate management'. He introduced costing techniques and improved systems of accountancy and was a pillar of the Railway Clearing House which assisted in the standardization of all railway practices. He disliked competition since, like war, it upset the steady tenor of railway business and reduced the profits from one of the largest accumulations of capitals in the world. He perceived the most profitable and efficient railway to be one with a highly controlled environment, with a constant traffic, without peaks. Such conditions would permit the largest business to be carried on with the smallest staff and without excess rolling stock. He might have enjoyed running a national railway system and may have considered the L&NWR as being large enough to form its nucleus: privately owned, under Parliamentary protection against competition but under Parliamentary obligation as regards its fares and dividends. But times were competitive, his Company was threatened by encroachment by others and, in pursuit of L&NWR security, he was obliged to establish a form of railway imperialism. In a sense he *was* the L&NWR, since it was entirely due to his astonishing manoeuvres during the period 1844–5 that the formative amalgamations took place. The L&BR had not wanted the merger, and the convoluted twists in the story of how, by blackmail and subterfuge, Huish brought it about are worthy of a Gilbert & Sullivan opera. He declared himself against monopoly in order to gain the financial support of businessmen in promoting three railways against the L&BR's interest, and even went so far as to forge the official seal of the Birmingham Company.[5] When they had served his purpose of forcing the GJR/L&BR merger, he not only repudiated his support but did his best to destroy them, so that they would not constitute a threat to his newly created monopoly. One of the railways was never built, the other was forced to build an expensive branch line under such conditions that it could never be used. However, the other part of this line was built, and entered the heart of Birmingham at Snow Hill in 1852 as the GWR.[6]

By 1850 the L&NWR was flanked, east and west, by rival lines. The Shrewsbury & Chester (S&CR) and the Shrewsbury & Birmingham (S&BR) railways opened in 1846 and 1849 respectively, and offered a route from Birmingham to Chester 29 miles shorter than that of the L&NWR. During the pre-construction phase, Huish had tried to buy the companies, but without gaining his end. On 1 August 1850 the Great Northern Railway (GNR) began running from King's Cross to York, via Peterborough, Boston, Lincoln, Doncaster and Knottingley. Although this was a roundabout route (the direct line via Grantham was under construction[7]) it at once affected the existing routes of other companies: the ECR's circuitous route from London to Peterborough, via Cambridge, Ely and March, was wiped out. The GNR had a branch from its main line at Royston to Cambridge, roughly parallel to the ECR's, and every town lying between the ECR and GNR main lines became the target for competitive railway projects, leeching away ECR and GNR money. The MR's York and Scottish traffic via Derby was threatened by the GNR, and would be lost once the direct GNR line was completed. The Nottingham and Derby coalfields, MR territory, were also being invaded by the GNR. The MR began to look for another route to Scotland, attempting to break into the L&NWR's Anglo-Scottish route in the north-west, and a full-scale war of competition exploded.

Impossibly cheap fares were offered in the hope of killing off the opposition, new railways were built as a defence against a larger neighbour or used by the latter to blackmail a smaller company into submission. The L&NWR indulged in all these activities and the results were as predicted by Herapath: its gross income nearly doubled between 1851 and 1860, but it suffered a 7½ per cent reduction in its

rate of return on capital invested.[8] In 1849–50 Huish set out to create
a cartel[9] – the 'Euston Confederacy' – to 'pool' receipts and agree fares.
This was not, however, to be an altruistic division of the spoils between
friends, but rather, an attempt by the imperially minded Huish to
entice or coerce other companies to become his colonies.

The Shrewsbury & Birmingham and the Shrewsbury & Chester
were not deliberately competing with the L&NWR. The two companies, co-operating, produced the shortest route between those places
and their fares were necessarily less than those charged by the
L&NWR. On 16 October 1849, Huish sent Mr Roy, Secretary of the
Shrewsbury & Chester, an elegantly worded threat:

> It is stated by the Shrewsbury & Birmingham than you are about to
> join them in opposing us, at low rates, between Birkenhead and
> Wolverhampton. Will you tell me if this is the case? I trust not and that your
> Company and ours may avoid the competition which has brought such loss
> on other parties. I need not say that if you should be unwise enough to
> encourage such a proceeding it must result in a general fight . . .[10]

Mr Roy replied in mild tones, declaring his Company's independence and its right to attend to its own business. In the final
paragraph he wrote: 'I have no doubt that your letter was written in
the hurry of business . . . if a "general fight" as you express it should
arise, it is not of our seeking nor from any unreasonable views on the
part of this Company.' Huish promptly ordered the S&CR booking-
office at Chester station – which was jointly owned by the S&CR and
the L&NWR – to be closed, and the booking-clerk to be thrown out
with his tickets. Under orders from Huish, S&CR cattle traffic
onwards to Birkenhead was refused by the Birkenhead Railway, a
satellite of the L&NWR, and a price war between David and Goliath
ensued, the L&NWR breaking legally binding agreements in the
process.

The lawyers took three expensive years to reach the only possible conclusion: that the L&NWR had acted illegally. Meanwhile
the mighty L&NWR carried at a loss, which it could stand, to force
the two Shrewsbury companies to carry at a loss – which they could
not. The final outcome of all this expense was an 'own goal' against
Huish. Instead of selling themselves to the L&NWR the Shrewsbury
companies fell into the open arms of the GWR, which thereby
obtained, ready made, its long-coveted, long-opposed route to the
Mersey.

On 17 April 1851 Huish brought the 'Confederacy' to life in a great diplomatic coup to prevent competition, with his 'Octuple' and 'Sextuple' Agreements. In the former he persuaded, or coerced, the eight companies involved in the Anglo-Scottish traffic – the L&NWR, Lancaster & Carlisle (LCR), Caledonian (CR), MR, GNR, York & North Midland (Y&NMR), York, Newcastle & Berwick (YN&B), and North British (NBR) – to make a 'pool' of their passenger and freight revenues earned on this trade. The 'Sextuple' Agreement applied to all but the CR and NBR, and covered everything apart from the Anglo-Scottish traffic.

The Agreement was complicated owing to the number of companies and routes involved, and depended for its operation on the impartial clerical services of the Railway Clearing House. After deduction by every company of its agreed working costs, the pool was divided 50/50 between the 'east coast' and 'west coast' companies. The latter, with a single, direct route, had their share apportioned to them on the basis of mileage. The east coast half had to be subdivided between two routes: Euston, Rugby, Derby, Normanton, York, and King's Cross–York.[11]

The Great Exhibition opened in Hyde Park in May 1851, and the no-competition agreement between the companies held for about two weeks, until cheap fares offered by sea between Hull and London forced the GNR to lower its fares – and this sparked off a fierce competition with the MR and the L&NWR. Lucky GNR passengers were travelling from Leeds and Sheffield to Maiden Lane (the temporary London terminus until King's Cross station was ready) for 5s and the GNR was saying: 'Whatever Euston charges, we will charge sixpence less'.[12] The GNR, which had new engines and rolling stock, and was able to provide more comfortable, more punctual trains than the L&NWR, proved a formidable adversary; but the GNR had to abandon the fight when the Company discovered that the tolls it was paying to the MS&L for the use of the latter's tracks between Sheffield and Retford was greater than its income from passengers.

There were longer-term threats to the L&NWR's supremacy, namely the possibility of the MR's breaking into the west coast Anglo-Scottish trunk at Low Gill on the Lancaster & Carlisle Railway, which was under lease to the L&NWR. The MR had obtained a route from Leeds north through the Aire valley to Skipton, 40 miles from Low Gill, in 1847. Acts of Parliament in 1846 and 1848 authorized the 'little' North Western Railway[13] to build a line from Skipton, through Ingleton to Low Gill, with a branch from Clapham, south of Ingleton, to Lancaster and Morecambe.

The NWR was supposedly an independent company but it had two of George Hudson's MR Directors on its Board. The NWR opened from Skipton to Ingleton, 25 miles south of Low Gill, on 30 July 1849. The necessary engineering works northwards to Low Gill were expensive and, in the desperate financial conditions after the 1847 crash, the NWR was unable to complete the line to join the Anglo-Scottish trunk. This was lucky for the L&NWR because their lease on the Lancaster & Carlisle was due to run out in 1857, when the L&CR Directors would be free to make agreements with whomsoever they pleased, and the L&NWR's pre-eminence in Anglo-Scottish traffic depended on keeping control of the L&CR.

All the smaller northern companies were jostling to advance their interests. The MR took the lease of the NWR for twenty-one years in May 1852. The GNR had extended its Doncaster–Wakefield line to Bradford in 1854, and was planning further northwards extension, even hoping to purchase the 'little' NWR, while the Lancashire & Yorkshire Railway (L&YR), the NBR, and the Glasgow & South Western (G&SWR) stood ready to ally themselves with any company which could breach the CR/L&NWR axis.

In the east Midlands too, the GNR and MR did battle. On 1 August 1852, the GNR was given access to Nottingham by a little company with a long name – the 'Ambergate, Nottingham, Boston & Eastern Junction'.[14] The latter had built a railway from a junction with the GNR just north of Grantham to a junction with the MR at Colwick, near Nottingham, and the MR allowed it to use their Nottingham station. The MR, which already had a line from Nottingham deep into GNR territory at Lincoln, thought they could eventually buy the small Company and get a route into the main line of the GNR. The Ambergate Company, however, gave the GNR permission to run over their line to Colwick Junction, and enter Nottingham Midland station – permission they had no power to give. When the first GNR train arrived at Nottingham, on 1 August 1852, its engine was captured by Midland engines and was dragged off to an MR shed, locked in and the tracks torn up. A fortnight later, Edmund Denison, Chairman of the GNR, wrote to Edward Ellis of the MR, asking if the hostilities could cease and suggesting that the companies ought to amalgamate. Ellis rejected the suggestion politely:

Our Board is equally alive to the serious evils of competition; the needless expenditure in running duplicate trains and still more the imperative necessity of preventing a reckless outlay on the construction of new lines. You are aware that for many years the L&NWR and MR companies have cultivated an intimate alliance and negotiations are on foot for a closer union.[15]

Shortly after this the L&NWR and MR jointly lodged a Bill in Parliament for the amalgamation of the two companies and the MR placed a Bill in the House for a railway from Leicester to the GNR at Hitchin. The GNR then promoted a Bill for a railway from its main line at Sandy to Bedford, in the path of the MR's route to Hitchin.

Sandwiched between the L&NWR and the MR was the very successful North Staffordshire Railway (NSR). Between 1845 and 1850 it had built 112 miles of route centred on the Potteries and meeting the two giants – the MR and the L&NWR – at various points, including Derby and Crewe. The MR seems to have been happy to coexist with the NSR, but the L&NWR envied the immense industrial wealth served by the NSR, saw that its route could make an excellent short-cut to Manchester, and recognized the danger if the GNR came from Nottingham to Derby and across the NSR to Crewe and Manchester. Huish eased himself gently into the NSR's affairs by concluding an agreement that each would offer the other 'every reasonable facility' for the use of each other's lines – for a toll, of course. While the NSR played by the rules, the L&NWR was slow in paying its tolls to the NSR and was even obstructive to NSR traffic where it junctioned with the L&NWR.

The NSR not only lost money through this but felt obliged to defend itself by proposing a blackmailing railway from Colwich to the GWR at Cannock. The legal costs of promoting the line were hard on the NSR but the L&NWR took the hint and in 1852 offered the NSR amalgamation. Together with the MR, this would have placed a sixth of Britain's railway mileage and most of industrial England's railways under one decisive management. Co-ordination of effort and a reduction in costs would have lowered fares and provided a better service. Parliament however, was thoroughly alarmed at the prospect of what was seen as a gigantic monopoly – even though Robert Stephenson and Carr Glyn had in the recent past offered to accept government control of fares and dividends in return for a reduction of competition. The result of this and other amalgamation proposals was that, on 9 December 1852, Edward Cardwell's Committee on Railway and

Canal Bills[16] was appointed. Its members included five ex-Presidents of the Board of Trade: Cardwell, Labouchere, Henley, Gladstone and Bright; a proposal to appoint Robert Stephenson to the Committee was defeated.

In evidence to the Committee, the great men of the railways urged amalgamation as the only way to protect existing investment and to provide a proper, national, railway system. Charles Saunders, Company Secretary and General Traffic Superintendent of the GWR, suggested the amalgamation of all railways into a few concerns, with specified territories. Samuel Laing agreed, and suggested that the Chatham, South Eastern, Brighton and South Western could be merged 'with great public advantage'. He pointed out that, in total, British railway companies had spent at least £70 million in obtaining their Acts of Incorporation. Robert Stephenson believed that to be an underestimate.

Cardwell's Committee sat from December 1852 until July 1853. By this time the MR had allowed the GNR into Nottingham and, in return, the GNR gave up its blackmailing Sandy–Bedford Bill. In April 1854 Cardwell told Parliament:

> If you look at a map of this country you see it covered with railways and your first impression is that there is a most easy and most uninterrupted transit from one extremity to the other. Examine more closely and you will find that this is not a uniform system [but] is divided into kingdoms, diplomacies and alliances, offensive and defensive and is altogether a more complicated affair than at first sight appears.[17]

From this, it seems plain that Cardwell realized the disadvantages of fragmentation where railways were concerned but yet, in his Fourth Report he recommended that 'no railway or canal bill containing any powers of amalgamation, purchase, lease, working arrangement or other combination of interest between different companies should be read a second time'. He recanted this very extreme position in his Fifth Report: 'Working arrangements between different companies for the regulation of traffic and division of profit should be sanctioned under proper conditions and for limited periods but amalgamations should not be sanctioned except in minor or special cases.'

The Railway & Canal Traffic Act resulting from his Committee, which became law on 10 July 1854, gave a legal framework to assist the companies to compete less and help the public more. Section 2 obliged every railway company:

according to its respective powers, to afford all reasonable facilities for receiving, forwarding and delivery and no such company shall make or give any undue or unreasonable preference, advantage or favour to any particular person nor shall any company subject any particular person to any undue or unreasonable prejudice or disadvantage in any respect whatsoever . . . every railway which forms part of a continuous line of railway communication shall afford all due and reasonable facilities for forwarding and receiving traffic by one such railway so that all reasonable accommodation by means of the railways of several companies, be at all times afforded to the public.

Competition, as Samuel Smiles observed, usually results in agreement or outright amalgamation between the competitors. Along the way, such competition will result in improvements for the passengers, provided that there is a steady increase in revenue, so that the added costs of greater luxury and/or lowered fares can be absorbed and a dividend maintained; and that there are temperate personalities to direct the competition in a sensible way – until even that level of competition becomes too expensive for the companies, and amalgamation is essential in order to maintain a reasonable level of profit.

Parliament, perhaps confused by the conflicting opinions expressed in the Fourth and Fifth Reports, adopted an arbitrary attitude towards amalgamations. It threw out the L&NWR/NSR/MR Amalgamation Bill but allowed the formation of the North Eastern Railway (NER) in 1854. This involved five railways which were themselves the combination of many others. In 1863 the Stockton & Darlington joined the North Eastern group, whereupon the NER had the monopoly of the entire north-east. The Company was a well co-ordinated organization, the first to study the use of precise statistics as an aid to the most economical operation, strong enough financially to provide a really good service, and co-operative towards any other railway which wished to use its tracks. The NER became a very great railway, although there was discontent among enthusiasts for competition in the Corporation of the City of Hull, which had been instrumental in creating the impecunious Hull & Barnsley Railway.

The East Anglian railways, serving a remote and rural area, had competed with each other into decrepitude and were desperate for amalgamation, yet in 1854 Parliament refused to sanction the mergers. All the companies were by then leased to the Eastern Counties Railway (ECR) but were still, legally, separate entities, and were thus able to sue the ECR and each other for various hurts, real or imagined, and to project fresh railways to which the others would object. They were so short of money that, in promoting a new railway, they would borrow thousands of pounds at 5 per cent for six months to cover their legal costs.[18] Only in 1862, when the East Anglian companies were *in extremis*, did Parliament agree to the merger to form the Great Eastern Railway (GER).

The competition between the MR and GNR was for years supported by a territory rich enough to produce the necessary annual increases in revenues to absorb the costs of competitively improved services, while maintaining the dividend. Even so, the companies would occasionally beg each other to 'cease hostile actions', but so long as they remained separate, feuds broke out. Robert Stephenson, in spite of his strong feeling against unbridled competition, assisted the contractor Samuel Morton Peto's attacks on the ECR, and Huish was happy to have Peto as an accomplice in his attacks on the GWR over the Oxford, Worcester & Wolverhampton Railway. Huish estimated that the GWR's competition between London, Birmingham and Chester cost the L&NWR £70,000 per annum.[19]

Huish had to protect his Anglo-Scottish traffic, worth £1.5 million annually, by controlling the fiercely competitive situation between – and in between – the west and east coast routes to Scotland. In 1854 the MR was still a vassal of the L&NWR, albeit a restless one. The management of the Manchester, Sheffield & Lincolnshire passed, in 1853, from James Allport, who became General Manager of the MR, to Edward 'Wrecker' Watkin. The former is said by Hamilton Ellis to have been a close ally of Huish; the latter had been a pupil of Huish and for years his colleague. Huish certainly felt, therefore, that he had both MR and MS&L under control.

On 4 August 1853 the MR obtained its Act for the Leicester–Hitchin line. The MR trains had previously to share the L&NWR main line south of Rugby so the new railway was intended to reduce congestion on the L&NWR, and to enable the MR to run a London–Carlisle service from King's Cross via Leicester, Leeds and Ingleton. The latter plan came to little, for in November 1854, Huish persuaded Allport to pool the entire receipts of both companies in the 'Common Purse' Agreement and receive an agreed percentage of the resulting fund.[20] The MR then had no incentive to compete with the L&NWR for the Scottish traffic.[21]

The GNR was subject to the 'Octuple' Agreement which pooled certain parts of the GNR's earnings and paid it an agreed percentage.

The GNR had been coerced into the Agreement and was therefore always mutinous, looking for ways of getting the better of the L&NWR. The GNR shareholders, having only recently raised a vast capital sum, were seeing it squandered by their management as they engaged in a furious competition with the L&NWR and the MR; the GNR was again charging return fares of 5s between Sheffield and West Riding towns, and London. Edmund Denison, MP, Chairman of the GNR, commented: 'If this goes on the great majority of my constituents, washed and unwashed, will be visiting London in the course of next week.'[22]

The GNR also cast eyes on the L&NWR's Scottish traffic. The GNR had gained access to Leeds in 1850, and in 1856 encouraged the 'little' North Western to bring a Bill to Parliament for running powers over the Lancaster & Carlisle (L&CR) and over the MR to Leeds, so as to connect with the GNR. The L&NWR and MR fought this tooth and nail and the NWR lost, but in the course of the argument their 'Common Purse' Agreement was revealed. Tens of thousands of pounds was paid out in legal fees by all four companies, the L&NWR spending £15,000 to achieve their victory.[23] Huish's victory was hollow because the 'Common Purse' Agreement was later ruled to be illegal, which broke the 'Euston Confederacy'. Watkin, for the MS&L, repudiated the 'Octuple' Agreement and, in August 1857, allowed the GNR to run their trains to Manchester and Liverpool, via Retford. The Manchester terminus was owned by the L&NWR, and the MS&L, merely a tenant, was now sub-letting to the GNR. Huish ordered the MS&L booking-clerks to be evicted, the offices and entrances used by the MS&L (and now the GNR) passengers to be boarded up, and the tracks they used to be occupied with trains of pit-props. MS&L/GNR passengers had to resort to unusual means of egress from the station, and the lawyers had a field day as the writs were issued. The outcome in the courts was yet another defeat for the L&NWR and the passing of the GNR/MSL Traffic Agreement Act on 25 July 1858.

The MR's Leicester–Hitchin Line was opened in May 1857, reducing both that Company's dependence on the L&NWR and the tolls received from the MR by the L&NWR. Mark Huish's imperial policy had failed. His attempts to control other companies had resulted in humiliating reverses for the L&NWR, the greatest company of any description in the whole world, and despite his best efforts, L&NWR net revenue had consistently declined throughout his reign. A group of his Directors, led by the granite personality of Richard Moon, were very much opposed to him; the Company's Chairman, Lord Chandos, did not support him; at the Railway Clearing House, other railway managers removed their support for his ideas.[24] Within the L&NWR, high ranking officers were resentful of his interference, as they saw it, in their departments. Huish tendered his resignation on 11 September 1858 and left the Company's service one month later.

15

Contractors and the Great Crash

A FTER THE DÉBÂCLE of September 1847 the money market was depressed for several years. Even in 1850 only three Acts for new railways were passed, authorizing 195 miles and the raising of £9.6 million. Since 1835 large railway contracting businesses had been developed, and the organizations these men had built up were, by 1849, lacking work. The public was sick of railway projects, and so the way forward for those major contractors, like Peto & Betts and Thomas Brassey – and for freelancing engineers like George Parker Bidder – lay in promoting and building their own railways in the hope of persuading some existing company to buy or lease their product.

From 1851 frozen money began to thaw and require investment opportunities – and not just in Britain. In France, industrial capitalism was cautiously introduced after 1830 through railway building, which required the development of the coal and iron industries. Until 1847 the work was financed to a significant extent by British money and built with British technical expertise. In 1848 France experienced another revolution and in 1852 the new order accelerated industrialization by permitting the establishment of two great investment banks – Crédit Mobilier and Crédit Lyonnais[1] – into which the ordinary people of France were encouraged to place their savings. These funds now began to invest in Britain.

Mr Gladstone, as Chancellor, reduced as many taxes and import duties as he could. Income tax fell to 7d [3p] in the pound, British and French financial confidence grew and a period of 'exuberant borrowing' ensued.[2] In 1853, with Bank Rate at a mere 2 per cent, the third railway mania began. Sixty-one new railways, amounting to 972 miles of route and requiring £15.5 million of new money, were authorized in that year.

The outbreak of the entirely unnecessary Crimean War in March 1854 immediately caused a tremendous inflation of prices which undermined all the recent investments. Income tax was at once doubled and the cost of labour and materials rose sharply. Contractors of all kinds, working on contracts taken at pre-war prices, were demolished. The great naval architect John Scott-Russell, his shipyard heavily mortgaged and burdened with the added misfortune of building Brunel's SS *Great Eastern*, went bankrupt in February 1856. The civil engineering contractor Fox Henderson went down in October. The rapid economic and industrial expansion then taking place in the United States was leading to financial instability and high interest rates, British gold was being drawn across the Atlantic and the British Bank Rate rose above 6 per cent in an attempt to hold it back.

In 1857, 674 miles of new railway requiring £10.8 million were authorized by Parliament. On 8 October 1857, 62 of 63 New York banks failed; the effect was quickly felt in Britain, the Borough Bank of Liverpool being the first to collapse on 27 October. By November the British Bank Rate was at a crisis 10 per cent and the Bank of England had issued £2 million-worth more notes than was legal under the 1844 Act.[3] On 12 November the Government passed the 'Bank Indemnity Act', making it legal for the Bank to have in circulation more paper money than it had gold to support it. The credit crash swept like a wave into France, embarrassing wealthy individuals who were unable to meet their obligations on the Bourse and causing them to decamp to the United States to avoid their debts. Highly respected financial names were sullied.[4]

The crisis of 1857 did not assume the proportions of that of 1847–8 because of the abundant supplies of gold coming in from California supplemented by more from the recently discovered gold-fields of Australia, and a providentially plentiful harvest. To stimulate business an Act was passed in 1858 permitting banks to take on the financial protection of 'Limited Liability', which held a shareholder liable for his company's debts only up the value of the shares he held in it. This privilege was granted to each railway company in its Act of Incorporation, and to other businesses by the Act of 1855. In 1862 'Limited Liability' was extended to cover finance companies, formed to grant credit for railways, mines – and armaments – around the world. Many people believed 'Limited Liability' to be an invitation to fraud.

Thus there came about the fourth railway mania. Between 1860 and 1866 British railway route mileage was increased by 45 per cent. As in the previous credit booms, sober observers of the financial world took a dim view of the 'overtrading' and the fantastic borrowing for railways was, as usual, singled out for particular criticism. The Master of the Rolls said, in 1865: 'Companies are promoted for the sole purpose of the Capital subscribed being divided between the promoters and their lawyers'.[5] The *Economist* magazine wrote:

> A railway is now-a-days got up to *sell* . . . A lawyer and an engineer get together in a district where there happens to be two small towns uncon-nected by direct railway communication and devise a railway to unite them . . . Out of legal and Parliamentary expenses they will fill their pockets. Whether the Bill passes or not is immaterial.[6]

The learned judge and the editor should have added 'contractor' to their condemnation of enterprising professionals. The two greatest railway contractors in the world at that time were Thomas Brassey, and Samuel Morton Peto (in partnership with Edward Ladd Betts, and sometimes also with Thomas Brassey). Peto was the most imaginative, energetic and capable property developer of his period. Large schemes requiring thousands of men, millions of bricks and millions of pounds sprang from his acutely businesslike brain. He became Member of Parliament for Norwich in 1847 and developed an enormous reputa-tion as a moral, Christian gentleman – and indeed, he invested in churches and chapels as he invested in everything else. His shining image encouraged both banks and small investors, many of whom sub-sequently lost everything. In 1845 Peto leased his own Lowestoft Railway & Harbour Company to the Norfolk Railway (NR), of which he was Chairman, making the latter responsible for his debts in the Lowestoft and guaranteeing the interest on his investment therein. By 1848 the financial burden had become too great for the NR to carry, so he offloaded the liabilities of both the Norfolk and the Lowestoft companies on to the ECR by means of a lease which commenced in September. This arrangement had not been approved by Parliament and was thus illegal, but Peto was a major creditor (if not *the* major creditor) of the ECR, and was on close terms with the Company's Chairman, George Hudson, MP, and the Deputy Chairman, David Waddington, MP, and it went ahead on the understanding that if, by 1855, Parliament had not been persuaded to approve the lease, the NR could re-purchase its rolling stock at the 1848 price. The lease resulted in the entire staff of the two companies being dismissed and replaced by ECR men,[7] and the ECR's miserable revenues were further depleted by prior payments of rent to the shareholders of the Norfolk Railway and the Lowestoft – principally Peto. The illegality lasted into 1849, when Parliament gave its approval.

In February 1849 Waddington and Hudson were ejected from the ECR by angry shareholders, and Edward Ladd Betts, Peto's brother-in-law, became Chairman. He and Peto, together with Brassey and the engineer George Parker Bidder, were then working hard to recover from the financial crash. Bidder and Peto had a longstanding plan for a large development of factories, houses and docks, served by a railway, all built over several square miles of marshland they had purchased before the 1847 crash. They were also arranging to construct railways in Norway and Denmark, by which farm produce would be brought to the coast to be shipped to Lowestoft in Peto's steamships while British coal and industrial products went eastwards.

In 1850 the four were trying to persuade the London & Blackwall and the ECR to raise the money to pay them to build a line to Tilbury. When it was built the contractors would lease it from the ECR at a rent equal to 6 per cent of the capital raised. The shareholders of the ECR were receiving little or nothing in dividends, the value of their shares was far below par and they were not inclined to take part in further adventures. Flushed with their recent success in getting rid of Hudson and Waddington, they resisted Betts's enthusiasm and in November Betts left the Company, on doctor's orders, on account of 'his late, serious, accident'. His place was taken by one Joseph Glyn, and during his tenure the ECR firmly refused all blandishments from Peto and his confederates until David Waddington was recalled as Chairman, in spite of considerable opposition, in March 1851.

Waddington had been recalled because 'his influence was too great to be lost to the railway'.[8] The other Directors and the shareholders were to live to regret their decision, but meanwhile they meekly withdrew their opposition in Parliament to the Tilbury line. Parliament however, threw out the Bill in June 1851 because the Committee did not like the proposed leasing agreement. Undeterred, the L&BR and ECR went back to Parliament in 1852 with a Bill for a jointly owned line, making no mention of the intention of leasing it to the people who built it – indeed, the shareholders were told that they would be free to choose whether or not to lease it.[9] As a result of this subterfuge the Bill received the Royal Assent on 17 June 1852 and a month later Peto wrote to the railway's Joint Board, rejecting the agreement giving him and Brassey 4 per cent profit and demanding 10 per cent. Since the Boards were chaired by Waddington and strongly influenced by Bidder, Peto's demand was agreed to one week later.[10] The Tilbury line was overtly a joint ECR/L&BR financial undertaking but separate from either the ECR or L&BR as such. Therefore, unless shareholders in either company bought shares in the joint concern they had no power to vote on matters affecting it. Peto, Brassey, Bidder, Betts and Waddington owned well in excess of £130,000 of the £400,000 capital. Meanwhile it was solely an ECR expenditure of £47,000 which created the locomotive and rolling stock fleet for the Tilbury line. This was then rented to the contractors, Peto and friends, at a fraction of the true cost.

In 1851 Peto, Brassey and Betts promoted the Halesworth & Haddiscoe Railway, the first phase of a system of railways to be known as the 'East Suffolk Railway', which would connect Yarmouth and Lowestoft to the Eastern Union Railway (EUR) at Ipswich, and would reduce their distance from London by about 26 miles compared with the existing route via Norwich, Brandon and Ely. When built it would divert all that traffic to the shorter route and commensurately damage the revenues of the long-suffering and highly obliging ECR.

The ECR and EUR were wasting each other's money in promoting rival lines along the peaceful East Anglian fields and hedges. The Norfolk was still legally a separate entity and the EUR tried to buy it. By 1853 the EUR had exhausted its resources and was leased, without Parliamentary permission, by the ECR in January 1854. Peto's East Suffolk was then under construction, and it seemed a foregone conclusion that he would be able to sell it to the ECR. He would expect Waddington to commit the ECR shareholders to a lease at a rent which would guarantee him, Peto, 10 per cent of the capital he had invested.

Peto's applecart was upset in July 1855 when the ECR shareholders refused to vote for a lease of the East Suffolk and set up a Committee of Investigation under the Chairmanship of Henry Love, to inquire into Waddington's actions as Chairman. Many skeletons were unearthed, including the fact that the ECR received £400 per annum on their outlay of £47,000 to equip the Tilbury line. Waddington was saved for the moment by Peto, Brassey and Betts, who bought up ECR shares and thus had the power to get him re-elected. He was finally ejected for outrageous duplicity in April 1856, three years before the ESR was complete.

The re-formed Board of Directors, chaired by Love and representing the wishes of the shareholders, wanted to stop all new capital expenditure and to concentrate on trying to make a profit out of what they already had. Peto thereupon promoted a Bill for a railway from Colchester, through Maldon to Pitsea, on the Tilbury line. If Peto built the Pitsea line he and the ESR would have a competing route to London, short-circuiting the ECR. The impoverished and threatened ECR had therefore to agree to buy the lightly built East Suffolk line at Peto's inflated price of £15,000 per mile, guaranteed fair by his friend Robert Stephenson. The Pitsea line Bill was at once withdrawn: suddenly it was no longer the great public benefit it had been the day before.

The ESR opened on 1 June 1859, and was undoubtedly very useful to the towns it served. Had the ECR grown stronger it might well, at some later date, have built the line itself; as it was, the heavy expenditure and the future costs had been literally forced upon the Company at a time when it was financially weak. The attitude of the ordinary investor to railway schemes and the vulnerability of existing companies to the self-interested schemes of contractors, is encapsulated in the words of Richard Moon, Chairman of the & L&NWR who, in 1862, declared: 'Not one of the great companies can raise sixpence without preference or guaranteed shares. There are no proprietors willing to come forward to make a railway. They are made by contractors, engineers and speculators who live on the *fears* of the companies.'[11]

There is no doubt about the great practical and financial abilities of Messrs Peto, Brassey, Bidder and Betts, who all played a large part in the development of Victorian London, its railways, stations and docks. They 'thought big', and drove all before them to accomplish their plans. While this was often damaging to existing companies, it kept their workforce – and their credit – afloat, and created work for thousands of people, directly and indirectly. In pursuit of their own interest, these men stretched the capitalist system to its limit and beyond.

The contractor's technique was, as Richard Moon implied, to insert a railway into territory where its presence would create a threat to an existing company or companies. In 1837 Parliament had ordered the South Eastern Railway – always known as 'The Dover Railway' – to use the London–Brighton line, from its south London terminus of Bricklayer's Arms, as far as Redhill, and there to break away due east for Ashford and Dover.[12] There was, therefore, an opening for a direct line from London to Dover, via Rochester, and in 1845 Parliament authorized the SER to construct the Greenwich & Gravesend Railway as an instalment of such a line. The purchase of the Gravesend & Rochester Canal enabled the SER to extend its line to Strood in August 1847 and there it stood, unable to proceed in the aftermath of the crash.

In Kent leading local figures, including Lord Sondes (who had lands in Norfolk and had worked with Peto) and Stephen Lushington, MP, decided to build the East Kent Railway (EKR), from Strood through Rochester to a terminus in Canterbury – in a direct line for Dover. Their Act was obtained in 1853 and gave them the right to use the SER from Strood to London. Thus what was potentially the direct route from London to Dover was placed in the hands of two companies, one no more than a country branch.

The EKR Directors were authorized to raise £700,000. In accordance with Parliamentary Standing Orders, eighteen names, including that of Mr Sadlier, MP, Deputy Chairman of the Company, were entered on the 'Subscription Contract', guaranteeing £380,000.[13] T.R. Crampton, locomotive engineer, promised to buy £12,500 shares, and the line's civil engineering contractor, Sir Charles Henderson of Messrs Fox Henderson, agreed to buy £31,875-worth and further, to pay the cash deposit of £36,250 into Parliament, in return for receiving 14,500 £25 shares at 90 per cent discount, which were to be considered fully paid up.[14] Thus the new Company's prospects were talked up, suppliers of rails could show their banks that they were about to sell rails to a vibrant new concern and thus keep their overdrafts going for a bit longer. It later emerged that another £40,000-worth of promises came from a lowly clerk in Fox's office, while Sadlier, too, had to withdraw from lack of funds. Fox Henderson went bankrupt on 29 October 1856, owing £320,000, of which £170,000 was unsecured. Without a contractor and with its finances sadly astray, the EKR Board was delighted when a 'fairy godfather' appeared in the form of Samuel Morton Peto.

Peto was one of a group of entrepreneurs who had purchased the

Great Exhibition building for re-erection on Sydenham Hill as 'The Crystal Palace', and who had also obtained an Act for a 'West End & Crystal Palace Railway' to connect the London, Brighton & South Coast Railway at Norwood, through Sydenham Hill, to the London & South Western Railway (LB&SCR) at Wandsworth and on to a Thames-side terminus at the site of the southern entrance to the proposed Chelsea Bridge. The railway opened from Crystal Palace to Wandsworth on 1 December 1856 and was operated by the LB&SCR. It reached Norwood a year later and the riverside terminus opened in March 1857, one year before the bridge.

Peto was close to the heart of London's development. He saw Belgravia and Pimlico being built; he saw the congestion and inconvenience of the SER routes, and realized the possibilities of making the East Kent and WEL&CPR the nucleus of a trunk system, crossing the Thames and making a new London terminus in fashionable Belgravia, a much more congenial location for the sort of people who would want to go to Paris than out of town to the dismal Bricklayer's Arms.

In 1859, with Peto's assistance, the EKR obtained an Act to extend from Strood to St Mary Cray, to meet an extension of the WEL&CPR. The rural EKR then changed its name to the 'London, Chatham & Dover' (LC&DR). At Peto's prompting, the newly promoted rural branch line borrowed millions to build its 'Metropolitan Extension' right into the heart of the City of London, across the Thames by Blackfriars Bridge (which cost, pro rata, approximately £1 million per mile), to Ludgate Hill station and Moorgate. Peto also promoted the 'Victoria Station & Pimlico Railway', from the WEL&CPR at Wandsworth, over the Thames on Grosvenor Bridge to a terminus on the north bank at 'Victoria', in Belgravia.

The LC&DR Company was financially completely indebted to Peto and had no choice but to raise the money for him to build any railway he suggested. The proposed route of the LC&DR to Dover, from the fashionable West End and as many as three stations within the City of London, was shorter and more convenient than that provided by the SER. It was also exceptionally expensive, and Peto would be the main beneficiary. As contractor for the LC&DR, he would receive the money his friends loaned to the captive Directors and shareholders; at one point, Peto obtained for the LC&DR a loan of £400,000 and allowed them to borrow it at 14 per cent.[15] There was not the slightest chance that the finished railway would return even 4 per cent.

Finance companies such as Crédit Mobilier, and, from 1862, Thomas Brassey's General Credit & Finance, could continue to promote the railways which the LC&DR – and the threatened SER – would then have to buy. Competition is a wonderful generator of bank loans and legal fees, which is why it is so popular among the piratical classes.

In 1865 the nationalization clause of the 1844 'Railways Act' became operative – if the Government wished to invoke it. To mark this milestone in railway history, the *Economist* published a leading article on 7 January 1865, urging that the railways be nationalized as an aid to the more rapid development of industry. The writer acknowledged that competition between railways had failed to produce low charges – quite the contrary. Since it was plain that the railways had become monopolies, they should be nationalized in the public interest.

The article pointed out that on the competitive railways there were too many types of charges, that these were 'inexplicable' and 'capricious', and that constitutionally they should be neither. 'High charges' on the railway were 'a heavy tax on commerce which was a hindrance to production', and 'No reform is possible when numberless boards of directors settle innumerable rates'. The writer held up the nationalized monopoly of the Post Office as an example of a successful government business which charged a clearly understood, low priced tariff for the public benefit and which had thereby encouraged a large expansion in communication and business.

While it was true that railway company barristers often found it difficult to satisfy a judge on the matter of their clients' charges it is hard to see how the railway companies were hindering business, since business was expanding during an unprecedented credit boom – which these same railway companies were encouraging by the building of very expensive new railways.

British money was poured into European and pan-American businesses: railways, factories and mines. Peto not only financed the LC&DR but in 1865 guaranteed the finance and construction for an American railway – the Atlantic Great Western, which would compete with the exceedingly profitable West Central Rail Road in Pennsylvania. This was an exceedingly risky business, since the American Civil War (1861–5) was then in progress; indeed, the British investment did not receive its returns, while the price of US gold rose 84 per cent above its pre-war level. The British cotton industry was severely affected, as the mills ran short of their slave-labour-produced raw material. This forced the mill-owners to purchase more expensive cotton from Egypt and India, and the sole method of payment was in gold. Consequently gold reserves began to fall.

The financial system trembled. Bank failures, linked to the failure of sugar refiners, cotton mills and merchants, began in Lancashire in late 1864. Some newly incorporated London finance companies suspended payment, bankrupting their clients. In Europe, governments were pareparing for war and removed their gold from the Bank of England. British gold reserves fell and the Bank Rate rose from 4 to 7 per cent in three days, and then to a crisis 10 per cent.

The collapse was precipitated by the failure of the financiers Overend Gurney & Co., Ltd, who ceased trading on 10 May with liabilities of £10 million. The Company originated in Norwich in 1817 as a partnership from among the Quaker Gurney and Barclay families. Their office in the City of London was known as 'the Corner Shop' and they built up a reputation for prudence and honesty which was spoken of with reverence in the City and around the world. After many successful years the partners became reckless, and by mid-1865 their partnership was insolvent by £4,246,000.[16] Keeping this secret, the partners converted to 'Limited Liability' status and continued to take people's money on deposit. In an attempt to get 'into the black' they became even more reckless, and began advancing money to Peto for the LC&DR, and for the Grand Trunk of Canada. The collateral Peto gave for these loans was often nothing more than 'Lloyds Bonds',[17] which were merely written promises to pay. When Peto (and the rest) were unable to repay their loans, Overend Gurney & Co., Ltd, failed, whereupon the entire banking community, already feeling nervous, absolutely lost confidence and literally panicked. *The Times* for 12 May 1866 described the scene in Lombard Street: 'The tumult became a rout. The doors of the most respectable banking houses were besieged – throngs heaving and tumbling about Lombard Street made that narrow thoroughfare impassable.' The Bank of England paid out £4 million in cash in a single day, and the Government was obliged once again to suspend the 1844 Bank Act.[18]

David Barclay Chapman, one of the original partners in Gurney & Co., wrote in Herapath's *Railway Journal*:

The principle of the House was to discount Bills representing current mercantile transactions and strictly to avoid paper [Lloyds Bonds] drawn simply for the purpose of raising money even though endorsed by a Country Bank or other substantial person. We were content with a very small return though it aggregated to sums that enriched us all.

The 1866 crash was the most devastating international financial disaster until the fall of the New York Stock Exchange in 1929. It was not brought about by any trade union activity, nor through large sums being paid out in welfare benefits to the homeless or other unproductive persons but solely by capitalists single-mindedly following their own best interests. Thus ended the fourth railway mania.

Peto had assiduously cultivated his public persona as a highly moral character with a talent for multi-million-pound speculations. He was in the public eye and the public perceived, rightly or wrongly, that it was he who had brought down Overend Gurney, which in turn had panicked the City. Charles Dickens was merely voicing the view of the time when, in a letter to a friend, he described the events of 1862–6 as 'a muddle of railways, in all directions possible, and impossible, with no general, public scheme, no general public supervision, enormous waste of money, no fixable responsibility.'[19] Speculation in railways was again seen as *the* cause of another Great Crash, but the cause lay in the system as a whole.

16

Debt, Overwork and Democracy

THE EFFECT OF the Great Crash on the railway companies varied considerably, their fate depending on the potential of their traffic and the financial state of their bankers. The value of L&NWR, GNR, MR and L&YR shares merely nodded to the crisis and moved on; it is surprising, perhaps, to modern eyes, to read of the near bankruptcy of the GWR; and for most companies the value of their stock was severely depleted, while dividends were reduced or even cancelled.[1] The LC&DR was bankrupted when Peto's credit failed on 11 May. Forty-two Warrants for abandonment of railways were issued.

The Great Western would have been bankrupt had its creditors pressed their claims. Interest at 8.7 per cent had to be paid monthly or bi-monthly on several million pounds-worth of debenture shares; the Company's bankers could not advance any money, the public refused to buy a new share issue to raise money to pay off these short-term loans, the Government was approached but could not become involved, and so the interest was paid 'out of the till', as were wages – leaving nothing for any Preference or Ordinary shareholders in 1866 or 1867. The GWR's new Chairman, Sir Daniel Gooch, introduced the strictest economy of working. He at once abolished all express trains; the refurbishment of broad-gauge carriages was stopped; the conversion of the gauge from broad to standard, the introduction of proper signalling and the improvement of stations were all postponed. So severe was the crisis in 1867 that the 28-man Board of Directors was reduced to sixteen.

The London, Brighton & South Coast Railway (LB&SCR) was temporarily embarrassed when their bankers crashed in May 1866. The Company paid no dividend in that year, or in 1867. The LB&SCR's troubles had, however, started over a decade earlier. The financier Leo Schuster had become Chairman of the Company in January 1855 when Samuel Laing was sent to India as Finance Minister. Schuster's business was lending money and, under the competitive system, railways had always to be building to protect their territory from rival schemes – or to make pre-emptive strikes. In his ten years of Chairmanship, Schuster engaged the LB&SCR in some strenuously competitive branch-line building, increasing the Company's capital from £7.7 million to £18 million. In 1862 Schuster, Thomas Brassey and Crédit Mobilier founded the General Credit & Finance Company to lend money to railways for schemes that regular banks would not have touched. This finance company advanced the money to the LB&SCR; Brassey, as contractor, received the money as payment for the work, and General Credit received the interest on the loan. Schuster's increased capital requirements for the LB&SCR enriched his finance company, while reducing the railway's gross income from 7s to 5s per train/mile and net receipts from 3s 6d to 1s 6d per train/mile.[3] By January 1866, Schuster had reduced the LB&SCR to penury. In July 1867 the Chair was resumed by Laing, who had returned from India. He found the railway physically run down and in need of £1.25 million of new money to pay for repairs. In the shambles of confidence after the crash, Laing could only sell the new shares at a 55 per cent discount, although the Company would, of course, pay the dividend percentage on the full face value of the share.

The vast sums that had been raised to increase the route mileage by 45 per cent in six years did not – *could* not – earn a proportionate return. Since most of the empty spaces in the kingdom were now served by railways, there was limited room for expansion. Between 1866 and 1886, the annual average for new railway opened in Britain was 328 miles, most of it simply contractors' speculations. The MR built the competitive Settle & Carlisle (S&CR), which opened in 1876, and the Hope Valley line (1893). The GWR opened the Severn tunnel in 1886, an extremely costly but very useful internal improvement and also a competitive link, favouring the GWR and L&NWR against the MR. There were also two entirely superfluous major works, fiercely competitive and very unprofitable: the Hull & Barnsley of 1880; and the London Extension of the MS&LR (1893).

A group of local optimists might try, with the encouragement of a hungry contractor, to construct a trunk line 'on the cheap'. Such lines usually went through empty places: the railways of North Norfolk are examples or, even more extreme, the Golden Valley line.[4] Little lines were also constructed by local groups in order, they hoped, to break the monopoly of a large company which they suspected of denying them their rightful profits: the Severn Bridge Railway (Appendix 3) was such a case.

In the USA between 1866 and 1886, railways continued to expand at an exciting average rate of 4936 miles annually; in 1886, 9000 miles was added to US routes. US railways cost half as much as British railways to build, so British investment in new railways tended to go to the USA, to the expanding Empire, or to South America. By 1886, 25 per cent of US railway securities were being sold in the London Stock Exchange. In financial terms, this was roughly equal to 50 per cent of the entire capital of British railways.[5] From now on the British railway system would have to compete for its investment capital with large overseas attractions.

The period between the financial crises of 1857 and 1866 coincided with a developing national awareness of the desirability of greater democracy. In addition to the widespread misery of bankruptcy experienced by the investing classes, tens of thousands of railwaymen, their wives and children, innocent of any responsibility for either débâcle, suffered lay-offs, wages cuts and an increase in already dangerously long hours of labour – and the public suffered a reduced train service.

A more liberal mode of thought was developing. In 1859, the year Charles Darwin published *The Origins of the Species*, J.S. Mill, the Aristotle of the Victorians, published *On Liberty*. Ten years later, pursuing the notion of individual liberty to its logical – but revolutionary – conclusion, Mill published *On the Subjection of Women*. In 1867, Karl Marx (who had, unlike Adam Smith, experienced the disadvantages brought about by self-interest) published his influential *Das Kapital*, his meticulous analysis of the problems of capitalism, together with his excessive remedies. In the same year, ignoring a ban, the Electoral Reform League held demonstrations in London. On 11

February 1867 a large demonstration marched through London to Hyde Park, chanting 'Gladstone and Liberty'; conspicuous in the procession was a large group of uniformed railwaymen.[6]

In August the Second Reform Act was passed, giving the vote to all (male) ratepayers and those living in lodgings rated at £10 per annum; 938,000 new voters were created nationwide, many of them railwaymen, and forty-five seats from little towns and villages in the wilds of Cornwall or Montgomeryshire were redistributed to growing metropolises such as Manchester and Birmingham.

A continuous stream of liberal reforms followed, from both Liberal and Conservative governments, whose purpose was to clean up the mess created by unbridled self-interest and to grant some power to the previously powerless classes. The Master & Servant Act[7] was amended in August 1867, to allow servants to withdraw their labour without fear of prosecution for breach of contract. At the Paris Exposition of 1867, the fact that British exhibits did not win gold medals as they had done at the Great Exhibition of 1851[8] was a shock to the British sense of superiority and gave weight to the arguments of the Birmingham industrialist, Joseph Chamberlain, that Britain needed a universal, free, state education system. The first Education Act, giving free education to all, was passed in 1870; access to the Civil Service was opened to anyone who could pass the entrance examination, and the practice of purchasing an Officer's Commission in the Army was abolished.

In 1871 the Trade Union Act legalized the movement, and the Associated Society of Railway Servants (ASRS) was founded. The following year, the iniquitous system of public voting was at long last replaced by the secret ballot. After the great collapse of 1866 these liberal measures, some of which Edwin Chadwick had urged (with small success) in the 'roaring forties' of totally free enterprise, became increasingly popular. An important contribution to the improvement of living standards was the advantage of rapid, relatively cheap transport.

Tens of millions of rail journeys were made each year, a large and growing proportion of them undertaken by individuals who would previously have been obliged to walk – if they had travelled at all. Thanks to mass transport by rail, there was also cheaper, rail-borne coal, homes were warmer, and suburban living replaced life in crowded slums.

The railways encouraged the mass-production of food, beer, manufactured goods and building materials and distributed these items, in bulk, to the ends of the land. This benefited consumers but was devastating for local producers, who could not compete. Bass, Brooke Bond, Bovril, Huntley & Palmers all became household words. In heavily industrialized areas the presence of competing railways provided factories with plenty of cartage to carry away their finished products and warehousing in which to store them. As traders or private persons, the public also enjoyed a better postal system, thanks both to the speed of railways and of the electric communications which the railway companies installed for their own and the public's use.

Railways also provided career opportunities for tens of thousands of boys of humble origins who would otherwise have remained farm labourers. They could join the railway and break through the boundary between the working class and middle class – provided that they possessed the constitution of an ox, to withstand wind, weather and long hours of work. Women, too, were brought into relatively secure employment on the railways. From the 1830s a few women were employed in domestic or catering roles, including such managerial positions as housekeepers in charge of hotels. Starting in 1886, the GWR employed women as industrial workers in the carriage works of the Swindon factory, where they were kept strictly segregated from the men.[9]

Upon the physical and mental fitness of the railwaymen depended the safety of millions. Never before had the ordinary people of Britain assumed such responsibility for (quite literally) running their country, taking the daily initiative in organizing and ordering the journeys of all classes.

The speed and frequency of trains had increased beyond the wildest dreams of 1830, but signalling, brakes and the hours of labour of the men had remained unchanged, and so the fatality rate among railwaymen and their public increased. Official inquiries blamed the unfortunate railwaymen but public opinion blamed the companies, and this swelled the tide of political feeling against 'the Big Battalions'. *The Lancet* made an inquiry into the dangers to health in railway travel and published its opinion, on 4 January 1862 and 29 July 1871, that the greatest danger to passengers' health was from the effects of exhaustion on railwaymen. The lives and limbs of the middle and upper classes were directly affected by the bad working conditions of the working classes, and for the first time the self-interest of both converged. On 20 August 1868 the incineration of the *Irish Mail* at Abergele caused the deaths of the Duchess of Abercorn, the Marquess of Hamilton, and Lord and Lady Farnham – which disaster brought down the wrath of Queen Victoria on the L&NWR and focused attention on the twin issues of the lack of safety devices and the exhaustion of railwaymen. The Inspector of Railways stated that one third of all fatal railway accidents in 1870 had occurred on the L&NWR.

The Government's response was to give the Board of Trade greater powers of inquiry into accidents. Much more effectively, two great newspapers took up the cause of overworked railwaymen on the grounds of danger to the public. In 1871 *The Times*'s Editor supported the idea of a railway trade union and the *Daily Telegraph* commissioned James Greenwood to write a series of articles on the abuse of railway workers. In one, Greenwood reported how a train guard, exhausted after 18 hours on duty, was ordered to take a train from Leeds to London. The guard protested to the Superintendent and was told: 'You've got 24 hours in a day and they are all ours if we want you to work them.' It was obvious that the lot of hundreds of thousands of railwaymen would have to be improved, for the safety of the travelling public and as part of a more general effort to create a civilized society.

Much less had been made of the railways' iniquities when they were in the full flood of expansion, creating exciting speculative opportunities and clamouring for vast bank loans. But from 1866 railways ceased to be exciting. Acts of Parliament in 1868, 1871, 1873, 1888, 1892 and 1894 laid obligations on the companies to produce their annual accounts to a standard, comprehensible format, and to provide annual statistics on their progress in installing expensive safety devices – such as putting brakes on trains. Acts also established 'Railway Commissioners', to hear complaints from the public against the companies. In this last thirty years of the nineteenth century, social conscience grew and was expressed through the extension of local government control and the provision of services. The great railway companies were seen increasingly as quasi-public institutions, and were expected to do their social duty and pay their (exceptionally heavy) social taxes.

To a nation looking forward to establishing the New Jerusalem through free trade, democracy, municipal swimming baths and sewers, the monopolistic railway directors were a convenient *bête-noire*. The railways became another sort of whipping boy, and one can read in the contemporary press of 'heartless', 'overcharging' railway Directors, 'the tools of scheming contractors'. The fact that a relatively large number of railway Directors were Members of Parliament did not pass unnoticed. There was a growing feeling that the companies had become too powerful for a democratic country and should be brought under state control 'in the public interest'.

Under the triple pressures of competition, the necessities of profit-making and efficient operation, railways had become by far the largest corporations in the world.[10] They charged thousands of different rates for carrying freight, giving lower rates for regular, bulk loads; the rate per mile was more on a short haul than a long haul. A new customer might be charged less to encourage his business, a practice which was frequently misunderstood as 'undue preference', forbidden by the 1854 Act. A railway company was occasionally challenged in court under that Act, to explain how it had arrived at a certain charge, what proportion was for carriage and what for 'terminal costs'. Failure to do so would be seized upon as certain proof of 'dictatorship', and *The Times* or the *Economist* would urge that 'these great, private, monopolies' be made to charge everyone impartially and cheaply – under nationalization. The fact that railway dividends were in single figures, almost all below 7 per cent, and most of them only half that or less, was ignored. They were monopolies and, as such, they stood condemned. The good the railways had done, and were continuing to do, to assist the national economy was taken for granted.

British express trains were the fastest and most frequent in the world; fares were only marginally higher than those charged for a much lower standard of service in Europe; 56 lb of luggage per person was carried free anywhere on the network – all this in spite of the heavy financial burdens borne by railways as the result of competition. The co-ordinating work done by the Railway Clearing House to create this national network out of the many opposed companies – the introduction in 1866 of national, ticket regulations to make tickets more interchangeable between companies[11] – this achievement was attributed either to 'wholesome competition' or to laws made to protect the public. Certainly no credit was given to the wicked companies.

Parliament grudgingly acknowledged that railways had to be in large units, but there was still the irritation that they had a monopoly – and the question remained whether Government should take over the railways or legislate to prevent the companies from abusing their position.

In 1867 the Royal Commission on Railways went so far as to

concede that amalgamation in large groups was necessary because, in building so many small lines, there had undoubtedly been great waste and disorganization; but they nevertheless concluded that the 'great waste' had been for the best:

> The system of considering each application [for a railway] upon its own merits without reference to any pre-conceived scheme for the accommodation of the country [as a whole] may have led to a larger expenditure of capital than was necessary but . . . the freedom from defined principles of action has led to a much more rapid development of the country than could otherwise have taken place.[12]

The great companies were in a predicament. Competition and speculative enthusiasm had created an enormous, unplanned infrastructure, much of which would not have been built had some rational plan been followed. Traders, shippers, factory owners, farmers, lawyers and bankers had benefited – but the railway companies had to operate it all at a profit and were required by law to provide the best of facilities for the public good. Further competition was not a pleasant prospect for the companies – yet they continued to compete.

17

The Midland Railway

THE MIDLAND RAILWAY is the best example in Britain of a great railway arising from a group of small, ruinously competitive, publicly inconvenient companies. It was fortunate in that its three[1] constituent companies amalgamated early, on 10 May 1844, despite Parliamentary opposition to 'monopoly', and thanks to the much maligned George Hudson. It thus avoided years of the sort of debilitating competition which ruined other companies, notably those in Kent and East Anglia. In 1846 the L&NWR was formed to the west and north-west of the MR, the GNR arrived to the east in 1850, and in 1854 the NER was formed to the north and north-east. The MR was thus 'hemmed in', which meant that the Company needed to be permanently expansive in its outlook. It pursued an adventurous, competitive policy, creating competition on a larger scale and at even greater expense.

The MR was successful in its competition because, unlike those railways in Kent and East Anglia, it was blessed with an increasingly heavy traffic which enabled it to pay the interest on enormous loans for its vast capital programme. However, its loan burden – and the increased working costs of the new lines, once built – ensured that proportionately increased profits did not accompany this expenditure.[2] By 1900, in relation to its route-miles of track, it was the most heavily capitalized railway in Britain (see Appendix 2, p. 342). Over many years, the Midland was transformed into a privately owned public institution, yielding a modest but relatively secure return[3] to investors and a lifetime of steady wages for its staff.

From amalgamation in 1844 until 1867 the MR was a provincial railway. During that period it built up a system of routes considered by its management to radiate from Derby to Sheffield, Leeds, Manchester, Leicester, Rugby, Birmingham, Bristol, Nottingham and Lincoln, and from Leicester to Peterborough. By other companies' metals its carriages could reach the north of Scotland and London. The MR's presence encouraged the sinking of coal-mines, the erection of engineering works, iron foundries, breweries and potteries. Cities expanded as a result. The investment made to construct the railway had a wider, longer-lasting and more profitable effect than merely paying dividends to the shareholders.

In terms of mileage and traffic, the MR was approximately the equal of the L&NWR, but the latter held it in check and there was always tension between them. From 1844 until 1848 all MR passenger, coal and merchandise trains used the L&NWR route from Rugby to Euston. From May 1848 some coal was also sent via Leicester and Oakham to Peterborough, whence it travelled south over the GNR or via March and Cambridge, on the ECR; in 1852 the MR hauled 325,000 tons of coal[4] to Rugby Junction, for onward haulage by L&NWR.

In 1846 the MR put a Bill into Parliament for a Leicester–Kettering–Bedford–Hitchin railway, countering a similar proposal from the GNR. In 1847, just as the financial world tumbled, Parliament decided in favour of the MR scheme but there was no money forthcoming to build the line, and the Act, so expensively won against the GNR's opposition, was abandoned under the 1850 Act. Only two years later the project was restarted and re-financed. The route was resurveyed, by Charles Liddell, and the lawyers briefed for another Parliamentary session. The MR's expenses were less this time owing to a remarkable outbreak of common sense. Realizing the long-term value to their estates of the railway, the main landowners along the route, the brewing family Whitbread and the Duke of Bedford, decided to forgo their short-term gain and sold the required land for its agricultural price of £70 an acre instead of the going rate of £300. Then, in February 1853, the GNR and the Midland reached a reasonable compromise, in place of former strife. The GNR withdrew its counter-proposal for a Sandy–Bedford line in return for the MR's agreeing to GNR trains running into its Nottingham station. It was a this point that the MR released the locomotive hostage it had imprisoned since August the previous year.

The Leicester–Hitchin Bill was passed 4 August 1853. The new railway was to be approximately 67 miles long, requiring 3,750,000 cu. yds[6] of earth to be moved by men wielding picks, shovels and wheelbarrows. There was to be one tunnel, 880 yds long, near Old Warden, 4 miles south of Bedford. Charles Liddell estimated that the whole line would cost £1 million to build. With the exception of the Old Warden tunnel, the entire contract was placed with Thomas Brassey. He took 3½ years to complete the work, only five months longer than promised, and kept within the contract price.

The line opened for coal trains on 15 April 1857 and for passengers on 7 May. Since its main purpose was to carry coal and merchandise to London, and it only had a local train service, the most important MR passenger trains continued to use Euston. South of Hitchin, MR traffic was hauled by the GNR until 1 February 1858 when – possibly as a result of the collapse of the pooling agreements between the L&NWR, MR and the rest – the GNR allowed the MR to haul its own trains to and from King's Cross. This was no great privilege: it relieved the GNR of the costs, while the Company still took its exorbitant tolls.

In April 1860 the GNR initiated a revolution in travel, and a war with the MR. The GNR's 12.20 p.m. Bradford–London express began to haul 3rd-class carriages. The MR at once put 3rd-class carriages on all its express trains to and from London, Leeds and Bradford. Both companies reduced their freight rates on these routes by 40 per cent.[7] Accommodation at King's Cross was stretched to the limit, and in 1860 the MR obtained an Act to construct its own coal depot and goods station, connected to the GNR, in Agar Town – known locally as 'Ague Town' because of its disgustingly insanitary condition. This district was a little to the north-west of King's Cross.

Coal was tumbling out of the Nottingham/Derbyshire coalfields and thousands of gallons of beer were gushing from the breweries of Burton-on-Trent: all served by the MR system. The coal and beer was destined for London, Bristol, the south of England and export – much of it to France, as a result of the 1860 Free Trade Agreement. In 1862 the MR carried 491,000 tons of coal to London using the L&NWR line south of Rugby, and another 216,000 tons passed on to the GNR at Hitchin.[8] The GNR main line south of Hitchin became as congested as the L&NWR line south of Rugby, and the GNR tried to discourage MR traffic by charging exorbitant tolls – 2s 7½d a ton in the case of coal. During 1862 the Midland sent freight over the GNR with a total revenue value to the MR of £88,741, of which the GNR took £60,000 in tolls; on the Rugby–Euston line, MR traffic worth £276,000 was charged £187,000.[9]

In 1859 the L&NWR installed one extra 'up' line, solely for goods traffic, between Bletchley and London, on which MR coal trains sometimes stood for days without turning a wheel. The situation was no better on the GNR. From south Bedfordshire, it was quicker to send perishable traffic – eggs, milk, meat – to London by road.[10] Many collisions on rail resulted from the combination of heavy traffic, miserable brakes and ineffective signalling.

The original signalling system for all British railways was by handsignal and time interval. For many years, trains had followed each other at the command of a lineside policeman, who would allow one train to follow another after a certain interval of time had elapsed. There was nothing to prevent the following train catching up with and crashing into the first train, yet the technology to keep the trains apart had existed since 1837 and was well known. Cooke's and Wheatstone's electric telegraph was installed between Euston station and Camden, at the top of the steep incline, as a means of telling the man in charge of the winding engine when to start hauling a train up the bank. In 1842 Cooke published a pamphlet showing how his telegraph instrument could be used to maintain a definite and inviolable distance, which he called a 'space-interval',[11] between trains.

Between 1854 and 1856 the GNR installed the space-interval or 'absolute block' system between King's Cross and Hitchin, which meant that one or two miles or so of track between each train remained empty. In 1855 the L&NWR installed the telegraph between Euston and Bletchley to work a 'permissive block' system, which permitted trains to follow each other closely, after the driver had been cautioned. This tended to defeat the object of the exercise but did permit every yard of track to be crammed with trains.

Not all accidents were caused by a lack of equipment; some occurred perhaps, as a result of the competitive spirit. At Hitchin Junction on 8 September 1859 the GNR signalman cleared his signals for an 'up' MR train which was whistling as it approached the junction. Shortly afterwards, he heard the whistle of the GNR's 'crack' Scotch express as it left Hitchin station. The signalman reversed the signals against the MR train and gave the road to the GNR express, with the result that they met head-on at the junction. Thirty-five passengers were injured.[12]

The 'absolute block' system demanded space and, with the advent of MR trains to the King's Cross–Hitchin section, space was not available. The line needed to be quadrupled but there was a cheaper alternative. In November 1860 the General Manager of the GNR, Seymour Clarke, told his Directors: 'There is no doubt that our system is very safe but it causes very great delays.'[13] The GNR then abandoned 'absolute block', except through the four longest tunnels between Welwyn and King's Cross, in favour of 'permissive' working. Thereafter, and until the MR ceased to use the route in 1868, there were 'numerous accidents'.[14]

An International Exhibition of Science and Industry began in London in May 1862. The GNR and MR fought each other with daily, even hourly, price cuts: Leeds to London return for 5s, less than ¼d per mile; Nottingham to London for 3s 3d return – and in covered carriages at that. Throughout the summer the price-war continued, until in August excursion revenues were pooled and divided 50/50. These very cheap fares filled as many trains as the companies could find carriages for, and the line south of Hitchin was jammed. There were many collisions. On 10 August an excursion train, having been allowed to follow a cattle train too closely under the 'permissive' system, crashed into it at Hitchin. The driver had not noticed the signals at 'Danger' and sixty excursionists were injured.[15] In July King's Cross station became so congested that the MR's trains were banished to goods sidings, where the passengers were obliged to enter and leave without benefit of platform: a potentially indelicate task for crinolined ladies. In spite of the chaotic congestion the MR still managed, during August alone, to carry 64,066 excursionists to and from King's Cross.[16]

A spectacular accident occurred in Welwyn North's 1066-yds-long tunnel, at half-past midnight on June 10 1866, when the engine of a 'down' GNR train broke down. The tunnel was worked by the 'absolute block' system, but the electrical system had failed and another goods train was allowed to follow. The guard of the first train, relying on the protection of the 'absolute block' system, had not got out of his van to put down detonators on the track to protect his train, and so the collision took place – nicely beneath a ventilation shaft. Wagons from both trains fell over on to the 'up' line where they were jammed within seconds by an 'up' express freight, loaded with Scotch beef. The wreckage piled up to the roof of the tunnel. A fire started and the ventilation shaft, which was about 80 ft high, acted as a chimney.

The heat was intense as a hundred wagons burned with a noise eye-witnesses likened to the roar of 'a mighty cataract,'[17] and the flames were fierce enough to reach high above the air shaft into the fields blazing like a beacon to the surrounding countryside. The only fire engine in the neighbourhood, a little one belonging to Lord Salisbury's estate, was galloped across the fields; but the heat at the tunnel mouth and the dense smoke was too great to allow anyone to enter for 17 hrs. All that day black smoke and the smell of roast beef poured out across the peaceful fields.

As a result of the 1857 collapse of Huish's self-interested efforts to control competition, and because Parliament was very slow to accept amalgamation as the solution to railway companies' problems, a complex and debilitating battle ensued between them. That year, the GNR and the MS&L made a 50-year non-aggression pact, and were colluding in Manchester, conspiring against the L&NWR to run from Manchester to London, via the MS&L to Retford and the GNR south-wards, and inflicting bitter competition from Manchester to Leeds and York on the L&YR. The GNR had penetrated the heart of the MR at Derby, together with the coal and industry-rich Erewash valley to the north, and had got as far west as Uttoxeter and Stafford, siphoning-off erstwhile MR traffic from the Potteries. The London, Chatham & Dover, the SER and even the LB&SCR were entangled in feuds in their narrow province in Kent. Paradoxically, the East Anglian companies were too weak to join in the wider mayhem, but once the Great Eastern Railway (GER) was formed, in 1862, it began to campaign for railways into the South Yorkshire coalfield, to York, Sheffield and beyond, finding an ally in the L&YR and adding to the woes of the GNR and MS&L.

The ambitions of the Midlands Railway, under the leadership of its progressive General Manager, James Allport, extended from Manchester to the south coast. The MR encouraged any company proposing the construction of routes from Cheltenham and Bath, across the GWR and into London & South Western Railway territory at Southampton and Bournemouth, and on its own account undertook superb, and very expensive, engineering works to reach London and the enormous commerce and industry of Lancashire, Manchester and Liverpool. In 1861 Allport concluded an agreement with the MS&L for the use of their part of Manchester's London Road station. The MR's Manchester route was constructed as an extension of the Rowsley branch, which forked north-west off the Derby to Leeds main line at Ambergate, up the valley of the River Derwent and was opened throughout in 1849. In 1863 the MR extended the line to Buxton, and, forking off the Buxton line at Millers Dale, climbed through the Peak and down to the MS&L Manchester line at New Mills.

Tunnelling from Darley Dale, to Monsal Dale, to Millers Dale, running at 60 mph along ledges cut out of sheer rock faces, over splendid viaducts, and climbing practically continuously on 1 in 125 gradients for 10 miles, the line reached a final 3-mile length at 1 in 90 to its summit at Peak Forest, 980 ft above the sea. From here the line tunnelled the northern escarpment of the limestone, in the 2984-yds-long Doveholes tunnel.[18] The course of the tunnel took it through an underground river, which the engineers had managed to divert, but the river broke in again before the tunnel was successfully completed, and the navvies who were working on it drowned. From the summit the line fell at 1 in 90 for 8 miles, and was only a little less steep for a further 10 miles to New Mills.[19]

The Midland opened its passenger service between King's Cross and Manchester on 1 November 1866. It was a cramped and rather bitter situation at London Road, where three companies shared one station, and indeed things were no better at King's Cross. By admitting the Midland to Manchester London Road, the MS&L had broken their solemn promise to the GNR, given in 1857 and approved by the Board of Trade in April 1861.[20] Now the MR had a route to London shorter than that of GNR and practically the same length as that of the L&NWR.

In 1864 the MR obtained an Act for a 13½-mile railway from Chesterfield, on its main line to Leeds, to the GNR stronghold of Sheffield. This had involved the purchase and destruction of brand new housing on the southern approaches to Sheffield at a cost of £500,000 in compensation to the landowner, in addition to the cost of construction. By the time the line was opened in 1870 it had cost the MR's shareholders £1,180,000, well over twice the estimated total, and still the GNR was taking half the traffic. While not significantly improving the Company's fortunes, the MR's huge expenditure in ameliorating the city's rail links with the south enabled a great deal of industrial development to take place, and raised the value of property in its vicinity tenfold.[21] The profit of outsiders was thus far greater than that of the Company's shareholders. Truly the 'Invisible Hand' works in unintended ways.

The substantial tolls paid by the MR to the L&NWR and GNR were insufficient recompense for the fantastic delays and danger caused by the congestion on their lines. The GNR now had so much traffic of its own that, even if the MR were removed, the capacity of the line would be overstretched. Clearly, the MR required its own main line into London.

The Midland briefed its lawyers to put the case to Parliament; on 3 March 1863 legal battle was joined to prove that it would be of the greatest public benefit if a new railway line were constructed from Bedford to London. The competitive system ensured that the greatest opposition possible was brought to bear to prevent this great improvement. There were seventeen petitions against the line,[22] the sternest opposition coming from the GNR and L&NWR – who stood to benefit most by getting rid of the congestion caused by MR trains. The case for the line was so overwhelming that it was proved fairly quickly, and Royal Assent for the 'Midland Railway (Extension to London)' Act was granted on 22 June 1863. This authorized a railway from the Leicester–Hitchin line at Bedford, through Luton, to a station in Somers Town, St Pancras, on the New Road (soon to become known as the Euston Road). The line would be 51 miles 4 chains long,[23] and to build it the MR would have to raise fresh capital of £750,000.[24]

The whole work, from Bedford southwards, was designed by, and under the supervision of, William Barlow, the Company's Engineer. The approaches to the site of the station, in the parish of St Pancras, crossed an area described by Charles Dickens in *Household Words* as 'stinking and full of cholera'. Ten thousand were evicted from this metropolitan swamp without any provision for their welfare, whereupon they crowded into adjacent slums, thereby reducing still further (if that were possible) their living conditions.[25] Furthermore, 10,300 coffins[26] were unceremoniously disinterred from St Pancras Cemetery, and the Fleet River – then virtually an open sewer[27] – had to be enclosed in a cast-iron pipe within a tunnel of brick. All this demolition, excavation, brick-making and construction on (and through) the most putrid and disease-laden clay was carried out by gangs of navvies, bricklayers and carpenters, supercharged on beef and beer and working with such enthusiasm that when occasion demanded, they could toil for 48 hrs without sleep[28] – one hopes in order to earn a bonus.

St Pancras station was designed by William Barlow (see Appendix 3) and occupied a site of seven streets, on 4½ acres, lying between the

Regent's Canal and the New (Euston) Road. In clearing the site, the Midland had to demolish the recently consecrated St Luke's Church and rebuild it in Kentish Town.[29] In order to give the canal barges headroom below the railway bridge, Barlow brought the line in on brick arches over the canal, and this left the station 20 ft above the Euston Road. The platforms were originally to have been built on an earth-fill, using the spoil from the MR tunnel to the Metropolitan Railway, in which case the platforms would have been covered by a two-arched roof. Instead, it was decided to make the space beneath the platforms earn a revenue by turning it into a warehouse for the storage of Bass beer from Burton.

The roof was designed as a single span, rather than a less expensive twin-span, to avoid a line of foundations down the centre of the basement, which would have interfered with the beer barrels, and with any future reorganization of the platforms that pressure of traffic might require. So it was that William Barlow, with considerable assistance in detail from R.M. Ordish, a specialist in the construction of large iron roofs,[30] designed the highest, longest, broadest single-span roof of any railway station in the world: 689 ft long, rising 100 ft above the platforms, with a clear span at platform level of 245½ ft.[31] It was constructed with 27 iron ribs, each weighing nearly 55 tons, placed at 29 ft 4 in. intervals – again a multiple of the measurements of the girth of a 36-gallon beer barrel.[32] The 100-ft-high timber framework on which the ribs were built up ran on rails, and was moved to each new position by navvies levering against its wheels with crowbars, their efforts co-ordinated by the beat of a gong.

Approximately 700 brick pillars were sunk into the ground below street-level, evenly spaced over the entire area to be occupied by the platforms above. The ends of the roof ribs were anchored to the outer rows of these foundations and the rest carried the cast-iron columns which would support a grid of 2000 girders on which would lie the platforms and tracks, and which would also tie across the lower ends of the roof ribs. The columns were spaced according to the girth of a 36-gallon beer barrel, so as to stand the barrels compactly between them.[33] Between the station and the Euston Road was the 'Midland Grand Hotel', designed by Sir Gilbert Scott (see Appendix 4). This was his heart's delight, an extravaganza approximating to fourteenth-century Flemish Gothic. It could pass for a gigantic convent, and it is rumoured that tourists have mistaken it for a church. Scott originally designed it with five storeys, but the financial disaster of 1866–7 forced a reduction to four; this is probably just as well, since it is dizzying enough as it stands: 565 ft of frontage from the great *porte-cochère* on the pavement at the western end, curving back into the main frontage, which rises 100 ft, pierced by serried ranks of windows, to the steep roof, itself lined with double ranks of dormers, each surmounted by a cross, and these in turn dwarfed by ranks of windy chimneys, 150 ft above the street.

As if all this were not enough to announce the arrival of the Midland Railway in London, there is the multi-turreted clock tower at the east end, 270 ft tall to the tip of its spire. The huge clock face glares down on London in general, and in particular at the hotel and terminus of the rival Great Northern, just across the street. Such was the competition between the two railways that, very often, not even their respective clocks could agree.

The interior of the hotel was a lavish, Gothic fantasy laced by the iron ceiling joists deliberately left exposed to show off intricate mouldings. Hard-nosed Midland businessmen could imagine themselves princes in the palace, as they paced the Minton-tiled corridors or escorted their wives, or mistresses, down the wide, helical staircases, under fan-vaulted ceilings. The medieval atmosphere was reinforced by a lack of central heating – each of the 400 bedrooms had a coal fire – but it was the first building in London to be fitted with revolving doors and to have a *ladies'* smoking room. Women had been segregated from men in hotels, even to the extent of having separate dining rooms, and the Midland Grand was big enough to overturn such barbaric practices. Mr Baedekker reported that it was the best railway hotel in London.[34]

It is estimated that St Pancras station, with its arched approaches, took 60 million bricks, 80,000 cu. ft of dressed stone and 9000 tons of iron to build.[35] The Midland Grand cost the Company £438,000,[36] a gigantic sum in those days. From the time of the granting of the 1863 'Midland Railway (Extension to London)' Act, the 51 miles from Bedford to the Agar Town goods depot took four years to complete; goods trains began working into the depot from Bedford on 9 September 1867.[37] The Great Crash caught the MR in the throes of completing the passenger station and also of its Sheffield Direct line. The Bedford line had cost many times over its budget and in the very depths of the post-crash depression the Company had to raise £5 million, £2 million of which was to pay for the line. St Pancras station opened to passengers on 1 October 1868.[38]

Work on the Hotel had barely started in 1867 when it was suspended owing to lack of money. It recommenced in 1868. The straight frontage was completed on 5 May 1873 and the curved, west wing in 1876. The full cost of the Bedford–London extension, including the goods depot, the great passenger station, its goods yards and its fantastic hotel, was £9 million.[39] The brick-makers, bricklayers, carpenters, plumbers, navvies and employees of the Butterly Ironworks no doubt remembered the Directors of the Midland Railway in their prayers!

18

The Cost of Intricacy

WHILE THE MIDLAND Directors were battling with railway building from Manchester, through the Derbyshire Peak, to the cemeteries of London, they were also engaged in legal and operational battles with L&NWR obstructiveness to their Anglo-Scottish ambitions via Skipton and Ingleton. In 1861 the MR had threatened to build its own main line to Scotland. The L&NWR, somewhat chastened, agreed to haul Midland coaches without the customary delays, north of Ingleton, and thus began an MR express service from King's Cross, via Leicester and Leeds to Glasgow, using Caledonian trains north of Carlisle. The arrangement was, however, far from satisfactory, since it depended on the co-operation of two indifferent (or actually hostile) companies; beyond Ingleton the L&NWR was attaching MR coaches to its goods trains.[1] In 1864 the MR again threatened to build an Anglo-Scottish main line. In response, the L&NWR offered the MR a joint lease of the Lancaster & Carlisle Railway but only on condition that the L&NWR dictate the fares charged by the MR to and from Carlisle.[2] The MR could not accept this and in 1865, deposited a Bill in Parliament for a main line from Settle to Carlisle.

The Midland had several allies. The North British Railway, already a link in the east coast main line, had in 1862 opened their Border Union Railway, or 'Waverley route', extending the Edinburgh–Hawick branch 43 miles south to Carlisle. Though the NBR had spent

£5 million on this line, it returned only branch-line profits because it depended on the Caledonian Railway for the final 1¼ miles into Carlisle station. Since the new route challenged the established 'Caley' route to Edinburgh, the latter charged heavily for the use of that 1¼-mile link line, while traffic for Edinburgh arriving at Carlisle was sent over the Caledonian route unless it was specifically labelled as via the NBR. To the west of the Caledonian, the Glasgow & Southern Western Railway (G&SWR) had a route to Carlisle, and was eager to find an outlet southwards independent of the L&NWR. The L&YR, too, was dependent on the L&NWR/CR and keen to break the monopoly.

The Parliamentary Bill for the £2.2 million[3] Settle–Carlisle line was deposited in 1865 when the MR was already engaged in large borrowing for extending its routes to Manchester, Sheffield and London. The L&NWR/Caledonian axis furiously opposed the MR's Settle to Carlisle Railway Bill but evidence of their highly monopolistic behaviour at Carlisle was submitted to demonstrate the need for a competing line, and the Bill received the Royal Assent on 16 July 1866. The Company was now legally obliged to build the line, and thus, to raise £2.2 million in post-crash depression, with the Bank Rate at a crisis level of 10 per cent. The MR sought to strengthen its financial and operational position by amalgamating with the G&SWR, but the Bill was thrown out in 1867, on the grounds that there was no physical connection between the two companies. By now the depression had deepened, and MR shareholders, anxious at the vast expenditures already made and proposed, agitated for the S&CR to be abandoned. Seeing the split, the L&NWR renewed its offer to the MR of a joint lease of the Lancaster & Carlisle. The MR gratefully accepted and in 1868 applied to abandon the S&CR Act – whereupon the Company found itself expensively opposed by its former allies, who still wanted an alternative route. The NBR in particular was anxious to make some kind of profit out of their £5 million outlay on the Border Union line. Parliament agreed and refused to sanction the abandonment. Work began in November 1869.

The completion of the Settle route would result in a huge loss of revenue to the L&NWR/CR; the former Company lodged a Bill in 1871 to allow it to amalgamate with the L&YR, while the CR proposed amalgamation with the G&SWR. The MS&L tried, unsuccessfully, to sell itself to the GNR or anyone else who would have it, and became known as 'the Railway Flirt'. If the L&NWR captured the L&YR, and the Caledonian the G&SWR, the Midland would lose them as allies, together with the heavy traffic and revenue from those companies which was vital to the success of its investment in the Settle line. The GWR and L&SWR, threatened by the MR's designs on the south coast and west of England, in 1871 jointly deposited a 'West of England Traffic Arrangements' Bill which, if enacted, would permit pooling agreements between the two companies and the purchase by the GWR of its allies, the Bristol & Exeter, South Devon, and Cornwall railways. In Kent, impoverished by competition, the SER, the LB&SCR and the LC&DR tried various permutations of togetherness, without success.

Parliament and most leading railways observers disapproved of these attempts at amalgamation. Captain Tyler, RE, Board of Trade Inspector of Railways, whose thankless task it was to persuade the companies to face up to their safety obligations, wrote to *The Times* on 30 November 1872: 'As the Companies grow larger they became more impervious to action from within or without.' He consistently advocated state ownership as did the *Economist*, which stated in 1871 that British railways – and therefore the public – suffered from 'inharmonius working, excessive fares and scanty accommodation'. The only outcome in the public interest must be state acquisition. The article pointed out that government could borrow money at a cheaper rate than individuals, and if it had purchased the railways in 1867, when the total value of their stocks was £119,311,000, plus 10 per cent for compulsory purchase, the property would have appreciated by 50 per cent in the ensuring six years, since the total value was now £163,735,000.

The situation was paradoxical. 'Inharmonious working' could only be cured by close co-operation, but when companies tried to draw closer together this was perceived by Parliament as 'monopoly'. The choice was between allowing inharmonious working to continue, in pursuit of an ideal concerning 'competition', permitting amalgamations to achieve greater efficiency and thereby risking monopoly, or, – since the drift was in that direction – that the monopoly should be owned by the state. The amalgamation proposals of 1870–72 caused Parliament to set up a Select Committee on Amalgamations[4] and until its report was issued all the amalgamation Bills were suspended.

In evidence to the Committee, Thomas Henry Farrer, Permanent Secretary to the Board of Trade from 1865 to 1886,[5] stated that

. The Derby Canal tramroad showing Jessop's tram plates on stone blocks and horse-drawn wooden wagons running on ordinary road wheels

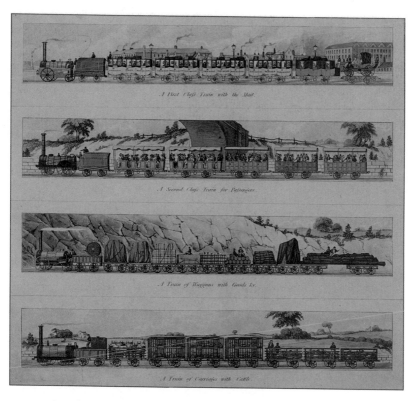

2. Liverpool & Manchester Railway trains in 1834: *Liverpool* hauling 1st-class carriages, a mail coach and a carriage truck; *Fury* with 2nd-class carriages; *North Star* with a goods train; and *Jupiter* hauling a cattle train

3. George Stephenson, 1845

4. Robert Stephenson, undated

5. Joseph Locke, undated

6. Isambard Kingdom Brunel, 1837

7. Carpenters, clerks, hod-men and shop-men pause for a moment for the camera before cramming themselves into the four-wheeled dog-boxes forming the 12.10 p.m. train from Liverpool Street to Enfield, 25 October 1884

8. The grimy environs of Pratt's Sidings, Stoke-on-Trent, are enlivened by the heraldic crimson magnificence of the North Staffordshire Railway's locomotive livery. To the right of the signal box a wooden mast supports the pulleys for overhead wires operating certain signals. One such wire exits low down in the box wall and rises to the top of the mast. c. 1895

9. One of Daniel Gooch's legendary '8ft Singles', *Dragon*, in its day the fastest thing on rails, here relegated to humble duties at the end of its career. It is hauling 'convertible' carriages, standard-gauge bodies on broad-gauge frames. Seen at Maidenhead *c.* 1891–2

10. A well turned-out horse and van of the Midland Railway, photographed on 10 August 1909, suggests that the van driver takes an interest and pride in his work

11. The Forth bridge in 1896, the zenith of Victorian engineering and the precursor of the twentieth century – the Age of Steel

12. The Grindleford end of Totley tunnel, a fine bridge completed, the tunnel beyond under construction. Temporary track, horse-drawn wagons and a hand-operated crane stand on either side of the bridge, 29 August 1893

13. Railways provided a lifetime of secure employment and were family affairs. This group at Gayton Road station, near King's Lynn, on the Midland & Great Northern Joint Railway comprises: (*back row, left to right*) platelayer Todd and porter Jones; (*front row, left to right*) ganger Whitby, station-master Arthur Youngman and his daughter Gladys, and signalman Bailey. Arthur's father, Richard, laboured with pick and shovel to build the line in 1880–83 and became a ganger; Arthur's son, Percy, joined the M&GN in 1923, became Chief Inspector and had the bitter job of supervising the demolition of the line in 1959

14. The M&GN made up for what it lacked in style and comfort with a stern enthusiasm. This is the scene beside the River Wensum at Norwich (City) station in 1925

15. Acres of coal at Peterborough, 11 May 1908. The costs of the British method of carrying coal by rail are obvious: tens of thousands of small wagons had to be built and then maintained, stored, shunted and hauled. Doubling their capacity would have halved the number in use, and if they could have been emptied and returned quicker, fewer wagons would have been needed

16. A 'Star'-class engine had just arrived at Paddington with empty coaches to accommodate Edwardian excursionists bound for Henley Regatta on 2 July 1908. On the platform beside the engine is the guard's handlamp and grub bag which he has dropped in order to hurry forward and unlock the doors of the six-wheel coach next to the engine

17. A 3rd-class dining-car of 'East Coast Joint Stock' for use in the Anglo-Scottish expresses from King's Cross to Edinburgh over the GNR, NER and NBR, June 1901. Competition has forced up the standard of 3rd-class accommodation, as evidenced in the damask table linen, plated tableware, mahogany and velvet chairs. Overhead the clerestory lets in extra light through engraved, frosted glass. The wonderfully ornate lamps are for night-time use

18. A Great Eastern Railway kitchen-car with gas-fired range in service on the Liverpool Street to Cromer 'Norfolk Coast Express', photographed in 1910. The chef is about to carve a joint of beef while a liveried waiter comes in with a tray of tea

19. The ultimate in commuter
travel: a 'Club' car for Edwardian
businessmen, built by the
North Eastern Railway.
This one is lit by electricity
and was built *c.* 1913

20. A spacious sleeping berth on
a Midland Railway express,
February 1907

21. The motor bus was appreciated as a feeder to, and cross-country link for, the trains. This is the Marlborough to Calne motor bus link at Marlborough, *c.* 1910

22. The Cinderford, Forest of Dean, branch train, optimistically formed with two arriages, waits in its bay on the Gloucester to South Wales main line at Newnham to onnect with the main-line train which is signalled. A passenger service was instituted on the formerly 'goods only' Cinderford branch on 3 August 1907: this view dates rom shortly after that. The carriages are new, equipped to enable the engine driver to operate his locomotive from a cab at the end of the carriage

23. The Charing Cross Hotel, designed by E.M. Barry for the South Eastern Railway, was opened in May 1865 and had 250 bedrooms. A further 90 were added when the Annexe was opened in 1878. This view dates from 1897

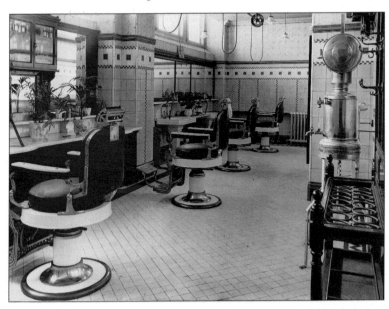

24. The railway hotels were opulent. This is the hairdressing salon of the 80-bedroom Liverpool Exchange Station Hotel opened in 1888. Overhead shafting provided the drive for mechanical hair clippers – a service not for the faint-hearted. This view was taken on 14 July 1914 as ultimatums sped between Berlin, Moscow, Paris and Vienna

25. During the Great War women were recruited to take the place of railwaymen who went to fight: as a result of their efforts they finally broke down the male prejudice against 'votes for women'. These two women are serving as porters at Paddington

26. During the period of the Great War, Foreman Fred Ward checks that all is well with the engine Fawley Court and its crew as they prepare to set out on the long haul from Paddington to Cardiff

THE DELIVERER.

LOCOMOTIVE (*stationary through strike*). "ONCE ABOARD THE LORRY AND THE GIRL IS MINE —NO MORE!"

27. The railwaymen went on strike in 1919 in an attempt to secure civilized working conditions. They thereby gave the somewhat piratical and dangerously unregulated road haulage industry the opportunity to appear before the public as the saviours of the nation, as depicted in this *Punch* cartoon

28. On the outbreak of war in 1939 the railways were expected to be – and proved – the most important carriers of passengers and freight. Efficient movers of large tonnages, they were not dependent on foreign fuel. Here, at Maidenhead, children await evacuation away from the bombing to the West Country, June 1940

29. Paddington, Platforms 5 and 6 looking west, on the morning of 22 March 1944 after an air raid. A German flying bomb fell on the station during the night, breaking one roof rib. The station remained in service: a train full of passengers is waiting to leave Platform 4

30. The Great Hall of Euston station, 1838–1962, the first and probably the most magnificent Temple of the Railway Age. The staircase rose to the door of the Directors' Boardroom, its portico crowned by a marble Britannia with shield and trident, supported by lions and with female figures representing Science and Industry. From the Boardroom some of Britain's greatest railwaymen and public figures, among them George Carr Glyn, Lord Wolverton and Lord Stamp, controlled the largest railway company in the world. This view was taken on 18 November 1962, not long before the building's demolition. It is difficult to comprehend the mentality that ordered its destruction

amalgamation strengthened companies and enabled them to provide better services and accommodation. He foresaw the time when all the railways of Britain would be amalgamated into one, and believed that the danger in such a development would be political rather than commercial. Sir Edward 'Wrecker' Watkin, a Director of several railways, whose competitiveness was a great spoiler of his own companies' and others' profits, declared that competition was essential to keep down fares, and pointed to the L&NWR as an example of low fares brought about by competition with others. Mr Thompson, Chairman of the NER, stated that his railway was the result of the amalgamation of a dozen companies which had previously engaged in 'virulent competition'. As a co-ordinated monopoly they now had rates and fares lower than those on the L&NWR. Mr Cawkwell, General Manager of the L&NWR, pointed out that 'Almost all traders make similar arrangements [agreements as to prices] and it is unreasonable to say that railway companies should not in their own protection do the same thing'.[6]

The conclusions of the 1872 Report were as follows:

1. Past amalgamations have not led to the evils feared [i.e. the monopoly abuse anticipated by Cardwell's Committee Report of 1853].

2. Competition is limited and cannot be maintained by legislation.

3. Amalgamations are increasing and will continue to do so.

4. It is impossible to lay down rules determining the limits of future amalgamations.

5. Can the self-interest of companies be enough to ensure that the public interest is adequately protected and if not, what improvements can be made consistent with the rights of the companies and the public interest?

6. There can be no doubt that the introduction of certain amalgamation bills which have been the reason for this Select Committee affords opportunities for imposing on the companies conditions which may be desirable in the public interest.

The outcome was the 1873 Regulation of Railways Act, itself an expansion of the 1854 Act. It instituted the Railway Commissioners, to whom aggrieved members of the public could refer cases of unfair trading practice on the railways' part. It also gave the Board of Trade power to refuse to allow a new railway to commence operations until it was properly equipped with interlocked signal and point-levers and the tracks were controlled by the 'absolute block' system, worked by electric telegraph. Never before had a privately owned business been so much under government control.

By the time Parliament had reached these conclusions the navvies on the Settle to Carlisle route had been hard at work for three years (their labours have been described in detail in several books).[7] At more than twice the length of the difficult Millers Dale line, it was the greatest work attempted by the Midland Railway, a *tour de force* of every human talent. The MR's Chief Engineer, John Crossley, outlined the route the line should take, but the surveying and detailed planning of the 73-mile route was given to a Mr Sharland. This he accomplished with the skill of eye and determination of a latter-day Brunel, travelling on foot and on horseback, scouting a far greater distance than that of the proposed route over those remote, inhospitable hills. He was often drenched, frozen – and, for three winter weeks, snowed-up in the Gearstones Inn,[8] 11 miles north of Settle. The result was a glorious conception which the engineer–artist Brunel would have been proud to own: a double-track, high-speed route sweeping through the Fells. Sharland's exertions led to his premature death and he did not live to see the line opened.

The route would cross the remotest country in England, rising to a summit of 1166 ft according to the MR's own survey.[9] The work was divided between four contractors, John Ashwell, Benton & Woodiwiss, Joseph Firbank and Eckersley & Bayliss, under the ultimate supervision of John Crossley, who deferred his retirement to take his part in the great work. Experienced though all these men were, they underestimated the weather in those northern Fells. Torrential rain would be driven by tremendous gales; snow would fall deep and the wind would fill the cuttings with it; bitter frosts would freeze the ground like iron. Nor did they fully anticipate the nature of the boulder clay, which sometimes had to be blasted away and then, in pouring rain, became like a glue, so that it could not be removed from the tipper wagons.

Contract No. 1, Settle to Denthead, was begun in November 1869. It included the Batty Moss or Ribblehead viaduct, 440 yds long and carrying the rails at a maximum height of 104 ft above the valley; and the 2629-yds-long Blea Moor tunnel, cut to a curve through millstone grit and shale.[10] By June 1871 the contractor John Ashwell was in financial trouble and in October the MR itself took over the work. By June 1873 the line was no more than half complete, the contractors were out of money and the Company's statutory powers had run out of time. The MR instructed the contractors to borrow and build, and promised to stand by them. The contractors duly borrowed on the strength of the MR's reputation while the Company itself went to Parliament to request power to raise more money and more time to finish the work.

Construction of the passenger stations was begun in late 1874. They were designed by the Company's own architect, J.H. Sanders, RIBA, who had also designed the MR station at Bath and Ilkley.[11] The Settle line stations are dignified and handsome, fitting perfectly into their surroundings, with gabled roofs over strong walls of local stone, pierced by large mullioned windows, smaller windows ornately latticed, and doors strongly panelled. There a sense of strength, but harshness is kept at bay by ornately carved barge-boards at the gable ends. The route was opened for long-distance goods traffic on 2 August 1875[12] after six years' work, rather than the originally estimated four – but what work had been achieved, and what enormous difficulties had been overcome! Although the gradients were very long, they were nowhere steeper than 1 in 100, while the curves were wide enough for 90 mph running. The cost was 60 per cent more than estimated: Blea Moor tunnel had cost £45 a yard or £1.5 million, against the original estimate for the entire line of £2.2 million. The final cost was £3,467,000, or about £47,500 per mile.[13] This was higher than the British average but the terrain was anything *but* average, and when the superb alignment of the line over such territory is considered it will be appreciated that the navvies gave the Midland Railway exceedingly good value for their wages.

While the cost in pounds sterling is known to the last penny, the full cost to the almost entirely anonymous and uncounted workforce in terms of life and limb is not known. At intervals along the route there rose shanty towns for the navvies, their wives and families, the largest of them at Batty Moss. With its traders' stalls, makeshift pubs, flocks of sheep and herds of cattle awaiting slaughter it had the atmosphere of an American frontier town. From such encampments the men set out daily to walk to the tunnels, the viaducts, the cuttings and the embankments, where they would slog for 12 hrs through mud and rock before facing the long walk home each night. In the camps men, women and children died from smallpox and assorted fevers, and from drinking too much whisky. The men also died from fist fights, from being blown off high scaffolding by the ferocious winds, from misfired charges of dynamite, from being run over by wagons. Many of them were buried at the church of St Leonard, Chapel-le-Dale, where a marble tablet commemorates their sacrifice.[14] What these people achieved was very great indeed. The architecture of the route and indeed, the route itself ought to be considered as works of art. Its contoured track-bed, bridges and viaducts, its station buildings and signal boxes form a perfect unity and enhance the lives of the people as well as the landscape. All this was produced by practical men: half a dozen engineers, an architect who understood craftsmen – and several thousand horny-handed sons of toil. Those unsuing heroes wielded saws, planes, picks and shovels for a Board of Directors who, though they had not wanted to build the line, honoured their legal obligation without parsimony.

The Settle to Carlisle line was opened to passenger trains and local goods traffic on 1 May 1876.[15] The MR's very own Anglo-Scottish expresses over the Settle & Carlisle began running without an official ceremony. There were no trains in Britain remotely comparable with these for comfort and all facilities were available to 3rd-class passengers. Green 2–4–0-type locomotives, hauling a train of crimson-painted, steam-heated, power-braked bogie clerestories and a pair of American Pullman cars (one for Glasgow, one for Edinburgh), were storming through the lonely Fells, the sound of their whistles and the rhythmic exhausts muted in the vastness of the space, as much as the hush of the wind and cry of the curlew. For all this magnificence the MR charged 40s 6d 1st class from St Pancras to Carlisle, compared with 47s 4d on the Euston–Carlisle route. The L&NWR reduced their fare to 40s 10d, and retained their original volume of traffic on their faster route.

The original construction cost of £3.5 million was by no means the end of the investment. A much larger station was required at Carlisle and the Glasgow & South Western Railway, which was to haul the MR trains to and from Carlisle, needed a city-centre station in Glasgow. In preparation for the opening of the S&CR line the G&SWR built a grand new station – St Enoch – which was fronted by an imposing 97-bedroom hotel, the first purpose-built railway hotel in Scotland. Both bore a resemblance to the station and hotel at St Pancras. These were not finally completed until July 1879, but the station was sufficiently advanced to be officially opened by the Prince and Princess of Wales on 17 October 1876, when they visited Glasgow. The new Carlisle Citadel Joint station was opened for public use on 4 July 1880 t was managed by a Joint Committee on behalf of all seven companies which used it, and almost at once litigation began between the companies and the Committee over the alleged unfairness of the tolls the former paid.

The S&CR line remained expensive to maintain and operate. It would have been more sensible for the MR to have leased the Lancaster & Carlisle with the L&NWR, but the L&NWR's fear of the MR prevented this. The MR's intention had been to establish a competitive route to Scotland, yet there was much grandeur in the achievement. The Company had created sane and decent employment in a public service and a powerful support to the communities of the Dales. The railway gave the Dales folk something extra to be proud of, even if they did not actually work on it – and more if they did. It became part of their lives, making the living easier, bringing in cheaper fuel and goods, enabling them to buy and sell at hitherto inaccessible markets, at Appleby, or even Carlisle. It brought the electric telegraph across the remote Fells by which messages could be sent out for a doctor or to advise of a homecoming son. In the deep snows of winter, the people were supplied with food by rail where before they were threatened with famine.[17] At Hawes Junction the station waiting-room doubled as the village library except on Sunday, when it became the chapel. The room below the locomotive water tank at the same station was equipped with comfortable chairs and a piano, and became a little dance hall and social club.[18] The Settle line is perhaps the best-known example – but by no means the only one – of how a railway became the focal point in the lives of those who worked on it or lived by it, bringing them together and fostering the development of communities from Carlisle to Melton Constable.

The distance from London to Carlisle was 299 miles by the L&NWR against 310½ miles by the MR. From London to Glasgow by the MR/G&SWR route was 426½ miles, against 401½ miles by that of the L&NWR/CR. Had the geography of the MR/G&SWR route been kinder this would not have mattered, but the main disadvantage for the MR Anglo-Scottish expresses was that, for 75 miles from Trent Junction, near Derby, to the north of Leeds, they had to pass through an industrial conurbation thick with private sidings to factories and collieries, large stations, complicated junctions with their permanent speed restrictions, and the ever-present possibility of delay from conflicting movements. Midland trains also had to contend with the Fell country for a much longer distance than the L&NWR, and cross a much higher summit. Because the MR engines had to work hard to counteract all these difficulties, they hauled fewer coaches than the L&NWR's Anglo-Scottish trains, but still took an hour longer for the journey. Thus the MR carried fewer passengers per train, yet competition obliged them to charge lower fares than the L&NWR.

In 1873, as part of the scheme for a direct Anglo-Scottish service, the Midland obtained an Act for a route from Trowell, a few miles north of Trent Junction, to Nottingham, Melton Mowbray and Glendon Junction, just north of Kettering on the main line from St Pancras to Leicester. It was a heavily engineered and very expensive short-cut, which avoided the complications of Leicester, Trent and Derby in exchange for those of Nottingham and the Erewash valley. In the 16 miles from Kettering to Manton Junction there were four tunnels, at Corby, Seaton, Glaston and Wing, totalling 4319 yds, and the 1275-yds-long Welland or Harringworth viaduct. The 22 miles from Melton Mowbray to Nottingham included another four tunnels totalling 3817 yds. This line was opened to passenger traffic in 1880.

Looking at the map of the MR, one sees that it was an exceptionally complicated network, taking on, very approximately, the shape of an inverted 'Y', the stem reaching Carlisle, the Manchester line joining the stem 10 miles north of Derby, and a forking at Derby for London and Bristol. Closer inspection reveals that the main trunks were divided into parallel routes, each serving one important town. Even worse, the enormously important industrial area of Bradford was, for the MR, at the end of a branch line, while Sheffield lay at the bottom of a deep valley, on a loop off the main line. There were also numerous lines interconnecting the trunks, such as that from Leicester to Birmingham, and long tendrils reaching out to York, Lincoln, Peterborough, and even to Swansea and Bournemouth. Because of the splitting of the main trunks a number of connecting trains had to be run from far-off places to provide the necessary through-service. All these interconnecting, long-distance trains had to run punctually through heavily built-up areas – and among all the other trains (see Map 6).

The intricacy of the MR's operation was its glory, in the view of the men who coped with it, but made it very expensive to run. Whether it St Pancras–Glasgow/Edinburgh expresses were profitable is open to question, since the carrying capacity of each train was low, and the Company had to guarantee the NBR and the G&SWR a profit on each MR express they hauled. The MR's paid-up capital per mile of route was, by 1900, the greatest of any major British railway company, while its fares were competitively low. Its competition to Manchester, the West Riding and Scotland forced the GNR – and, eventually, the L&NWR – to improve their services; but all was well so long as revenue increased in line with costs, so that the dividend could remain more or less static after the vast outpouring of capital.

19

The Great Western Railway

T HE GREAT WESTERN was a special case among railways, brought
into being and guided for many years by the most talented
group of people ever to serve one company. It was designed by
Isambard Kingdom Brunel (1806–1859), probably the greatest civil
engineer of his period, who remained in his post from 1833 until his
death. Brunel's genius for civil engineering was complemented by the
mechanical engineering genius of Daniel Gooch (1816–1889), the
finest locomotive engineer of the period. Gooch was Locomotive
Superintendent from 1837 until 1865, when he became Chairman of
the Company, an onerous task he fulfilled until his death. Charles
Russell (1786–1855), MP for Reading, was Chairman of the Company
from 1839 until ill-health forced his retirement in 1855. From 1840
until 1863 the Company Secretary was Charles Saunders (1796–1864),
who was also financial adviser to the Board, General Manager and
Superintendent of the Line. When he retired, three new Officers had
to be appointed to fulfil the duties he had carried out for 23 years. His
successors were honest and non-speculative, and nurtured the growing
Company, steering carefully past the rocks and whirlpools of competition. They had a lifelong commitment to the success of the Company
and understood intimately the workings of Parliament, finance and
railway operation.

The idea of a railway between Bristol and London was first mooted
in 1824 and remained an open subject. Early in 1832 two Bristol land

surveyors, William Brunton and Henry Price, proposed a railway from Bristol, which would follow the route of the coach road (the present A4) to a terminal in the vicinity of Paddington. The suggestion stirred the powerful businessmen of Bristol, and on 21 January 1833 a Committee, formed from members of the Corporation, the Dock Company, the Merchant Venturers and the Chamber of Trade, met to discuss the benefits and decided to press ahead with the project. Brunel knew about the proposal by 4 February, almost certainly from his friend Nicholas Roch of the Bristol Dock Company, who was also on the Railway Committee. On that day Brunel used the initials 'BR' in his journal for the first time when recording a meeting he had with Bristol Railway Committee member William Harford, when the possibility of a survey was discussed.[1] The second time Brunel mentions 'BR' in his journal is on the 21st, when he records a meeting with Roch at which the latter told him:

A sub-committee was appointed for the purpose of receiving offers from me in conjunction with Townsend and probably also from Brunton and Price [as to] what terms and in what time we would make a survey and lay down a line on what terms we would afterwards undertake to lay our line for Parliamentary plans.

'Townsend' was William Townsend, the Engineer of a coal-carrying tramway from the Floating Harbour to coal-mines at Coal Pit Heath, north of Bristol.

Brunel had for years been anxiously looking for work on a scale to match his talent and ambitions. Now here was a magnificent opportunity, but he was being tied to a mediocre local man and told to produce the cheapest solution. Brunel wanted to do great things, not penny-pinching things. At the end of his journal entry for the 21st he writes of Townsend: 'How the devil am I to get on with him tied to my neck I know not.'[2]

Brunel was implacably opposed to the Committee's intention to give the job of surveyor to whoever offered the cheapest price, and was further dismayed that the post of Engineer of the line was to go to the person giving the lowest estimate for its construction.[3] The railway he would build would be the best – not the cheapest.[4] He hammered away at the point that competition for cheapness was not the way to approach the project. On the 23rd he 'pointed out to Mr Roch the difficulties attending a competitive survey', but Roch was emphatically in favour of a competition, and Brunel was obliged to enter, protesting all the while. In his journal for 23rd he records: 'Before breakfast wrote to the Committee, explaining my views of the proposed survey etc etc and ending with a joint offer from Townsend and myself to undertake the survey, at cost, for £500.' On the 24th he wrote to a Mr Sweet in London, asking his help in forming a London Committee for the Bristol Railway and also for his assistance in pacifying the landowners in the vicinity of Lambeth and Rotherhithe. It would appear from this that he had already decided on an approximate location for his terminus, which was not to be Paddington.

On 1 March Brunel went to Bristol Council House where Roch was chairing a Committee on the railway. Roch came outside to speak to Brunel, who 'pointed out strongly [his] feelings against a competition'.[5] Roch immediately invited him to repeat his arguments to the Committee – which he did, 'to some effect'. He also showed his grasp of the situation by impressing on them the importance of bringing the railway to the attention of London, and of forming a London Committee, with which those present agreed. Despite this, Brunel seems to have been seized by one of those bouts of depression to which he was prone. The following day he told Townsend of his 'intention not to engage in a competition and as I did not want to involve him in any withdrawal I wished to know his intentions'.[6] On the 3rd he began putting on paper his views on the inconveniences of a competition, a task which occupied him until the 4th, when he handed it to Roch and then left for London.[7]

He returned to Bristol on the morning of 7 March, and at 2 p.m. he was informed by Roch that he had been appointed to survey a route for the Bristol Railway by a vote of 15 to 14, although the Committee Chairman, John Cave, had voted against him.[8] It seems to me probable that the Committee had been entirely in favour of building the cheapest railway, but that Brunel's protestations had converted a slim majority to a longer-term view. To have disagreed absolutely with the entire selection panel and still to have got the job was a truly Brunellian feat.

Brunel's route to London was a masterpiece of strategic planning. Where ordinary mortals would have taken the obvious, parochial route, through narrow river valleys and across high ground, following the old turnpike road, Brunel conceived the unexpected route with easy gradients, which would pass over a summit at Swindon half the height of that at Marlborough and be strategically placed to extend into west Wales, for Ireland and the Midlands, and north-west through

Oxford. The first public meeting of the Bristol Railway took place on 30 July, when Brunel explained his proposals. He was confirmed as Engineer of the line on 27 August and that evening, recording the fact in his diary, he invented the title *Great Western Railway*, and wrote those magic initials: GWR. He and his assistants set out on a thoroughly detailed survey of the 120 miles of route on 7 September and this was deposited in Parliament, along with the Bill, in November, ready for the 1834 Session.

The proposed route from Bristol corresponded approximately to that of today as far as Ealing, where it turned south-east through Brompton to the proposed terminus at Vauxhall Bridge, Lambeth. The strategic siting of the route was supported by George Stephenson and Joseph Locke. Stephenson told the Select Committee investigating the public benefit of the proposal: 'I can imagine a better line but I do not know one so good.' Brunel assured the Committee that his railway would be so perfect, in every respect, that it would have the *monopoly* of its part of the country, and that, rather than build competing lines, people would wait until the GWR arrived. Since he was in all other respects an extreme Liberal, supporting free trade and freedom of individual choice, his monopolistic aspirations are surprising; but there again, he really believed that only he could produce perfection. Brunel was questioned for eleven of the Committee's fifty-seven days, but the Bill was thrown out because of the objections of some Noble Members who owned ornamental parks between Ealing and the river at Vauxhall.

In 1835 the GWR presented Parliament with another Bill for the same line from Bristol to Ealing but which would then veer north-east to a junction with the London & Birmingham (L&BR) at Kensal Green and run to a common terminus at Euston. There was opposition from the London & Southampton Railway, which contended that Bristol and London would be better served by an L&SR branch from Basingstoke to Newbury, Hungerford, Devizes, Trowbridge, and along the Avon valley to Bath and Bristol. This was foiled by geography, the hills which Brunel had deliberately avoided providing a perfect defence. The Commons passed the GWR's Bill, a Committee of the House of Lords reported to their Lordships that no more evidence of the need for a railway from London to Bristol was required, and they then spent forty days arguing the matter. The Bill received the Royal Assent on 31 August 1835.

On 15 September Brunel wrote to his Directors proposing the use of the 7-ft gauge. Though his reasoning for preferring a 'broad gauge' was clever, he could have achieved all he desired on Stephenson's gauge, while maintaining the vital continuity of railways. He saw the existing gauge as that of coal carts, and unworthy of the magnificent new transportation system he had in mind. He sprang the idea on his Directors like a thunderbolt, and while his Directors accepted it the Stephensons did not, and at once began to hang back in their arrangements to accommodate the GWR at Euston. Brunel badgered Robert Stephenson continuously, but was obliged in December 1835 to abandon the scheme, despite having the legal sanction to carry it through. The Company now had to find a new London terminus, which entailed the expense of another Act and of buying the extra land. The Act for the Paddington Extension was obtained in July 1837 and added about £1 million to the cost of the railway.[9] The permanent benefit of the move to Paddington was that the railway obtained the most perfect exit from London of any railway. Brunel was well aware that Brunton and Price had intended to use Paddington and one wonders whether this was why Brunel had tried to avoid using it: he did not want to admit that they were right in any degree. Brunel's Vauxhall Bridge terminus would have required a steadily uphill start for about 6 miles to Ealing, whereas the Euston site was at the foot of a 1-mile gradient so steep as to require rope-haulage of trains.

Brunel wanted to combine smooth riding and speed, and believed that this could only be achieved safely by designing carriages with a low centre of gravity, running on axles with reduced friction in their bearings. He chose the 7-ft gauge in order to place the carriage bodies between the wheels[10] so as to obtain a low centre of gravity, and intended to use 4-ft-diameter wheels which would revolve more slowly at any given speed than the usual 3-ft or 3 ft 6 in. wheels and thus, reduce friction in the axles' bearings. Sometimes Isambard was far too clever for his own – or his shareholders' – good.

Brunel brushed aside the problem of the break of gauge just as he was later to brush aside the problems of the atmospheric railway. 'A very simple arrangement', he declared – not specifying what form this would take – 'may effect the transfer of the entire loads of goods from the wagons of one company to that of another while the passengers will merely step from one carriage into the other.'[11] One supposes Brunel envisaged detachable goods containers and coach bodies being hoisted from a broad-gauge to a standard-gauge flat-bed wagon, but the broad-gauge container or carriage would have to be built to conform to the standard loading gauge, and the nuisance of having to change over would always exist.

The only passenger vehicles Brunel designed with the wheels outside the bodies were some 1st-class saloons, magnificently upholstered within, whose bodies rested on rubber air-bags mounted on the frames. They had a clerestory running the length of the roof, giving a maximum headroom of 6 ft, and were 7 ft 6 in. wide at seat-level, reducing to 6 ft wide at the floor. The seats were arranged around the walls, with a table down the centre. The carriages' bodies were 18 ft 6 in. long and carried on two axles, which were 10 ft apart. Only a few of these fine carriages were built. The majority of the original broad-gauge carriage fleet were constructed in the conventional way, with the bodies above and overhanging the wheels, which, being 4 ft in diameter, came through the floor and were enclosed in a metal cowling – a system that remained the broad-gauge standard until 1875. Like the grander saloon, these carriages had 18 ft 6 in. bodies, but these were carried on two axles spaced only 7 ft or even 6 ft 6 in. apart. Since the axles were 7 ft long, the wheelbase was square or even less than that. How Brunel could have thought this sensible is one of the great mysteries of his life.[12] These vehicles came into service on 4 June 1838 for the opening of the line from Paddington to the old Maidenhead station,[13] and were at once in trouble for the obvious reason: the wheelbase was far too short to give a stable ride.

To make matters worse, Brunel's original track was very badly designed. He had accepted the conventional wisdom that it should consist of an unyielding surface. In pursuit of this ideal, all engineers except Joseph Locke (who used a relatively flexible track of rails on timber cross-sleepers) placed their wrought-iron rails on stone blocks. Cross-sleepers was seen as a temporary expedient, and in 1838 the L&BR was spending copiously to replace their cross-sleepered tracks with the primitive stone block system. Brunel did not see the virtue of Locke's system, and tried to make his track perfectly unyielding.

He designed a wrought-iron rail of inverted 'U' section and supported it continuously on a 6-in. longitudinal sleeper, laid on really hard-packed sand. At 15-ft intervals, these sleepers were fixed to timber piles – about the size of present-day telephone poles – driven deep into the ground. (The tremendous effort involved in lifting these upright and then creating the means to get above them in order then to hammer them into the ground can be imagined.) Brunel thought that these piles would hold the longitudinals tight against the hard ground;

but what actually happened was that the weight of the trains forced the sleepers into the ground towards their centres, while the piles held them up at each end. This created a roller-coaster effect which, with the extremely short wheelbase carriages, produced a shockingly uncomfortable ride and caused many derailments.[14] In December 1838 Brunel abandoned the piling idea, which created more expense, as the huge piles had to be removed from about 25 miles of double track.

Although the 1st-class saloons were extremely comfortable and had a well-designed wheelbase, they were found to be 'of little general use'[15] and gradually withdrawn from service. The others were a disaster. Brunel drew up fresh designs late in 1837 and the first carriages of new design appeared from 1839.[16] These had their bodies above and over their wheels and were carried on a very practical six-wheeled chassis which became the standard on the GWR for 40 years. First-class carriages had 24-ft-long, 9 ft 6 in.-wide bodies; 2nd-class were 27 ft long, their axles spaced at 7-ft and 9-ft centres respectively. This well-spaced, three-axle construction produced a very smooth, steady ride, though that would also have been the case even on the standard gauge. For at least 30 years a six-wheeled carriage chassis was standard practice on the GWR.

By 1877 the maximum width of any broad-gauge carriage had reached 10 ft 6 in., with 8 ft 6 in. to 9 ft 6 in. as the norm. But one does not need to have excessive width between the rails in order to have wide carriage bodies; neither was the ultra-low centre of gravity necessary for speed. In the 1840s and 1850s Great Western trains were the fastest in the world, yet the carriage bodies were set above and overhanging their wheels: Brunel could have had wide bodies on the standard gauge, had he not been so obsessed with bursting upon the world like a comet. The essential requirement in respect of wide carriage bodies is to keep lineside structures further away from the rails. (This is most evident on South African 3 ft 6in.-gauge railways, or the standard-gauge railways of the USA, both of which have carriages at least as wide as the widest on the broad-gauge GWR.) Having provided the 7-ft gauge in order to put bodies between wheels and almost immediately abandoned the idea, Brunel then cramped his style by putting station platforms close to the rails and making his ordinary brick arches across the tracks no higher than those designed by Robert Stephenson for the London & Birmingham. By 1874 the Midland had 8 ft 6in.-wide carriages, and in 1904 the Lancashire & Yorkshire Railway introduced electric trains to their

Liverpool–Southport service with bodies 10 ft wide. It was the loading gauge, not the width of the rails, which determined carriage body width, and locomotive power which determined speed.

The broad-gauge locomotives built to Brunel's specifications were poor machines, and the fact that their axles were 7 ft long did not compensate for their severe design defects. Brunel was fortunate in having Daniel Gooch as his Locomotive Superintendent. Born in 1816, Gooch grew up in Bedlington, Northumberland, with its coal-mines, iron foundries and engineering workshops. In 1825 he had a Saturday job driving pit ponies in a coal-mine owned by George Stephenson.[17] Gooch learned mechanical engineering from Tredegar foundries in 1831, moving to Charles Tayluer's 'Vulcan' foundry near Warrington in 1834, and to Robert Stephenson's Newcastle factory in 1835. He was as strong-willed as Brunel, and far cleverer at mechanical engineering. The two men complemented each other. Brunel's magnificently engineered main line from Paddington to Exeter would not have been the success it was without Gooch's locomotives, and these could not have shown off their paces so well but for the scores of miles of 'Brunel's billiard table'. Gooch's engines were the best in Britain: well-proportioned in their boilers, valves and cylinders, they would have worked just as well mounted on axles 4 ft 8½ in. long. Indeed, the first proper locomotive on the GWR was designed at Robert Stephenson & Co. for a 5 ft 6 in.-gauge railway in New Orleans, but was sold instead to the GWR – whereupon its axles were lengthened to 7 ft.[18] The new engine was very handsome and Brunel poetically named it *North Star*, the forerunner of a whole fleet of 'Stars'.

Brunel created a wonderful road, with minimal gradients, from Paddington to Bristol and for another 50 miles beyond that. The summit was at Swindon, 77 miles from Paddington station and approximately 220 ft above it, and 41 miles from Bristol station, which lay about 250 ft lower than Swindon. He came west from Paddington to Swindon on an almost continuous and imperceptibly rising gradient, with a few short, level stretches. Obstacles were cut through or leaped over, irrespective of cost. West of Swindon he had to include two relatively steep inclines of 1 in 100, each less than 2 miles long, the more westerly coinciding with the Box tunnel. From Box to Bristol he created his most splendid architectural effects as he decorated the various stations, tunnel mouths and lengthy viaducts in a variety of Brunellian adaptations of mock castles, Jacobean, Tudor and Classical styles. The Company paid dearly for their road and for Brunel's exquisite taste, but the line's ultimate perfection must have saved an enormous sum in fuel costs in the long-term. The line from London to Norwich, designed at the same time as the GWR, was built as cheaply as possible and faithfully replicates, in 115 miles of switchback gradients, the rolling meadows and ploughlands of Essex, Suffolk and Norfolk: had more money been spent on construction the annual fuel bill of the railway would have been substantially reduced (see Map 7).

It is open to question whether the GWR's high construction cost was entirely due to the heavy works required to produce such perfection, or whether there was an additional cost because Brunel was the Engineer. He cost the GWR an extra million at Paddington – but the railway obtained a far better terminal than Euston; his artistic sense certainly created extra expense without any balancing technical advantage, but it enhanced the beautiful countryside from that day to this. He was, however, a difficult man to work for; 'tyrannical' and 'overbearing' were words commonly used to describe his attitude by those who had the experience, and he was often slow to pay his contractors. After a year of searching, he had been unable to find a really strong contractor for the 1¾-mile-long Box tunnel. This may have been because the really competent, solvent contractors, Peto & Grissel, Hugh McIntosh or William McKenzie, for instance, were busy elsewhere, or that word had got around and they were wary of working for Brunel in such a risky operation as the greatest tunnel yet contemplated. Whatever the reason, the Box tunnel was driven by two contractors with insufficient resources, and the work, admittedly extremely difficult, certainly took longer than it would have done with financially stronger and more competent contractors.

On 14 June 1841, the GWR was opened throughout from Paddington to Bristol, and the Bristol & Exeter Railway, leased for nine years to the GWR and engineered by Brunel, was opened as far as Bridgwater. The only large-scale feat of engineering on the B&ER was the 1092-yds-long Whiteball tunnel through the ridge of the Blackdown Hills between Somerset and Devon; apart from that, it ran through many miles of flat country between Bristol and Taunton. The line was opened to Exeter on 1 May 1844, having cost no more than the original estimate. The B&ER was entirely independent of the GWR, although it was to form the extension of the trunk rail route to the west. The only common feature was that the companies shared the services of Brunel. The result of the B&ER's independence was that it started from a junction on the London side of the GWR station at Bristol, obliging all its trains to and from the west to reverse in or out of the GWR terminal. When the GWR lease expired the B&ER regained its independence, which meant buying its own fleet of locomotives and carriages, erecting extensive locomotive repair workshops, goods-sheds, offices and a separate terminal station at Bristol: a splendid example of the expense of individualism applied to railways.

The Great Western Railway cost £6,150,000[19] to construct and equip, nearly three times the original estimate. No one could have anticipated the Parliamentary expenses of £118,000, nor that the other legal fees, engineering and direction fees would amount to £295,000, nor that land purchase and compensation to landowners whose land had been compulsorily purchased would swallow £743,000; the total costs of non-constructional activity came to £1,156,000,[20] or about 20 per cent of the capital raised.

The Great Western was a peaceable company and tried to make agreements on allocation of territory with the London & South Western, to prevent penetration of the GWR trunk. Unfortunately the L&SWR did not understand the financial benefits of coexistence, and the GWR was obliged to create a line of railway from Newbury, through all the town threatened by the L&SWR, to Weymouth. This amounted to a sort of defensive outwork protecting GWR territory, and might not otherwise have been constructed (or perhaps not as soon after the main trunk had been built). The trunk line westwards from Bristol, all of it engineered by Brunel, was constructed by independent companies. As each company was opened, it joined in the financing of the next lap of the journey to Penzance. The GWR, B&ER and the Bristol & Gloucester (B&GR) all assisted at the birth of the South Devon Railway (SDR), incorporated on 4 July 1844, which would run from Exeter to Plymouth. The Cornwall Railway (CR), incorporated in August 1846 from Plymouth to Truro and Falmouth, was supported financially by the GWR, B&ER, B&GR and SDR. The line from Truro to Penzance was built by the West Cornwall Railway (WCR), and incorporated on the same day as the CR, although the WCR demonstrated its fierce independence from the GWR and its allies by installing the standard gauge. At the time, this amounted to self-strangulation. The CR and WCR were still under construction when the 1847 crash occurred; their contractors were badly hurt, and the openings were set back several years. The WCR got ever deeper into debt and was leased to the GWR in 1865, whereupon the broad-gauge rail was added.

On the SDR, Brunel experimented disastrously with the 'atmospheric' system of haulage, in effect pouring nearly £½ million of his shareholders' funds into a vacuum tube.[21] Brunel's obsession left the SDR bankrupt in all but name; however, blessed with very generous mortgage-holders it was able to continue operations. Its main creditors, who were owed 6 per cent interest annually, received no interest for three years, and then agreed to accept a much smaller amount.

It was on the remote Cornwall Railway that Brunel achieved his greatest triumph: the Royal Albert bridge across the Tamar, and also the dozens of spectacular stone pier and timber trestle viaducts across the steep-sided, deep Cornish valleys. The viaducts appeared too lightly constructed to be safe, but they *were* safe and they enhanced the landscape with their terrifyingly dramatic aspect. They were *tours de force* of economy: Brunel pioneered a unitary principle of construction, whereby the viaducts were constructed to one of a strictly limited number of standard designs, each type having interchangeable components.

Into Wales from Grange Court, near Gloucester, the South Wales Railway (SWR), enacted 4 August 1845, was supported by the GWR, with Brunel as its Engineer. There were no other railways to oppose it, and the only challenges were to Brunel's engineering genius – the greatest being the very difficult crossing of the Wye at Chepstow, which he achieved with a typically remarkable bridge, clever and relatively inexpensive.

In January 1845, the Birmingham & Gloucester and the Bristol & Gloucester decided on a working union, after Parliament refused to permit their formal amalgamation. The GWR at once tried to purchase them both but was beaten by an offer from the MR to lease the route, take over all its debts and pay the shareholders a guaranteed 6 per cent. The lease was signed in February 1845, and in it the Midland stated that they had taken the action: 'under the conviction of the absolute necessity of a uniformity of gauge between the northern manufacturing districts and the Port of Bristol'.[22]

The GWR did push northwards, from Oxford to Banbury and Birmingham in 1850–52, and into the Black Country by means of the Oxford, Worcester & Wolverhampton Railway (OW&WR), incorporated in 1845 as a broad-gauge line, engineered by Brunel and supported by the GWR, which agreed to lease it, paying the OW&WR shareholders a guaranteed 3½ per cent on their capital of £1.5 million, plus half the profits of the line. The construction of the

OW&WR involved the GWR in tremendous legal battles as the corrupt and perjured management of the former tried to sell the concern to the MR and the L&NWR. It was fully opened in 1853, with mixed gauge; but apart from the Board of Trade Inspection train, it never carried a broad-gauge train. The route was a source of trouble to the GWR for another eleven years, as the L&NWR managed to run expresses from Euston to Worcester over it, and Peto tried to build a new railway from London to join it just north of Oxford, which attempts the GWR was obliged to fight in Parliament.

While it was still a relatively simple trunk line the GWR paid a reasonable dividend to Ordinary shareholders (6½ per cent in 1848); but later, most of the fresh capital required for new lines or other purposes could only be raised by offering a guaranteed interest to investors, and thus there was less money available for Ordinary shareholders. From 1849 to 1853 they received 4 per cent. In 1854, during the good times between two recessions, the GWR leased the Shrewsbury & Birmingham (S&BR) and the Shrewsbury & Chester (S&CR) – in spite of Mark Huish's ploy of forging the S&BR seal in an attempt to prevent the merger. Such leases benefited the public because they provided a through-route under one management, but the GWR had to pay rent in the form of a guaranteed interest to the shareholders in the old companies, which diverted GWR revenue away from its own shareholders. The capital employed by the GWR at this stage was equal to £61,000 per mile and in 1854 the Ordinary dividend fell to 3 per cent, melting down to 1 per cent in 1858.[23]

When the 1857–60 recession passed and money was again available, albeit only at the cost of guaranteed interest, the Company embarked on another series of very useful, necessary but costly amalgamations. In August 1863, the GWR purchased the South Wales Railway and the West Midland, which by then included the OW&WR. Two years later, the GWR bought the Vale of Neath Railway and West Cornwall Railway. In purchasing the companies the GWR also took over their debts. By the end of 1865 the GWR was short of money and the Ordinary dividend was a mere 2 per cent. By the time of the 1866 financial crash, the GWR had loans totalling £16 million, borrowed at nearly 9 per cent, the interest on a proportion of this to be paid monthly. Unable to do this, the GWR tried to raise new loans at a lower rate to pay off the high-interest short-term loans. In the wake of the crash the public would not look at railway shares – not even GWR Debenture shares, which by June 1866 were selling at a 54 per cent discount,[24] though the Company was earning a gross income in excess of £1 million per annum.[25] On 7 March 1867 Sir Daniel Gooch (knighted in 1866 for his work in laying the first transatlantic cable, and recently appointed Chairman of the GWR), accompanied by the chairmen of two other, severely embarrassed railways, Edward Watkin and Samuel Laing, went to interview Benjamin Disraeli at Downing Street with the extraordinary request that 'the Government should authorise the Bank of England to loan the GWR £1 million and that the Government should make itself responsible for the repayment of the loan'. The ambush was too obvious. If Disraeli acquiesced to Gooch's request he would have been pounced on by the MS&L, the LB&SCR and several others. The request was tantamount to asking Disraeli for nationalization of railways. Gooch received the following reply from Disraeli:

> Downing Street
> 13 March 1867
>
> Sir Daniel Gooch,
> Paddington.
>
> Sir,
> I have not failed to consider very attentively your letter of 11th instant, in which, after referring to the statement made to me respecting the financial position of the Great Western Railway, when I had the pleasure to receive you, with Mr. Laing and Mr. Watkin on Saturday last, you proposed that the Government should authorize the Bank of England to advance £1,000,000 to the Company and should make itself responsible to the Bank for the repayment of the loan.
>
> I regret to have to inform you that, with every wish to look favourably upon your request and to avert as far as possible the distress to which grave embarrassment on the part of the Company would no doubt give rise, the Government find it impossible to entertain the proposal which you made. Without entering into the details of your application, I may state that, while they reserve to themselves complete freedom of action, the Government are not prepared to admit that it is their duty to interfere in the affairs of the Company which you represent and that they cannot therefore undertake to propose to Parliament the adoption of so exceptional a measure.
>
> I am Sir,
> Your obedient servant,

That such a powerful character and staunch a Tory as Gooch, that man of such vast experience of government finance as Laing, should have made such a suggestion, must indicate a state of mind akin to panic on their part.[26]

A regime of extreme operational economy was instituted, and the interest and principle of these short-terms loans was paid 'out of the till' – which left (literally) nothing with which to pay holders of Debenture or Preference shares from January 1867 until September 1868. By mid-1867 the market value of the best GWR shares had dropped 62 below par.[27] The strict economy regime was directed by George Nugent Tyrrell (1816–1893), who had entered GWR service in 1842 and in 1864 was the first to hold the post of Superintendent of the Line, taking over this responsibility from Saunders. Tyrrell was ideally suited to the task. He disliked show and speed and he was contemptuous of competition, feeling that the GWR was great enough not to concern itself with what the rest did. Until he and Gooch retired, in 1888 and 1889 respectively, the GWR remained a majestically slow, stately, superbly well-engineered railway.

From 1870 the worst was over and the GWR was feeling sure of itself. Supported by its large revenues and its enormous assets in land and property, and by dint of stern economy in operating, it had weathered the terrible storm. Profits were increased by improving access to and from the GWR for standard-gauge trains; the GWR obtained a mileage payment for 'foreign' wagons passing over its metals. This process started in December 1856, when a third rail was added with the 7-ft gauge to allow OW&WR traffic to run through to the L&SWR at Basingstoke via Reading West and the South Eastern Railway at Reading station. On 1 October 1861 the mixed gauge reached Paddington.

The next stage was to abolish the broad gauge. In six days in August 1869, Gloucester to Hereford via Grange Court was converted to standard gauge. In fourteen working days, mainly at weekends during May 1872, 188 miles of double track from Swindon to Gloucester and Grange Court to Whitland, and 48 miles of single-track branch lines, including all the point-work in stations as large as Newport, Cardiff and Swansea, was converted to standard gauge without stopping the traffic. Work began on the construction of the Severn tunnel in 1873. In May 1874 the mixed gauge was installed between Swindon and Bristol while from Thingley Junction, near Chippenham, to Westbury, Salisbury and Weymouth was converted to the standard gauge. A total of 140 route miles was involved.[28]

In 1876 the GWR purchased the Bristol & Exeter Railway, which had completed the installation of mixed gauge from Bristol to Taunton in 1875. From Exeter to Falmouth the line was purely broad gauge with the mixed gauge over the West Cornwall Railway for Penwithers Junction, near Truro, to Penzance. The South Devon and the West Cornwall railways were amalgamated with the GWR on 1 August 1878. The Cornwall Railway, leased to the GWR since its opening in 1859, was absorbed into the larger concern on 24 June 1889. The broad-gauge rail was retained from Paddington to Penzance via Bristol for an ever-dwindling number of trains until final conversion, when, in a single weekend (21–3 May 1892), 423½ track miles from Exeter to Falmouth, including all branch lines and sidings, were narrowed to conform to the standard gauge. Posthumously Brunel cost the GWR large sums of money.

Work on the Severn tunnel was exceedingly dangerous but thanks to a heroic driver called Lambert, who twice risked his life to save the work, and the anonymous daily heroism of hundred of workers, the tunnel was opened to goods traffic on September 1886, and for passengers on 1 December. The tunnel, 7768 yds long, cost £1 million and was of great strategic importance to several companies. It gave L&NWR carriages access to Bristol and the west, taking traffic from the MR, and it gave Welsh coal a much more direct route to the infant port of Southampton, enabling the L&SWR to transform it into a major, transatlantic centre. The tunnel's full potential for the GWR was not realized until 1903, when the Wootton Bassett–Patchway line was opened (see Map 8).

Between 1870 and 1892, the Great Western was at its most Jovian and, judged by route mileage, the largest railway company in Britain. Its management virtually ignored the minimal competition from the L&SWR; it had agreements with the L&NWR in the west Midlands and co-operated with the L&NWR between Shrewsbury and Bristol. As on the L&NWR under Sir Richard Moon, economy was the watchword. The GWR's trains were relatively slow, its carriages reasonably comfortable for the time, and improvements were made gradually with measured excellence. The Company installed its own version of the automatic vacuum brake from 1876; in 1877 it introduced its first two sleeping-cars, 1st class only, with 10ft 6in.-wide bodies. Passengers brought their own bed-linen. Third-class sleeping-cars running on bogies, appeared in 1878.[29] For those twenty-two years the GWR was more or less at peace with the rest of the railway world: a gilt-edged investment for three-quarters of its shareholders.

20

Speed, Comfort and Insanitary Practices

FROM 1845 UNTIL 1853 the Great Western ran the fastest trains in the world with no more effective means of stopping than the fireman's handbrake on the tender and the guard's handbrake in his van. From December 1847 until March 1852 the 9.50 a.m. Paddington–Exeter *Flying Dutchman* was timed to run the 53 miles to Didcot at an average of nearly 58 mph. On 11 May 1848 the train carried a group of scientific observers and ran to Didcot in 47½ mins, an average of 66 mph.[1] Top speed must have been 80 mph. From October 1852 until January 1853 two Oxford–Paddington expresses were scheduled to average 54½ mph over the 63½ miles.[2] The best speeds on other railways in this period varied from 30 to 45 mph,[3] but even 40 mph is a frightening speed for 150 inadequately braked tons. By 1873, 60-mph running was commonplace on all major railways, but the method of stopping a train was what it had always been: the driver would whistle for the guard to apply his handbrake; when the former felt the train draw back against his engine he would tell his fireman to apply the tender handbrake, and then he would put his engine into reverse. The railwaymen certainly became skilful at handling this difficult operation, but there would still have been considerable jarring as the coaches were tugged back by the van brake, and then collided with the decelerating engine and tender, jostling each other as their buffer springs reacted.

Before 1874, when the MR introduced better carriages, passengers undertaking a 50-mile journey on any railway would have had a fairly tiring time, even in a 1st-class carriage. Up to that time competition between railways concerned prices and journey time, and had not extended to improvements to comfort or safety. Prior to 1874 British railway carriages were no better than those of 1850 or even earlier: always unheated and badly lit, frequently noisy and, with the possible exception of the GWR, insufficiently long in the wheelbase. The swivelling bogie had been patented in 1844 but was not used on public carriages in Britain for thirty years. In 1861 the L&NWR developed a system of carriage heating using the locomotive's exhaust steam, which was described as 'clever and economical',[4] but the L&NWR did not install it for thirty years – not even in the Royal saloon.

In 1874 a typical carriage on any railway except the Great Western would have been 15 to 21 ft in length and carried on four wheels; 30 ft would have been 'long'. On the L&NWR 30 ft was the maximum length for any carriage until after 1886. The carriages of the GWR were atypical because they ran on Brunel's 7-ft gauge, and were as much as 10 ft 6 in. wide. They were normally between 24 and 28 ft long, and generally (but not always) carried on a six-wheeled chassis.[5] In 1842 the GWR built the first eight-wheeled carriage in Britain, to Brunel's design, for Queen Victoria. This was also the first carriage to have a lavatory.[6] In 1848 the GWR built a new Royal saloon and this was carried on four-wheeled bogies. The first public eight-wheelers were a few built by the Eastern Counties Railway for their suburban services in 1847; the South Eastern also built a few at about the same time.[7] The first eight-wheeled carriages for express work were the 38-ft-long, 10 ft 6 in.-wide and 7 ft 2 in.-high 'Long Charleys', built by the GWR in 1852 for their Birmingham expresses.[8] Though these were for 1st- and 2nd-class passengers only, their lighting was 'miserable', to quote the Company's historian. All the above-mentioned eight-wheeled public carriages had fixed axles, with some radial movement built into the outermost axle boxes at each end of the coach.

The typical carriage of 1874 (GWR or otherwise) was divided into self-contained compartments by a partition the full width of the coach, with a door at each side. Space and comfort was, of course, allotted according to class: the 1st-class compartments had most leg-room, the most comfortable upholstery and perhaps two oil lamps per compartment – although knowing passengers who wanted to read after dark brought their own lamps with them. There was no fitted heating system in any railway carriage before 1874. Temperatures in unheated railway carriages dropped below freezing in winter. Those who could, came well supplied with rugs and, if they could afford it and were of the right class, hired a footwarmer.[9] Some companies provided these – metal cans filled with boiling water, or a reactive chemical which created heat, which could be hired at a cost of between 3d and 6d. The GNR is thought to have introduced them in 1852. The GWR provided them solely for the 1st class in 1856, for the 2nd class in 1879 and, in the winter of 1873, for 3rd-class passengers, after representations from the Railway Clearing House.

Second-class seats were reasonably padded except on the GWR, where seats and backs were stuffed hard with horsehair and covered in cold, slippery, black American cloth. Third-class carriages had half-height partitions so that one oil lamp could flicker over the whole length of the coach. Third-class passengers sat on bare boards, and 3rd-class carriages on the Midland were described by Hamilton Ellis as 'miserable coops'.[10] The North London and the Metropolitan (Met.), the latter running mainly in tunnel, had gas-lit carriages from 1863, but some of the South Wales railway companies' carriages had no interior lights until the GWR took them over in 1922.

When travelling at 45 mph in relatively short-wheelbase, four-wheeled vehicles, all passengers, regardless of class, would have been given a good shaking – accompanied by the roaring of iron wheels on the rails. Until 1848, carriages ran on iron, spoked wheels which were both very noisy and inclined to shatter occasionally. The solution to this was invented by Richard Mansell, Carriage & Wagon Superintendent of the SER. In 1848 he patented his wooden wheel-centre. It consisted of an iron boss, into which were socketed 16 tightly fitted segments of teak, to form a solid disc, around which was fitted the wrought-iron, flanged tyre. This wheel was all-but silent; a total of 21,760 pairs were made between 1848 and 1874 and none was known to have broken.[11] The improvement was very slow to be taken up by the companies, probably because of the royalties they would have had to pay Mansell. The GNR began using the patent in 1861 and the GWR from 1866. By 1874, 50 per cent of GWR standard-gauge carriages were running on Mansell wheels but only 38 of the 587 broad-gauge carriages were so fitted: just enough to form the trains of the GWR's most prestigious expresses.[12]

Whether it is worse to travel in the freezing cold or in dire need of a lavatory is a difficult question. In British railway carriages it was commonplace to suffer both inconveniences until the mid-1890s. The first carriages to be equipped with a lavatory were the Royal saloons of the early 1840s; the first public carriages to have this facility were the family saloons of 1860 onwards, which were hired by the wealthy to convey themselves and their servants to the grouse shooting or a seaside holiday. Since the passengers were well known to each other, they could have a water closet. The American Pullman cars had always had them, but Americans did not feel embarrassment at being seen entering or leaving a lavatory; the lack of a lavatory in British carriages was to some extent the result of the proverbial British 'reserve'.

The first sleeping accommodation in Britain was introduced in 1873 by the NBR,[13] quickly followed by the L&NWR, GNR and the other major companies. At first the sleeping arrangements were of the convertible armchair or fold-down sofa types, and the vehicles were neither heated nor equipped with a lavatory. In 1877 the GWR built two six-wheeled sleeping-cars with separate quarters for ladies and gentlemen. The occupants of the dormitories lay 'in close packed rows like recumbent cod on a fishmonger's slab'.[14] From each dormitory there was access to a lavatory. In 1881 these vehicles were withdrawn and replaced with the first modern sleeping-cars. These were bogie-mounted, 46 ft 6 in. long, with six double berths, no upper bunks, and a side corridor giving access to three lavatories.

In the same year the GNR put into service on their 'crack' Anglo-Scottish expresses, the first side-corridor day coaches in Britain. They ran on six wheels and were for 1st-class passengers only. The corridor was there only to provide access from each compartment to the lavatory at each end of the vehicle. Only gradually did this improvement become standard in all main line carriages of the companies. Male passengers sometimes relieved themselves through the open door of their compartment, an insanitary practice for those downwind, and dangerous for the culprit. Surgical suppliers catered for this demand with a curious apparatus of pipes and bottles – but this was of no use to women, who simply had to suffer in silence through the long hours of the journey.

All passengers had to bring their own food on long, non-stop journeys until the companies got around to providing on-train eating facilities. The 'luncheon basket' originated on the L&NWR's 'Irish Mail', which had been running daily between Euston and Holyhead since 1848. Not until 1876, when the journey had been cut to a mere 13 hours for the journey from London to Dublin, were the passengers able to buy a basket of provisions at Chester. There were two to choose from and they were shrewdly named: the 'Aristocrat', comprising a pint of claret or ½ pint sherry, chicken, ham or tongue, bread, butter and cheese, for 5s; and the 'Democrat', consisting of cold meat or pie, bread, cheese and a pint of beer for 2s 6d.[15]

The L&NWR, MR and GNR/NER stopped their Anglo-Scottish expresses for 20–30 mins to enable passengers to buy food and relieve themselves: the MR stopped at Normanton, the L&NWR at Preston, the GNR/NER at York. The GWR expected their west of England express passengers to do all they had to do in a mere 10 minutes at Swindon. At Preston there was double confusion because the 'up' and 'down' Scotch expresses were timed to arrive simultaneously, passengers pouring into the refreshment room from both sides, jostling for attention. Over the fireplace in the refreshment room at Carlisle was a well-meaning – but easily misunderstood inscription – in Latin, like a Gothic curse: 'Faciam ut Hujus Loci Semper Memeris', which might translate as '[I will] make things so that you will always remember this place'.[16] Sensations subsequent to a gulped meal of pork pie and beer would linger in the memories of most passengers.

When the MR opened its St Pancras terminal, its carriages were among the worst of any main line in Britain; even the 1st class rode in short wheelbase four-wheelers.[17] James Allport (see Appendix 5), the MR's General Manager, was the first railway manager in England to see the justice (and the profit) in making travel more comfortable for the largest section of the population, and set out to increase his revenue by making his railway the most popular in Britain, positively encouraging people to travel. From 1869 he put 3rd-class carriages into some of his best trains, providing passengers with express speed at one penny a mile – although they had to bear the discomfort of the MR's unreformed carriages for a few more years. In April 1872 the MR and the GER put 3rd-class carriages on all their express trains.[18]

Allport toured the USA to see how they ran their railways – and was impressed with the Pullman car, which ran on bogies and was fitted with the Westinghouse brake. George Pullman, originally a cabinet-maker, had introduced his luxurious cars in 1858, hiring them to various railroads. The interiors were open-plan, entered from verandahs at each end and centrally heated by hot water radiators supplied from an oil-fired boiler – and there were lavatories. Allport graciously agreed that Pullman should build one sleeping-car for the MR and run it – at Pullman's risk and expense – in MR trains. In May 1873,

Allport extracted from the GWR works at Swindon the formidable T.G. Clayton, fresh from his triumphs in supervising the rapid construction of large, stone-built carriage and locomotive workshops there. The perfect 'Project Manager' and a fine designer, he became the Midland's Chief Carriage & Wagon Superintendent. It would seem that there was many a dry eye at Swindon when he left.[19]

The splendid Pullman car was built in Detroit, shipped over to Derby in kit form, reassembled, and left the works on 25 January 1874. To people used to the little four-wheelers of the time it must have looked gigantic: 58 ft 5 in. long, 9 ft wide and 12 ft 2 in. high to the top of its clerestory roof. It was exceptionally well built, using oak for the bogie and main frames, oak and mahogany for the body. In its principle of construction the vehicle was as modern as an all-steel coach: it was built all in one piece, a wooden box-girder mounted on bogies. The heavy car, upholstered in red velvet and carpeted, ran silently and smoothly on its Mansell wheels and, in the event of a smash, was much safer than a conventional British coach. The Pullman protected its passengers not only through its box-form body but because the verandahs at each end took the inital impact, whereas the conventional British coach body, bolted to a chassis, could and did shear off, while the flimsy end walls afforded no protection from the iron buffers of the following coach.

In February 1874 Clayton produced his design for a fleet of standard express coaches accommodating 1st- and 3rd-class passengers. By June that year all the Midland's best express trains were formed with the new coaches. One hundred had been built at Derby, another hundred by contractors. All four-wheeled carriages were destroyed as fast as the works could build modern replacements. The new carriages were very handsome, and, with 54-ft-long bodies under a GWR-style clerestory roof, they were the longest in Britain. They had three 1st-class, four 3rd-class and one luggage compartment, and were mounted on an iron chassis rolling on a pair of four- or six-wheeled bogies with Mansell wheels. They had well-sprung, warmly upholstered seats for 32 passengers, weighed 22½ tons – and all were fitted with the Westinghouse brake. These were tremendous and pioneering improvements, but still they had not better lighting than in 1840, no fitted heating and, unlike the solitary Pullman car, no lavatories.

The instant increase in MR revenue brought about by selling express travel at 3rd-class fares was so great that, on 1 January 1875, the MR reduced 1st-class fares to the 2nd-class rate of 1½d a mile, abolished the designation '2nd-class' and redesignated those carriages '3rd'. The other companies were alarmed at what seemed to them to be outrageous competition, all the worse in that it brought the 3rd class, the travelling ghetto of the 'lower orders', nearer to equality with their 'betters'. The companies protested vigorously to the MR, but Allport actually did have a sense of mission to improve the lot of the lower-paid – quite apart from the urgent need for the heavily capitalized Company to increase its revenue. The L&NWR reduced its 1st- and 2nd-class fares although, loftily secure in its heavy, regular middle- and upper-class traffic, it did nothing for 3rd-class passengers. The GNR retained its 10 a.m. King's Cross–Edinburgh *Flying Scotsman* as '1st- and 2nd-class only', and accelerated it by 30 minutes to put Edinburgh within 9 hrs 5 mins from London – inclusive of the 30-minute refreshment stop at York; but they also added a new train – the 10.10 a.m. from King's Cross, carrying 1st, 2nd and 3rd class to the pre-1875 *Flying Scotsman* schedule. Even so, the GNR was still building four-wheeled carriages for its Anglo-Scottish services in 1878.

South of the Thames, the L&SWR was the first, in 1877, to abolish all its supplementary fares for express train travel and to admit 3rd-class passengers to all its trains. In the same year, the GWR, that 'Jovian'[20] railway, ran only two trains which could properly be called 'express': the 'up' and 'down' *Flying Dutchman*. All the others were 'wretchedly slow',[21] and for this service the GWR charged the highest fares of any major railway in Britain. At this time it was not moved by any competitive spirit, nor had it been for many years; like the L&NWR it had a regular, heavy traffic and saw the economy of proceeding at a genteel pace. The L&SWR's fare reductions attracted away much of the GWR's traffic for Exeter and beyond, but it was not until June 1879 that the GWR Directors responded to the pleadings of their Officers and put on really fast train to the west, comparable to the *Flying Dutchman*. Like the *Dutchman* it did not deign to carry 3rd-class passengers. The railwaymen at once dubbed it the *Zulu*.

Since 1855, the GWR management had not run a fast service to Birmingham in competition with the L&NWR. The L&NWR route was 113 miles compared to 129¼ by GWR, and both companies had been happy to coexist. In 1880 the L&NWR took about 3 to 3¼ hrs for their Birmingham run, the GWR anything from 20 to 40 mins longer. It was good business for both companies: speeds were economical in fuel and GWR fares were high. In June 1880 the GWR accelerated one train in each direction to cover the distance from Paddington to

Birmingham in 162 mins, 20 mins faster than the L&NWR expresses. Immediately dubbed the *Northern Zulu*, this train conveyed 3rd-class passengers and there was no express supplementary fare.

On the entirely non-competitive South Wales route, the GWR's passengers were charged express supplements for so-called expresses which averaged 34 mph between London and Cardiff, going via Gloucester prior to the opening of the Severn tunnel. In June 1881, one train from Paddington to Cardiff was accelerated to cover the 170¼ miles in 263 mins, an average of 38 mph. A year later, the GWR abolished the express supplement and allowed 3rd-class fares on all its trains except the most prestigious broad-gauge expresses – the 'Limited Night Mail' and *Flying Dutchman*. These two remained sacrosanct until 1884 and 1891 respectively. As each express train admitted 3rd-class passengers the Company's Officers complained that the train had been 'degraded'.

The L&NWR route to Manchester, via Nuneaton and Crewe, was 14 miles shorter than the MR's via Derby or 29 miles shorter via Nuneaton and Stoke on Trent. Richard Moon's trains got to Manchester faster than those of the MR or the GNR, carrying more passengers per train and at less cost to the Company in fuel, wear and tear. The L&NWR was indeed an exceptionally well-maintained railway but it was usually the last of the three major northern companies to introduce any innovation in speed or comfort, while its competitors were always spending hard, trying to catch up. The L&NWR could afford to look on while the MR spent large sums of money on splendid coaches, in which passengers travelled at reduced fares as the engine blasted its way over hill and dale in a strenuous effort to get from St Pancras to Manchester or Carlisle taking only half an hour longer than trains out of Euston. The east coast companies had a tacit agreement with those on the west coast on the timings of their Anglo-Scottish trains, and only very gradually improved on them.

In their attempts to break into L&NWR territory in Lancashire the MR, GNR and MS&L found common cause and co-operated. In 1875 the MR opened the 'Marple curve' near Stockport to enable their expresses to run directly to the joint GN/MS&L (or 'Cheshire Lines Committee') route to Liverpool, and then introduced Pullman sleeping-car trains.[22] Sharing the costs with the NER, the Midland helped to build a 20-mile-long link from the MS&L at Swinton, north of Sheffield, to the NER at Ferry Bridge, south of York, which afforded MR trains direct access into York and over which the MS&L had running powers. This was opened in 1879. In 1880 the Midland opened its Manchester South District Railway, giving access to a new station called Manchester Central, the latter a joint venture with the Cheshire Lines Committee. As the MS&L, GNR and MR no longer had to cram into London Road with the L&NWR, they would be able to improve their London services and establish a very fast service between Manchester and Liverpool, in opposition to the L&NWR and the Lancashire & Yorkshire Railway.

The GNR was the first to introduce the conservative British 1st-class passengers to dining-cars when it put on a Pullman dining-car called *Prince of Wales* between King's Cross and Leeds on 26 September 1879. The car weighed 22 tons, more than one ton per passenger carried. Gangway connections between corridors were more than a decade away, and so those who wanted dinner on the train had to get into the carriage at King's Cross or Grantham. As soon as Manchester Central opened, the GNR put Pullman dining-cars into this service. A GNR Manchester express typically consisted of five side-corridor six-wheelers and a Pullman diner, hauled by one of Patrick Stirling's '8 ft Single' locomotives. This relatively light formation was essential to cover the greater distance and higher summits in a time close to but still slower than that of the leisurely North Western. The schedule for the 105 miles from Grantham to King's Cross was 117 mins, an average of just over 50 mph although requiring a top speed of 75 mph over many miles. The MR's Manchester expresses were also formed of only five or six eight- or twelve-wheeled carriages, and had no dining-car until 1882. The Company did not put dining-cars on the Anglo-Scottish expresses until 1884.

Between 1861 and 1891, under the chairmanship of Richard Moon, the L&NWR's gross income increased 300 per cent, although dividends did not increase at all, alternating between 6 and 7 per cent. Rising operating costs had much to do with this, but it is also true that the railway was maintained in perfect order, and that improvements were made to harbours, stations and signalling, tracks were widened and bridges strengthened, while each year a large sum was carried over into the reserve; a 7 per cent dividend for the Ordinary shareholders was considered ample. Economy also meant keeping out of the competitive race – which meant less passenger comfort, especially for the 3rd class. The L&NWR applied the 'economy' principle ruthlessly to items large and small: the gas lamps at Euston were dimmed at any platform where a train was not standing.

The L&NWR's passenger rolling stock continued unchanged in essentials until the Company's chief Carriage Engineer, Richard Bore retired in 1886. He had held the post since 1846 and, like Moon, was opposed to anything which would unduly increase the running cost of the Company. When the 'Bank Holidays' were established by Act of Parliament in 1871, Moon discouraged the running of seasonal 'extras'. Forming and running extra trains upset the regular working schedules of coaches, engines and crews, increasing costs and often causing delays. At holiday times, extra coaches and family saloons were attached to regular trains.

Bore was opposed to long carriages, to bogies, power brakes and the steam heating of carriages. Even the Queen's saloon is recorded as suffering from frozen lavatories because of a lack of heating.[23] Express trains during Bore's incumbency were formed of carriages as far as possible of equal weight, in tight-coupled sets, running noisily but smoothly at 40 mph, on iron wheels, over the best maintained track in Britain. He was supported by the Locomotive Superintendent F.W. Webb (see Appendix 8). The L&NWR never used Pullman cars believing that a heavy carriage among lighter carriages was very dangerous – and this would indeed have been the case if the vehicle were braked with the L&NWR brake: 'Just wait till there is an accident – then you will see a pile.'[24] Bore designed some 42 ft eight-wheelers the inner axles were fixed and the outer had Mr Webb's radial axle-box to allow some 'give' around curves. It is possible that Webb's antipathy to bogie trucks and power brakes had something to do with the fact that he got a royalty from the L&NWR for every carriage using his patent axle-box and patent brake. Bore's successor, C.A. Park, did not at once design bogie-mounted carriages; he had first to persuade Moon to accept the increased cost, not just of heavier carriages but of more powerful engines to haul them. The L&NWR's first dining-car came into service, on the Manchester run, on 1 March 1888. It was a six-wheeler, for 1st-class passengers only, and was well known for shaking soup and gravy into the laps of the illustrious diners.

21

Standardization and Brakes

REEDOM FROM DEFINED principles of action', referred to approvingly in the 1867 Select Committee Report, had been successful only in creating disorganization at a national level, against which the Railway Clearing House and even the companies – when they could forget their rivalries – battled. Clearly defined principles of action were obviously required if the railways of Britain were to be a truly national carrier of passenger and freight. By 1874 there was railway communication from Penzance to Thurso and the system was crying out for one track gauge, standardization of certain vital aspects of the rolling stock, and common purpose. This was most important with regard to the carriage of freight, since tens of thousands of wagons wandered the system. Convenience demanded that one wagon and one payment should carry the load across all company boundaries – in short; that there should be 'through-rates'. This therefore required a standard type of wagon acceptable to all routes and a standard accounting procedure for all companies. What had begun as a few private companies, each with no broader vision than that of a private individual, had now to become positively communal if the system – which had so haphazardly grown up – was to realize its full potential. The benefit to the companies would be an end to debilitating competition, that to the customer would be an efficient service and, possibly, lower charges.

The GWR joined the Railway Clearing House in 1857, the southern group of railways joined in 1862, and in 1865 the RCH established the 'Normanton Rates Conference'. By 1872 the Parliamentary Select Committee on Amalgamations was able to report that: 'there is no active competition between different railways in the matter of rates and fares'.[1] Competition continued only in such small matters as the differing provision of cartage facilities. The impartiality and clerical expertise of the RCH was vital to making the system work for the benefit of the public and the companies.

British railways gave the best freight facilities in the world. The Act of 1854 obliged them to provide the facilities required by the public at any location, while local competition encouraged the companies to maintain high standards of collection, warehousing and delivery services. In any case, it was in the interests of the Company to make its service attractive to producers, so that the railway could carry the produce. The railway companies' status was ambiguous: each had been enacted to be a privately owned, self-interested corporation, but the 1854 Act obliged them to provide a public service – on request – irrespective of whether the Company thought it was profitable. The British Parliament tried to have the best of both worlds, individualistic and collectivist: by so doing, they increased the railway companies' costs and thus, their charges to their customers.

Thousands of rural stations sent wagons on their journey with half a load or less. The rural porter did not wait perhaps two days or more to fill a wagon; in the interests of prompt dispatch for the customer who had come that day, he would send the wagon to its destination. In Europe, where rail charges were lower, rural freight wagons were not sent on their way until they were full. In heavily industrialized districts the companies visited each factory twice or even four times a day, carrying away the produce, delivering empties, giving good service and saving the factory-owner the cost of cartage and storage. All this wagon-load and quarter-wagon-load traffic had to be collected, sorted in marshalling sidings, and transfer trips worked between marshalling yards within major centres. Once delivered to the destination station, wagons would remain loaded for days, or even weeks, the consignee using the truck as a store until he was ready to clear it. The returned empty wagons owned by other railway companies or private traders would also have to be shunted, formed into trains and hauled back to their owners. The customers took all this for granted, but demanded to know why their railway charges were so high.

The carriage of coal by railway in Britain and, therefore, the price of coal to the consumer, was made unnecessarily costly because the railway companies were not allowed to act as coal merchants.[2] Had they been coal merchants, railways would have arranged block train contracts with the collieries at very favourable rates to both sides, since bulk haulage would have saved on the railways' operating cost. Instead, a vast fleet of colliery-owned and coal-merchant-owned railway wagons carried coal, relatively speaking, piecemeal. The cost of shunting, to sort loaded and empty wagons into destinations, was considerable. Traders used coal wagons stored on sidings as warehouses, and refused to pay for the privilege; this created a permanent shortage of wagons and required a larger fleet than would have been the case with a quick 'turn round'. The British individualistic principle reigned supreme. It is true that railways did drastically reduce the cost of coal to inland towns and villages, but this was because its cost had previously been inflated by the expense of having to horse-haul it about in small quantities. If the disorganized principles referred to above had not been allowed to flourish, coal for inland places would have been even cheaper.

The first, insignificant amount of rail-borne coal reached London in 1845, but the majority of the tonnage came by sea from South Wales and Northumberland until 1867, when, for the first time, the amount arriving rail-borne equalled the amount coming in by sea.[3] Over the period 1845–85 the supply of coal to London increased by a factor of 5, while the population of London only doubled.[4] The London coal market was swamped, yet the price did not fall until the onset of the long depression in 1874, when prices of all commodities fell. This contradiction of the laws of supply and demand arose because carrying coal by rail was as expensive as carrying it by water. In 1887, a total of 12,192,000 tons of coal came to London, of which 60 per cent (7,327,770 tons) was rail-borne,[5] and arrived in hundreds of thousands of small wagons, to be re-marshalled and hauled to every suburban London station and 155 railway-owned coal depots.[6] The MR and L&NWR had invested heavily in miles of sidings at Cricklewood and Willesden especially for the sorting of coal trains, and from these and other centres the coal was hauled into the capillaries of the London railway network – and the empty trucks returned to be sorted yet again for the run back each to their home colliery (see Appendix 6).

The increase in freight traffic required larger trucks and faster trains, but goods trains, and especially coal trains, continued to be formed out of an assortment of utterly basic, badly designed, low-capacity wooden trucks. The railway-company-owned wagons were usually of better quality than those tens of thousands owned by collieries, coal merchants or other 'private owners' (PO). All coal wagons lacked a power brake, and access to the handbrake was on one side of the wagon only. The latter gave rise to constant difficulties, delays and dangers for train guards and shunters. Coal wagons ran on inadequately lubricated axle bearings which tended to overheat, while their tyres were often riveted on to the wheels. Private-owner wagons had all these faults and were the last to be rebuilt to a more satisfactory design. A feature particularly associated with PO wagons was the 'dumb buffer': projections of solid wood where the sprung buffers should have been.

The urgent need for a standard design of wagon had first been raised with the Railway Clearing House by Mark Huish on 25 June 1846. In December 1856 an RCH sub-committee, comprising a group of General Managers of the great railways, reported 'very serious differences' in the design of wagons, and again urged that there should be a standard design. Since the companies had to haul 650,000 privately owned trucks, there seemed little point in standardizing their own. Private-owner wagons were a remnant of the 'turnpike' railway, and these in particular ran overloaded, with worn-down axles and tyres because there was no proper system of inspection. By 1890 there were at least 200,000 coal trucks with dumb buffers; in 1903 it was reported that these wagons had been the cause of 333 accidents. No wagon owner was ever prosecuted for negligence, let alone manslaughter.

In the 1890s the major railway companies began to lubricate the axle bearings of the goods wagons with oil instead of the traditional 'yellow fat'. Oil flows better than grease over the moving surfaces and reduces the risk of a bearing collapsing from overheating. Private-owner wagons were described by John A. Aspinall, General Manager of the Lancashire & Yorkshire Railway, as 'the bane of English railways, a hindrance to progress, involving risks to safety and a constant source of unprofitable expense,'[9] – but even in the 1930s there were still plenty of PO wagons running on bearings lubricated with 'yellow fat'. Goods trains travelled at low speed out of respect for the lack of brakes and poor lubrication of some wagons. At the top of modestly steep inclines – 1 in 100 for instance – they had to stop to allow the guard to walk along the train to pin down the handbrakes. The relatively small capacity wagons available to carry the increasing traffic required more shunting and more trains to be run. Thus as traffic increased so did the expense of carrying it.

The railway companies agreed a common specification for open wagons, box vans and cattle trucks in 1904, and would have banned all others from their tracks, had they not met with total opposition from the wagon-building firms and private owners. It was not until 1914 that the railway companies managed to ban 'dumb buffered' wagons from their tracks. As late as 1918 the 'Advisory Council of the Ministry of Reconstruction' reported that British railway freight wagons were 'a riot of individuality',[10] with 200 different kinds of axle box and 40 types of handbrake, and that all wagons were of insufficient capacity. One hears much about the costs imposed on railway companies by the men demanding pay rises and little or nothing about those imposed by penny-pinching businessmen.

The companies, worried about their rising costs, were reluctant to spend on safety, and yet the costs of accidents were so great that, according to *The Engineer*,[11] any company fitting power brakes would recoup their outlay within two years. The companies' objection to power braking was that since the various, newly invented braking systems were untried they did not know which to choose. The North London Railway (NLR), a satellite of the L&NWR, was the first railway in Britain to use power brakes: in 1855 it used Miles's steam, then Jackson's hydraulic and finally Kendall's air brake.[12] The latter used an axle-driven pump to charge a reservoir with air at 45 lb psi. By the turning of a cock, this pressure entered the train pipe and was carried to a brake cylinder on each carriage. Within the cylinder a pair of pistons were forced outwards by air pressure to apply the brakes.[13] It was smooth in operation, powerful and continuous throughout the length of the train. Its disadvantage was that, in the event of an air hose breaking, the whole train was left without a brake; but in ordinary conditions it was a far better system than the LNWR's chain brake, to which the NLR then regressed.

In April 1874 the *Quarterly Review* commented in robust, period style: 'Instead of some-one being hung for an accident there is a mysterious controversy about points and signals between the Board of Trade and the railways.'[14] A Bill introduced in that year to enforce the installation of continuous braking was defeated by the influence of 24 railway Director-MPs and a fair sprinkling of railway Directors in the House of Lords. The railways' illiberal public image was thus reinforced, and in the General Election year of 1873, the magazine *Punch* advised its readers not to vote 'on any account' for a candidate who was 'a railway Chairman, Director or official of any kind'.[15]

The railway accident rate rose – although death and injury on railways nationwide was always far less common than on the streets of London. The public, inured to the latter, became thoroughly incensed with railway fatalities and demanded that the 'dictatorial' railway Directors at once install proper brakes, interlocked signalling, and 'absolute block' working; and furthermore, that they reduced the hours worked by railwaymen as an aid to safer working.

In mid-1874 a Royal Commission on Railway Operation was established. On Christmas Eve that year a terrible accident occurred on the GWR at Shipton-on-Cherwell. Two engines were hauling a fourteen-coach train when the tyre, riveted on to a carriage wheel, disintegrated. The drivers, looking back and seeing the derailed coach, immediately whistled for the guard's brake and then put their engines into reverse. There must have been an element of panic, for the men handled their train too roughly. The carriages were entirely without brakes and so ran into the suddenly decelerating engines; the leading carriage was crushed against the tender by the weight of the others ramming from behind. Derailed, unbraked carriages bounced about the track, tripping over wreckage, falling down the embankment. Thirty-four people were killed and sixty-five injured.

The sitting Royal Commission instigated comparative trials of braking systems, and these were held on the Midland Railway near Newark during June 1875. Six major companies took part, the GWR standing aloof. Under trial were four systems: the Fay & Newall and the Clark friction-clutch chain brake; the Smith non-automatic or 'simple' vacuum brake; the Sanders automatic vacuum brake; and the Westinghouse automatic air brake.

The friction-clutch chain brakes required coaches to be in 'permanently' coupled sets of five. Longer trains were thus made up of separately braked sections. The brake was available to the engine driver or the guard, and when applied, caused the carriages to decelerate sharply, tugging back against the engine and creating the danger of a breakaway (this actually happened during the trial). The danger was amplified when the train was made up of more than one set of chain-braked coaches (as would normally be the case), because then the two or more guards had to operate their braking mechanism simultaneously.

The Smith 'simple' vacuum brake was the invention of J.Y. Smith an American engineer whose misfortune it was to invent a third rate brake at about the same time as a fellow American, George

Westinghouse, had invented a first-rate system. The Smith brake consisted of an air ejector on the engine, connected to the 'train pipe' which was itself connected to the top of a large-diameter brake cylinder on each carriage. Each brake cylinder was permanently open to the atmosphere below the brake piston, but the space above the brake piston was closed. The train pipe was fixed to an airtight 'stop' at each end of the train. When atmospheric pressure existed above the brake piston, the brake was 'off'. When the driver operated the air ejector, air was drawn from the train pipe and from the brake cylinder above each brake piston, so that atmospheric pressure below the piston drove it upwards; this movement was used to force the brake blocks against the wheels. This was a smooth-acting, powerful brake, but it could not be used by the guard or a passenger, and if the train pipe came apart – as would happen during a derailment, or when a vehicle broke away from the train – the vacuum could not be created and there would be no brake.

The Sanders 'automatic' vacuum brake, was 99.9 per cent fail-safe. In this system the brake cylinders were closed vessels. The air ejector on the engine drew air out of the train pipe and the entire cylinder, above and below the piston, to a depression about 10 lb psi below that of atmosphere. The brake piston dropped to the floor of the cylinder under its own weight. To apply the brake the driver, the guard or a passenger would open a valve to admit atmospheric pressure (equal to about 10 lb psi) to the train pipe; this pressure entered each brake cylinder below the brake piston and lifted it, since there was a vacuum above the piston – a one-way value preventing air from reaching the space above the piston. The beauty of this system was that the brake was 'off' only for as long as a vacuum existed in the pipes and cylinders. If the train pipe was broken, atmospheric pressure replaced the vacuum in each brake cylinder and the brakes were applied on all vehicles.

The Westinghouse brake did all that the automatic vacuum brake did but because it acted more quickly, it stopped the train within a shorter distance (see Appendix 7). On dry rails it took only 19 secs and 913 ft to stop an MR train weighing 203 tons and travelling at 52 mph. On wet rails, the Fay & Newall chain brake stopped an L&YR train, weighing 186½ tons and travelling at 48½ mph, in 27½ secs and 1165 ft.[16] The Westinghouse was, however, very complicated and considerably more expensive, and required greater maintenance for its very intricate valves and its steam-operated air compressor (see Appendix 7). The Report of the Royal Commission in 1876 observed that the railway companies would rather pay compensation for a few accidents than pay for a good safety system, and recommended that: 'Every train should be provided with sufficient brake power to stop it absolutely within 500 yards at the highest speed at which it travels and upon any gradient.' This was supported by the Board of Trade, and a Bill was introduced that November to make automatic brakes and the 'absolute block' system obligatory. The Bill was debated early in 1876 and was defeated by the combined influence of the 120 or so railway Director MPs and Lords.[17]

In February 1876 James Staats Forbes, General Manager of the London, Chatham & Dover Railway (LC&DR), told his shareholders, with regard to continuous brakes, block telegraph and signal/point-lever interlocking, that he 'had had these things urged upon him for some time but he had been reluctant to involve the shareholders in a single shilling of outlay which could be avoided'. He required 'not mere theory but the strongest evidence that these things were required'.[18] The London, Brighton & South Coast Railway (LB&SCR), however, chaired by Samuel Laing, was more conscientious, and without waiting to be forced, began the process of installing power brakes. In December 1877 the Company informed the Board of Trade that it had fitted fifty engines and 500 carriages with the Westinghouse brake.[19] In 1878 the GWR began a rapid installation of the Sanders automatic vacuum brake.[20] The L&SWR followed in 1882.[21] The GER, NBR, NER and MR standardized on the Westinghouse, although the Midland later changed to the automatic vacuum after falling out with George Westinghouse.

The Manchester, Sheffield & Lincolnshire and the South Eastern Railway, both chaired by Sir Edward Watkin, took up the Smith brake, which forced the Great Northern to use it, since they were running over the MS&L.[22] Various other companies, including the Great Northern of Ireland, installed the Smith brake; it was cheap to build and, since there were two infinitely superior, systems to choose from, perhaps Smith was not asking a lot in royalties. Cheapness undoubtedly appealed to the businessman in Watkin, and his Chief Locomotive Engineer, the kindly Charles Sacre – who should have known better – dared not disagree.

The L&NWR, under the penny-pinching management of Richard Moon, continued with the cheap and dreadful chain brake. In 1880 Francis Webb patented a modification to it, fitting each wheel with a pair of clasping brake blocks; thus it became the 'Clark & Webb' brake and Webb received from the L&NWR a royalty for every vehicle fitted, despite the fact that the brake could not bring a train to a stand within the distance recommended by the Board of Trade, that it was useless if the carriages broke away, and that it had already contributed to some terrible smashes.[23] At the Annual General Meeting of L&NWR shareholders in 1883, Moon told the assembled throng the most outrageous lie: that it was 'impossible to have a better brake' than the Clark & Webb chain brake.[24]

In 1881 representatives of twelve companies who had chosen the 'vacuum brake' met at Euston, under the Chairmanship of Francis Webb (see Appendix 8) in an attempt to agree on a common system. Nine of the companies used the dangerous 'simple' vacuum brake and refused to change, but it was agreed that for vacuum brakes, whether simple or automatic, the MR's pipe-end coupling would be adopted as the standard. Webb could now fit a 'through' pipe beneath his chain-braked vehicles so that L&NWR rolling stock could be coupled into any vacuum-braked train without interrupting the continuity of the train pipe – even though the L&NWR vehicle would be without a brake.

Although the companies had agreed on a standard pipe-end coupling they could not agree about the positioning of the vacuum pipes on the vehicles, which meant that the brake pipes of different companies were likely not to reach across the gap between vehicles to be coupled. Caledonian Railway brake pipes were mounted in the centre of the buffer beam, Furness Railway put theirs 2 ft 8 in. from the centre. It was not until 1902 that the railway companies agreed, through the RCH Regulations, that all new rolling stock from that date would have the pipes as near the centre of the buffer beam as the coupling hook would allow.[25]

Only in 1884, when the entire passenger stock of the L&NWR had been equipped with the Clark & Webb patent chain brake, did Webb permit a change to his patented, dual system of automatic/Smith vacuum brake – and collect patent royalties as before. Webb's combined system allowed the driver to run with his brakes working under the Smith 'simple' or the Sanders 'automatic' system, and was potentially more dangerous than Smith's brake because a driver might become confused as to which system he was operating.

Fairly frequently accidents occurred as a result of using Smith's brake. On 16 July 1884 an MS&L express, fitted with the Smith brake, was derailed on the curve at Bullhouse colliery, Penistone.[26] The engine, designed by Charles Sacre, had broken its driving-wheel axle. Unbraked once the train pipe had parted, the carriages ran on until they fell off the embankment. Twenty-four men, women and children were killed. The Board of Trade Inspector, Major Marandin, criticized the brake. Since the engine driver was not to blame, no one could be charged with manslaughter. Sacre resigned his position on the MS&L, but Watkin and all the others using the brake continued to do so – and Smith continued to draw his royalties. By June 1887, 8010 coaches and 1616 engines in the British Isles had been fitted with it. Board of Trade figures[27] (see Appendix 9) for that month showed that out of a total of 8472 locomotives and 52,808 coaches, fewer than a third of the former and only half the latter were fitted with an automatic and fail-safe brake. Parliament, which had for half a century vigorously promoted a debilitating competition between railways, was curiously lethargic when it came to legislating on safety.

Then came the catastrophic Armagh crash of 12 June 1889, where the lack of every possible safety device was responsible for the large number of fatalities. Out of 600 passengers, 78 were killed and 250 injured,[28] numbers so terrible that at last common decency overcame *laissez-faire* principles and a 'Regulation of Railways' Bill was rushed in. For reference, there were the rejected Bills of 1871 and 1877, while the railwaymen's unions had been campaigning since 1882 for improvements to brakes and signalling. The Bill was presented to Parliament by Sir Michael Hicks-Beach, President of the Board of Trade, on 15 July, but had to be withdrawn on the 29th. It was re-presented on 3 July, had its First and Second Readings on 1 and 2 August and received the Royal Assent on the 30th. The Act obliged all railways to install continuous, automatic, fail-safe brakes on passenger trains, to pass trains along the line by the 'absolute block' system of signalling, combined with fool-proof interlocking of point- and signal-levers. The work was already well advanced on many lines (see Appendix 9), and a period of 18 months was allowed for all companies to bring themselves up to scratch.

On being forced by nothing less than Act of Parliament to install the automatic vacuum brake, after years of risking the lives of his passengers – including Queen Victoria – and his staff, Moon had the cheek to say of the automatic vacuum brake: 'This is not quite so certain in its operation as the old Clark–Webb brake.'[29] Smith and Webb had made a lot of money out of bad brakes, though it is only fair to say that Webb made amends posthumously by bequeathing the whole of his somewhat ill-gotten wealth to charitable causes within the railway town of Crewe. Charles Sacre was plagued with a terrible but honourable agony of guilt after the Bullhouse crash. On 3 August 1889, when the Bill to ban the Smith brake had passed its Second Reading, he shot himself.[30]

22

Guilty until Proven Innocent

THE 1889 REGULATION of Railways Act, dealing as it did with safety and thus with the provision of handsome signal boxes, with locomotives and carriages, is well known in railway history. The Railway and Canal Traffic Act of 1888[1] was no less important: in seeking to control railway charges it led to a severe curtailment of the railways' ability to cover their costs. This Act was the culmination of years of agitation against railways by farmers, traders and industrialists, who blamed their lack of prosperity on high railway charges. Up to 1874 there had been a comfortable annual increase in national wealth, but then until 1896 the trade of the country was generally considered to be in depression. In particular, foreign and colonial food, grown in bulk on vast acreages opened up by railways, was imported by the ship-load and transported by rail around Britain, undercutting local prices to the great detriment of British agriculture.

In 1886 Parliament convened a Select Committee on the Trade Depression. The Report[2] showed that British industrial output had actually increased during this period but that German and American goods were being produced at a faster rate and more cheaply. Newly unified, the Germans were well organized and state-directed, and because the state owned the railways, German industry was subsidized through very cheap rail transport charges. Bulk imports of grain and meat into Britain from the Empire, together with increasing home industrial production, gave the railways plenty to carry, and their gross revenues rose annually through the period of depression. The railways' 'image problem' became worse. Of necessity large corporations, they were perceived as 'monopolists' who, by definition, must be charging extortionate rates. Their reluctance where safety was concerned appeared as arrogance and increased the resentment of their critics. The greatest complaint was that they were overcharging the home market while giving concessions to foreign imports. A.H. Tatlow, of the Glasgow & South Western Railway, wrote:

The railway rates policy has developed long and short distance traffic and has aided the opening of new industries: fruit, vegetables, flowers, potatoes, milk, fish were all developed due to sympathetic railway rates. The bringing in of all this extra traffic has kept the [railways'] modest dividends going although carrying the traffic has increased the Companies' costs [see Appendix 10].

No protestations the companies could make would convince their customers, however, and the 1888 Act established a new Railway and Canal Commission, with wider powers of control. Under Section 7 local government authorities or Chambers of Trade were permitted to make a complaint to the Commissioners against a railway company on any matter over which the Commissioners had jurisdiction – even on matters in which they, the complainants, were not directly involved. Section 10 reinforced the Commissioners' jurisdiction over any railway charge judged by them to be 'unreasonable', and Section 11 gave the Commissioners the power to order a railway to provide such traffic facilities to the public as they, the Commissioners, felt was 'reasonable'.

All this was harking back to earlier Acts, but Section 24 was devastatingly new. It obliged the railway companies to 'submit to the Board of Trade a revised classification of merchandise traffic and a revised schedule of maximum rates and charges applicable thereto and fully state the amounts of all terminal charges'. Since the dawn of railways there had been constant argument over the payment necessary for services rendered at the terminal or the end of the haul: whether a company could make such a charge and, if so, how much the charge should be.

The companies had, in 1867, asked for a legal recognition of their right to charge this extra sum, and had been prepared in return, to accept a legal maximum terminal charge, irrespective of the service rendered. As with earlier reasonable proposals from the companies, Parliament had refused this; now, however, it obliged the railways to codify precisely what their charges were for the thousands of different items they carried, and to define exactly what their terminal charges were for each item at all the different terminals in every country siding and city station in the land. It was Parliamentary interference at its worst, prejudice blundering in on the square wheels of dogma and destroying the carefully negotiated prices between companies and customers. In 1889, when the laboriously revised schedules were handed in to the Board of Trade, they were accompanied by 4000 objections from traders.[3] Between 1889 and 1891 Sir Courtenay Boyle, the Permanent Secretary to the Board of Trade, Lord Balfour of Burleigh and representatives of the companies spent a total of eighty-five days thrashing out the maximum rates to be charged for the different classifications of goods.[4]

The companies were represented by their greatest managers and these men outwitted the Board of Trade. They agreed to the reduction in the maximum charge for some classifications but, by bringing pressure to bear, obtained a rise in the maximum level for others. This pressure consisted, in part at any rate, of threatening to withdraw all Bills then before Parliament which sought powers to enlarge and improve their respective railways.[5] However, they 'one and all'[6] disclaimed any intention of raising some charges to the new maxima in order to recoup their losses where the old maxima had been reduced. The increases were there solely to cover the future eventuality of a rise in costs of fuel and labour.

Mr Henry Lambert, General Manager of the GWR, declared: 'I do not know how we are to recoup ourselves for these heavy losses. After discussion with our customers we have arrived at rates which are mutually satisfactory and we could not, without interfering with trade in a serious manner, increase those rates which will be below maxima'.[7] Sir Henry Oakley of the GNR made a similar statement. Sir George Findlay, General Manager of the L&NWR, stated to the Board of Trade on this occasion: 'When our new rates are issued, I think the traders will find that they are very much as they were before . . . there will be very little, if any, material alteration in the rates.'[8] Relying on the good faith of such great railwaymen, the Board recommended to Parliament increased charges on a large number of classifications.

Parliament debated the new maximum charges and made them legally binding by Statutory Orders referred to in a new Railway &

Canal Traffic Act of 1892.[9] Over 50 million separate charges had been agreed,[10] and people thought that, on the whole, the benefit would be to the trader. In September 1891, however, the chief men of the railway companies met and agreed to recoup themselves as far as possible for the losses which would be made on the new, lower, maximum charges.[11] The new schedules took effect from 1 January 1893 and at once the maximum rates were charged. Some rates fell but others rose by 50 per cent and more. Contrary to the intention of the 1888 Act, the railways had gained more than they had lost, Parliament was inundated with complaints and the Government was at once annoyed and embarrassed.

Legally the companies were entitled to their action, but they had broken their promises. From such great corporations as the L&NWR and GWR it was a very public and extremely foolish show of bad faith. Sir George Findlay had been appointed by Sir Richard Moon, whose standard exhortation to all his Officers was: 'Remember first that you are a gentleman, remember next that you are a North Western Officer and that whatever you promise you must perform – therefore be careful what you promise but having promised it, take care that you perform it.'[12] Moon, who had retired from the L&NWR Chair in January 1891, had no responsibility for these broken promises but he would have been well aware of Findlay's bad faith. Still in office, Findlay died in March 1893, ten weeks after his treachery became public knowledge.

Mr Mundella, President of the Board of Trade, promised traders that if reasonable rates had not been submitted by Easter the Government would 'bring in a measure which shall have the effect of bringing the railway companies to their senses'. He went on: 'If the companies ask me "What are reasonable rates?" I would ask them in return, "What were your rates before 1 January? If they were then reasonable why have you now departed from them?"' In response the railway companies might have asked why they had spent nearly three months revising their charges if they were not then to be allowed to use them. In an attempt to prevent the companies from using the maximum rates it had only just sanctioned the Government passed yet another Railway & Canal Traffic Act in 1894. It consisted of a single section:

1. Where a railway Company has alone or jointly since 31 December 1892 directly or indirectly increased any rate or charge then if any complaint is made that the increase is unrea-

sonable it shall lie on the Company to prove that the increase is reasonable and for that purpose it will not be sufficient to show that the rate or charge is within any limit fixed by Parliament.

The railways had been put in the position of 'guilty until proven innocent'. The companies reduced their charges by private negotiation with individual traders, based on the usual commercial considerations – length of haul, regularity of the traffic, full wagon loads, full train loads – and the pricing situation returned, more or less, to how it had been prior to the upheavals of the 1892 Act. Writing in 1914, the railway official and historian Cleveland Stevens, observed: 'The 1892 Act was more destructive of competition than amalgamation because the most enterprising competitor will hesitate to reduce his prices if he knows he will not be allowed to raise them again.'[13] This was true but there is no doubt that companies did sometimes manage to increase charges.[14] However, there was a severe restriction on the companies' maximum charges, and this at a time when they were making greatly increased expenditure on better locomotives, rolling stock and facilities.

The period from 1889 to 1914 was a time of great social unrest and important political changes. Unemployment was rife, people worked incredibly long hours, and there were many strikes, some of them lasting weeks or months. The Fabian Society, the 'gas and water Socialists', was formed in 1884 and dedicated to reforming British society along non-competitive lines. Through the trade unions, ordinary working people were actively trying to improve their lives, and tens of thousands of railwaymen joined nationwide trade unions, forming a large political weight directed at obtaining a greater democracy and better standards of living for working people.

The railway companies, bred by Private Enterprise out of Adam Smith, were now in the Age of Social Responsibility. Lever Brothers built a garden village for their workers at Port Sunlight in 1887; the Cadbury family did the same at Bourneville in 1889. Times had changed – and the presence of railways had helped to bring about the change. Few railway companies were directly involved in social improvements, although the GWR operated a unique, medieval welfare service at Swindon and the MR established an orphanage – St Christopher's – at Derby (see Appendix 12). In the burgeoning mood of democracy, railway companies were expected to provide all good things to everyone; to the traders, frequent, fast and cheap goods trains; to the passengers, trains which were frequent, fast, cheap and luxurious, every one of them with a dining-car; to their workers, better pay and shorter hours; to the parishes through which their rails passed, large sums in parochial rates. The railway Company was usually the largest ratepayer in a parish even when nothing was more complicated than a length of plain track traversed its boundaries.

Some members of the Liberal Party and all the new-born Socialists wanted railways nationalized – either on the Marxist principle of 'democratic ownership of the means of production', or on the Liberal principle that, since they had the monopoly of transport which was vital to the national well-being they ought to be owned by the state to protect the public from alleged overcharging. The railways' shareholders also expected respectable dividends. Thus the companies were being squeezed from both sides.

There were several matters in the field of social responsibility, where the companies had a moral duty which, if taken up, would be very costly to them. One was to reduce the cruelly long working hours of the men; another was to rehouse city slum-dwellers displaced by railway works. The companies had not only paid landowners handsomely to buy their slums, but had in addition paid generous compensation for their loss. Costs had to be saved somewhere, so the vulnerable, evicted poor were ignored.

A very few voices were raised in their defence, prominent among them that of Charles Pearson, Solicitor to the City of London. He had agitated continuously from 1845 until his death in 1862 for the railways to be under statutory obligations to rehouse those who had lost their homes to railway building. He gave evidence before the 1846 Committee that established the 'Quadrilateral', to advocate a single terminal for London in order to avoid so much destruction of housing. He wanted model villages built on the fringes of London and exceptionally cheap trains to bring the working men and women from them into the city centre. He was ahead of his time, but as the liberal conscience of the nation developed, his ideas were taken up.[15]

In May 1864 the GWR and the Met. voluntarily honoured an agreement made earlier with Pearson, by running workmen's trains from Southall. The LC&DR's 1860 Metropolitan Extension Bill for a railway from Loughborough Junction, through Brixton and Battersea, to Victoria, was intended to give a route from the City to the West End. It cut through a dense concentration of housing and displaced thousands of poor people. The LC&DR's Act obliged the Company to run two workmen's trains daily between Loughborough Park and Ludgate

Hill at fares 'that would not pay for the coke', as one shareholder put it. The trains began running on 27 March 1865.[16] The GER obtained an Act in 1864 to extend its line to a new terminus at Liverpool Street. Again, thousands of people would be made homeless, and the Act contained a clause obliging the Company to run trains the 21¾ miles from rural Enfield through Lower Edmonton, then a market gardening area, to Liverpool Street, for 2d return.[17] The line was opened in 1872 and the cheap fares stimulated house-building. Very soon the market gardens of Edmonton disappeared under regiments of red-brick houses. In 1871 the population of Edmonton was 14,500; ten years later it had risen to 23,500.[18]

The provision of cheap trains became a favourite with politicians and social reformers, as a way of enabling working people to leave the slums for decent, suburban housing. From 1860, Acts for railway widenings or enlarged stations in London always contained a clause obliging the Company to run workmen's trains to the suburbs.

The railways, as usual, could not gain public approval. They ran more than their legal quota of these trains – although this may have been because the engines and carriages used on this kind of work were unsuitable for anything else but needed to be kept busy. A demand was certainly created by the cheap fares, and the crowded conditions – thirty to a compartment, boys in the luggage racks – soon became a favourite scandal for the London newspapers, with the railways being blamed for squeezing a profit out of the poor working man. Following the recommendations of the 1882 Select Committee on Artisans and Labourers' Dwellings, the 1883 Cheap Trains Act[19] gave the Board of Trade and the Railway Commissioners the power to order the companies to run workmen's trains, and abolished the government tax on train fares of 1d a mile or less. The 'cheap fares' theory worked well in that it helped persuade people to move into the new suburbs, but it did nothing at all for the poorest majority: unskilled men who worked as casual, day labourers, close to home.

The companies believed that the cost of running ultra-cheap trains was less than the cost of building new houses for the displaced poor. In fact they now had to provide, in perpetuity, a social service with little or no profit.[20] The cheap trains were crowded only at certain times; earlier and later services ran half-full, and at best, did no more than break even. In order to run these cheap services, many engines and carriages had to be specially built. The runs involved frequent stopping and starting, hard acceleration, and the engine burned an inordinate amount of fuel. The increase in track occupation eventually required expensive widening of tracks and enlargement of terminal stations. Liverpool Street station, for instance, opened in 1874 at a cost in excess of £2 million,[21] had to be greatly enlarged in 1890, mainly to accommodate trains carrying passengers paying very cheap fares.

In 1874 a House of Commons Standing Order[22] was made, whereby any Bill seeking powers to widen railways and demolish the houses of the labouring classes should have a clause obliging that Company to rehouse those whom its works displaced. For ten years the Standing Order was ignored or evaded. In 1884 a Royal Commission on 'The Housing of the Working Classes'[23] was established at which the veteran campaigner for social justice, Lord Shaftesbury, gave evidence:

It is terrific to see the condition of the people before a demolition begins. It is perfectly true that notice is given according to form but poor, working men cannot attend to that sort of thing and in fact they delay to begin to act because they have no time to look about for houses and they rarely act until the men come to pull the roof off their heads and then I have seen the people like the people of a besieged town running to and from and not knowing what on earth to do.[24]

Parliament thereafter made 'a serious attempt' to enforce the 1874 Standing Order on rehousing.[25] In 1888 the London County Council was established by Act of Parliament. Invoking the new Railway & Canal Traffic Act, the new LCC was able to champion the rights of London's poor when these were trampled by a railway company. When the GER and L&SWR had to demolish slums to widen their stations at Liverpool Street and Waterloo, the reform-minded LCC insisted that the 1874 Standing Order on rehousing was obeyed. The railway companies were thus forced to build houses as well as run the cheap trains made obligatory by earlier Acts. In 1890 the GER and L&SWR opened the first railway-built rehousing scheme.[26] In 1897, the GCR constructed the Wharncliffe Gardens estate of six, five-storey tenement blocks near Marylebone station, to rehouse some of those displaced by railway construction. Nevertheless, the railways were always strongly opposed to rehousing: none of them built new housing before existing houses were demolished; nor did they make an honest tally of those to be displaced, which meant that no railway company ever rehoused all the people it rendered homeless.[27]

The idea that railway companies should build houses for those their works displaced was not universally accepted. In an article, 'The

British Railway Position',[28] written in 1902, the contemporary econo mist Sir George Paish expressed the view that it was 'the height c unwisdom to increase the cost of transportation by compelling th railways to rehouse the working classes'. He thought that, since th improvements causing the displacement were for the good of every one, the cost should fall on the taxpayer (see Appendix 11).[29]

23

The Forth Bridge, Strikes and the 'Golden Age'

THE PERIOD 1890–1914 has been described as the 'Golden Age' of railways. It was certainly a 'Golden Age' of great engineering magnificence, both in fixed structures and rolling stock, of greater speeds and improved comfort for the passengers; it was also 'golden' in terms of the vast amount of money expended by the companies. On the other hand the golden expenditure did not produce golden profits even though railwaymen of every department worked long hours, usually for low wages. Between 1888 and 1894 Parliament had placed financial restraints on the companies. The combination of high capital outlay and a comparative lack of freedom to raise charges for their improved services was unfortunate. The period should in fact be divided into three: an Age of Intensified Competition, which could not be sustained; followed by an Age of Agreement where standards were maintained static; and the only railway 'age' which actually did last from 1890 until 1914: the Age of Industrial Unrest, as the railway workers set out in earnest to achieve proper pay and working conditions.

The enormous steel web of the Forth bridge, completed in 1890, is the perfect emblem of the 'Golden Age' of railways. It was then considered to be the greatest triumph of British engineering, the apogee of a long period of constant development. Its impact went beyond railways and long outlasted the 'Golden Age'. For sixty years the image of the bridge represented the excellence of British products in general – honest, reliable, supremely practical – and was respected as such appearing as a symbol of quality on items as diverse as tins of biscuits and advertisements for ladies' stockings.

The need for a Forth bridge had been felt for years, but until railways were able to amalgamate in order to increase their financial strength and to produce a strong enough common purpose, such a vast undertaking was impossible. The North Eastern was formed in 1854 and enlarged in 1863, the North British Railway was formed in 1862 after the dust of the 1866 crash had settled, these two, together with the Great Northern and the Midland, formed the Forth Bridge Railway Company (FBR) in 1873. The bridge was to have been a suspension bridge designed by Thomas Bouch, who was the Engineer of a bridge then being erected, under his supervision, across the Firth of Tay. Bouch's Tay bridge was opened to traffic on 1 June 1878, just about the time that the first stone pillar for the Forth bridge was under construction. Towards the end of June Queen Victoria was taken across the Tay bridge on her way from Balmoral to Windsor, and the following day she knighted Bouch for his great achievement. Eighteen months later, on 28 December 1879, the Tay bridge was blown down during a particularly fierce gale. A train was crossing at the time and all seventy-three people on it were killed. The subsequent inquiry found that Bouch had not designed the bridge properly, and that he had allowed the contractor to get away with outrageously bad workmanship.

The collapse of the Tay bridge destroyed Bouch, severely damaged the reputation of British engineering, and caused the FBR temporarily to abandon its project. The Company was re-formed by the same group of railways and a new Act was obtained on 11 July 1881. The MR, already in possession of its Settle route to Scotland, subscribed one million pounds, a third of the required capital.[1]

As well as crossing 1¼ miles of water, the Forth bridge had to redeem the reputation of the British engineering profession. It was designed in steel by Benjamin Baker and Sir John Fowler, proponents of the use of steel in bridges when wrought iron was the accepted material, and was fabricated and erected under the direction of William Arrol (see Appendix 13). For the GWR crossing of the River Severn they had proposed a 1000-ft single-span steel bridge in 1864 and two 800-ft spans in 1871,[2] but they had been unable to convince Gooch and his engineers; the following year, the GWR set out to construct their great tunnel, vastly expensive to build and to maintain. The Forth bridge used a Brunellian idea inasmuch as it depended on the inherent strength of metal tubes, although the method of utilizing their strength differed.

The double-track railway approached the river on a deep lattice girder, supported at intervals on stone pillars until it reached the support of the cantilevers. The southern, or 'Queensferry' approach viaduct is 1743 ft long, and the northern, or 'Fife' approach viaduct 1047 ft. The railway tracks are carried over the water by three canti-levered spans which support between them two 350-ft-long, ordinary girder spans. The central cantilever is founded on Inchgarvie Island at mid-stream and is known as the 'Garvie, the southernmost cantilever is the Queensferry and the northernmost, the Fife. At both its north-ern and southern extremities the 'Garvie cantilever supports one end of a 350-ft girder bridge; the other ends of these bridges are supported by the Queensferry and Fife piers.

The cantilever principle allowed the enormous structure to be self-supporting under construction, so that it did not have to be built on supportive timbering rising out of the water. As they grew, the main tubes carried not only the steam cranes and hydraulic cranes which hoisted the plates and other supplies from the barges on the water, but also the giant hydraulic riveting machines and oil-fired rivet-heating furnaces – the latter weighing half a ton apiece. The cantilevers sup-ported the same deep, lattice girder that was used on the approaches, and this 'internal' girder was made strong enough to support a 3-ton crane at the outer end of 100 ft of its unsupported length, to enable the small bridges to be erected beyond the reach of cranes mounted on the extremities of the cantilevers.

The core of the design are the three self-supporting 'towers', each formed of four 12-ft-diameter tubes of 1½-in.-thick steel plate. Each of these tubes is anchored to its own column of Aberdeen granite, founded in bedrock. From these columns, which are arranged four-square, the tubes rise in pairs, inclining inwards towards the other pair, until their upper ends are 330 ft above the Firth. All four tubes were tied at the bottom by 12-ft-diameter horizontal tubes; they were cross-braced diagonally by 8-ft tubes and horizontally by latticed struts. The three central towers took a year to erect and cost the lives of seventeen men.[3]

Each granite column was built within a 70-ft-diameter metal

caisson, 90 ft high to break the surface of the water. The men entered through an air lock and worked by electric light in a pressurized compartment at the base, the compressed air preventing the ingress of water. The firm of contractors for this work was French, and they used French, Italian, Belgian and German labour. Some men died from 'Caissons Disease', caused by bubbles of compressed air getting into their bones and expanding in ordinary atmospheric pressure to give terrible pain and, ultimately, to destroy the bone. Under these conditions the men created the massive columns, using 740,000 cu. yds of the hardest Aberdeen granite and 21,000 tons of Portland cement.

After the central towers had been erected, the top and bottom cantilevered tubes were built out from them, extending north and south from the tower, keeping the weight on each side of the tower approximately the same at all times. Some plates were cut to shape and drilled on site, other parts were fabricated in steel foundries in Motherwell, Glasgow and Swansea. William Arrol modified his patent hydraulic riveting machines to fit within the tubes and to move up as the tube extended. Fifty-two thousand tons of steel plates were rolled to shape and transported to the bridge, in the order in which they were required, 8 million rivets had to be manufactured and transported, then heated white-hot in furnaces mounted on the tubes, 8 million holes had to be drilled in thousands of tons of steel plates, with matching precision, and each hole reamered parallel. By no means all the rivets were closed by machine: much of the structure was inaccessible to the machines and millions of rivets, approximately 1 in. in diameter and from 1 in. to 11 in. long, were pushed into their holes, white hot, and hammered into place by hand.[4]

The riveting gangs consisted of three men and a boy. In the tradition of shipbuilding, boys were employed to heat the rivets and to throw them, using long-handled tongs, to the riveters. The speed with which the bridge was built actually depended on how fast these teenage boys could heat the rivets, how accurately they could throw them – and the men could catch them. Eight hundred rivets per day per boy was the usual rate. They were paid by the hundred rivets at around 4½d per hour; adult riveters got 8d an hour. A gang could heat and close 800 rivets a day, and a bonus was paid when they were working in high winds or freezing cold. Nothing appears to have stopped the work, neither summer heat nor autumn gales nor winter frost. Tools or pieces of equipment were knocked off working platforms, falling on to men below. William Baker reported that he saw a spanner fall 300 ft and pass through a 4-in.-thick timber plank at the bottom of the drop. Sometimes men became numb with cold, and fell into the water. Boats were permanently on station to rescue the fallen.

On 2 June 1887 six men fell from a considerable height. Two of them struck a girder and were killed, two fell into the water unharmed, two clung on to girders high over the water. The man nearest to the main part of the bridge told his rescuers to concentrate on the man further out because he had a less secure grip and was more in danger of falling. Both men were saved. Another danger was from the electric carbon-arc lighting, intended to make life easier. When an arc failed, the entire circuit ceased, plunging the whole workforce into that especial darkness which follows the cessation of bright light.

As the bridge grew, the workforce expanded until there were 4600 men and boys at work on the structure. According to Arrol, drunkeness was 'the curse of the Works', forcing him to import more foreigners to replace the Scots. Arrol gave the drunks at least a second chance, not sacking them at once but sending them home with instructions to come back when they were sober. The men on the bridge were brave and reckless – great spirits. They learned to live with constant peril and became blasé. All the exhortations and safety measures could not stop people taking deliberate risks, like jumping the gap between opposing girders when drunk – or sober. Arrol built a reading-room and a dining-room, and set up a Sick and Accident Club, membership of which was compulsory. He contributed £200 to start it off, and every worker had to give an hour's pay to a maximum of 8d. For this they got free medicine, ambulance and hospital attention. Pay when off duty sick was 9s to 12s per week, there was a lump sum in case of disablement, and widows were helped with funeral expenses.[5]

A vital and very difficult job was that of continuously fixing the longitudinal centre-line of the bridge and of indicating it clearly to those on the bridge whose task it was to join up the various parts. The problem arose from the expansion of the steel, the 'whippy-ness' of the long tubes, and the force of the wind. The bridge ran north/south and the sun's rays fell on it from the east and then the west as the earth rotated. This caused the metal to heat and expand on one side, bending the tubes away from the sun, first towards the west and then towards the east; the effect of strong wind also distorted the inclination of the tubes to a considerable extent. The tubes of each central tower had to be tied with diagonal members all the way up their length, but before they were permanently joined the tubes had to be pulled precisely and centrally into position, above the centre-line of the bridge at rail-level. There was the same problem with the 600-ft-long tubes arching out over the water to form the cantilevers. To provide a proven datum line through the centre of the bridge was a vital task, maintained with precision even in the worst winter weather conditions by Mr W.N. Bakewell. Despite great care, the bridge tops and cantilevers were built 2 in. off-centre along the whole length of the bridge, the bias being towards the east. This might have been caused by the prevailing westerly winds and the fact that the westerly, afternoon sun is hottest.[6]

The junctions between the 'Garvie cantilever and the 350-ft spans on each side of it are constructed to allow for longitudinal expansion and contraction due to changes in temperature, and for lateral movement due to wind pressure, but where these 350-ft spans meet the Queensferry and Fife cantilevers they are bolted tightly to them and are, for all practical purposes, part of them. Vertical deflections, arising from loading by trains, are taken up by the elasticity of the steel.

The expansion and contraction of the steel caused great difficulty in joining the sections of the bridge in the first instance: a rise or fall of one degree Fahrenheit resulted in an expansion or contraction of an eighth of an inch.[7] The junctions between the top and bottom tubes of the 'Garvie cantilever and the girders of the 350-ft-span central bridges on each side of them had to be made when the air temperature was 60 degrees Fahrenheit. This was a matter of great skill and patience. After several days' waiting, on the afternoon of 10 October 1889, with the sun on the west side, the temperature rose sufficiently to expand the tubes on that side and the bolts were pushed through their holes. But on the side of the bridge in shadow the tubes were ¼in. short. Rags soaked in oil were placed 60 ft inside the tubes and fired, the tube expanded and the bolt holes, coming into line, allowed the bolts to be pushed home. The process had to be repeated at the other end of the 'Garvie pier for top and bottom booms, and not until 14 November were all the tubes connected. The last rivet was hammered in by Edward, Prince of Wales, on 4 March 1890, in a squall of wind and rain. William Arrol and Benjamin Baker received knighthoods and Sir John Fowler received a Baronetcy. The Forth Bridge Company spent about £3,227,000 in bridging the Forth, out of which £378,000 went not to steel plate, but on legal fees in Parliament.[8] The cost should also be counted in the lives of the fifty-seven men killed during construction.[9]

Like the Severn tunnel, the benefit of the vast investment in the

Forth bridge was not felt until more money had been spent to connect it to the rest of the system. While the cost of the bridge had been shared, that of the approach lines and of a new route, some 30 miles long, to connect the bridge with Perth via Dunfermline, had to be borne solely by the NBR. These new routes reduced the mileage from Edinburgh to Dundee from 91¼ miles to 59¼ miles, while the rail distance from Edinburgh to Perth was reduced from 70¼ to 47¾ miles.[10]

Before the Forth bridge was opened, the NBR station at Edinburgh had been saturated with trains. Their Waverley station in Edinburgh had last been enlarged in 1860 and even then it was inadequate; by 1890 the lack of platforms, sidings and goods loops – and the fact of only having double-track approaches – created, according to Professor Foxwell, 'scenes of confusion so chaotic that a sober description of them is incredible to those who have not themselves survived it'. *The Engineer* magazine stated that 'The North British has been notoriously mismanaged for some time. The block of traffic at Edinburgh since the opening of the Forth bridge has become a disgrace.'[11] The NBR's Glasgow–Edinburgh expresses took 3½ hrs for the 47 miles, and the fastest expresses from London were subjected to the indignity of a 2-hr crawl for the three miles from Corstophine into Waverley.[12]

The delays created by the NBR's mismanagement increased train crews' already over-long hours of work. The NBR systematically overworked their men; at holiday times train crews might work 25 hrs consecutively, and in 1890 an average working day for a North British train crew was 13½ hrs.[13] Because they were paid for their time according to the scheduled time of their train in the timetable, they received no overtime pay. It was normal to work 90 hrs in a week and receive pay for 60. Work done on a Sunday received no extra pay. This was the general situation throughout industrial Scotland, and a huge wave of resentment had been building up against the injustice. The men were held in check because they knew well the consequences to themselves and their families of striking. The additional congestion and long hours following the opening of the Forth bridge tipped them over the edge, and the long-threatened, all-Scotland railway strike was precipitated on 21 December 1890.

The companies recruited some 'blackleg' labour to run a few trains which then ran the risk of hitting boulders placed on the line by striking railwaymen. Through weeks of bitter cold the railwaymen held out for better conditions of work. Those railwaymen living in railway houses were evicted under riot conditions, with 25,000 iron workers and miners supporting the railwaymen and a regiment of cavalry supporting the railway Company.[14] Scottish industry was severely curtailed and workers suffered lay-offs. The strike was called off on 29 January 1891, with no gains to the men beyond a promise to consider their grievances and not to prosecute any striker.

The outcome of the companies' deliberations was that they agreed to pay the men extra for working on a Sunday and an effort was made to book train crews off duty after they had been at work for 12 hrs; nevertheless, the Company's requirements remained paramount. Beyond this, however, public attention had been focused on the dangerously long hours worked by railwaymen, and Parliament was obliged to conduct a public investigation.[15]

The NBR obtained an Act of Parliament in July 1891 to purchase the land needed to quadruple the line for several miles on each side of Waverley station, and to rebuild the station itself. The quadrupling required a strip off Princes Gardens, which caused great anguish among the City Fathers – the Lord Provost vowed that not an inch of ground would be sold at any price – but the problem of rail congestion was so great that the City had to give way. Three new tunnels were driven and a 23-acre site was purchased and cleared of houses, not only for a grand station but also for a hotel of 'international' proportions. The work began in 1892 and the upheaval must have made delays even worse. It was finished towards the end of 1898: the new Waverley station had nineteen platforms with a total length of 4660 yds under a magnificent glass and iron roof. The station was then able to (and did) handle fifty-seven trains per hour.[16]

Work on the North British Railway Hotel at Edinburgh Waverley station was commenced in 1895. The hotel was designed by William Hamilton Beattie[17] and had ten storeys, rising from the platforms below street-level to a clock tower 90 ft above the roof. It was a massively solid, severe-looking block, 'combining the Old Scottish architecture of the Old Town with the rather severe Classical style of the New Town'.[18] Inside were 700 rooms, including a central Palm Court on the street-level floor, the 'Mahogany Room', a ballroom and shops. There were over 300 bedrooms and all ten storeys were connected to platform-level by steam-operated lifts. By the time it was opened, in October 1902, it had cost the NBR over £500,000; so magnificent was it, that its first General Manager was paid £1000 per annum.[19]

The Caledonian Railway could not stand idly by and let their great rival overshadow them. At the opposite end of Princes Street, within sight of the North British, the Caley raised an equally expensive, huge and magnificent hotel, which opened in December 1903.[20]

The opening of the Forth bridge in 1890 does coincide neatly with the dawn of the Age of Competition. In 1888 the L&NWR and GWR lagged behind the MR and GNR in terms of speed and passenger comfort on long-distance expresses (local trains on any railway were primitive), but with the Old Guard out of the way the new managements at once began to catch up. The GWR's Superintendent of the Line to replace Tyrrell was N.J. Burlinson. He was in charge for only five years, 1889–94, but in that period the number of 50-mph express trains on the GWR rose from nine per day to thirty-five daily and the mileage covered at that average speed from 310 to 2245.[21]

The GWR had no restaurant-cars until 1896, but on 7 March 1892 it introduced the first modern express train in Britain. This consisted of four 56-ft-long bogie-coaches, seating 1st-, 2nd- and 3rd-class passengers. The carriages were steam-heated by under-seat radiators supplied from the locomotive, they had corridors with connecting gangways between them, were built with a clerestory roof for added height and light, and were equipped with lavatories. These coaches were panelled with walnut and satinwood and upholstered in broadcloth – buttoned, Morocco leather in the 'Smoking' compartments. In each compartment there was an electric bell-push by which the guard could be summoned, and they were the first carriages in Britain to be equipped with passenger access to the train's vacuum brake. The old idea of a 'communication cord', running under the eaves of the carriage roofs to a bell on the engine, was utilized, though this was now attached to a valve at the end of each carriage so that, when pulled, it opened the valve to allow air into the vacuum train pipe. In 1900 the 'cord' was brought inside the carriages. The train was put into service on the Paddington–Birkenhead run, in competition with the L&NWR, which was also building luxuriously expensive trains.

On 2 June 1890, after many years of abortive plans, considerable expense, and sometimes working through 'front' companies, the L&SWR managed to create a double-track route from Exeter, around the north of Dartmoor, through Okehampton and Tavistock, to Plymouth. This gave them a main line route from Waterloo to Plymouth North Road 16¾ miles shorter than the GWR's – even though the L&SWR route between Exeter and Plymouth was 5 miles longer than that of the GWR and passed over a summit twice as high.[22] The L&SWR

route east of Exeter also contained longer and steeper gradients than the equivalent stretch on the GWR.

Whether the L&SWR was wise to spend money on lonely, moorland railways is very much open to question. Its true vocation was to run from Waterloo to Southampton and Bournemouth, over which route it had a monopoly. The Company did not abuse its power; Southampton and Bournemouth owed their developing prosperity entirely to the fine train service of the L&SWR which, in return, gained a heavy traffic over a relatively short line.

West of Exeter on the GWR in 1890, the route was purely broad (7-ft) gauge, and until this was converted to the standard gauge the GWR was unable adequately to respond to L&SWR advances. In the past the GWR had hardly bothered to compete: Gooch had felt they had traffic enough without fighting expensively for it – but Gooch had gone. The conversion to standard gauge of 213 miles of broad-gauge track, from Exeter to Penzance, in a single weekend in May 1892, was a magnificent example of GWR engineering expertise and organization (and, of course, of the skill and commitment to the job of hundreds of workmen). Thereafter, the GWR was free to modernize its west of England route – beginning with the introduction of its superb, new corridor trains. The L&SWR (with Surrey Warner, an ex-GWR Swindon Carriage Works man, in charge of carriage design) had to respond, and so the spiral of passenger comfort – and costs – rose.

Since the 1850s the GNR and MR had attempted to invade East Anglia, while the incumbent of East Anglia, the Great Eastern Railway, spent heavily to break out into the north Midlands and Yorkshire. Between 1870 and 1900 the GER forced its way most expensively north-east – building railways jointly with the GNR or funding railways competitively against the GNR and MS&L – to reach the coalfields and industry of Doncaster and Sheffield, and thus, to siphon off GNR, MSL *and* MR traffic.

In November 1892 the GER realized an ambition dating back to 1836 and, with the co-operation of the GNR and NER, got a route to York. This was 26 miles longer than the GNR route, which had better gradients and far fewer junctions to restrict speed. Undaunted, the GER ran express trains from Liverpool Street to York, via Cambridge, March, Spalding and Lincoln. It also instituted the 'York Continental', to and from York and Harwich, for the Hook of Holland. This was Britain's first 'all class' dining-car express.

On 1 July 1893 the MR and GNR jointly purchased the bankrupt

Eastern & Midlands Railway for £1.2 million. Out of their respective revenues, they each guaranteed a permanent 3 per cent dividend, equal to £18,000 a year, to E&MR shareholders. One reason why the E&MR was bankrupt was because the MR had reneged on an earlier agreement to route traffic over it, but had instead treacherously handed Norfolk traffic over to the GER at Peterborough.[23] Having bought the line cheaply, there was no more handing over of traffic to the GER. The 170 miles of routes were now vested in a 'Midland & Great Northern Railway Joint Committee', a semi-autonomous colony based at Melton Constable under the leadership of its Engineer and Locomotive Superintendent, William Marriot. After meeting all its working and maintenance costs it contributed to the owning companies an annual surplus varying over the years to 1914 between £80,000 and £90,000 per annum, out of which the £36,000 was deducted.[24]

While the Midland was buying into the Cambridgeshire fens and the sweetly pretty slopes and beaches of north Norfolk, it was also battling to complete a railway through the Hope valley, west of Sheffield, to make a route to Manchester in competition with the long-established route of the MS&L. The MR's routes was opened to passenger traffic on 25 June 1894, at a cost of one million pounds. This included the 6230-yds-long Totley tunnel into the Hope valley at the Sheffield end, the 3702-yds-long Cowburn tunnel at the valley's western end, and a large new station at Heaton Mersey.

The MR and GNR wanted to develop the east coast holiday traffic, encouraging tourists while capturing the GER's traffic in coal, fish, grain and agricultural produce. This meant doubling the line, strengthening the bridges and bringing on more powerful locomotives and better carriages. Investment poured on to the light loam and sandy beaches of north and east Norfolk, enriching the scattered community. The poor little fishing village of Sheringham suddenly sprouted redbrick and stockbrokers' Tudor, and the holidaymakers promenaded on the sea wall constructed by the Midland and Great Northern. An optimistic German named Krundell built a hotel on Waybourne Hill, just above the railway station.[25] An entirely new coastal resort town was instigated by the M&GN Join Committee at Mundesley, at the end of a branch line from North Walsham built as the joint property of the M&GN and the GER.

Cromer got a second station, to which the enthusiastic MR and GNR ran as many excursions from the Midlands and London as they could, doubling the number of visitors to Cromer's hotels and board-

ing houses and creating a boom in land prices and the building trade
Small towns like Aylsham, Fakenham and North Walsham also
acquired a second station. The brickworks in the little village of
Barney, previously 8 miles from a railway, now had a station on it
doorstep, and so it was in many remote places. Parish workhouses and
roads benefited from an increased income, since the railway company
had to pay parochial taxes in accordance with its profits. Labourer
who had no better prospects than a lifetime on the farm were given th
chance of a career.[26]

L&YR coaches came to Cromer from Manchester, and Midland
and London holidaymakers arrived at Yarmouth and Cromer on
dining-car expresses; there was even an MR 'through-carriage' daily
from Gloucester. Commercial travellers were provided with their own
trains on Mondays and Fridays to convey them and their hampers of
samples from and to the industrial Midlands and north Norfolk
Norwich and Yarmouth. The GNR's route from London to Norwich
Cromer and Yarmouth was circuitous compared with that of the GER
However, from 1895 the GNR ran the 3.00 p.m. King's Cross–Cromer
express, stopping only at Finsbury Park and Peterborough before
Melton Constable, and reaching Cromer, 168½ miles from London
in 225 mins, an overall average of 45 mph. In 1898 a second GNR
'London–Cromer Tourist Express' was instituted.[27]

The GER's response was to convert certain locomotives to oil-firing
in order to increase their range and power; to lay in locomotive wate
pick-up troughs at Ipswich and Tivetshall so that there was no need to
stop for water; and, with a new curve at Norwich that would avoid the
terminal station, to run Liverpool Street to Cromer expresses (first
stop North Walsham, 130 miles), completing the 138-mile journey in
175 mins, an average speed of 47.3 mph.[28]

On 1 November 1875 the MR had leased – jointly with th
L&SWR – the bankrupt Somerset & Dorset Railway. The main ben
eficiary of the lease was its contractor, Charles Waring, MP, who had
been responsible for the construction of the western section of the
M&GN. The S&DJR consisted of 7½ miles of semi-derelict, steeply
graded single track, from Bournemouth to Bath, with a 24-mile
branch from Evercreech Junction across the Somerset marshes to
Burnham-on-Sea, and two more branches off that. The track was in a
terrible state, the engines and rolling stock unequal even to the task of
running a local railway. Leasing this line looks more like an act
of mercy than a commercial venture, and there seems to be some

evidence that the companies did not fully realize what they were taking on.[29] However, as with the M&GNJR, a great human epic grew out of the expenditure.

The MR and the L&SWR spent heavily to bring the Somerset & Dorset line up to main line standards, the MR supplying larger engines and better rolling stock while the L&SWR carried out improvements to the civil engineering works and signalling. Between 1886 and 1892 the line was doubled – with the exception of the 4 miles from Bath to Midford, 1¼ miles of which was in tunnel – and heavy rails were laid to take the heavier engines. Express trains began running between Bath and Bournemouth from about 1890, with a fleet of five MR-built 4–4–0 locomotives hauling 'through carriages' from Birmingham, Derby and Manchester. These engines, good as they were, could not cope with the gradients over the high Mendips and in 1903 the Midland found itself producing larger machines for the line.

During the 1890–1903 period, the MR's enterprise covered not only a new main line between Sheffield and Manchester and expenditure on the two 'Joint' railways at opposite ends of the country; the Company also made loans totalling £244,000 to the bankrupt Midland & South Western Junction Railway, to which it had no formal ties.[30] The M&SWJR was a contractor's speculation, a ramshackle route from the GWR near Cheltenham to the L&SWR at Andover, but with MR money and an energetic Manager, Sam Fay, seconded from the L&SWR, its track and rolling stock was brought up to a reasonable standard. Although neither the MR nor the L&SWR ever owned or leased the line, it gave both companies a direct route from north to south, something particularly coveted by the MR. This route became famous for conveying Cunard liner crews between ships at Liverpool and Southampton, and for the vast quantities of Burton beer it carried into the southern counties. During the Great War it was of major strategic importance.

The railway companies had, since the late 1840s, taken people to the seaside and built hotels. It could be argued that the railways initiated the British hotel industry and set the standards of excellence. Torquay benefited from the railway in 1848, Eastbourne and Folkstone from 1849. In 1859 the Quaker family of Pease – still directing the Stockton & Darlington Railway – extended the S&DR line from Redcar to the tiny fishing village of Saltburn and, with the approval of the land-owner, Lord Zetland, established an 'Improvement Company' to build the Zetland Hotel and Britannia Mansions on the towering cliffs and to develop Saltburn into a resort. The NER, which absorbed the S&DR in 1863, developed Scarborough into one of the most important resorts in Britain.

The MS&L, having already transformed Grimsby into one of the most important fishing and import/export docks on the east coast, now went into the seaside entertainment business and built the colonnaded delights of Cleethorpes; while the GNR, not to be outdone, built the railway to bracing Skegness and so established 'Nottingham-by-the-Sea'. From 1865 the Lynn & Hunstanton Railway (worked by the GER) turned the humble hamlet of Hunstanton into a very genteel seaside resort from which day-trippers were excluded by the simple expedient of not running day excursions there. Heacham, a few miles south of Hunstanton, took the 'trippers'. The L&SWR helped Bournemouth to develop a gentility rivalling that of Torquay – by not running excursion trains but tending instead towards the 1st class. On 21 April 1890 the dawn of the 'Golden Age' was marked by the inauguration of a very fine Pullman dining-car train, which became known as the *Bournemouth Belle*.

From 1888 to 1890 the railway companies of the north-west competed with each other to develop the holiday potential of Blackpool and the Fylde district. With Richard Moon no longer in command at Euston, the L&NWR contributed wholeheartedly to cheap and cheerful Blackpool by putting on all those day excursions abhorred by Moon as expensive nuisances, jamming the tracks for regular trains. The L&YR ran luxurious, dining-car express, 'Club' trains daily between Blackpool and Manchester, while the MR, on which Thomas Cook had chartered his first excursion in 1840, fought back with day-trips to nearby Morecambe.

Throughout the 1890–1914 period the GNR ran excursions from London to Skegness in trains formed with the best coaches and hauled by the most powerful express engines. Skegness, 132 miles from London, was reached in 3½ hrs, an average of 38 mph. This expensive capital investment in rolling stock, the additional mileage and extra wages for staff, was provided for passengers who paid at the rate of one penny for 8 miles. Once one company started an improvement, the others were drawn into the race. The GER and GNR had to include a dining-car/kitchen-car section in their Norfolk expresses and modern bogie-coaches with corridors and lavatories. Luxurious corridor carriages carried no greater number of people per ton of dead weight than the older, cheaper, six-wheelers and restaurant- and kitchen-cars increased the dead weight without increasing seating capacity. Train weights doubled in a few years, necessitating more powerful engines.

As the 'Golden Age' got up steam the overall financial situation of the fifteen major British railways was that gross revenue was increasing, but a considerable percentage of the increase was absorbed by escalating working costs, parochial rates and other taxes. Board of Trade figures[31] show that, for English railways as a whole, gross receipts for 1890 rose by 3.9 per cent but working expenses rose by 7.5 per cent. The best individual result was from the MR, which increased its net profit by £56,000, although this added only ¼ per cent to the Ordinary shareholders' dividend (see Appendix 2, p. 343).[32]

24

The Destructiveness of Self-interest

FROM THE PANOPLY of powerful egos that constituted Victoria railway officials, Sir Edward Watkin (1819–1901) stands out a the most extreme example of the competitive spirit in action 'When I ope my lips let no dog bark', was how one of his shareholders summed up his attitude. Professor Jack Simmons describes Watki as 'a megalomaniac and gambler'.[1] The competition he generate ought to have produced the best of services for the people his railway served; the contrary was, however, the case, while his own railway and those with whom he competed were damaged, in some case severely so.[2]

Watkin began his career in 1845 as Secretary of the Trent Valle Railway (TVR) which, while still under construction, became part the newly formed L&NWR in 1846. He then came under Mark Huis who liked his energetic approach and appointed him his person assistant, using his abrasive talents wherever there was a company be bullied – even, indeed, the Railway Department of the Board Trade. Watkin's management style was simple: domination of every thing and everybody. He resigned from the L&NWR in 1853 become Manager of the MS&L, and in 1856 he turned against Hui and embraced the enemy – he became a Director of the Oxfor Worcester and Wolverhampton Railway. When the OW&WR w bsorbed into the GWR in 1863, Watkin had – briefly – a seat in the oardroom at Paddington.

Sir Edward had a hugely ambitious idea: to link Manchester by rail ·ith Paris, through a Channel tunnel. He probably conceived the idea n the early 1860s, when the great boom in finance companies and con-·actors' railways was getting under way. He would have stood a reater chance of success had he not allowed his ferocious antagonism ɔ lead him off into blind alleys of competitiveness.

In 1864 he became Chairman of the Board of the MS&L, after eleven ears as its Manager. In that time the fortunes of the MS&L had not nproved, neither did the shareholders benefit from his tenure of the :hair. The Company continued to struggle to pay interest even on its ¡uaranteed' shares, while Ordinary shareholders received 2¼ per cent n 1864, 1¼ per cent in 1868, and 2 per cent in 1877. Watkin poured 1S&L money into Grimsby docks and Cleethorpes beaches, to the reat advantage of the inhabitants, and had for years tried to sell the 1S&L to the L&NWR, the Great Northern or the Midland – or some ombination of the three. This involved making friends with two com-anies and attacking the third; and then, when he could not get what e wanted, turning on the erstwhile ally and trying to 'make a deal' ·ith those he had recently been attacking.[3] At one time the MR offered 1S&L shareholders a guaranteed and very generous 4 per cent if they ould sell to Derby, but Watkin lost this opportunity by insisting on ¼ per cent. The shareholders were lucky to receive 3 per cent from Vatkin, but even so, he managed to persuade them to refuse the Aidland's 4 per cent.[4]

In 1864 he added the South Eastern Railway to his list of)irectorships, and became its Chairman in 1866. The SER, serving)over, would be needed in any Channel tunnel scheme, but rather han pressing on with the great plan Watkin became involved in a futile eud with the other railway in Kent, the London, Chatham & Dover. 'he General Manager of the LC&DR was James Staats Forbes 1823–1904). He was an Aberdonian, but began his railway career on he Great Western in 1835, on the construction side. When the line ·pened in 1838 he became a clerk at the first Maidenhead station and ose quickly to become Goods Manager at Gloucester in 1844, when he 'change of gauge' controversy was raging. He later became Aanager of the Dutch Rhenish Railway and rescued it from ·ankruptcy.[5] In 1860 he was offered the General Managership of he GWR, but refused, and went instead as General Manager of the embattled LC&DR. The Company was being crippled by the debts [ ] had incurred under the influence of its contractor, Samuel Morto[ ] Peto, MP, also by the huge costs of fighting off the plans of the con[ ] tractor, Charles Waring, MP[6] – and in fare wars with the SER. Forbe[ ] became Chairman *and* Managing Director in 1873. Like Watkin, h[ ] was 'extremely autocratic'[7] and liked nothing better than to fight a[ ] opposing railway Company. To the shareholders and public he coul[ ] be 'courtly and charming',[8] an attitude Watkin neither shared no[ ] trusted. To have such aggressive personalities in charge of the tw[ ] transportation companies of Kent was a great misfortune for th[ ] public, shareholders and railwaymen.

The LC&DR locomotive fleet was a shambles of inappropriate odd[ ] and ends, of all shapes and sizes, often built by contractors for foreig[ ] railways, purchased as cheaply as possible and maintained at th[ ] Company's workshops at Longhedge, in south London. In 186[ ] William Martley, an ex-GWR locomotive engineer, was appointe[ ] Locomotive Superintendent. The following year six locomotives, buil[ ] by Sharp Stewart in 1856 for the Dutch Rhenish Railway, were pur[ ] chased by the LC&DR and used for the Dover expresses. After Forbe[ ] carried out his great coup in 1862, capturing the London–Dover Roy[ ] Mail contract from the South Eastern, they were used on the mail train[ ] Peto, the LC&DR's enterprising contractor and financier, owned th[ ] 'Canada' locomotive works in Birkenhead, in partnership wit[ ] Thomas Brassey and the locomotive designer T.R. Crampton, whos[ ] ideas were more appreciated in Europe than in Britain. In 1862 Peto wa[ ] able to sell the LC&DR twenty-four of Crampton's locomotives. The[ ] were badly designed and damaged the track to the extent that the nex[ ] following, fast train was sometimes derailed; indeed, they were th[ ] cause of two derailments and five deaths in three years.[9] By 186[ ] Martley had to rebuild them; using their boilers to power a new class o[ ] his own design, he built ten of the new engines at the 'Canada' work[ ] It was not until 1869 that the first new locomotive was constructed a[ ] Longhedge works. Martley named it *Enigma* because he had had suc[ ] difficulty in obtaining the money to construct it that it was a myster[ ] to him as to how it came to be built at all.[10]

Early in 1866, LC&DR £100 shares were worth £27 10s.[11] Whe[ ] banking collapsed in May 1866, the LC&DR was formally declare[ ] bankrupt and Forbes became its Receiver. He worked with great ski[ ] to rebuild its finances: the enormity of the task can be measured by th[ ] fact that it required two Acts of Parliament to regularize matter[ ]

Meanwhile the war of fares and new railway building went on. That summer, the 3rd-class return from London to Dover had been reduced to 2s 6d and the SER was threatening to charge 2s. On 10 August the two companies agreed to charge a proper fare, to pool their London–Dover receipts and share the pool – the alternative being to carry passengers for nothing. But price wars elsewhere on their systems continued, producing a fiendishly complicated fare structure.

In 1867 the SER, LC&DR and the London, Brighton & South Coast Railways (LB&SCR) agreed to a 'working union'. A Bill was put into Parliament in 1868 to obtain the necessary sanction, but Parliament destroyed the accord by insisting on lower maximum charges than those agreed between the companies.[12] Parliament was worried about the consequences of such a monopoly and so the three companies continued to battle it out with proposals for new railways, most of which were never built but drained money from the antagonists into legal fees. Those that were built usually duplicated existing services. Between 1881 and 1888, the SER spent nearly £500,000 to build a line less than a mile long, parallel with that of the LC&DR, from Strood (SER) into Rochester (LC&DR).[13] This gave the public more stations, but worse carriages and slower trains as the money ran out. On 26 August 1868 Watkin informed his shareholders that joint working with the LC&DR would have saved £100,000 a year, which would have allowed the Company to provide better track, carriages and dividend.[14]

Had the companies entered into a working union, the SER would not have had the expense of creating an entirely new main line in order to shorten their route to Dover. The new line ran from New Cross to Sevenoaks and Tonbridge. The gradients were long and heavy and there were two expensive tunnels: Polhill (2610 yds) and Sevenoaks (3454 yds). The new line considerably reduced the SER mileage to Dover, but it included such steep inclines that new, more powerful engines had to be built specially for it. The boat trains of both companies ran on to the Admiralty pier at Dover, approaching from opposite directions. Local railwaymen, cabbies and others around the station used to bet on which company's train would arrive first. The signals of each company would be lowered, the SER train could be seen approaching for some time as it ran along the sea-wall and would seem to be the winner; but then the LC&DR train would burst into view, and reach the pier first, so the excitement was great (see Map 9).[15]

Forbes appears to have been willing to reach agreement with the LB&SCR and SER, whereas Watkin always 'threw a spanner in the works' – unless Parliament did it for him. After the 1872 Select Committee on Railways had reached the conclusion that 'amalgamations have not brought with them the evils which were anticipated', the SER and LC&DR began fresh negotiations for a working union or outright amalgamation. In April 1874 the companies publicly announced their forthcoming marriage but in May they disagreed. Watkin was holding out for the last impossible detail. The shareholders, who had visions of a rise in the value of their shares to somewhere near par, were extremely disappointed.[16] In August 1877 Forbes told his shareholders: 'If the two companies were put together we could save something and, by improved administration, increase profit and attend to the wants of the country.'[17] In 1878 there was a fresh attempt and an amalgamation Bill actually got into Parliament but was withdrawn by Watkin. For a further ten years the impoverishing competition continued, to the benefit of no one.

Late in 1887 William Abbott, a shareholder of the LB&SCR, tried to restart peace talks between the LB&SCR, SER and LC&DR, conducting a correspondence with Samuel Laing, Chairman of the LB&SCR and ex-Finance Minister for India, Watkin and Forbes, publishing the letters, and the replies he got, in Herapath's *Railway Journal* for 7 January 1888. Abbott sought: 'The termination of all disputes and rivalries which have for so long occupied the attention of the respective Boards as well as Managers and officials of the Companies, involving a very large wastage in competitive working, heavy expenses in legal and Parliamentary charges.' Laing replied:

> I can have no difficulty stating my general concurrence with the principles laid down as to the vital importance of those Companies working in harmony to secure the best results for the shareholders and the public. I have always endeavoured to act on those principles, but as to your specific inquiry, 'Whether I can see my way to unite with the Chairmen of other Companies to bring about such a desirable result', I am obliged to answer with considerable reserve.

The problem was, in Laing's view, Watkin:

> I had hoped that the Chairman of the SER would have been satisfied with my last speech at the Annual General Meeting and that our two Companies might have rested in tranquillity. Unfortunately Sir E. Watkin has revived his claims and so I cannot pledge myself to any course other than that laid out at the last AGM.

Forbes replied to Abbott that he was entirely in favour of 'working unions' and reminded Abbott that 'several years ago [1878] a Bill actually passed the Committee stage in the House and in the Lords only to be withdrawn by SER to the accompaniment of protests from LC&DR and LB&SCR. The terms were equitable to the Companies and the public, Parliament agreed – and then the SER withdrew.' He went on:

As to the benefits to be secured, they are correctly set forth [in Abbott's letter]. An enquiry as to the waste of power and money going on under the present 'armed truce' between one of the Companies and the other two would reveal startling results and notwithstanding great extravagance in expenditure – much of which would have been spared under a united management – the public are being badly served in many particulars where they might be well served. If ever circumstances of any line justified concentration of administrative power and the solidification of important properties into an harmonious whole such a course is especially desirable for these three Companies.

Sir Edward Watkin instructed his secretary, William Stevens, to reply to Abbott that it was he – ABBOTT – who had persuaded the *Brighton* shareholders to reject the 1878 Bill 'although its terms had previously received their unanimous approval'. Sir Edward claimed he had repeated these proposals in 1885 when, according to him, Laing had stated that: 'anything like a fusion of interests between the three companies is completely impractical'. This does not sound to me like a saying of Samuel Laing's, who had, since the 1840s, urged the amalgamation of companies.

On 14 January 1888 Abbott placed an advert in Herapath asking each shareholder of all three companies to ask their respective Boards that: 'No further time should be permitted to elapse before a vigorous effort is made to terminate the long standing hostility, friction, restlessness manifested by the SER Co. towards the LB&SCR and LC&DR Cos.' A futile round of accusations, denials and counter-accusations ensued, in which even the 1865 SER/LD&CR Continental Traffic Pooling Agreement became a bone of expensive contention. Watkin fought legal battles over this until, in 1893, he finally took the SER case to the House of Lords – which gave judgment in favour of the LC&DR. The total cost to both companies in this one legal argument was £250,000.[18]

The feud between Watkin and Forbes spread to the transport system of central London in the 1870s, and was allowed to disrupt and damage what ought to have a great public work. The railways concerned were the Metropolitan (Met.) and the Metropolitan District (MDR) railways. The 1846 'Quadrilateral' ruling, which kept railways off the streets of central London, seems to have given rise to the idea of putting them underground. The Met. was opened on 10 January 1863 from Bishop's Road, Paddington, to Farringdon, running beneath the New Road for much of the way. The MDR was incorporated by Act of Parliament on 29 July 1864 to build a railway from South Kensington to Mansion House via Westminster. Four members of the MDR Board were Directors of the Met., including William Wilkinson, its Chairman; Sir John Fowler was Engineer of both railways, Peto & Betts and Kelk & Waring were the contractors. On the day the MDR was incorporated, the Met. obtained an Act to extend from Edgware Road to the MDR at South Kensington, and from Farringdon to Tower Hill. The Met. agreed to work the MDR for 45 per cent of the gross income, and everyone assumed that they would amalgamate in due course.[19]

The MDR opened from South Kensington to Westminster on 24 December 1868, and to Blackfriars on 30 May 1870. The Company's advisor on operating matters was James Forbes. He encouraged MDR dissatisfaction with the way the Met. operated their line so that they gave notice of their intention to take over the operating on 1 July 1871, with Forbes as the Managing Director.

This was too much for Watkin. Forbes was still General Manager of the LC&DR and there was now a chance that the LC&DR could break out, through the MDR, into regions denied to the SER. At this time the finances of the Met. were in a low state, owing to the machinations of its Chairman, John Parson – he who had committed perjury against the GWR while Chair of the OW&WR, had bought land to sell at a profit to his own Company, and who had paid Met. shareholders 7 per cent dividends out of their own capital, thus masking his bad management and draining the Company's resources. In 1868 his methods were challenged in court and found to be 'false, fictitious and fraudulent'[20] – yet Parson did not go to prison, nor even lose his chairmanship until Forbes joined the MDR, and Watkin felt obliged to counter his influence by becoming Chairman of the Met. Parson was duly ejected and replaced by Watkin on 7 August 1872. Now 'the fat was in the fire' as Watkin carried his feud with Forbes into the underground.

The MDR had cost £1,000,000 per mile.[21] Revenue was disappointing, share values plummeted and amalgamation with the Met. was discussed; meanwhile the MDR considered extensions into the south-western ruralities of Richmond and Wimbledon to develop housing and increase its traffic, and also proposed to build a link from Mansion House to Aldgate. On 7 August 1874 the Metropolitan Inner Circle Completion Company was formed; Watkin 'exerted all his influence to prevent the Company raising the necessary capital and his efforts were crowned with success'.[22]

The impasse was only solved by an Act of Parliament on 11 August 1879, ordering both companies to build the link jointly. Huge capital sums were raised for this most important, public benefit project, which entailed diverting sewers and building an entirely new street – Byward Street – but still thousands of pounds were wasted in legal battles (Watkin, for instance, making objections to the route where it passed near the SER's Cannon Street station). The link was opened on 6 October 1884. Having been forced to act sensibly, the two companies had high hopes of a large traffic from a 'Circle Line' but these were not fulfilled. The problem was that trains were sulphureously steam-hauled through the tunnels, while up in the relatively fresh air of the surface, there were hundreds of horse-drawn cabs, trams and omnibuses – whose more organic fumes were well known and accepted. In spite of the relative lack of success of the 'Circle Line' and the consequent great financial burdens bearing down on it, Watkin never ceased to attack the MDR with litigation, costing both companies tens of thousands of pounds.

Watkin's great urge to make something utterly stupendous was realized only in part, and even that only very slowly – and he probably had only himself to blame. The spirit was willing but the financial resources were weak. In 1875 he had used £20,000 of SER money[23] – and Forbes's LC&DR had contributed an equal amount – towards the costs of trial bore-holes for a Channel tunnel, but it was not until 1882 that Watkin could form the South Eastern & Channel Tunnel Company, and it was a further nine years before he was able to lodge a Bill in Parliament for an Act to commit his impoverished MS&L to building a 93-mile main line from Annesley, south of Sheffield, through Nottingham, Leicester and Rugby, to a junction with the Metropolitan Railway at or near Quainton, 7 miles north of Aylesbury. The route would connect with the SER through the tunnels of the Met. and so reach Dover.

The proposed route came south, crossing and re-crossing the

Midland – whose profits it would particularly attack, as well as those of the GNR and L&NWR's, while doing nothing at all to enhance its own. The threatened railway companies strongly opposed the Bill in Parliament. There was also opposition from the artists, poets and publishers of St John's Wood and, fiercest of all, from right-thinking Englishmen in general and the Marylebone Cricket Club in particular at the proposed sacrilege of making a 'cut and cover' tunnel underneath Lord's ground. The fact that the temporary cutting would cross a corner of the ground never used for playing cricket, and that, when the cutting was roofed over and the grass restored, no one would know the railway was there, did nothing to ameliorate the feelings of outrage. The notion of sacrilege was so great that Parliament threw out the Bill, and the legal expenses of the MS&L went for naught.

The MS&L soothed the opposing railway companies with promises of 'running powers', reassured the delicate inhabitants of St John's Wood that not a navvy nor a cart of earth would desecrate their peaceful streets, and finally (and most importantly), gave suitable obeisances to the MCC. The Bill was re-presented and became an Act on 28 March 1893. Work began on the new railway the following year. The obligation to the MCC was that the sacred turf be carefully removed and laid respectfully on one side while a cutting was dug and roofed over, whereupon the soil and turf would be replaced – all this within the close season (September to May) so that nothing should disturb The Game. An orphanage for children of the clergy adjoining the cricket ground and its 1¾ acres of gardens was purchased, the orphanage demolished and the large site presented to the MCC. The orphans, meanwhile were rehoused in a brand new orphanage, built by the MS&L, in Bushey.[24]

The strain on Watkin of negotiating with all the aggrieved parties, and of arguing two Bills through Parliament, caused him to suffer a heart attack in 1894, and he was forced to retire. Only then could a co-operation between his companies and those he had attacked begin to develop.

On Watkin's SER 4 per cent dividends were paid to Ordinary shareholders in 1892 – but only at the expense of not carrying out maintenance. Competition had so reduced profits that in 1898, twelve out of nineteen steamships owned by the two companies were unfit for service.[25] The MS&L changed its name to Great Central Railway (GCR) in 1897; in July of the following year coal trains began running over its London Extension, and on 15 March 1899 a regular passenger service commenced between Sheffield and London, competing for the same traffic with three other companies.

It was just at this time that the SER and LC&DR formally gave up their ruinous competition by obtaining the South Eastern and London, Chatham & Dover (Working Union) Act. This was not an amalgamation but a 'burying of the hatchet', an opportunity to reduce working costs. The expected financial savings from SER/LC&DR co-operation were not, however, realized. The LC&DR locomotive works at Longhedge was closed in favour of the SER works at Ashford, but the track of the LC&DR was so badly worn out that it had to be entirely replaced. Over the years the number of workers on both railways' staffs had been reduced in order to cut costs, which meant that to produce an efficient operation, the new Committee had to employ an extra 2000 men. The Chairman of the Managing Committee, Cosmo Bonsor, bravely told the SER shareholders that the SER and LC&DR had been 'more or less absolutely starved in efforts to create dividends for the shareholders but I have endeavoured to absolutely ignore the question of dividend in the endeavour to bring this undertaking into a sound commercial position'.[26]

The financial problems of the SER were exacerbated by the utterly desperate state of the LC&DR. The nominal value of the LC&DR's capital was £11.2 million but the market value of those shares in 1900 was only £4.8 million. Money had to be raised to repair the depredations of 30 years of competition and to carry out improving works – quadrupling the line and making useful junctions between the erstwhile rivals – but who would buy shares in such an unprofitable venture when there were so many more profitable places in which to invest? In the first half of 1900 Ordinary shareholders in the Harmsworth Press received 25 per cent, *Kelley's Directory* 8 per cent, *Illustrated London News* 7 per cent, George Newnes 10 per cent, Armstrong Whitworth 20 per cent, Vickers 20 per cent, and South Hetton Colliery, 17.5 per cent.[27]

Because the South Eastern Railway was in a better state, materially and financially, it had to guarantee interest repayments on any money raised for LC&DR; and, as a result, SER shareholders received lower dividends after the formation of the Working Union. Gross revenue of the joint concern increased by £40,000 in the first half of 1900, but the total expenses increased by £100,000.[28] There was too much capital, too many shareholders, too great an expenditure – and not enough revenue.

25

The Trade Unions

THROUGHOUT THE NINETEENTH century, any railway company had complete power over its workers. Railwaymen were spoken of and treated as if they were servants in a great house or on some vast estate. This could hardly have been otherwise in 1830, but the stern paternalism lasted long after the railways had become vast, technical-industrial giants. 'We claim the right to deal with our own servants as we think expedient', said Mr Harrison, General Manager of the L&NWR on 8 December in the Golden Age of 1896.[1] The working conditions of the railwaymen depended entirely on the relative humanity of their employers. The Directors interviewed each applicant for a post on their railway; indeed, they personally recruited large numbers of them, so the men felt some personal loyalty towards them – which might have been dissipated by experience. The Directors dispensed or withheld largesse according to their prejudice; hired, fired and believed in their own righteousness with a religious zeal against which there was no appeal.

From 1838 until 1865, the Traffic Department and clerical staff of the Great Western Railway was appointed only after an interview with the Board, and they would be reprimanded or dismissed in the same way. Daniel Gooch, subject to Brunel's approval, appointed men to the Locomotive Department; the original GWR footplatemen were all from Lancashire or the north-east.[2] In 1848, on the GNR between Lincoln and Peterborough, 110 out of 135 men were actually recruited by the Directors.[3] On the GWR from 1838, policemen, switchmen and locomotive crews received a biennial bonus for good working and good conduct. There were issues of free or cheap coal. Locomotive men had to find their own white corduroy clothes for work but all other grades were given a uniform. These conditions were typical of those to be found on the better-led railways.

The GWR Provident Society was established at the start of operations 'for the purpose of affording relief to its members in sickness, accident or old age and the means of decent burial for themselves and [their] wives'. As a craftsman, Daniel Gooch believed in looking after his tools and established an additional, Locomotive Department Sick Fund in 1843; in 1844 he set up the 'GWR Mechanics Institute' at Swindon, after noticing that some of the workmen had, the previous year, started their own library. The Institute was to provide technical information in books and lectures and to encourage 'rational amusement amongst all classes of people employed by the GWR at Swindon'.[4]

In the wake of the financial collapse of 1847, Gooch had been obliged to lay off hundreds of factory workers. Those still in work were on short time but volunteered to contribute towards the upkeep of those laid off. Gooch had to encourage his workforce to remain at Swindon and await better times. At this time the GWR provided no medical assistance to workshop employees either in the extremely dangerous environment in which they worked or in their homes. If the Company could supply some very minimal medical attention, Gooch thought that this would be an incentive to hold the workforce at Swindon and might also help to prevent some epidemic in the sewerless town which would cause the people to leave.

It appears from the letter Gooch wrote to the Directors in November 1847[5] that any injured GWR workshop employee would be liable not only for the doctor's call-out fee but also for the bandages and splints – although he would often be assisted by his workmates and, occasionally, by Gooch. In his letter Gooch pointed out that the L&NWR paid their doctor at Crewe £50 a year and gave him a free house, in return for attending to all accident victims free in the first instance; after the first call-out the injured man was responsible for the doctor's fee. Gooch asked that the GWR allow Doctor Rae a free house, worth £30 per annum, in return for his attending free the first call to an accident in the works; to this the GWR Directors agreed immediately. This was the genesis of Medical Fund Society,[6] paid for by the factory workers and the Company.

The fund provided treatment and medicine for the employees of the works and their families. Membership was compulsory; the workers' contributions were deducted from their pay and graded accordingly. During the next twenty-five years Swindon Works people, led by Gooch, arranged their own finances and built a remarkable welfare system for themselves, with assistance from the Company. The GWR built for the children of works employees, a school and then a larger school. Healthy drains were laid. The Medical Fund opened a bath-house on Faringdon Road providing ordinary baths, Turkish baths and a swimming-bath; later, a bathhouse was built opposite the works, close to the engine-shed. In 1871 a cottage hospital was opened containing a four-bed ward, a doctor's surgery an operating room, a dispensary and mortuary. The following year Sir Daniel Gooch was awarded £5500 by the shareholders of the GWR for rescuing the Company from bankruptcy and donated £1000 of this to the cottage hospital endowment fund. No welfare provision on this scale existed on any other railway (see Appendix 12). The railway companies had always to provide housing where they had workshops in remote areas, such as at Crewe and Swindon, and also in cities where there was a shortage of decent housing for working people. At times of industrial unrest the chance of losing your home by going on strike was a strong incentive to remain at work.

Wherever there was a sufficient concentration of people, choirs, silver bands, drama groups and sports clubs grew up. During the French invasion scare of 1859–60, the L&NWR and GWR each raised a regiment of militia from their factory workers at Crewe and Swindon – the close-knit railway spirit easily transformed in 'regimental spirit' (see Appendix 12). Individual railwaymen organized technical training – the Mutual Improvement Classes – for young hands long before the greatest companies established formal training colleges at a very few major centres. The Enginemen's & Firemen's Mutual Assurance Society (always known as 'the MAS') was started in 1867 by a few GWR enginemen. Daniel Gooch, by then Chairman of the Company, provided clerical and accounting facilities to the MAS and sanctioned an annual Company subscription to the fund. In the first instance this was £500 but it was increased to £1000 in 1879 in a successful attempt to avert a strike of footplatemen, after his Locomotive Superintendent, William Dean, had reduced the weekly wages and increased the hours of work of locomotivemen.

Most companies allowed their employees to complain personally to the Directors about their pay or working conditions or their treatment at the hands of a railway official, but of course, the justice of the case was subordinate to the Directors' opinion and their word was final. If the Directors had harsh notions of 'discipline' a plaintiff might find himself in hot water for complaining. Occasionally a Company was run corruptly with tragic results for the men. In April 1850, the Eastern Counties Railway, under the Chairmanship of Edward Ladd Betts, MP, appointed John Gooch, brother of Daniel, as its Locomotive Superintendent. Betts gave John Gooch permission to take 2½ per cent of the amount by which he reduced the Company's working costs. Had the agreement been approved by the Board and minuted, had the Company known what the working costs were before the arrival of Gooch, and had there been an independent assessment of the amount he had saved each year, the arrangement would have been fair. As it was, Gooch told the Company's accountant what he had saved and pocketed his 2½ per cent. Betts was replaced as Chairman by David Waddington, MP, who made himself responsible for the Stores Committee of the ECR. Gooch made an agreement with the coke merchant, E. & A. Prior, that they would pay him 3d a ton for every ton he ordered from them and this was not challenged by Waddington; Gooch even went so far as to sell the Company's brand new stores to outside firms, and pocketed the proceeds.

Gooch reduced costs by sacking men and offering them their jobs back at lower rates, and by deducting from those reduced wages large fines, as a punishment for anything that went wrong with their engine or train, from a lack of punctuality to the snapping of a coupling or the collapse of a connecting-rod. The men seethed so much at the daily injustices inflicted on them that, on 12 August, 178 drivers, firemen and fitters very courageously handed in their notice to quit unless Gooch was removed. Gooch stayed and 178 new loco-men were found from other railways, and by new recruitment. In addition, the 178 were vindictively blacklisted so that they would not be employed on railways elsewhere. Gooch and Waddington continued their depredations against the ECR for six years until the shareholders caught up with them.[7] Their punishment was that their contracts were not renewed, and they went on to a life of luxurious retirement.

The effects of inefficient management could always be mitigated by taking money from the men. Sir Edward Watkin opposed any power structure for his employees, and indeed, when there was a strike among London workmen he withdrew all those 'workmen's' cheap tickets on the SER that were not obligatory under the law; and yet he freely admitted the large debt that railway shareholders owed to the railwaymen when he told his shareholders in 1871 that their dividend 'depended on the sacrifices of the men' – that is to say, low wages and long hours.[8]

The railway companies permitted themselves their own pressure group, the Railway Companies Association, of which Daniel Gooch was Chairman from January 1881. There were also over 120 Directors of railways, including Gooch, who sat as Members of Parliament (see Appendix 14), but the employees were denied any power at all. British society had always been proud to boast of its 'freedoms', but as the industrial century wore on, more and more people realized the inequality and lack of freedom of working people.

Establishing a trade union was one thing, getting the companies to recognize it, and the men to join it, was a very different matter.[9] On the GWR the unions had a particular problem in that large numbers of the footplatemen placed a considerable trust in Daniel Gooch. In 1862, a Bill was introduced into Parliament, by Mr J.M. Cobbett (1800–1877), Liberal MP for Oldham, to limit the hours of work of locomotivemen. An anonymous letter purporting to come from 'a GWR engine driver' appeared in *The Times*:

> I am surprised to see by the motion of Mr. Cobbett . . . that Great Western enginemen are classed with those who claim the protection of Parliament. I am requested by the above to say that they have authorised no-one to use their names in any petition asking for the protection of Parliament . . . so long as our respected and esteemed Chief Superintendent Mr. Gooch is at our head we want no other protection for we know that we can get no protection so just and generous as we receive at his hands.[10]

Some railwaymen had Tory sympathies and distrusted the unions as being allied to the Liberals, or even the Radicals. More were apathetic towards the idea that anything could be done against the power of the companies, and still more were afraid to belong, for fear of the repercussions from their Company. The companies always denied that they dismissed men for being too active in the union but there were far too many instances for them to be coincidences. Fred Evans, a clerk employed by the GWR at Bristol, was a pioneer of the Associated Society of Railway Servants (ASRS). Evans had helped canvas support among railwaymen in Exeter during the November 1873 General election for the election of Sir Edward Watkin. Watkin had agreed that, if elected, he would support in Parliament a 'Workmen's Compensation Act'. In January 1874 the GWR (Sir Daniel Gooch) dismissed Evans. Watkin offered him a job on any one of his railways – but only on condition that Evans gave up his organizing work for the ASRS. Evans refused, whereupon Watkin donated £50 to a subscription started for Evans's benefit. In October 1874 Evans was elected General Secretary of the ASRS.[11]

The Associated Society of Railway Servants was founded with the Parliamentary and financial assistance of four Liberal MPs, including the millionaire brewer and Member for Derby, Michael Bass,[12] who held £100,000-worth of MR shares. Canon Jenkins of Aberdare became the first President of the union and the Liberal Earl de la Warr,[13] Vice-President and spokesman for the railwaymen in the House of Lords. The declared aims of the ASRS were:

> To promote a good and fair understanding between employers and employed; to prevent strikes; to protect and defend members against injustice; to secure 10 hours for a fair day's labour and one day's extra pay for 8 hours' overtime; the payment of the same rate for Sundays; to afford a ready means by arbitration or otherwise for the settlement of disputes; for granting temporary assistance to its members and to provide legal assistance where necessary; to make grants to members who desire to emigrate and to found a superannuation fund for old and disabled members.[14]

In 1869, when the MR was in financial difficulties, its footplatemen loyally volunteered to give up their guaranteed minimum weekly wage and to be paid only if and when they were sent out on a job. The guarantee was restored in 1873 – two years after the Company's fortunes were restored. The GWR gave wage rises to all their men in 1873 and introduced a guaranteed weekly wage for their footplate staff. In 1870, 38.8 per cent of GWR gross income was swallowed by working expenses; by 1879 the proportion had risen to 52.3 per cent. Many factors affect working costs: actual wage rises can inflate these, but so can a great increase in traffic, in terms of extra time worked and extra fuel consumed. The national 'boom' was short-lived; a decline began in 1874 and by 1879 the general trade situation in the country was described in Parliament as 'the culmination of distress'.[15] The major railways' profits were not, however, 'distressed' at this time because they were busy hauling the imports helping to cause the distress, particularly in home agriculture. The GWR's dividend in 1879 rose slightly to a modest 4⅛ per cent and Gooch chose this moment to withdraw the guaranteed week's pay of his footplatemen, reduce the wages of all staff and lengthen the working day.

The GWR dividend then increased to 6 per cent in four years – paid for, in part at least, by the workmen (and their families) in shifts of 12 to 15 hrs a day, five days a week, without overtime pay, the sixth day being a 'day of rest', spent carrying out maintenance to their engine on shed on half pay. The GWR was, however, the most humane of companies. Particularly notable among the companies for overworking their men were the Cambrian, GER, L&SWR, MR and NBR; on the LB&SCR the enginemen lived in actual terror of John Craven, their Locomotive Superintendent from 1847 to 1869.[16] William Birt, General Manager of the GER, gave it as his reasonable, well-educated opinion, that a man working 15 hrs a day six days out of seven would still have 'ample time' to see his children.[17] If a man could be booked off 'early' after only 12 hrs at work, it would be done, but everything depended on the requirements of the Company. What it would not do – if it could possibly avoid it – was to take on more staff.

Sir Daniel Gooch, 'the engineman's friend', refused till the day he died to recognize the men's right to a trade union. True, he would always grant an individual an interview; but one man can hardly have a pay rise without the rest, so an individual interview was rather a pointless exercise. On 21 June 1883, when the total railway union membership of the whole country was only about 10 per cent of those employed, eleven GWR engine drivers, members of the Associated Society of Locomotive Engineers & Firemen (ASLEF), went as a deputation from their colleagues to interview Sir Daniel Gooch with various complaints and suggestions. Gooch replied:

> What I complain of is that a number of men come here without having any complaint to make in their own case. If a man has a grievance let him come himself and he shall have a hearing. [Driver] Hughes made a statement the last time and a few days later I received a statement signed by every engine man on the Metropolitan trains – whom he said he represented – saying that he did not represent their views.[18]

The years of hardship and injustice (and not just on the railway) developed some men's resolve to do something positive to improve matters. In August 1889 the disgracefully badly paid dockers of the Port of London went on strike. They were asking for, and had been refused, 6d an hour – the 'Docker's Tanner', the price of one cigar smoked by the Chairman of the London Dock Board.[19] They also wanted a guaranteed minimum of 2s (10p) a day and an end to the practice whereby the Dock Foreman only hired those who were willing to pay him a bribe. Within their own ranks they found leaders – John Burns, Ben Tillet and Tom Mann – of sufficient ability to organize with perfect honesty, throughout the two months of the strike, the distribution of £51,000 and tons of food from sympathizers. Help came from the international trade union organization. Australian trade unionists sent money, while in Britain it was not only the working class who came to their aid, as the large sum of money raised in so short a time demonstrated. Cardinal Manning (1802–1892), well respected by the workers for his efforts to improve the lot of the poor of London, and of sufficiently high caste to be acceptable to the employers, became arbitrator of a compromise. The dockers got their 'tanner' an hour.

The trade union movement received a great boost from the dockers' victory, and ASRS membership, which had declined from 8500 in 1880 to 6300 in 1882, and which showed only very modest increases thereafter, took off in 1889.[20] So it was that the railways' 'Golden Age' coincided with the intensification of the struggle between the railway workers and their companies. The hours of labour of factory workers had been regulated by Act of Parliament since 1833, but nothing was done to protect railwaymen from overwork or unfair dismissal. The Board of Trade was powerless against the companies in these matters – even though overworked men were a threat to public safety.

Gooch died in September 1889. In January 1890, and again in May, GWR enginemen petitioned the Directors that a 10-hr day or 150 miles should constitute a day's work; that time or mileage worked in excess would be paid for; that Sunday work would be paid for at 'time and a quarter'; and that the guaranteed week's pay would be restored. The GWR Directors, without the 'engineman's friend' to restrain them, agreed. In the same year, the NER men asked for a guaranteed week's pay and for a working week to be six days of 8, 10 or 12 hrs, depending on the amount of daily work to be performed; shunters in busy yards (whose work Parliament acknowledged was the most dangerous employment in Britain) asked to work a 48-hr week. To all this the NER Directors agreed.

In southern Scotland, on the North British, Caledonian and Glasgow & South Western railways, it was common enough for train-crews to work between 19 and 25 hrs continuously in 1890. They worked a 'trip' system, whereby they were paid a certain number of hours to make a journey. The result was that the men routinely worked when they were still out on the track after the allotted time for their journey had expired. The overtime was incurred because of the congested state of the tracks across southern Scotland and, in particular on the approaches to Edinburgh after the opening of the Forth bridge On 21 December 1890, 7000 out of 8000 Scottish guards, drivers firemen and signalmen struck work.[21] It lasted through six cold hungry weeks, long enough to alarm the leaders of the business community. The Lord Provost of Glasgow and Mr Haldane, QC, both of whom considered the men's demand for a 10-hr day for those employed on busy main lines and a 12-hr day for others very reasonable, were willing to act as intermediaries; but the Directors of the Scottish railway companies were not interested in being reasonable they wanted to punish their 'servants'.

They raised the wages of any who would remain 'loyal', brought in 'blacklegs' from England and prosecuted strikers under the Conspiracy and Protection of Property Act of 1875. The courts threw out these prosecutions but the intimidating circumstance existed until that happened. All industrial Scotland seethed; sometimes tens of thousands of workers were on the streets in support of the railwaymen. There were riots by the workers and baton charges by police and army. The companies seemed willing to risk anything, rather than talk to their men, and baton charges against Boards of Directors, to 'bring them to their senses', were unheard-of. In the end, on 30 January 1891 the railwaymen were obliged by cold and hunger to call off the strike without any gains having been achieved.[22]

The railway Company always referred to the striking men as 'Disloyal' – as if the men had an obligation to suffer unprotestingly any indignity and hardship the Company liked to put upon them. The fierce rivalry felt by the men of the Caledonian, NBR and G&SWR companies is a matter of recorded fact: there was no one more loyal to the G&SWR than a G&SWR driver with a 'Caley' driver on the opposite platform at Carlisle. These were the men who flung caution to the wind and risked their lives at suicidal speeds for the honour of their Company, in the 'Race to the North' between the west coast and east coast routes from London to Edinburgh in 1888. The Company was always right: the thought never seemed to occur to the Directors that they were being disloyal to their very loyal workforce, and that they themselves had caused the strike by driving their men beyond endurance.

The Scottish strike shook the companies a little; there was some reduction in the hours worked, while any time worked on a Sunday was, from March, paid at 'time-and-a-half'. The NBR decided to widen the tracks into and around Edinburgh to accommodate the extra traffic generated by the presence of the Forth bridge, and so relieve the congestion that caused the delays and unpaid overtime. The NBR claimed £20,000 damages from the Scottish ASRS under the 1875 Act, and the Scottish union, whose funds were exhausted by payments to the men on strike, now finally agreed to amalgamate with the wider ASRS.

The greatest achievement of the strike was to bring about the first ever Parliamentary debate into railwaymen's working condition. It took place on 23 January 1891 and lasted 7½ hrs. The outcome was a Select Committee on Railway Servants (Hours of Labour), which started hearing evidence on 10 March. The Committee consisted of twenty-three MPs but only five made a quorum, and eight of the total were Directors of railway companies.[23]

The railway companies ran their systems 'undermanned' and did not want to take on more men – which they would be forced to do if their men's hours were limited by law. Such a law might also force them to modernize their old-fashioned layouts, to deal with the modern demand. Tracks might have to be widened and stations rebuilt, in order to abolish the 'bottle-necks' which caused the congestion and lengthened the men's hours. A legal maximum to the number of hours a railwayman might work would be very costly, and the companies tried to frighten Parliament by claiming that: 'A strict limit to hours would oblige the railway companies to refuse to carry the mails, passenger and parcel traffic or to employ an immense additional staff whose services would not be required at other periods of the year'.[24]

Not all railwaymen wanted their hours restricted by law, and those who did want a 10-hr day and extra hourly rates for overtime had differing views on how to achieve this. Some wanted the Board of Trade to have the power to regulate their hours; others said they had 'no faith' in the Board's ability to do this. The Scots wanted a 10-hr day but were prepared to concede that in some places a 12-hr day would be reasonable. Some ASRS members, brought before the Committee to speak in support of a 10-hr day, actually spoke against it when the time came. The Secretary of the Tyne Dock ASRS, Robert

Collingwood, told the Committee that he did not regard working 80 hrs a week as too much and did not want Parliament to interfere, and Edward Ellis, a North Eastern goods guard, said he was 'perfectly satisfied' with working an average of 66 hrs 48 mins a week during the previous twelve months.[25] Perhaps, at existing levels of wages, they could not afford to have their hours reduced, or perhaps they were too frightened for their jobs to complain against their Company, since the Chairman of the Committee, Sir Joseph Pease, was also Chairman of the NER. But there was also a petition against legal limits on hours, signed by 1354 GER drivers and firemen. They were concerned that they would be booked off, away from home, at the far end of a journey.[26]

This conflicting evidence was very unfortunate because there were undoubtedly a number of companies who, from lack of care, or money, employed too few people and routinely required their men to work excessively long hours – and some statutory maximum was essential. Shunting was a particularly gruelling job because it had to be done come rain, snow or heatwave. The goods trains arrived at a meeting of routes, the wagons had to be sorted according to destination, marshalled into new trains and sent on. Shunters walked miles on each shift, worked the longest hours and suffered the greatest number of fatalities and mutilations of any class of worker in Britain – only British merchant seamen suffered greater casualties and longer hours.[27] At Didcot in 1891 the shunters routinely worked 14 hrs a day or night, six days or nights every week.[28]

The only companies that attempted a self-imposed limit to the number of working hours were the GWR and the L&NWR, who instructed their men to ask for relief before, or at, a 12-hr maximum, but the difficulty arose if there was no relief. The others, great companies and minor ones, expected their men to work 'as required'. The abuse of the men on the Cambrian Railway amounted to recklessness, but 24-hr shifts were also worked on the M&SWJR. What has immortalized the Cambrian's abuses was the management's lack of sorrow for their actions. This Company had, for at least twenty years prior to 1891, booked men on duty for 36 continuous hours as a matter of routine and there were cases where men worked continuously for 47 hrs.[29] This dreadful and dangerous state of affairs was exposed to the Select Committee by Mr Bather, a miller from Oswestry, who had collected sworn affidavits from the men concerned. When the General Manager of the railway, Mr Conacher, was cross-examined on this, he insisted that he had no knowledge of it – although it had been going on for twenty years. He was also questioned about an accident on the junction points at Ellesmere at 3 a.m. on 6 November 1887, which had been blamed on the porter, Humphreys, who had been on duty for 19 hrs at the time of the accident, and who was dismissed for allegedly causing the derailment. Conacher told the Committee that the excessive hours worked by the man were necessitated by the incompetence of the Ellesmere station-master John Hood. The true reason for the derailment was sleepers so rotten they resembled compost; Conacher ordered these to be replaced during the interval of several days between the accident and the arrival of Colonel Rich, the Board of Trade Inspector. Hood stated publicly that the cause of the derailment was the rotten track and signed a petition for the reinstatement of Humphreys. As a station-master, Hood was expected to support the Company rather than justice, and he was punished by a fourteen-day suspension and transfer to Montgomery, where the station-master's pay was less than at Ellesmere. Hood left Ellesmere with a purse of gold sovereigns donated by the locals.

John Hood read in his local paper what Conacher had told the Committee and at once asked Conacher for permission to defend his (Hood's) good name in the local press and before the Select Committee. Conacher was too arrogant to take Hood seriously, refusing him permission to write to the press and ignoring his request to go to Parliament. Having written again, and receiving no response, Hood wrote to Parliament and was invited to appear before the Committee on 16 July. He showed to their satisfaction that he had asked for a reliefman for Humphreys, and that it was Conacher who had refused to send one. With his name cleared, Hood went home and that might have been the end of it but for the vindictive liars in the top echelons of the Cambrian Railway: Manager Conacher and Chairman Buckley.

Conacher searched around and dug up a two-year-old instance where Hood had sent a hamper to his son by L&NWR and somehow the sum of 1s 7d was in dispute, but which had faded from notice until that moment. Without any further ado Hood was ordered, on 10 August to leave the Company's service and his house that same day. Hood was so highly trusted and esteemed that the Mayor of Montgomery, the landed gentry, the clergy and the tradesmen all signed a petition for his reinstatement. On 30 September Hood was interviewed by a Committee of the Cambrian Board, consisting of Chairman Buckley, Directors John McClure, MP, and William

Hawkins, and Manager Conacher. They told him to justify the remarks he had made *before the Select Committee*. After a severe browbeating from all four he remained dismissed. He had been punished for giving evidence to the Parliamentary Committee on overwork – and one of his executioners was a Member of Parliament.

Other Parliamentary investigations were pending into the abuse of working men, but with the example of John Hood before them, witnesses were actually dissuaded from giving truthful evidence. Parliament had been treated with contempt and undermined, even by one of its own, and yet Parliament was slow, if not reluctant, to take action against the miscreants. On 24 March 1892 the Committee on overwork reported to Parliament that the four Cambrian Railway officials had punished Hood 'in a manner calculated to deter other railway servants from giving evidence to your Committee'.[30] On 7 April Buckley, Conacher and Hawkins were summoned to appear before the House, McClure standing in his place among the MPs. After being allowed to reiterate their denial of any wrongdoing where Hood was concerned, they expressed 'unqualified regret' if they had 'unintentionally infringed any of the rules of Parliamentary privilege'. After a fiercely argued debate, where some MPs tried to stiffen the punishment by obliging the four miscreants to make amends to John Hood, they were merely verbally 'admonished' by the Speaker of the House 'for the breach of privilege they have committed'.

The 'Act to Amend the Law with Respect to the Hours of Labour of Railway Servants',[31] passed on 27 July 1893, was as weak a thing as the Speaker's admonition of the Cambrian Directors. The title is misleading, since it did not lay down the maximum hours which could be worked, neither did it specify what interval of rest there should be between shifts, nor did it apply to clerical or workshop staff. Section 2 gave the Board of Trade power to 'bring the actual hours of work within reasonable limits, regard being had to all the circumstances of the traffic and the nature of the work'. The companies could still overwork their men and express regrets later.

In 1892 and 1893 the railway companies were saddled with the Act intended to restrict fare rises. The intensified competition demanded more capital expenditure on increased luxury and speed, and the gap between the companies' gross income and working expenses closed somewhat, reducing the dividend and creating a problem for those companies who were trying to raise fresh capital. Under these conditions a railway train union activist, demanding shorter hours and more pay, had to be brave, willing to risk losing his job for his beliefs – yet trade union membership increased. In October 1897 the ASRS held a conference in Birmingham to define what improvements railwaymen – nationally – needed, and to prepare for a national strike if they did not get what they wanted. In response the major railway companies, led by the GWR and L&NWR (but with the notable exception of the NER, which suggested that arbitration would be sensible), voted to oppose any agreement with the unions and made arrangements to help each other in the event of a strike. Meanwhile the companies continued to try and disrupt the trade union movement by 'divide and rule' methods: give pay rises to a few, reduce other men's wages, harass or dismiss anyone with the courage to complain.[32]

This went on throughout the 1890s and was particularly nasty on the exceptionally wealthy Taff Vale Railway. Yet relations had once been good, during the humane chairmanship of James Inskip,[33] who believed that 'workmen have the same right to negotiate the price of their labour as a landowner who has something to sell'. Under Inskip, working costs in 1889 were taking 59 per cent of the gross, but since 1881 the shareholders had received a dividend averaging 12¾ per cent.[34] In 1889 the Barry Railway opened, providing the TVR with competition for the first time since it opened in 1840, and forcing the latter to reduce its coal charges by one third and its dividend to 5⅛ per cent. In November 1891 the railway appointed a new General Manager, Eamon Beasley, an arrogant 'hard man'. Inskip resigned the Chair and Beasley proceeded to reduce working costs by reducing wages, increasing hours of labour and bullying his workforce into a state of grumbling subjection.

The Boer War broke out in 1899 and a year later the average railwayman's living expenses had risen by 5s a week. The men of the Barry, Cardiff and Rhymney railways negotiated a pay rise of 4s a week with their Directors, but Beasley, scenting an advantage in working costs over his rivals, gave only small rises to a few men. In 1900 Beasley got his working costs down to 57.7 per cent of gross income, and the Company was able to pay an 8⅛ per cent dividend. The demand for coal quadrupled, and so did its price. The miners, coal-mine owners and shipowners all reaped the reward. The railway companies continued to carry the increased flow at the old price; had they made the effort, they could have agreed a small increase in charges and thus, been able to pay their men extra.

The ASRS wanted to discuss matters. Beasley absolutely refused and continued to bully anyone with the courage to protest. Signalman John Ewington of Abercynon was a leading ASRS representative. He was forty-five years old and had served the Company faithfully for twenty years. On 28 April 1900 he was ordered to move to a signal box at Treherbert, 16 miles from his home. He would get 2s a week extra there but he was well entrenched where he was, with an off-duty job which brought him in 5s a week. He appealed but was ordered to do as he was told. Ewington fell sick with rheumatic fever in July and both his job at Abercynon and the job at Treherbert were filled. Ewington's treatment by the Company was interpreted by the men as harassment; it was the last straw and, on 19 August 1900, they went on strike.[35]

Prior to the strike's being called, Beasley had arranged for entirely untrained 'blackleg' labour to be supplied by William Collinson's London-based 'National Free Labour Association' – 'free labour' being a very desirable goal. Collison's organization had broken 300 strikes in ten years and he charged the TVR £100 to break theirs,[36] thinking that it would only last two days. He later declared[37] that he knew nothing of the men's grievances but had to smash the 'tyranny' of the trade unions – as if the union was something alien, superimposed on the men, rather than the men themselves, driven to defend themselves and their families from a cruel management. On the day the strike was called, Beasley immediately intimidated some of the men by evicting them and their families from their TVR-owned houses, even though the rents had been paid for the whole week commencing 20 August.[38]

The ASRS picketed Paddington and Cardiff GWR station, distributing a leaflet to the would-be strike-breakers recruited by Collinson, informing them of the true situation. This strategy was very successful in the short term and many of them men did indeed go home, after a meal at the ASRS's expense and on a ticket purchased for them by the ASRS. But the handbill made use of the word 'blackleg', which was deemed in law to be 'intimidation', while the shadowing of the strike-breakers by pickets was 'harassment'. Beasley applied on 23 August for an injunction to prevent the latter activity. Richard Bell, MP, General Secretary of the ASRS, tried to open negotiations to end the strike, but Mr Beasley refused to talk to him. He was Master and his men were going to have to learn their lesson.

On 24 August Mr James Inskip wrote to *The Times* (see Appendix

15), pointing out that 'hundreds of thousands of pounds' of business had been lost because Beasley would not negotiate with the ASRS. In the same paper Sir W.T. Lewis, an important Welsh industrialist, suggested a 'Conciliation Board' to deal with any industrial grievance in the South Wales area. The next day, the TVR Directors agreed to meet Richard Bell and negotiations began. They concluded on the 30th when Mr Justice Farrell delivered an interim injunction restraining ASRS officials from organizing picketing. The strike was called off late that same day. The TVR promised to take back all those on strike, to cease all legal actions against their employees, to guarantee pension rights of the strikers, to set up a Conciliation Board to arbitrate between their men and themselves, and to refer signalman Ewington's case to the Board of Trade's arbitration.

On 5 September Mr Justice Farrell made a devasting extension of his interim injunction, ruling that a union could be sued in its registered name for losses suffered as the result of a strike; he further declared that Richard Bell, MP, had issued an intimidating leaflet.[39]

The effectiveness of the trade union movement to stand up against injustice would be seriously crippled if Farrell's judgment were to stand. The ASRS went to law to test the legality of the ruling and the Master of the Rolls, Lord Justice Collins, ruled that there was nothing in the Trade Union Act 1875 which rendered a union liable to be sued in its registered name. Beasley took the case to the House of Lords, and on 21 July 1901 Justice Farrell's interpretation of the 1875 Act was upheld. The ASRS were obliged to pay the TVR £23,000 damages and £19,000 in costs; but worst of all, from the point of view of trade unions, was the fact that they were no longer able to picket a workplace.

The companies were so pleased that they gave Beasley £2000, a pair of silver candelabra and a pendant brooch for his wife. The proper order was re-established: they could do as they liked, while the men were defenceless. In 1902 the ASRS brought a civil action against the TVR for compensation for Ewington, alleging victimization. The case was heard by Mr Justice Wills, who concluded that Ewington had been victimized, and saw in the incident 'a great deal of the sort of thing which would raise the strongest feelings in the men'.[40] From 1903 profits began to rise. For the railwaymen there was a reduction in real wages through rising food prices – and a realization that they needed a more sympathetic government.

The ultimate result of Beasley's vindictiveness was that membership of the union and of the infant Labour Party grew, and the public generally saw the injustice of overweening power. In the election of 1906, the Conservatives were swamped in a Liberal landslide – and twenty-nine Labour Party MPs were elected out of the fifty who stood. That same year, the enormously powerful Trade Disputes Act became law.[41]

26

Competitive Excellence

FROM 1900 THE RAILWAYS began to work as they had never worked before, but against a weakening financial background due to a reluctance among investors to buy railway shares. The average dividend paid to Ordinary shareholders that year was 4.75 per cent, and the average financial yield from Ordinary shares was £3 8s per cent.[1] The MR was permanently damaged by Watkin's reckless competition: all MR stocks were below par, and even MR Debentures were selling at a 14 per cent discount. MR Ordinary shares had been worth 153 in 1893 but had tumbled to 91 at the opening of the GCR's London Extension, and were at 71 four years later. The GCR Ordinary shares were, of course, almost worthless.

The L&NWR's gross earnings were greater than those of any company except the GWR, but neither was able to keep working expenses down while spending large sums on the long-neglected modernization of their respective systems. Euston and Crewe, both cramped and narrow, required rebuilding. The entire layouts had to be enlarged and at Euston this was extremely difficult, involving the demolition of private housing and of its own hotel and offices, as well as the construction of several tunnels below the approach tracks to keep empty carriage and suburban train movements clear of the main lines. The quadrupled track from Euston to Bletchley had to be extended to Rugby; there were quadruplings around Wigan, new marshalling yards, fleets of larger locomotives, superb new corridor trains.

In response to the GWR's and MR's challenge on the Anglo–Irish sea routes (from Milford Haven and Heysham respectively), the L&NWR purchased two new steamers for the Holyhead–Dublin service and carried out improvements to Holyhead harbour. The vast building and rebuilding programme at Euston, including tunnelling under main lines, was carried out with the least possible interference to the trains: not for the engineers of the L&NWR the amateurish solution of closing Euston or Crewe for six months while the layout was rebuilt.

Between 1890 and 1900 the value of L&NWR Debentures, a 'gilt-edged' stock for sixty years, fell from 200 to par, and for the first time the Company experienced difficulty in raising money through share issues. By 1900, like the MR, it was experiencing that new phenomenon – a deficit in its capital account, in the L&NWR's case, of £1,859,000. Gross receipts in the second half of 1900 were £211,000 better than the same period in 1899, but working costs increased by £238,000, depleting net revenue by £23,000. By carrying forward to the following year a mere £8500, a tenth of the usual amount, the dividend was maintained at 7¾ per cent.[2] The GNR and GER managed to pay Ordinary shareholders 2½ per cent only by drawing on their savings.[3]

In spite of these worrying signs the companies went flat-out to provide for the increased demands of a more prosperous nation. They were also spurred on by competition among themselves and by the need to prevent traffic moving to the roads. Each company strove conscientiously to improve standards of speed, comfort and punctuality. They had to provide larger stations with more tracks leading into them, even brand new routes, complete with new stations, to make short-cuts or bypass congested districts,[4] while at the same time the amount they could charge for their services was curtailed by the legislation of 1892 and 1894.

Main line express coaches were magnificently upholstered and decorated, but remained for the most part gas-lit, although electricity was creeping in; more humble coaches were dimly illuminated with the usual oil-lamps. Carriage bodies continued to be made of wood, bolted to steel underframes and coupled together with screw-up shackles. They looked splendid, but in the event of an accident wooden bodies broke away from their underframes, 'telescoped' inside the one in front, and then caught fire when the gas supply exploded.

An MR express crashed near Hawes Junction on Christmas Eve in 1910. The gas cylinders exploded and the wooden train burned cremating twelve passengers, but still the Company did not begin to install electric lighting, even in its finest carriages; on 2 September 1913, sixteen MR passengers were burned to death after a collision near Ais Gill, yet electric lighting of carriages did not become widespread until after 1921.[5]

In 1893 a law was passed in the USA making automatic couplers obligatory on passenger and freight cars. These couplers were (and indeed still are) massive iron castings which interlock like the curled fingers of two opposing fists; they reduced the risk of death and injury to shunters and, in the event of a derailment, were much more likely to hold the train upright than if it were fitted with screw couplings. In 1900 a Royal Commission on Accidents to Railway Servants strongly recommended the use of automatic couplers.[6] Only the GNR responded, adopting the device known colloquially as 'the buck-eye' for its best coaches. The GWR waited twenty-two years before introducing the 'buck-eye' experimentally. The use of this type of coupling gradually became more widespread but only after the railways were nationalized did it become obligatory.

Unsafe though they were in a crash, the carriages of the greatest companies were extremely well made and proportioned, anything from 57 to 70 ft long, and superbly finished. Starting in 1895, the L&YR – 'the Businessman's Line' – went to the expense of building 'club' saloons of bordello-like sumptuousness, each with its liveried attendant to provide tea and stronger drink, and ran them in trains of normally upholstered 1st-, 2nd- and 3rd-class carriages on the Manchester–Blackpool route. The L&NWR followed suit between Manchester and Llandudno. These luxurious saloons were doubly exclusive: to enter one, a passenger not only had to have a 1st-class season ticket but had to be elected to the fraternity of the carriage by the 'Club Carriage Committee'. Although the patronage was small; the L&YR did well out of them because the users agreed to guarantee the Company a certain minimum income. In 1902 and 1911 even bigger and more sumptuous saloons were built for the service.[7]

Dining-carriages were now carried on all long-distance express trains, the lengthy stops for eating at stations were abolished and journey times reduced. Passengers were attended by waiters and sat in some splendour, beneath ceilings moulded with geometric or floral patterns, on seats of buttoned velvet in polished mahogany frames, the carriage walls of french-polished, walnut panelling inlaid with gold-leaf scroll-work. The tables at which they sat were covered in white, damask linen, beautifully woven with the Company's heraldic device.

The cutlery, cruets, coffee-pots, trays and their covers were usually plated to look like silver, the crockery was so well finished as to appear to be good china, when often it was in fact earthenware: beautiful yet robust enough to withstand the rigours of rail travel. The design of all these objects was conservative, comfortably of the period, never avant garde. The GCR's Sheffield–Marylebone expresses, forcing their way into a market already saturated with trains, were decorated even to the extent of stained glass in the clerestory roof lights. By 1906 the major companies formed their best trains from matching sets of these dignified, liveried carriages, sometimes (as on the LB&SCR) interspersed with Pullman cars. Hauled by a handsome, highly polished locomotive these were the fastest and most comfortable trains in Europe, the best that craftsmanship and money could produce.

Competition between companies raised standards of comfort and speed, but even if there was no direct competition on routes between two cities the 'monopoly' Company still considered it worthwhile to give their best service in order to encourage more traffic. The LB&SCR had a complete monopoly of Brighton traffic but positively pampered the place. The 'Brighton' was the second Company in Britain to use Pullman cars, and included one – *Jupiter* – in the formation of its 10.45 a.m. express to Brighton in November 1875. By 1895 this train had become an all-Pullman, seven-car affair. The 8.45 a.m. Brighton and 5 p.m. Victoria were known as 'the City Limited' and consisted entirely of 1st-class saloons and Pullman cars. On 1 November 1908 the LB&SCR instituted the all-Pullman *Southern Belle* – London to Brighton, 51 miles in an hour.

Sometimes there was competition between two towns. Bournemouth and Torquay, two very fashionable seaside resorts, competed for custom with the enthusiastic participation of the L&SWR and GWR respectively, both of which provided a magnificent service of dining-car express trains, although each Company had the monopoly to these places from London.

Competition did not assist passengers on the lesser trains of any company – indeed, the amount of money put into the top 10 per cent of trains probably starved the rest of investment. Passengers on more modest trains had to put up with the hand-me-down, and some had been handed down a long way. The GER found it very difficult to provide enough carriages cheaply for the increasingly heavy tidal flow of humanity morning and evening. In January 1900, Herapath's *Railway Journal* reported that a man standing in a packed compart-

ent of a GER suburban train had violently prevented another pas-
nger from boarding. The pugilist was summoned for assault but the
agistrate discharged him – in acknowledgement of the 'habitually
stressing' circumstances within GER suburban trains.[8] However, the
se judge warned the defendant that the 'chucker-out' of today might
come the 'chucked-out' of tomorrow, and advised him against the
actice. In 1908 the GER was still building six-a-side, four-wheeled
ammers, holding eighty people in a body 27 ft long by 9 ft wide. Old
dies were widened by cutting them longitudinally and inserting
foot-wide strip of wood in roof, floor and end walls. Suburban
rriages on bogies appeared in 1911 but these were merely two old
-wheeled bodies on new, longer frames.[9]

The GER was a line impoverished first by geography and thereafter
nultaneously by mismanagement and competition. It had made huge
pital outlays to build railways *out* of East Anglia in the hope of
pping the coalfields and some large centres of population. The
ER/GNR joint line from Spalding to Lincoln and Doncaster opened
1882. In 1892 the GER got the co-operation of the NER to run from
oncaster to York. After tremendous expense it got a line into
effield in 1900. While these developments were taking place, GER
venue for the London–Norfolk seaside traffic was reduced by
mpetition from the GNR. By 1906, while the GER was attempting
improve its services of fast, dining-car expresses to Lowestoft,
rmouth and Cromer, in response to the GNR, its income from the
ndon suburbs was severely depleted by competition from the more
nvenient trams. Money was hard to come by, and there was a large
ce of railway on which it had to be spread.

The railways tried to accommodate every kind of traffic. The 1854
t obliged them to do so, but their service to the public went far
yond mere legal obligations. It was in the companies' interest to
courage trade and they often initiated a new industry by providing
nsport and facilities. The L&SWR opened its route to the harbour
wn of Padstow on 27 March 1899, thereby putting this remote
rnish backwater in direct connection with London. During 1900,
tons of fish was carried by rail from here; the total for 1911 was 3074
ns, earning the L&SWR £6879, a small contribution towards repay-
the huge investment which had created the line – and employment
r Padstow.[10]

Thanks to the investments and hard work of the GWR, farmers on
Scilly Isles and the Channel Islands were able to sell to London, the

Midlands and the north. The large-scale cultivation of flowers, pot
toes, tomatoes and broccoli developed because of the services offer
by the Company. The produce was shipped in to Penzance a
Weymouth, in the latter case on specially built, railway-owned stear
ers. Weymouth benefited from a heavy investment made by the GW
between 1895 and 1900, when 20 miles of single track was doubled a
14½ miles of new railway was built in order to permit shorter journ
times for express passenger and goods services.

The West Cornwall Steamship Co. brought Scilly Isles produce
Penzance daily. If the load of flowers was moderate they went by t
4.50 p.m. mail train to Paddington; vans for Manchester were detach
at Bristol, those for Birmingham came off at Didcot. All the flowe
arrived in the early hours of the following day. If there were mo
flowers than could be put on to the mail, one or more special trains ra
carrying only flowers. From December to March the special trai
rolled with flowers and vegetables. The Cornish soil and climate w
good for potatoes and broccoli, and every year tens of thousands
tons were carried. Even the flower traffic was measured in hundreds
tons: they were packed in light, wooden, boxes made of specially th
wood sent from London, in kit form, by goods train.

To carry the traffic the GWR had to overcome difficult operati
conditions. The entire route out of Cornwall was single-tracked a
eventually it had to be doubled, which entailed rebuilding all t
viaducts. Meanwhile, the extra traffic required careful timetabling a
special priority over other goods trains, and indeed, over some p
senger trains: 'Where serious delay to a flower special can be prevent
by making a slight delay to a stopping passenger train, the flower tra
is to be given precedence.'[11] The trains of empty vans had, of cour
to be worked back to the West Country. This and other extra traf
meant that, whether existing staff worked overtime, or more staff we
taken on, the Company's working expenses were increased. Signalm
normally booked off-duty at nights or weekends had to be broug
back to their boxes to enable the heavy traffic to pass without del
During the season, additional engines, drivers, firemen and guar
extra porters and shunters were posted to Penzance and Weymou
from other parts of the system. Similar situations existed on oth
companies' lines.

The wholehearted enthusiasm of the GWR and the other compan
for conveying a huge volume of special traffic, did not protect the
from the perennial accusation that they were overcharging, or that t

ailways were carrying imported produce cheaper than the same, ome-grown products. In the latter case the companies would always oint out that imports came in such large quantities as to ensure a teady traffic in full train-loads, which reduces costs and allows a lower rice to be charged. It was ordinary commercial logic. In 1898 the ;WR Chairman, Lord Emlyn, declared: 'If the [British] farmers were o organise themselves and "bulk" their produce before they bring it o the station it could be taken for less. Farmers must learn that it is not nough just to farm – they must learn business.'[12]

Express passenger trains were often made up of coaches for separate estinations, the sections detached or picked up at various junctions. Another device was the 'slip coach'. Here, a coach at the rear of an nportant express was uncoupled, at full speed, a mile before some nportant junction or even the station of some minor market town. 'he GWR made 74 'slips' a day before 1914. This was a good service or passengers but it was an added expense for the railway, since it equired an extra guard to operate the slip coach and the provision of hunting power at the station to retrieve the coach and attach it to some ther train for its onward journey.

At the turn of the century, the GWR was planning hundreds of miles f high speed railway in order to shorten its routes to Birmingham, 'lymouth, South Wales, and Birmingham to Bristol, and thus, to ompete with the L&SWR, L&NWR and MR. The GWR route to xeter and Plymouth, via Bristol, was 15 miles longer than that of the .&SWR, and had single-track sections between Exeter and Newton Abbot, followed by severe gradients from Newton Abbot to 'lymouth. New, double-track railways were built through Wiltshire nd Somerset to shorten the route, and the single track in Devon was oubled, which entailed the widening of tunnels. The GWR's new oute from Paddington to Plymouth, via Westbury and Somerton, was pened on 2 July 1906; it cut 20 miles off the distance from Paddington o Taunton and points west, and gave the GWR a 5-mile advantage and omplete superiority over the L&SWR. Still the L&SWR kept up the xpensive competition. Whole trains of the finest type of corridor oaches, complete with dining-cars, were designed by both the GWR nd the L&SWR and a large catering operation was essential to keep assengers supplied with food.

The capital cost was high and the money not entirely forthcoming rom investors. On 10 August 1905 the GWR Chairman, Mr Alfred saldwin, announced that the Company had a deficit in its capital account of £125,972. The GWR was thus the last of the great compa nies to become the owner of a capital account overdraft.

The most intense competition faced by the GWR was with th L&SWR for passengers and bullion off the transatlantic liners a Plymouth. Because the boat trains ran according to the arrival of th great ships, they could not have a set timetable, and yet they were th fastest trains on the railway, the signalmen finding them their patl through the other traffic. Absolutely nothing was supposed to dela an 'Ocean Special'.

The shipping companies were encouraged to drop anchor i Plymouth Sound to save their passengers one day in the journey fron New York to London. On 9 May 1904 the GWR train ran the 24 miles from Plymouth to Paddington in 227 mins, including a stop t change engines at Bristol. The engine from Plymouth was No. 344c the *City of Truro*, which touched 100 mph running down off th eastern flanks of the Blackdown Hills towards Taunton. The best tim the L&SWR could manage for the 230 miles from Plymouth t Waterloo was 243 mins, including one stop, at Templecombe, to refil the engine's water tank. The GWR had gone to the expense o installing four water troughs with their associated pumping stations to enable their engines to refill their tenders by scooping up water a speed. The two companies raced each other with these Ocean Special until, on 1 July 1906, the L&SWR train crashed at 70 mph passin; Salisbury station. The death toll was twenty-eight, including four rail waymen, and cost the Company £30,000 in repairs and compensation After this, the L&SWR Ocean Specials had to stop at Exeter an Salisbury and were scheduled to take 268 mins from Plymouth t Waterloo.

Special traffic became more and more a part of railway work, bring ing with it complication and expense. The holiday peaks grew eve more intense, creating problems solved only by suspending the norma service and re-drafting the timetables at peak times and by providin; special trains of vans for the bicycles and luggage of the holiday makers. The impecunious Cambrian Railway served a very beautifu rural and maritime area. Thanks to railways, holidays in these lovel places became very popular for the populations of the smokiest part of Britain. Factories in the Potteries disgorged their workforces e *masse* on to North Staffordshire Railway special trains to Aberystwytl and Barmouth. People from Manchester, Derby, Birmingham an London came to stay in the spa villages of Builth Wells, Rhyader an

landidloes as well as the obvious seaside resorts. In Edwardian sum-
mertime, the 10.25 a.m. Euston was formed in four sections, for
Liverpool, Manchester, Aberystwyth and Swansea, with dining-cars in
the first two sections only. The Welsh coaches were detached at
Stafford to form a separate train, via Wellington to Shrewsbury. Here
the Swansea and Aberystwyth coaches were parted, coaches from
Liverpool and Manchester added to each and then sent on as separate
trains, the Cambrian hauling the L&NWR along with its own. The
journey was spartan since there were no Cambrian Railway dining-
cars – and indeed, the Company did not build any corridor-connected
carriages until 1905.[13]

It seems unlikely that anyone would go from Euston to Swansea
in 10 hrs when they could go from Paddington in 4¼. The Swansea
carriages were sent from Euston to increase seating capacity as far
as Stafford and to form a Stafford–Swansea service thereafter. The
L&NWR did, however, provide the best route from London to
Aberystwyth until 1910. The 9.30 a.m. Euston arrived at Aberystwyth
at 4.20 p.m. The GWR made no attempt to improve on this until it had
opened its expensively engineered, shortened route to Birmingham,
via High Wycombe, in 1910. Then one could leave Paddington at 9.50
a.m. and arrive in Aberystwyth, via Shrewsbury and the Cambrian, at
4.15.[14]

Competition made the MR's operation as a major trunk railway
particularly difficult and expensive because of the peculiar complication of its routes in the Midlands and north. Because the main
centres served by the MR were each on a different loop of the 'trunk',
more trains had to be run to provide them all with a service than
if the Company had had a conventional trunk route system. It is
significant that, in the period around 1907, only fifteen MR express
trains ran non-stop over distances in excess of 100 miles, while on
the GWR the figure was thirty-three and on the L&NWR, forty-
nine. The MR was more suited to fast, relatively short-haul, inter-city
business: Derby–Leeds; Sheffield–Manchester; Birmingham–Derby;
Birmingham–Bristol.

The MR Birmingham–Cheltenham–Gloucester–Bristol line actually was a straightforward 'trunk': a monopoly and a valuable profit
earner, giving excellent service between the Midlands and the west. The
MR lost its monopoly in July 1908 when the GWR opened its rival
route from Birmingham, via Stratford-on-Avon, to Cheltenham,
although this was 10 miles longer and had long, wearisome gradients.

The MR route had better gradients – the two miles of the Lickey incline excepted. From Cheltenham, the GWR route ran alongside the MR to Standish Junction, 7 miles south of Gloucester; and from there, by virtue of running powers dating back to 1845, GWR trains ran on MR tracks to Bristol. The MR challenged these powers in court and the legality of the GWR's position was upheld. This MR route had once carried all traffic from Lancashire and Scotland destined for Bristol and the west. After the opening of the Severn tunnel the traffic could come south from Crewe, through Shrewsbury, Hereford and Newport, so that now the MR had to share its west Midlands traffic with the GWR.

The MR's Anglo-Scottish expresses over the Settle line, while apparently not very profitable, were very grand and important to the Company's prestige. R.E. Charlewood, a well-known contemporary observer of the pre-1914 railway scene, noted that while these expresses were well patronized for inter-city work south of Leeds, running to St Pancras, non-stop in 215 mins, north of Leeds they often carried no more than ten passengers.[15] The MR Anglo-Scottish express which crashed near Hawes Junction on Christmas Eve 1910, the peak of the holiday season, was very lightly loaded.[16]

The MR route from London to Carlisle was only 9 miles longer than the L&NWR's, but the real hindrance for the MR was the heavy congestion of their route, the large number of junctions and complex stations to negotiate. The MR operating people had to look sharp to keep their heavy freight and stopping passenger traffic out of the way of these 'crack' trains – and also clear of the important connecting services.

The MR timed their Anglo-Scottish expresses to leave London 30 mins earlier than their L&NWR counterparts, and by running hard with few carriages and few stops to pick up fare-paying passengers they could arrive at Carlisle 5 mins ahead of the L&NWR. The 7.20 p.m. St Pancras to Inverness 'Highland Express' stopped only at Derby and Leeds before Carlisle, and an additional train had to run to cover the station the 'crack' express missed. The 11.30 a.m. St Pancras–Carlisle, calling at Luton, Leicester, Leeds and Hellifield made the stops the 11.50 St Pancras–Edinburgh/Glasgow could not, if it was to arrive in Carlisle ahead of the rival L&NWR train. At Luton passengers from Cambridge joined the train; at Leicester, passengers from Cromer, Yarmouth and Norwich were waiting; at Leeds there might be passengers off an express from Bristol, Birmingham and

Derby. At Hellifield a connection was made with an L&YR service from Liverpool and Manchester. A great deal of legendary hard driving was done to keep these connections on time so as not to delay the Anglo-Scottish express in its race with the east and west coast companies.

The 11.50 a.m. St Pancras to Glasgow and Edinburgh ran to Carlisle non-stop except to change engines at Shipley. It had only five vehicles and *two* of those were Glasgow and Edinburgh restaurant-cars. One wonders how much profit the MR made from such a train, with its limited seating capacity and the fact that a second train had to be run to call at the stations it missed.

The really fast MR 'Scotch' expresses usually ran with only five or six coaches, one section for Glasgow, the other for Edinburgh – and one carriage in each section was the restaurant-car. If there was a shortage of seating, passengers rode in the dining-cars but had to give up their seat at lunchtime or dinnertime, or else order a meal for themselves. Beyond Carlisle the Edinburgh carriages were hauled by the NBR which the MR guaranteed minimum earnings of 2s 1½d per mile, money which was meant to come out of the revenue earned by the train north of Carlisle. Between June 1903 and 1907 the MR paid the NBR £5090 for the 1.30 p.m. St Pancras–Edinburgh, and £6097 for the 7.20 p.m. St Pancras–Edinburgh. During this period ticket revenue was insufficient to cover this charge, which left the MR out of pocket.[17]

The MR had many miles of cross-country secondary main lines to service (Nottingham–Lincoln, Leicester–Birmingham, Leicester–Burton-on-Trent), much of these in competition with the GNR, GCR or L&NWR. Timetabling was as complicated as the routes. The MR and the L&YR established a system of centralized train control, whereby men known as 'Controllers' sat before large-scale maps of the district and, keeping in constant communication with the signalmen and the staff at stations, marshalling yards and engine sheds, logged the movement of every train and engine and gave instructions to signalmen and others (which instructions had to be obeyed) as to which train was to have precedence at junctions. They also allocated relief crews to trains, arranged for engines to meet freight in the yards, tried to get the most out of the men and the equipment and to make the vast, complicated machine run punctually. The decade 1904–14 was remarkable for the intricacy of train services. Carriages were shunted from train to train, trains were combined and parted at junctions, slip carriages abounded on most major lines, and the firemen bent their backs as their drivers blasted their engines over hill and dale to keep time.

In 1904 the GWR and LB&SCR began a co-operation to run from Birkenhead to Brighton via Kensington. The Midland and the L&NWR replied in 1905 with a service of through-coaches, between their northern cities and the south coast resorts. The L&NWR trains came up the main line to Willesden, where LB&SCR engines took over, through Kensington to Latchmore Junction, a three-way junction on the edge of (and giving access to) the Clapham Junction complex. MR trains had no easy access to Kent and Sussex. Trains would come to Kentish Town, change engines and then dive into the tunnel below the main lines, underneath St Pancras station, swinging eastwards to run parallel to the Metropolitan (Circle Line) before plunging steeply to cross beneath the Met. at Farrington, rising again and turning south for the SE&CR at Blackfriars. The GNR had a service from its main line stations to Bournemouth using the same route (reopened in 1988 under the title of 'Thames Link').

On 2 July 1906 the LB&SCR and GWR began a remarkable co-operation with a Paddington–Brighton service offering through-tickets between any GWR and LB&SCR station along the way. LB&SCR locomotives hauled the trains throughout and created quite a stir. For a brief period, while it was a novelty, the train was well patronized, but people soon lost interest when they discovered how slow it was – 100 mins for 54½ miles – and the service was withdrawn exactly one year later, in the middle of the holiday season.

The most successful of these cross-London, cross-country trains was the dining-car train which the L&NWR and LB&SCR inaugurated on 1 March 1905: the Liverpool, Manchester and Birmingham to Brighton and Eastbourne train – the 'Sunny South Special' (later, 'Express'). The GWR/SE&CR ran a very long-lived service to and from Birkenhead–Birmingham–Dover, via Oxford and Reading. Passengers from Worcester were brought in conveniently to catch the train at Oxford. A Bristol and South Wales to Dover service was supplied by an 'up' express which slipped coaches at Southall. These were hauled to Kensington, where they were attached to L&NWR coaches from the north, and the whole was worked forward by an SE&CR engine. The carriage roofboards, a throw-back to stage-coach days, were yards long, boldly proclaiming the route and adding a certain grandeur to the occasion.

All over the country, the different railways developed and dealt with their special traffics. The L&YR ran daily, 1st-class-only, dining-car expresses from Liverpool to York. There were 'tourist' tickets, combined 'lake and rail' tickets, 'rail and river' tickets, tickets to cricket matches, the theatre, the races. Special trains took racehorses from the great training centres at Newmarket and Lambourn to wherever the meeting was to be – Aintree or Ayr, Bath or Doncaster. On Grand National Day the L&YR ran an all-day shuttle service of electric trains from Liverpool Exchange station to Aintree, each train consisting of seven ordinary six-wheeled carriages seating a total of 500 people and hauled with an electric motor coach at each end.[18] The L&NWR Royal Train from Euston had to be accommodated, the L&NWR 1st-class only, all dining-car express, on which every seat was reserved, and then as many as thirty more steam-hauled excursions including a dining-car express from the GER. All this was handled at the two stations close to the race course: Sefton Arms, near the grandstands and the specially built Racecourse station on what was, for the rest of the year, a goods line.

This required inter-company co-operation with route planning, timetabling, engine and crew changes. At Aintree there were no vast acres of sidings on which to park the trains as they waited – as at Doncaster on St Leger day – and some very careful staff work was required to ensure that the trains arrived in the correct order for their departure, and that all the passengers knew which train was theirs and at what platform it could be found – and when. Precision and costly intricacy describes railway operations then, of which Aintree provides but one example. The operating was planned and executed by ordinary working people, using their native wit and many years of experience.

There were even special trains to carry pigeons, in wicker hampers, to the point at which they would be released to fly back to their lofts. The porters at the destination station released the pigeons and filled in the time of release on a label attached to the hamper. The vans were then reloaded with the empty hampers and the whole lot returned whence it came. How this could have paid the railway Company is a mystery of public service. The railways carried produce from market gardens in Hertfordshire, crockery from Stoke-on-Trent, straw hats from factories in Luton, pork pies from Calne, strawberries from Axbridge, plums from Pershore, coal from Newcastle, iron castings from Coalbrookdale, bricks from Peterborough: all factories or sidings to be visited daily – twice daily to bring in raw materials and clear the traffic. Thousands of cumbersome wagons had to be sorted by destination into trains, swapped from route to route with as much speed and facility as flimsy envelopes in the mail system. It has been said that for every hundred miles a wagon travelled on the main line it travelled 75 miles in shunting.

The increase in traffic brought the need to enlarge facilities for passengers and freight. By 1907 the railway companies were wishing for a cessation, or at least an abatement, of competition, through working agreements or amalgamation. Meanwhile, the fact that some industrialists and most farmers grumbled about the companies' 'overcharging' was used as ammunition by those who wanted to see the railways nationalized.

27

Individualism on Wheels

E VERYONE – WORKMEN, TRADESMEN, shareholders, passengers
and paupers – wanted their portion of the railway companies'
profits, and the share taken by the paupers, or at least by the
parochial rates, was a very heavy burden, a sum sufficient to add one
per cent to the GWR dividend, for instance. The method used to discover the rateable value of a property had been established by the
Poor Relief Act of 1601, when the property to be taxed was simply
farm land probably rented under a landlord–tenant relationship.
When this antique system of assessment was applied to a highly
capitalized property which extended through hundreds of parishes, it
created situations 'based on legal fictions, some of them of a rather
fantastic character'.[1] The gross unfairness of the system was apparent
to William Gladstone who, in 1844, set up a Committee to investigate. Its Report stated: 'The Committee are satisfied that peculiar
difficulties attach to the application of the ordinary laws of rating in
the case of railways which give rise to great uncertainty and inequality . . . the subject is one which will properly call for the attention of
the Legislature . . .' There followed a series of appeals from a bewil-
dered judiciary to Parliament, begging the latter to simplify matters
and make them more equitable; occasionally these appeals resulted in
another Select Committee, but the railways made a wonderful milch
cow, which no one wanted untethered. The GWR complained in
1908:

Competition has compelled the companies to build more powerful engines, heavier, more luxurious, heated, carriages; continuous brakes on goods trains, the latest signalling instruments, more commodious stations, more trains. English railways' net revenue has increased by 7.6% between 1899–1906 but rateable value has increased 12%.[2]

To add insult to injury, some of the money the railways paid in rates went towards the upkeep and improvement of roads, on which, even then, motor cars and motor buses were running, and even towards the construction and subsidy of municipal electric tramways.[3] While railway companies had to pay the cost of their own track maintenance and paid parochial rates on every square inch of ground they used for their business, motor car, buses and trams ran on roads through the same parishes without paying a penny towards the rates – although the garage in which the bus or tram was housed was liable for rates.

The capital cost of constructing a tramway was miniscule compared with the costs of a railway; tramways paid very little for land and legal fees, they had no earthworks, no viaducts, no signalling, no stations; and thus, fares could be much lower than on a railway. Some electric tramways had shareholders to pay, but still had a tremendous advantage over the railways. The municipal tramways had no need to make a profit beyond the 1 per cent required to cover the costs of renewals and maintenance, and the deficit, if any, was subsidized out of the rates – paid very largely by the railway Company.[4] The tramways were easier for the public to reach than a railway station, they could afford to charge exceptionally low fares, and offered a widespread 'workmen's' ticket system and a frequency of service for 22 hrs a day which no railway could equal. For cross-London journeys even up to 12 miles long the trams were more convenient than trains.[5]

Although tram and motor bus competition was limited to relatively small areas within cities, these were areas where some railways had invested huge sums. The GER's investment in cheap trains had encouraged a large area of artisan and middle-class housing as far as Enfield, Edmonton and Tottenham by the 1880s.[6] In 1900 the tramways reached Enfield and Wood Green and took away much of the railway's income. Not knowing when it was beaten, the GER then decided to build a speculative railway in the hope of developing a new empire of housing estates – as if the trams would not also lay their rails to them. The Company opened two new railways: from Woodford, on its

Enfield line, through Fairlop to Ilford; and from Edmonton to Cheshunt, paralleling its Cambridge main line. Even while the railway line was under construction, Ilford Corporation built a tramway parallel to the Fairlop line and opened this in March 1903. The GER opened their line in May, by which time the trams had much of the traffic. The Edmonton–Cheshunt line did not attract much housing until the Metropolitan Electric Tramway Co. opened its route to Cheshunt in December 1907. Since 1901, East Ham and West Ham Corporations had been building tramways, on the rates, into London's East End and docks, taking away traffic from the GER's expensively constructed lines. The GER felt obliged to spend more on increasing their services in an attempt to retain a declining traffic, but people would not walk a quarter of a mile past a cheap tram to catch an expensive train which would drop them half a mile from where they actually wanted to be.

In 1901, a 12,000 volt overhead catenary system had been installed on the Berlin (Marienfeld)–Zossen military railway. The 50-seat coaches were driven at 130 mph by 2000 horsepower electric motors. The system was developed by Siemens & Halske and was a jointly financed project between the Imperial German Government, Siemens and German banks. In unregimented Britain the Government let competition blow wherever it might, like the wind. The need for electrification was recognized in Britain, but the difficulty was that such work required substantial additions to a railway company's capital at a time when returns on the existing capital were not enough to excite the markets; investors in railways were thin on the ground and only a handful of railway electrification schemes were completed prior to 1921. The first important[7] electric railway in Britain and the first elevated electric railway in the world was the Liverpool Overhead Railway, enacted specifically for electric haulage in 1888 and opened in 1893. It was known as 'the Dockers' Umbrella' because most of its 6½ miles was raised on girders above the streets. The steam-hauled Mersey Railway was electrified in 1903, and a connection between this and the LOR was opened on 1905. The L&YR electrified their Liverpool–Southport route in December 1904. These were purely suburban lines and used a 500 volts d.c., with a ground-level, 'third-rail' conductor.

The GER was endangered in 1901 when two Bills were submitted to Parliament for electric railways to connect the City with the suburbs to the north and east. The Bills' promoters argued that a better service could be provided by an all-electric railway. Electric trains could accelerate from a stand better than existing steam-engines, and a more frequent service could be run. In order to defeat these excellent proposals, the GER's Locomotive Engineer, James Holden, designed and had built a massive tank engine with ten driving wheels. On test in 1902 it was able to accelerate 335 tons at the same rate as an electric unit: from a stand to 30 mph in just under 30 secs. The point was made, the electric railways Bills were dropped – and the GER then turned its super-passenger tank into an eight-wheeled goods engine.

In 1903, the SE&CR spent thousands on an Act to electrify some of its suburban routes, and then, having obtained the Act, could not raise sufficient money to carry out the work. The LB&SCR's passenger carrying from south London to London Bridge was halved in two or three years, owing to the electric street trams – even though the trams were forbidden, until 1906, to cross the Thames,[8] so that passengers had to walk across from one tram to the other. Having a stronger financial base, the LB&SCR was able to raise enough money for electrification of their route from London Bridge to Crystal Palace in 1904, and gave the contract to the German company AEG. The trains, using an overhead catenary to carry the electric current, came into use the following year. The LB&SCR's outlay quickly restored their passenger carrying to 1902 levels – but the trams nevertheless carried off the bulk of the traffic. The MR set out in 1904 to electrify the 9 miles from Lancaster (Green Ayre) to Morecambe with an overhead catenary system, and brought it into use in 1908.

One of the four grandest railway companies from the 'Golden Age', the NER had a regional monopoly and gave splendid service to its public. Until 1896 NER new issues of Debentures and Preference shares were sold at whatever premium the Company placed on them; but from 1897 the first signs of a definite loss of interest in railway stocks emerged – even those of the NER. At the end of 1897 the NER had acquired the unthinkable: a £606,000 overdraft to cover the gap between capital income from share issues and capital expenditure on new works. On 8 February 1901 Herapath's *Railway Journal* noted: 'The NER is splendid in everything but net result'. Nothing more clearly illustrates the disastrous tendency of the times for railways than to find a magnificent increase in gross receipts reduced by expenses to a (net) increase of merely £2000. In May 1901 the NER issued £2.25 million in shares, of which £1.6 million remained unsold three years later. This large residue was handed over to the stockbrokers Rowe &

Pitman, who took 700,000 Ordinary shares at 140, 700,000 Preferences at 117 and 200,000 Debentures at 94.[9]

In 1912 the NER wanted to electrify the 18 miles from Shildon to Middlesbrough and was unable to raise the capital by any means. Although the Company had improved its profits that year, the investors were not impressed. The Company's capital account was by then £3.8 million in the red and the dividend was only a few per cent. There were more exciting places to put your money. In December 1913 the Chairman of the Company, Lord Knaresborough, told his shareholders: 'There has been such a depreciation in first class railway securities in the last few years that the public are now anxious that when they invest their £100 – it should be repayable.' Happy in his ignorance of the future, he added: 'In ten years I hope times will be more favourable to the raising of new capital.'[10]

The North London Railway was extremely vulnerable to competition from the new, electric trams. From 1901 the number of passenger journeys on the NLR began to fall, and in order to keep what traffic it could, it had to run more trains, thereby increasing its costs. Electrification was known to be the way forward, but the NLR was too small to do this on its own, and the L&NWR, whose satellite the NLR was,[11] was not rich enough in 1901 to assist it. The L&NWR and the GNR considered electrification of their suburban areas, but they carried a heavy coal and merchandise traffic, and the advantages of electric traction would have been lost if the new trains had to run among coal trains. Obviously, dedicated tracks would be required at the cost of adding extra tracks and duplicating tunnels. As late as February 1913 the GNR Board was of the opinion that the necessary capital outlay required for electrification was too great in relation to the profits it would generate.

In six months in 1905, the L&NWR suffered a decrease of 742,000 passengers, 542,000 of them from the 3rd class, and the Chairman, Lord Stalbridge, attributed this largely to the competition from trams.[12] One wonders whether the companies were wise to attempt to compete with the trams at all; suburban traffic had become too expensive for railways to handle, and was best left to someone else. As early as 1905 the L&NWR planned to build an entirely new, all-electric railway, paralleling their main line from Euston to Watford, but had to postpone the work because it could only raise the money by guaranteeing interest at a rate higher than the expected return from the new railway. Lord Stalbridge commented: 'There can be no doubt that the

[Watford] line is much needed. Owing to competition from trams and motor omnibuses in cities and especially in London, railways need to electrify their trains and modernise their signalling.'

By contrast, the L&SWR was able to increase its capital by £7,853,000 between 1895 and 1906, and continued to produce some of the very lowest working costs and highest dividends of any major railway in Britain. Its investment had been quite fruitfully spent on rebuilding Waterloo station, closing the ancient Nine Elms locomotive works and opening a new locomotive factory at Eastleigh, developing Southampton Docks, and purchasing the Waterloo & City Railway. In 1912, with the prosperity of Britain as a whole at a peak and the L&SWR uniquely paying 8 per cent on Ordinary shares, its Directors announced their first electrification scheme.

The decade 1900–1910 was perhaps the GWR's most competitive period. During that time the Company built most of its new main lines and a brand new, international harbour at Fishguard. The GWR's new route to Taunton made the GWR unbeatable to Plymouth and allowed the Company to attack L&SWR Ocean Liner traffic at two points, while also competing powerfully for the L&SWR's ordinary West Country traffic. The GWR's new route from London to Birmingham was 3 miles shorter than that of the L&NWR, and the MR was challenged by the GWR's new route between Birmingham and Cheltenham. Throughout all this large-scale building programme the GWR continued to pay 5½ per cent on Ordinary shares and the capital account went into no more than a minor deficit.[13] The GWR's suburban service depended on the outer areas, free of tram competition; it ran from Reading, Henley and Windsor into the Paddington terminus and, through Bishop's Road station, into the Met. and MDR underground system. The Company made a shrewd deal with the Central London Railway in 1911. Starting in 1912, the GWR built the 4½-mile Ealing & Shepherd's Bush line, while the CLR extended westwards half a mile from their Wood Lane terminus to meet them. The passenger service was opened in 1920 and operated by the CLR.

London's underground railway system in 1900 consisted of the steam-operated Met. and MDR[14] and the electrified City & South London. This was incorporated in 1884 to build a cable-hauled route from Monument to the Elephant & Castle, through deep-level tunnels. In 1888 the Company adopted electric traction, and the line was opened from Monument to Stockwell in November 1890. The Clapham extension opened in June 1900 and to the Angel, Islington,

n November 1901. Avoiding years of personal feuding between
Chairmen, as had happened with the Met. and MDR, was a great
uccess.[15] British money was, however, reluctant to invest in electric
ailways, even in London. The Charing Cross, Euston & Hampstead
Company (Charing Cross) got its Act in 1893 but was then unable to
aise the capital to build the line. The Baker Street & Waterloo (Baker
t), also incorporated in 1893, met the same fate – and then a worse
ne: it was purchased by Whittaker Wright, Chairman of the London
& Globe Financial Corporation and sundry shady mining companies.
His frauds caught up with him and in 1900 he was sentenced to seven
ears in prison, but committed suicide in the court waiting-room while
waiting transport to prison.

In America at the turn of the century, home investment was satu-
ated and the big banking syndicates were looking abroad for a place
o put their money. The Whitney–Elkins–Widener Syndicate, repre-
ented by Charles Tyson Yerkes (1837–1905), bought the Charing
Cross Company for £100,000 in 1900,[16] and the Baker St in 1901. In
March of that year he also gained financial control of the MDR. Yerkes
hen took on board the financiers Speyer Brothers of London and
New York and, in July 1901, formed the Metropolitan District Electric
raction Company to electrify the District and build a power station
o supply it. The Brompton & Piccadilly Circus was purchased in
902.[17] Yerkes was fortunate in securing as Deputy Chairman and
General Manager for his semi-derelict or entirely unbuilt underground
ystem the brilliant railway manager George Stegmann Gibb
850–1925). Trained as a solicitor, Gibb joined the GWR in 1877 and
om 1882–91 was Solicitor and General Manager of the NER, where
e pioneered scientific management of railways. The Yerkes/Speyer
oup of railways were together to form the 'Underground Electric
ompanies of London', or 'Underground' for short.

They were soon involved in a drastic price war with the London
nited Tramways (LUT), owned by the US financial syndicate
Pierpoint Morgan, and fares tumbled to dangerously low levels,
hich was pleasant for the passengers while it lasted – but not the
ay forward. Speyer Brothers managed to buy control of the LUT
September 1902, whereupon the trams became feeders to the
nderground rather than competitors.

Gibb got the various sections of the Underground's system built and
ened by March 1906, and quickly succeeded in organizing the
ondon Passenger Traffic Conference to co-ordinate the work of all

the underground railways and the trams. But even the electric unde
ground lines had their profits reduced by electric street cars and mot
buses. Sir Henry Oakley, Chairman of the GNR, was also Chairma
of the CLR (popularly known as 'the Two-penny Tube'), and
February 1908 he warned the tram and bus companies that the CL
had suffered a large decrease in passengers, and threatened that 'unle
they conducted themselves in a reasonable manner', the CLR wou
reduce their fares to one penny for three stations east or west of t
boarding station; however, the existing minimum fare of two pen
would be maintained if the 'surface competitors' would do the san
The CLR had benefited from through-booking arrangements with t
Baker St and the Charing Cross, and would make similar arrangemer
with the Piccadilly & Brompton once the engineers had worked o
how to make connections. There was also a working agreement wi
the C&SLR. Thus the greatest managers and financiers of the day la
the foundations of a co-ordinated transport system for London.

After what John Loudon McAdam had described as 'the calamity
the railways', the main roads of England, which were maintained I
Turnpike Trust companies, became practically deserted and fell in
real decay. Curiously enough, because locals had to get themselves a
their produce to the local railway station, the 'parish', non-turnpi
roads tended to be improved. The turnpike roads were in such a b
state that in 1864 Parliament recommended the abolition of t
Turnpike Trusts and that their roads be handed over to local authori
control. There were 854 Trusts in 1870 and two in 1890. The la
Turnpike Trust in Britain, owning the Anglesey length of t
London–Holyhead road, was abolished on 1 November 1895. A ye
later there came into force the law which, had it arrived the year befor
might have revitalized the toll road. On 14 November 1896 t
Locomotives on Highways Amendment Act abolished the requir
ment for a man with a red flag to precede a powered vehicle, and rais
the speed limit to 14 mph for 'light locomotives weighing less than
tons'. In moving the Bill's Second Reading Mr Henry Chaplin, MP f
the farming constituency of Sleaford, noted that the motor car w
already in use in USA, France and Germany, and commented: 'If t
car was freed from *all* restrictions it would lead to an enormous tra
and a vast amount of employment. Farmers could use them to tran
port their produce at much less cost than at present (hear, hear) a
they would force [railway] passenger fares to be reduced.'[18]

Railways, at their best, were fast, comfortable, even luxurious – b regimented. They required to take over completely the persons of those they carried. Through seventy-five years of development, railways had shown that they worked best as very large, centrally co-ordinated monopolies – and not particularly profitable monopolies at that. It was also the case that these large organizations created a more or less anti-capitalist working class, a significant political weight. Not only did motor cars represent individualism on wheels, and offer hitherto unknown freedom of movement, but even before the Great War, the car was *chic*. Perhaps it was its Frenchness; the Michelin Man with his champagne glass raised to his rich clientele. Railways in general could never be *chic* – although it is significant that, from the early 1900s, the railways tried to present a smarter or more elegant image by the use of some very beautiful advertisement posters.[19]

Between 1830 and 1866 railways had been financially dynamic, but after 1866 their financial importance declined, and by 1896 railways were no longer attracting much capital. The motor car was new technology and promised a whole new world of investment – and unregulated expansion. Mr Mundella, President of the Board of Trade, prophesied: 'There [is] in the future a vast industry in motor cars . . . we have handicapped ourselves by too much legislation already and for that reason we are so much behind [the rest of Europe and America] in the matter of electricity and telephones'.[20]

A whole new world of business was waiting in the wings. The Val de Travers, the Limmer Asphalte Paving and Trinidad Lake Asphalte Companies had been contractors for paving the streets of the City of London since 1869. The Standard Oil Company (later 'Esso') owned by Mr Rockefeller, and the Royal Dutch Oil Company and Burmah Oil, were already producing. The forerunner of Anglo-Persian (later BP) was formed in 1903. There were 200,000 miles of roads to be rebuilt and much petrol to be sold.[21] Here was competition indeed for railways: the competition for returns and investment capital on the money markets of the world. And railways were 'old hat'.

Until Ford and Morris began to mass-produce cheap cars, the car was the exclusive status symbol of the upper classes. Even in those early days the deaths and injuries caused by motorists numbered thousands a year,[22] and the dust clouds thrown up by cars were a very serious nuisance. The future Lord Harmsworth, the newspaper magnate, was an enthusiastic motorist in 1900. The Conservative Prime Minister in 1903, A.J. Balfour, was so enthusiastic a motorist as to be up frequently before the 'beak', charged with speeding; when

Parliament was debating the Motor Car Act of 1903, it was jokingly said that 'nothing in this Act shall apply to the present Prime Minister'.[23]

Although the potential for new industries connected with cars had long been recognized, only a few people regarded the motor car as a *serious* mode of transport. The GWR Chairman, Alfred Baldwin, told shareholders at the AGM on 10 August 1905:

> The Officers of the Company *do not quite agree with me* but I think that the present *craze* [*sic*] for motoring has got something to do with the loss of First Class fares. Last Thursday at Henley Week there were at least 400 motor cars counted and most of these would have been carrying people who would otherwise have travelled by train from Paddington.[24]

In 1909 David Lloyd George, then Chancellor of the Exchequer proposed the construction of 'motorways', 'bypasses', and the modernization of county roads. He noted that the Great North Road was under 72 separate Authorities. Roads were to be under a central authority – the 'Road Board' – which would manage a Road Improvement Fund created by the money raised from taxes on motor vehicles and petrol. The Board and the Fund were established in May 1910. In that year 144,000 cars were registered in Britain and the Board granted £14,300 to County Councils. This was mainly to lay asphalt on road surfaces although some new roads were constructed in the London area.[25] In 1914 there were 389,000 cars and £18,000 was laid out in grants by the Road Board.[26] There were howls of criticism from the motor car industry and the motorists' organizations: they were paying their tiny licence-fee (or none at all) and were not getting their motorways! They suspected that this had something to do with the fact that the Chairman of the Road Board was none other than that great proponent of statistics and transport integration, the railwayman Sir George Gibb.

28

The Companies Close Ranks

IN SPITE OF the comfort and speed of express train travel, in spite of the increasingly fast freight services – both much better than anywhere else in the world – the railways of Britain were not beloved by the farmers or manufacturers. The Board of Trade acknowledged the existence of a 'superficial discord', beneath which lay 'a general harmony of interest between the railway companies and the public they serve'.[1] Whether this was true is hard to say, but it is worth noting that although the cost to the plaintiff of bringing a complaint against a railway company before the Railway Commissioners was between £2000 and £2500, the Commissioners still heard about 120 cases a year.

The pricing policy of any railway company was, to outsiders at any rate, incomprehensible, and arose from individualistic market forces. Discounts and facilities were negotiated with traders either as competitive measures against another railway or to encourage a certain traffic to make more use of the railway. There was competition in some areas and 'no competition' agreements in others, charges of monopoly, and government Acts to control suspected abuses of power. Traders perceived ridiculous anomalies in charges (and the companies very often agreed), but these anomalies could often only be removed by amalgamation – which the traders denounced as 'monopoly'.

In 1895 the L&SWR was brought before the Railway Commissioners in what became known as the 'Southampton Case', under the provisions of the Railway & Canal Traffic Act 1854, Section 2: 'No company shall make or give any undue or unreasonable preference . . . provided that the different fares were being charged for *the same or similar service*.' The L&SWR demonstrated to the learned judge that taking full train-loads of imported goods from ships was not 'the same or similar service' as taking the occasional barrel of butter in the brake van of a branch-line train, or a truck of potatoes from a village station. That same year John O'Dowd, MP for Sligo North, complained in Parliament that 'small traders in Ireland are charged prohibitive rates for conveyance of their goods whilst manufacturers and wholesale merchants enjoy the privilege of specially reduced rates', and asked: 'What steps can be taken to equalise rates?' Mr Sydney Buxton, President of the Board of Trade, replied: 'It is a recognised practice to charge a lower rate for large and frequent consignments than that charged for small lots.'[2]

The railways' efforts to compete with each other in the number of services they ran, their speed and luxury, did nothing for profitability. The L&YR's traffic was so great in 1906 that its gross income increased by £88,000 but this sufficed only to maintain the dividend at 4 per cent because working costs had swallowed £74,000 of the extra revenue. The GNR increased its gross receipts by a remarkable £103,000, whittled down by increased working expenses to a mere £8000. In the first half of 1905 the L&NWR increased its net profit by £33,000 but paid the same 7 per cent dividend.[3] The MR increased net profit in the first half of 1906 by £227,500 and raised the dividend by ¼ per cent. The NER had a second-half increase of net profit of £294,500 in 1906, and its dividend rose by only ¾ per cent.[4]

Dividends of the major companies could have been higher if the half-yearly surpluses had been 'divided up to the hilt', but the companies were well aware that fair weather could turn foul, and they preferred instead to make small increases and put larger sums into reserve, or spend revenue to keep the railway in first-class order. This was noble and magnificent on the part of the Directors but also rather pessimistic; no wonder then, that the investors went away from railways to exciting, expanding, new industries like rubber and oil, which were supplying the exciting new, expanding car market; or to Imperial Tobacco, which was literally growing money – using a capital which was a tiny fraction of that employed by any major railway company – and yet which was able to pay its shareholders large dividends and bonuses.

By 1906 the railways' working costs took, on average, 62 per cent of gross income,[5] and wages formed a large part of this. Even so, railway-men were less well paid than other workmen. The passing of the Trade Disputes Act heralded an immediate increase in union membership among railwaymen. Inflation had been rising faster than wages since 1900, and there was also still the question of long working hours. In November 1906 the ASRS put forward their request for an 8-hr day for drivers, firemen, signalmen, guards shunters and platelayers, 10 hrs for all other grades, and a minimum rest period of 9 hrs between shifts. They also wanted a 2s a week pay rise for everyone. The com-panies conferred through their own union – the Railway Companies Association (RCA) – and, as one, refused to talk to the railwaymen's unions. They insisted that individual employees come before the Directors with their grievances. The effectiveness of the individual approach can best be summed up by the statistics issued by the ASRS early in 1907: 39 per cent of railwaymen had a standard weekly wage of less than £1 a week, 11 per cent earned in excess of 30s; 7.5 per cent worked an 8-hr day, 66 per cent a 10-hr day, and 26 per cent a 12-hr day. These were the mandatory hours for a day's pay; under-manning required overtime to be worked, and there were, in 1907, many instances where men worked 18 hrs a day. These figures were verified in a Board of Trade survey published in 1912.[6]

In the first half of 1907, thousands of railwaymen marched through London to demonstrate for union recognition and improved working conditions, while the union executive asked repeatedly to meet with the companies. On 11 October 1907 the railway companies, through the Railway Companies Association, collectively dismissed the men's collective request with the excuse that companies could only act indi-vidually.[7] *The Times* of 3 October 1907 supported the Directors, while the *Economist* believed the Directors were wrong. Meanwhile ASRS activists were singled out for dismissal by the collective policy of the companies.

The railwaymen were now prepared to go on strike. On 2 Nov-ember Lloyd George invited Richard Bell of the ASRS for talks on the 6th. Lloyd George had already told the companies that they would escape the need to recognize trade unions if they agreed to accept a 'Conciliation Board' for each Company. The scheme – almost entirely the work of Sam Fay, General Manager of the GCR – was a magnifi-cent device for time-wasting. Each Board was to be composed by a 'Sectional Committee' and, above that, a Central Conciliation Board comprising an equal number of members from the workforce and the management, who would deal with problems arising from pay and hours, the Company alone dealing with matters of discipline. Every problem had to be submitted to the Sectional Board; if not solved there it would be sent to the Central Board, and thereafter, if necessary, to arbitration. This was presented to Richard Bell on the 6th as a *fait accompli* and he was given 20 mins to accept it. This he did, although he knew that the railwaymen were fully prepared to go on strike.

The scheme was hailed by the national press as Mr Lloyd George's brilliant compromise, imposed impartially on the companies and the unions. The companies appeared to accept it grudgingly as an alternative to recognizing trade unions.[8] Richard Bell accepted the scheme as 'Hobson's choice', and the railwaymen accepted it because it came from Lloyd George and was recommended by their leader Richard Bell.[9] The railway companies were confident they had arranged a seven-year filibuster, but early in the New Year of 1908 Britain's trade collapsed in the wake of a similar recession in the USA.[10] In 1909, to compound the loss of traffic suffered by the railways, coal prices rose by 22 per cent. Any pay rises conceded through the conciliation service were very small (the companies pleading poverty), and agreements which were made were then binding for seven years, during which time inflation grew.

While denying their workers' right to combine in negotiations, the companies themselves now began to combine and co-operate to put an end to the fierce competition which had cost them dear. In 1905 the competition between the L&NWR and L&YR ceased with an informal agreement; the GNR and the GCR brought a Bill to Parliament to sanction their 'working union' in 1907; and in 1908 the NBR and Caledonian entered into a pooling agreement,[11] and the MR made a 99-year pooling and co-operation agreement with the L&NWR. At about this time the GWR and L&NWR made a valuable wagon pooling agreement which saved wasted mileage and made more wagons available.

On 11 February 1908 Mr G.A. Hardy, MP for Stowmarket and a Member of the Board of Agriculture, proposed the following motion in the Commons:

In view of the widespread complaints on the part of traders, agriculturalists and the general public with regard to railway charges and facilities and particularly with regard to preferential treatment of foreign goods, the time has come to consider how far these evils could be remedied by the State purchase of railways as foreshadowed by the Railway Regulation Act of 1844.[12]

Hardy had misread the 1844 Act. It did not allow unconditional state purchase. Rather, if a company paid 10 per cent to its Ordinary share-holders, it could be purchased – and after 1844 few companies ever paid 10 per cent. Hardy attributed the lack of profit suffered by those he represented to the railways' preferential charges to foreign imports, and was of the opinion that, if the railways were to be taken over by the state, 'all inhabitants of all parts of the country could pay the same rate for the same traffic', and that 'unnecessary and wasteful services should be abolished'. By what criteria he would judge a service to be 'wasteful and unnecessary' he did not say, but if he meant commer-cially unprofitable or duplicated lines then a large part of the railways in his native East Anglia would have had to be closed.

Speaking against the motion,[13] Mr Bonar Law, the Glasgow iron merchant soon to be the Leader of the Unionists, agreed that the 'present position of railways' was 'unsatisfactory', but thought that matters could be remedied without such a drastic step as nationaliza-tion. He reminded the House of the waste of money in getting railway Bills through Parliament: 'I have forgotten the amount but it was a sum almost fabulous and the money so spent was just as much capital as if it were spent in construction.' He went on: 'The real hope for the prosperity of the railways – and upon that largely depends the prosperity of the trade of the country – was the doing away with unnecessary competition. Much of this was utterly wasteful and among railway managers there was a strong movement on foot to put an end to it.' Law urged the President of the Board of Trade to assist rather than retard such arrangements. Traders, said Law, opposed these large groupings as 'monopoly', yet they had to pay higher costs as a result of maintaining the competition.[14]

Lloyd George, then President of the Board of Trade,[15] declared that the problem under discussion was not simple but 'gigantic' – and went on accurately to sum up the situation: 'Considering all the difficulties of the case I believe that our railways are very ably managed . . . and have done their best for the general public of this country.' He agreed with Bonar Law that the responsibility for high railway charges in Britain relative to Europe rested – primarily – 'not on railway direc-tors, nor even on stockbrokers but on the House of Commons'. He described both the cost of the Parliamentary legal processes through which a Bill had to go, and the compensation permitted to landown-ers, as 'a story of scandalous pillage from beginning to end'.[16]

He cited Prussia as the prime example of the benefits which could accrue from a state-owned railway system, calling it 'a very powerful machine for the purpose of developing and helping German industry and fighting foreign industry'.[17] He pointed out that many British trains ran two-thirds empty to the same destinations at about the same time of the day.[18] Fifty-three trains a day ran between London and York by the GNR, GCR and GER, the last two going by circuitous routes. This was the service which competition brought about, but it was wasteful of the companies' resources, and the public had to bear the expense of it in higher charges elsewhere. Lloyd George summed up the situation:

> The railway companies are themselves beginning to realise that the present system is impossible. They are pressed for increased wages, shorter hours, cheap trains for workmen – whether or not this is commercial for the rail-ways – and for greater facilities. The companies could not face all these demands under the present system. Unless the investor gets a fair return for his money the railways will not get the capital necessary for essential development demanded by the traders who are the industry of this country. Between the two, the companies are in real danger of being crushed.[19]

Hardy's motion got no further.

In 1909 the GER joined with the GNR and GCR to promote a Bill proposing a 'working union'. The three companies maintained collec-tion and delivery services for identical areas and in 1906 the GER spent £207,000 on cartage, the GCR £207,500, and the GNR £307,500 – delivering to the same streets. Obviously an amalgamated company could make very large savings in the withdrawal of overlapping ser-vices like these – and through the laying-off of large numbers of workmen.

Winston Churchill, by now President of the Board of Trade, was in favour of the amalgamation and said he had ensured that there were clauses to prevent the amalgamated Company either raising fares or reducing facilities. Mr Mond pointed out that he had made no mention of any clause which would oblige the Company to *reduce* its charges. In response to Labour members' concern over job losses, Churchill stated:

> I have devoted special attention to protecting the position of the railway servants. I think they ought not to suffer through an amalgamation in the

public interest. The railway companies have agreed to the insertion of a clause which makes it impossible for them to dismiss any man in consequence of this amalgamation.[20]

In spite of the assurances the Bill was thrown out; but Churchill promised that the question of railway amalgamations would be examined by a Committee of his department.

The GWR was perhaps the last great company to cease competition, having been the last to enter the field. It was in an unassailable position on the apparently competitive London–Birmingham, London–west of England and Birmingham–Bristol routes and had the good fortune to employ George Churchward as its Locomotive & Carriage Superintendent. Churchward's large, standardized locomotives, better-designed, better-made and longer-lasting, reduced the factory labour force and running costs. The latter took 64 per cent of income in 1904 and 60.9 per cent in 1909 and 1910, even though GWR train mileage had increased since 1906 by 500,000 miles.[21] On 13 May 1910 the L&SWR gave up the unequal struggle in the west of England, and agreed on fares and the pooling of Plymouth revenues; henceforth the GWR would carry all the 'Ocean' traffic to and from Plymouth to London.

From the beginning of 1910 the trade depression lifted and the railway companies' gross income increased, while their various co-operative arrangements allowed some reduction in working costs. The deliberately Byzantine rigmaroles of the Conciliation Boards (known to the men as 'Confiscation Boards') enabled them to hold off their employees' request for better pay and more humane hours; many claims took years to grind through the machinery to reach arbitration. Railwaymen observed that the arbitrators, paid £52 10s a day, were dismissing claims for pay rises from men earning 19s a week.[22] J.H. Thomas, an ASRS Member of Parliament, said of the Boards: 'They were intended to be a safety valve. The companies insisted on sitting on it and there was bound to be an explosion.'[23]

In the summer of 1910 Thomas warned the Government that if railwaymen's wages were not increased and their hours of work reduced,[24] there would be a railway strike within a year. In 1911 the Board of Trade issued its lengthy report into railway amalgamations.[25] The Investigators were of the opinion that 'the balance of advantage to the railway companies and the public lies in a properly regulated extension of co-operation rather than a revival of competition'. Paragraph 181 pointed out that, while railwaymen's wages were relatively low, they had a job for life, which was a great benefit to them and their Company. This benefit did not, however, buy bread nor improve low wages at a time of rising inflation. Unrest was rife, especially in the docks, where the men were already on strike and railwaymen were refusing to handle trains of cargo. Liverpool was at a standstill and the City was under guard by two warships on the Mersey and 7000 troops on the streets. The first national railway strike began in Liverpool, among the L&YR men, who were the worst-paid railwaymen in the area. They did so without union instructions – in fact the majority of those who first withdrew their labour were not union members.[26]

On 15 August, with 50,000 railwaymen on unofficial strike, the combined railway unions ASRS, ASLEF and GRWU[27] gave the companies 24 hrs to reply to the question of whether they were prepared immediately to meet the unions to negotiate a settlement. The following day the railway companies and the Government (in the form of the President of the Board of Trade, Sidney Buxton) met. The companies told Buxton they wanted 'a fight to the finish' with their hard-working men.[28] Without any discussion with the unions, the Government at once gave the companies written permission to call on whatever military force they required to guard railway tracks, installations, and railwaymen who remained at work.[29]

On 17 August the Prime Minister Mr Asquith and Sidney Buxton met the union representatives and told them brusquely that their claims as to the shortcomings of the Conciliation Service would have to be proved – by a Royal Commission, which would investigate and report what amendments, if any, were desirable to promote a satisfactory settlement of their grievances. This offer of another 'talking shop' was rejected in favour of a strike starting at once. The claim was for the recognition of the right of the men's unions to negotiate with the railway companies an 8-hr day for all railwaymen, and an immediate pay rise of 2s a week. Winston Churchill, now Home Secretary, mobilized 58,000 troops and declared martial law, giving the army power to act against civilians without the usual request for assistance from the civil authority.[30]

Many other workers used the railwaymen's strike as a vent for their own discontent. On the 18th, soldiers were summoned to Llanelli by the local magistrates to pacify a 'mob' of railwaymen and other workers who for 24 hrs had blockaded the line at a level-crossing near the railway station. The railwaymen had prevented any damage being one and the blockade was entirely peaceful, although it undoubtedly caused great hardship to the passengers on the blockaded trains. The troops cleared the gates, and some thirty trains passed in the next 20 hrs. At 2.30 p.m. on the 19th, men coming off shift from the nearby copper works saw a train slowly approaching, noticed there was no military guard and stormed the engine, ejecting the crew and bringing the train to a stand down the line. When soldiers arrived they were subjected to cat-calls and a barrage of stone-throwing; one soldier was knocked unconscious. The Riot Act was read and the Officer in charge of the soldiers, Major Stuart, drew out his watch and bawled the order to his men to open fire in one minute. Almost immediately five shots were fired. One man was killed, four were wounded. A riot ensued with a great deal of burning and looting, while the troops cleared the streets at bayonet-point, causing injuries to civilians in the process.[31]

These terrible events shocked everyone and had the effect of shortening the strike. The Government was also alarmed at the unexpectedly severe effect the strike had had on industry. There was also at this time, war in the Balkans and a serious international crisis between France and Germany which could lead to a general European war.[32] If that happened the underpaid railwaymen would be even more important to Britain. For all these reasons the strike could not be allowed to continue.

On 19 August Lloyd George and Sidney Buxton gathered representatives of the railway companies and unions into one room for the first time ever. The Government asked the railway companies to concede a small pay rise to their men, and promised that in return an Act would be passed relaxing the conditions of the 1894 Act so that the railways could recoup the cost of wage increases by putting up fares and charges. The unions were promised 'no victimization' and a speedy Royal Commission to investigate their complaints. The companies and the unions agreed and the strike was called off that day – much to the disgust of many railwaymen. The railway companies remained obdurate in their refusal to talk to the unions and were the only major employers in Britain to maintain this attitude. In spite of the 'no victimization' agreement, some railwaymen were sacked and some of these emigrated to British-owned railways in Argentina. The service records of GWR men who had gone on strike were secretly marked at the head of the page with a capital 'D' for 'Disloyal' and, in some cases, with remarks such as: 'Made himself very prominent. Gave open air address.'[33]

The Government passed the Railways Act of 1912, which permitte
the companies to raise their charges by a maximum of 4 per cent t
offset the cost of wage rises. This caused another outcry against th
companies, so much so that Lord Claud Hamilton, Chairman of th
GER, commented in February 1914:

> I do not think it wise to impose the increase. We could not impose it whe
> there are trams and we could not impose it in the country because we ar
> largely dependent on farmers and agricultural people . . . many have a har
> struggle for life. We carry an increasing quantity of milk each year and
> would not be wise to discourage this by raising prices.

The increase in wages was to some extent balanced by a better us
of rolling stock and motive power, and by a reduction in competitio
which allowed a cut-back in train services. The GWR, L&NWR an
GER suffered a rise in costs in 1912, but the MR, NER, GCR an
GNR enjoyed a reduction. Dividends increased and share values ros
The Chairman of the L&SWR, Henry Drummond, looking back o
1912, observed early in 1913: 'In spite of a serious coal strike in Marc
and April [of 1912] the year will be remembered as one of phenomena
prosperity for every trade and industry in the Kingdom.' In the la
few years before the Great War the companies stopped fighting eac
other and found peace and a prosperity they had not had for fiftee
years. At the end of 1913 the L&NWR paid 7 per cent against 6 p
cent in 1912, and placed £120,000 in reserve. That same year, the GW
paid its highest dividend ever on Ordinary shares, 8 per cent, again
7¾ per cent in 1912, and placed £200,000 in reserve.[34] The railwayme
were still asking for the 8-hr day, union recognition and a 5s a wee
pay rise when the Great War broke out. These men, hundreds of the
marked down as 'Disloyal', at once suspended their agitations (such a
they were) and threw themselves so wholeheartedly into the war effo
that they had to be restrained by regulations from volunteering for th
armed forces.

29

Railwaymen, Loyalty and Sacrifice

I N 1912 THE GOVERNMENT had consulted Sir Frank Ree, General
Manager of the majestic L&NWR, on the best way to organize
the railway system in wartime. With the benefit of a lifetime's
experience with his superbly well co-ordinated Company, he recommended that the entire railway system should be directed by a
Railway Executive Committee' (REC), under the powers granted to
government by Section 16 of the 1871 Regulation of the Forces Act.
On 4 August 1914, the day Great Britain declared war on Germany,
all but 2 per cent[1] of the railway mileage of England, Scotland and
Wales was placed under the orders of the REC; Irish railways were
not immediately included. One hundred and thirty companies were
affected, with a total capital value of £1.2 billion and 21,546 route
miles – of which 19,114 were owned by twenty-one companies. The
Government did not control any of these; they were instructed to
carry on as usual, subject to the control and co-ordination of the
REC'.[2] They still appeared to be independent companies, but under
the REC all receipts were pooled,[3] as were all wagons, sheets and
ropes; and individual companies no longer 'canvassed' the public for
traffic.

On 15 September the Government placed a notice in *The Times*
which in part stated:

His Majesty's Government has agreed with the railway companies that subject to the undermentioned condition, the compensation to be paid them shall be the sum by which the aggregate *net* receipts of their railway for the period during which His Majesty's Government are in possession of them fall short of the aggregate net receipts for the corresponding period of 1913. This sum, together with the net receipts of the railway companies taken over, is to be distributed amongst those companies in proportion to the net receipts of each company during the period with which the comparison is made.

The compensation to be paid under this arrangement will cover all special services, such as those in connection with military and naval transport rendered to His Majesty's Government by the railway companies concerned and it will therefore be unnecessary to make any payments in respect of such transport.[4]

Under Section 16 of the Act this payment was in compensation 'for any loss or injury . . . sustained by the exercise of the power of the Secretary of State under this section'. The Agreement was to be renewed *weekly*, an arrangement reflecting the comfortable view that a European war would be as short as the Franco-Prussian War of 1870.[5] On 5 August the REC stated: 'In view of the probable great decrease in traffic it is anticipated that there will be no difficulty in dealing with rolling stock'.[6] This was optimism on a par with 'It will all be over by Christmas'.

The railway companies had agreed to accept a payment to maintain ordinary profits as the legal 'compensation' for 'any loss or injury' mentioned in the Act. This was a bad bargain, hastily made in the first fine flush of patriotism when no one but a few military experts realized that the war would last for years rather than weeks. The companies never asked for, nor were they given, a specific contract.[7] The Agreement was ambiguous: it failed to specify *when* the Government would pay the compensation, and the latter had in mind paying when hostilities ceased – with the result that, as the war dragged on, the companies carried the additional traffic, and the additional costs, without any payment, until they were running short of ready money. They then asked to be paid an estimated sum of compensation, monthly, or account – and the Government agreed.[8]

Then there was the problem of paying for 'abnormal wear and tear' and the impossibility of maintaining the usual expenditure or renewals. The combination of pressure of traffic and a lack of man power meant that such work was not carried out to the same extent as n peacetime; the consequent drop in working costs created the impression that net receipts were greater, which reduced the amount of monthly compensation. But the wear and tear was real enough, and at the end of the war the companies would be obliged to make it good with insufficient funds. The Government told the companies to submit their account for damages at the end of the war.

No financial allowance was made, initially, for the capital expenditure incurred by the companies in the years leading up to 1914; the GWR, for instance, had built hundreds of miles of new railways between 1900 and 1914, and had also constructed some very useful, turbine-powered ships. The Government took possession of the GWR's (and other companies') ships and had the benefit of modern equipment and shorter routes – while the Company continued to pay interest on the capital they represented. At a cost of £3 million,[9] the GCR had constructed Immingham Docks, 1000 acres of harbours along 1½ miles of the River Humber, equipped with the latest in handling and repairing facilities. The docks were opened in 1912, and on 4 August 1914 they were handed over entirely to the Royal Navy. The Government agreed to pay the Company's interest at 4 per cent – but only on capital used to bring works into use after 1912.

The L&SWR was the 'Military Line', with 176 large barracks or camps on its route, including those at Aldershot and on Salisbury Plain. Southampton, with its docking, repairing and warehousing facilities developed entirely by L&SWR capital, was taken over by the Government as 'No. 1 Military Embarkation Port'. Through Southampton in the course of the war came a total of 21 million soldiers, carried in 58,859 special trains – a figure which should be doubled to account for the trains of empty coaches leaving the docks.[10] The expertise of the men of the L&SWR was equal to the skilled professionalism of the British Expeditionary Force. In both organizations the equipment, morale and training was of the highest quality, as was demonstrated by their respective achievements.

On 2 August the L&SWR was in the process of delivering the 1st London Division, Territorial Army, to Wareham in Dorset. Ten train-loads had been sent during the 2nd and 3rd, and eight more were actually in transit when war was declared. These were stopped and sent back to London, while ten trains of empty stock had to be marshalled immediately and sent to Wareham to bring back the 14,000 men, 1387 horses and 78 field guns already at camp. Meanwhile a Territorial Army division on exercises on Salisbury Plain was ordered home, and

the L&SWR at once marshalled thirty-eight trains, improvised a time
table and distributed the same to the relevant signalmen and loc
sheds and entrained the troops at Amesbury. By 5 August all thes
Territorials had been redeployed throughout Britain.[11]

At the same time the British Expeditionary Force had to be shippe
to France through Southampton. Four Divisions – 2825 Officers an
66,022 other ranks, 21,500 horses and 2400 wheeled guns – had to b
railed in complete secrecy. The movement did not start until Sunda
10 August 1914 and was expected to take eight days,[12] during the ver
period when the L&SWR also had to contend with their advertise
August Bank Holiday trains. The fact of the war excited rather tha
depressed people and holiday traffic was exceptionally heavy. On
wonders where the Company found enough locomotives, carriage
and crews to accommodate everyone.

The first military 'X' train was due at Southampton Docks on 1
August at 8.48 a.m. and arrived at 8.15 a.m. The last was due in at 6 p.m
on the 17th and arrived at 5.38 p.m. Between 10 p.m. on the 21st an
6 p.m. on the 22nd, seventy-three trains conveying 17,000 men, 458
horses and 72 guns were dealt with. In eight days 334 'X' trains ran wit
perfect punctuality, without locomotive breakdowns, points failure
or shortages of staff. Reinforcements for the BEF were also carried an
by 31 August a total of 670 trains had converged punctually an
methodically on Southampton – and departed again – carrying 118,00
men, 37,650 horse, 314 guns, 5221 horse-drawn vehicles, 1807 bicycle
and 4557 tons of baggage and stores. The *Daily News* of 18 Augu
wrote of the departures from Aldershot: 'It was a wonderful achieve
ment of toil done in the light of flares and arc lamps. Not a wagon or
field piece was damaged. When the medals are distributed, the railwa
workers should certainly receive them. The automatic regularity o
departure of trains was truly marvellous.' On 7 September the Com
mander of the BEF, Sir John French, wrote in his first dispatch: 'Th
transport of the troops from England to France was effected in the be
order and without a check. Each unit arrived at its destination in th
country [France] well within schedule time and the concentration wa
complete on the evening of 21 August.'[13] What a wonderful thin
praise is – and how quickly it is forgotten.

A less dashing but equally vital exploit of the railwaymen was th
working of the Admiralty coal trains from South Wales. In peace
time the steam coal for the Grand Fleet's boilers was shipped t
Grangemouth, the main coaling base of the Royal Navy, on the Firt

f Forth; but now, to avoid the 'U' boats it had to go overland. The oal came out of the Valleys eastwards, over a mountainous route, own to Pontypool Road on the Newport–Shrewsbury main line. Here the lumbering, unbraked, wooden wagons were made up into maximum load for an eight-coupled goods engine to haul north through Hereford, Shrewsbury and Crewe to Grangemouth. By 1918, 6,000 wagons were engaged in this traffic. Known officially as Admiralty Coal' the trains were promptly nicknamed 'Jellicoes' (after he Admiral of the Grand Fleet) by the men. The 'Jellicoes' were sig-alled along the line, through the signal boxes with the special bell ode 3–4–4 and were made up to at least fifty wagons for haulage by a GWR 28 class 2–8–0 or an L&NWR 'Super D' 0–8–0. In August 1916, 90 'Jellicoes' were run; in October 1916, 348; in June 1917, 466; in March 1918, 988: the highest for the war.[14] (Those figures do not include the empties coming south.) These trains of primitive wagons were unbraked, and of necessity slow-moving. The wagons were not always well maintained, especially the 'private-owner' wagons now in he common-user pool, and overheated axle bearings were a common-lace cause of delay; yet their load was vital and these slow trains had riority over all civilian traffic.

The GWR had forty-seven government munition works on its ystem and another 230 non-government factories making munitions. All of these required freight and passenger services several times a day. The Hayes shell-filling factory produced enough shells to fill 3800 wagons a month, and therefore required 3800 empty wagons inwards, quite apart from wagons of raw materials. Every day, one hundred pas-enger trains were required to ferry thousands of workers to and from he factory.[15] The shell-filling factories at Rotherwas, near Hereford, nd at Avonmouth, had similar requirements. From these factories he shells were hauled to the ports of Richborough, Newhaven, ittlehampton and Southampton.

Nitro-glycerine was made at a factory built at Lando, near Pembrey Carmarthenshire. Here, 5000 people a day required rail transport. his highly volatile explosive had then to be carried daily to Faver-ham in Kent and Chilworth in Surrey, via Reading, in hermetically aled, steam-heated vans. The railway's official telegraphic codeword describe these trains in operating telegrams had a nice touch of allows' humour: 'Ignite'; and 'Ignite trains' they promptly became in he vernacular – although none of them ever did.

By 15 November 1914, 12,339 railway-owned wagons and 9025

'private-owner' wagons were in use. The REC had considered th
ample, given a 'common-user' policy; but there was at once a gre
increase in the demand for wagons to carry military stores, occasion
by the diversion to rail of certain bulk loads which normally we
'coastwise'. Prior to 1914 pig-iron from Barrow to Glasgow went b
sea; by 1917 the Furness Railway was carrying 14,000 tons a month
Coal for south Devon, which even in 1914 was largely brought by s
from Newcastle, now transferred to the railways. The official total
former coastwise freight carried by rail in 1917 was 15 million ton
The railways lacked the capacity for this volume of extra traffic, b
carry it they had to. The wagon shortages were made worse by th
demands of the army abroad: the MR, to name just one company, se
seventy-eight locomotives, 6000 10-ton wagons and fifty brake va
overseas,[17] and at home there was also delay in unloading and wast
ful routeing. At Parkestone Quay, fifty-four railway wagons stoc
loaded from August 1914 until 30 June 1916; at Grimsby three wago
of ammunition, received on 14 November 1914, were not unloaded b
the military until 30 August 1915;[18] while at Reading Central Goods,
1222 wagons of oats were received for the army between 1 and 1
September 1915 and 1077 were sent away, still loaded, to other destin
tions. Wagons were often delayed because of a dire shortage of rop
to secure their loads, or of tarpaulins to cover the loads. There w
large-scale unofficial 'commandeering' by the squaddies and th
matelots. Trains became mobile storage space as thousands of tons
freight were hauled around the system because the sidings and yar
were full and could not accept more wagons.

The wear and tear on the track and rolling stock of all the railwa
was considerable, but the GWR, L&NWR, MR and NER were bett
maintained and equipped to cope than the smaller railways, such as th
SE&CR, which were not in the best of condition at the start of the wa
Others, such as the Caledonian, GS&WR and NBR, serving the gre
dockyard areas on the Clyde and Forth – and, even worse, the light
equipped Highland Railway and Great North of Scotland Railway
started well but became very worn down. The HR and the GNSR we
both mountainous, single-track railways, which suddenly assumed
vital strategic importance because the Grand Fleet was based at Scap
Flow in the southern Orkneys. The HR ran from Perth to Inverne
and Thurso (for Scapa Flow) and GNSR (jointly with the Caledonia
operated Aberdeen, which became the central stores depot for th
Grand Fleet.

Invergordon, a little village on Cromarty Firth served by the HR, became an important engineering, repair and oil-fuelling base for the Royal Navy. Three camps for 7000 men had to be built, the materials, the men and their food coming in by train, and thereafter all the military stores associated with a great naval depot. Scapa Flow required defence works, and all that material came to Thurso by train. Meanwhile, Scottish pit-props in hitherto unimagined quantities were required for coal-mines to the south, and camps for regiments of foresters had to be constructed and the men supplied. Domestic coal for use in HR territory which had previously come by coasting steamer, now arrived by rail. Inverness became the main store for naval ammunition so suddenly that train-loads of ammunition were on their way from the south of England before the branch line was built from Inverness station to the harbour. The HR completed the work in ten days.[20]

All this traffic had to be worked from near sea-level at Perth, over the Druimochadar Pass (1484 ft above sea-level), to Inverness, 118 miles away – or if to Thurso, 272 miles. The railway was mostly single track with only 75 miles of sidings. The signal boxes were, on average, 5 miles apart. In the 154 miles from Inverness to Thurso, ten signal boxes had no loop where two trains could pass each other.[21] The Company had 3000 staff in 1914, but 756 had left to join the forces. There were too few fitters to cope with engine repairs, there was a crisis with locomotives as early as June 1915, and by August a third of the motive power was out of action. Twenty locos, 1500 wagons and extra fitters were sent from other companies.[22]

The remoteness of Scapa Flow created enormous problems for personnel coming and going on postings and on leave but not until 1917 was a dedicated train instituted. The famous Euston–Thurso Naval Special left Euston at 6 p.m. and Thurso at 3.30 p.m., a journey of 717 miles each way for which the schedule allowed 21½ hrs going north and 22 hrs southbound – and its record of punctuality was good. At first it went via Crewe, Carlisle, Carstairs and Perth, not calling at Edinburgh, but it was soon re-routed over the NBR 'Waverley' route from Carlisle to Edinburgh, then across the Forth bridge to Perth. The service ran every weekday from 15 February 1917 until 30 April 1919.[23] The standard formation was fourteen corridor coaches, but often the demand was so great as to require one or even two extra trains. The mail for the Fleet was equal in volume to that for a city of 100,000 people; that from the south was loaded at Euston, and that from the West Country and Midlands at Crewe; English national daily newspapers were rushed out from Manchester to meet the Special at 10.15 p.m. at Preston. The *Glasgow Herald* and the *Scotsmen* were loaded on to the train at Edinburgh at 3.15 a.m., and all personnel, mail and daily papers were on board the Grand Fleet by 4.30 p.m.

The GNSR and the Caledonian had begun the enlargement of their joint station at Aberdeen to thirteen platforms in 1912; it was completed in 1915. To Aberdeen there came a never-ending procession of stores trains, each one scheduled for a certain day with a specific load: fresh food, dry food, meat, medical stores, machinery stores, petrol, paraffin, oil, cement, wooden huts, aircraft, firebricks for ships' furnaces – 30,000 items required to service the world's largest fleet of enormous battleships and their supporting warships.

Curious byways, perhaps the worst-engineered in Britain and often owned by financially weak, independent companies, suddenly assumed the status of 'vital artery'. These were the lines which cut across the great trunk routes radiating from London, and included the M&SWJR, which linked the MR's Birmingham–Bristol main line at Cheltenham with the L&SWR at Andover and Southampton, connecting en route with the GWR at Swindon and Savernake and serving the military area of Salisbury Plain at Ludgershall. The exceedingly ramshackle Stratford-on-Avon & Midland Junction, otherwise known as the 'Slow Moulding & Jolting', which ran through ironstone country, became of some importance when the shortage of foreign ironstone made the local ore of commercial value. At King's Sutton, 3½ miles south of Banbury (GWR), an exceedingly unsuitable single track, also owned by the GWR, turned west and, by way of the shaky Hook Norton viaduct, the Kingham flyover and Stow-on-the-Wold's narrow station, traversed the breadth of the Cotswolds, tipping over their western edge at Notgrove, down 9 miles of severe incline to the main line near Cheltenham. A heavy traffic in iron ore, iron and steel ran over this serpentine byway to and from South Wales and the Midlands, and the management of the heavy trains, which often required two locomotives, called for a very high standard of enginemanship.

The short cross-London railway routes formed connections of crucial importance. There were four: from Kew to Poplar, which could loosely be called the 'North London Railway; from Willesden through Addison Road (Kensington) to Clapham, known as the 'West London Railway' (WLR); the 'East London Railway' (ELR), connecting the

GER and MR with the SE&CR and LB&SCR through Marc Brunel's Thames tunnel from Rotherhithe to Wapping. The fourth was by way of the 'Metropolitan Widened Lines', giving access from Paddington, St Pancras and King's Cross to Ludgate Hill, and so across the river on Blackfriars Bridge into Kent (see Map 10).

Between 1907 and 1912 the SE&CR had, at considerable expense, rebuilt the disgustingly decrepit Ludgate Hill station in an attempt to make rail travel more attractive to the City clerks and lure them from the LCC trams, but barely two years later the war came. Between 4 August 1914 and 25 February 1915, 2738 troop trains – return empty-stock trains would perhaps double that figure – passed over this north/south link.[24] During the first two weeks of 1915, 2935 goods trains passed through: 210 a day. Passenger services between the SE&CR, GNR and MR were suspended intermittently to make way for this traffic, and on 3 April 1916 they were entirely withdrawn, making the Ludgate Hill investment a dead loss on the SE&CR.[25]

The working conditions for the steam-engine crews and guards in the tunnels from King's Cross to Farringdon had always been bad, but with the more intensive use of this route it is hard to imagine how the men could live in the sulphurous atmosphere. The steepest gradients came where the line crossed below the Met., just west of Farringdon; Here they were 1 in 40, and the engines blasted their hardest. The trains were always fully laden because there was so much to move, and the maximum load for an engine was only sixteen wagons, or twenty-five with a bank engine assisting at the rear. The crew of the latter was particularly vulnerable to asphyxiation from the fumes of the leading engine, yet these men – most of whom were marked down as 'Disloyal' in 1911 – daily risked their lives, inglorious and unsung, for their country.

The WLR was able to take the longest and heaviest trains; over this line went millions of tons of explosives and back came hundreds of thousands of casualties. All the wagons loaded with military stores destined for Dover and Kent came to Lillie Bridge (West Brompton) Goods station (and of course the empties came back, all to be remarshalled and sent on). There was also the daily ammunition train from the Hayes factory direct to Richborough, double-headed by a pair of SE&CR engines.

Dover was at first the only landing point for casualties from France. At the outbreak of war Dover Marine station was so new that it had neither platforms nor roof when the first ambulance boat arrived with

1500 casualties on 12 October 1914. On 23 December, work began to supply the deficiency and by 2 January the platforms were built and the roof erected. Dover was soon unable to cope with the army of wounded, and the hospital ships were obliged to make port at Southampton, Folkestone, Thurso, Plymouth and other places, the casualties being taken on by ambulance trains to the military hospitals. A train including 200 cot cases and 300 walking wounded could be loaded at Dover in 45 mins. Although the majority of Dover ambulance trains passed over the WLR, others, up to sixteen coaches long, passed between the SE&CR and GER/MR using the ELR.

The ambulance trains were either constructed new or converted from existing carriages in railway workshops for use at home and in various overseas locations, from France to Egypt. The standard Home Service Ambulance Train consisted of eight-wheelers: a guard's van, a medical officers' and nurses' car, a dining or sleeping-car, three ward cars, a pharmacy car, a kitchen-car, and another van for the guard's and orderlies' stores. The vehicles were all steam-heated and electrically lit, and the ward-cars were ventilated with electric fans. The train accommodated 500 patients, was 550 ft long and weighed 250 tons empty.[26]

From August 1914 until 7 April 1919, 2,680,000 sick and wounded allied soldiers, as well as wounded German prisoners, were received into ambulance trains. MR staff dealt with 3982 ambulance trains at twelve receiving stations and gave up their own time to care for the wounded, getting them from train to motor ambulance and into hospital. More and more ambulance trains were needed, giving the railway workshops plenty of extra work; at Swindon guns and ambulance coaches were made practically side by side. A large department was required to supervise the construction of the trains, to supply their stores and staff and to organize their actual running.

Holiday traffic was very heavy throughout the war on all the major railways. In January 1915 the SE&CR issued the following notice:

> In consequence of the very large and increasing demands made by the military authorities it has been found necessary to reduce the passenger train services. The Managing Committee regret the inconvenience to the travelling public and hope that no further restrictions may be necessary. So soon as it is possible the cancelled services will be restored.[27]

From February the other companies began to restrict service and withdraw cheap fares, without, however, discouraging the holidaymakers. The GNR was running restaurant-cars on its local services and managed to keep this service until the general withdrawal of all restaurant-cars in April/May 1916: those fateful months when conscription was introduced. Passengers were asked voluntarily to restrict their luggage at Christmas 1915, and in December 1916 the limit was set officially. Holiday traffic grew so heavy that the Government cancelled the 1916 Whitsun Bank Holiday, but so many people still went away that passenger receipts for June 1916 were 18 per cent higher than in June 1913. August Bank Holiday was also cancelled but traffic on the GWR to south Devon resorts was heavier than ever, in spite an absence of extra trains and cheap fares, and the strict limits on luggage.

The *Great Western Railway Magazine* for September 1916 stated that during the fortnight ending on 5 August 1916:

The Cornish Riviera 'Limited' Express left Paddington in three parts [as three separate trains] on 8 occasions conveying a daily average of nearly 1400 passengers, a record being reached on Saturday 9 July 1916 when the three parts carried 2027 passengers and their luggage. Passenger traffic throughout the GWR system was abnormal and the efforts of the depleted staff were severely taxed by the quantity of luggage to be dealt with. The assistance of men from departments other than the Passenger Departments was necessary and a number of clerks acted as emergency porters.

As greater numbers of skilled railwaymen – and rolling stock – were being sent to France and yet more government trains had to be run, the populace were implored by the Government not to travel, but without effect. In January 1917, fares were raised for the first time since 1914, by 50 per cent (the cost of living was then 106 per cent above that of 1914[28]); passenger train services were severely curtailed, and a speed limit was imposed to enable locomotives to haul more coaches. L&NWR and GWR tickets between London and Birmingham were made interchangeable so as to enable either route to be used. More stations were closed; whole branch lines were lifted and the track sent to France. No extra trains were run for Easter, Whitsun or August 1917, but on every holiday vast crowds turned up at the London termini, expecting to be carried away. Many people were earning very high wages and were in a mood to spend; they protested bitterly to the companies and the Government at the hardships they faced when going on holiday with only 100 lb of luggage per person, at full fares, in crowded trains. In April that year, the Battle of Arras began, and the intense carnage continued through

Whitsuntide, to explode into the third Battle of Ypres, otherwise known as Passchendaele, on 31 July.

The railways, which had never been adequately staffed, were now carrying unprecedentedly heavy traffic, while tens of thousands of their men went away to the war. In June 1915 the companies' newspaper, *Railway News*, stated that, with 80,000 railwaymen away in the armed forces the railways were operating at the minimum manning levels for efficient working. The paper's idea of what constituted 'efficient' was strange: to cover for those away at the front, the rest had to work incredibly long hours – most especially train crews. In June 1917 the L&NWR Chairman told his shareholders that 12,000 fewer men than in 1913 had shifted 1 million more tons of freight.[29] Taff Vale footplatemen were routinely working 20-hr shift with 9 hrs between turns. This was the norm on all railways. Footplatemen left home for their booked shift, not knowing when they would return, often staying away for days on end; and once a man had eaten the sandwiches supplied by his wife, the only food he ate was what he could scrounge from the canteens set up to provide free food for servicemen. There was no patriotic glow to be got out of feeding sooty railwaymen who were hauling the ammunition and ambulance trains, and they were often turned away. Not until 1918 was any provision made to provide emergency rations for footplate crews.[30] By then 55,942 women[31] had been recruited as ticket-collectors, carriage cleaners, engine cleaners and porters, but the running and repairing of trains was done by an overworked male staff.

Railwaymen's wages, barely adequate in July 1914, were by Christmas far from adequate, thanks to hyper-inflation and criminal businessmen who took advantage of shortages to force up prices. In January 1915 the Board of Trade assessed the increase in the cost of food as 19 per cent: *The Times* believed this to be an underestimate. Within five months of the outbreak of war the price of eggs had risen by 60 per cent, that of tea by 50 per cent.[32] The railway unions supported the war effort and at no time during the war did they support a strike. They saw, however, more clearly than the Government, that underfed railwaymen would be useless to the war effort. J.H. Thomas General Secretary of the National Union of Railwaymen,[33] suggested a 'War Bonus' additional to wages – which were still at 1911 levels – and asked for 5s a week. The trade unions met directly with the companies and Government for only the second time in history and, after a great deal of haggling, the bonus was set between 2s and 3s a week, the lowest-paid getting the greater bonus. The Government agreed to pay 75 per cent of the increase and the Agreement was signed at the Midland Grand Hotel, St Pancras, in February 1915. Even the pro-management *Railway News* expressed surprise that the men had gone so long without making any complaint.[34]

The buying power of money declined by the month throughout the war, and the resentment felt by the men intensified as they saw their wives and children becoming weaker while 'profiteers' cornered the markets and forced up food prices. The railway unions were unable to increase the war bonus and unofficial strikes broke out locally. In September 1916 the railwaymen, not the NUR leadership, threatened a national strike, and the unions were summoned and lectured by Asquith on the vital role of the railways: the trains must not stop even for an hour. J.H. Thomas asked whether it would not have been better to have called in the companies so that they could be told of their responsibilities as well as the railwaymen. The men were underfed and overworked, and since their work was so important they deserved to eat. The bonus was increased by another 5s a week. By successive bonuses, wages for low-paid railwaymen were increased by as much as 183 per cent over 1914 levels, to 51s by 1919. The express train drivers' bonus increased only by 68 per cent, because they were better paid to start with; the differential was eroded, and this they did not like.

The unions had suspended their agitation for an 8-hr day and a 5s a week pay rise at the outbreak of war and the only agitation during the war had been used to draw attention to the fact that railwaymen (and their families) were facing starvation while they hauled around the country the sinews of war. Without the efforts of the railwaymen the war would have been lost. They were short-staffed by 184,000 men who had joined the armed forces: of those who went away 18,957 were killed.[35]

30

Broken Promises

THE WAR CAME to an end on 11 November 1918. The British people were split between those who longed for a 'better world', to come out of the ghastliness; for the state to arrange a more equal, better-ordered society, with no return to the days of subservience to the masters – and those who wanted a prompt return to the familiar conventions of 1913 and the removal of the state from their lives. Lord Claud Hamilton, Chairman of the GER, who had unreservedly praised the railway workers for 'behaving so well' during the war, now asked the Government to 'remove the velvet gloves it had worn too long'.[1]

Since 1916, the Prime Minister had been the Liberal David Lloyd George. After the Representation of the People Act of 1918, the right to vote was extended to every male over the age of twenty-one and to every woman over thirty. The electorate was trebled and the outcome of the General Election of 14 December 1918 – the 'Khaki Election' – was the return of Lloyd George as Prime Minister at the head of a coalition government. He did not believe in 'iron laws' of economics which maintained the rich at the expense of the poor, and in this he had the support of the working class, some Liberals, and intellectuals such as the economist J.M. Keynes, the social planner William Beveridge, as well as that great believer in economic planning, the ex-Deputy General Manager of the NER, First Lord of the Admiralty and honorary Major-General, Eric Geddes.[2] Lloyd George hoped to realize his wartime promises of 'a new heaven and a new earth' by continuing his pre-war radical Liberal reforms. He had promised to place under government direction road, rail and water transport, electricity, housing, health-care, town and country planning; to expropriate the big landowners; and to re-colonize the countryside by giving tenant farmers the right to purchase their farms and making farm land available to those who wanted to work it. There was also to be a Forestry Commission. To improve matters for town dwellers there would be garden cities like the one already existing at Letchworth.

On 12 September 1918, in Manchester, he declared:

> We want neither reaction nor revolution but a sane, well-advised steadiness of bold reconstruction. That is why the whole field of national enterprise, national education, national resources is being examined with a view to immediate action – one people, one spirit, one purpose to lift our native land above the wretchedness, the squalor, the horror, the misery which so many endure.[3]

But his Government was not only a coalition with elements of the Conservatives and seventy-three Labour MPs: it was riven with an internal division between his own brand of radical Liberalism and the more conventional aspect represented by Herbert Asquith, later to become the first Earl of Oxford. There were also 179 MPs who were Directors of companies – forty more than in 1916 – 'men who looked as if they had done well out of the war', to quote the future Conservative Prime Minister Stanley Baldwin.[4] Thus the coalition was not a good tool to force through such unconventional and sweeping changes. Out in the great cities there were tens of thousands of hungry, impatient people. Meanwhile the influenza epidemic which began in 1917 was still raging in February 1919.

Long before the war the railway companies had amalgamated to control the wasteful effects of 'the free play of market forces'. One might say that these were the first steps towards the 'planned economies' which attempted to abolish the fluctuations, uncertainties and expenses of competition and 'market forces'. During the war, railways had carried more traffic using fewer men and wagons: there was much to be said for common-user co-ordination and planning. It seemed that when the greatest economy and strength was needed, as in a wartime emergency, the only way forward was to adopt a socialistic system. Geddes and Lloyd George believed that the stronger, wartime methods should be used to rebuild the country in peacetime. Lloyd

George favoured this way as the means to a more just ordering of society. Industry would remain in private hands but would be directed and co-ordinated through the government ministries. For a brief period it looked as if the country would be run like one of the great railway companies with fifty expert railway managers in charge of the departments and ministries.

The 'Ways and Communications' Bill, introduced in February 1919, sought to establish a Ministry of that name 'for the purpose of improving the means of and the facilities for, locomotion and transport'. The Minister in charge was to assume all powers and duties of any government department in relation to railways, roads, canals, docks and harbours and electricity supply. Clause 3 extended the period of government control of railways for two years after the Act, 'with a view to affording time for the formulation of the policy to be pursued as to the future position of undertakings'; Clause 4 gave the Minister power 'to purchase, by agreement, or compulsorily if need be, any ... railway, light railway, tramway, inland waterway, dock or harbour undertaking'.[5] An Electricity Supply Bill introduced in 1919, had it been passed in its original form, would have given the Minister the authority to control the generating industry so as to create a National Grid and supply electricity, without competition, cheaply and universally.

Mr Brace, Under-Secretary to the Home Office, stated: 'There is a vast body of opinion among the working classes that we can only hope to meet successfully in the difficult times ahead by placing the great interests of the country upon a National basis (Labour cheers).'[6] There was also a large group who saw in 'state direction' a brake on individual profit making and, in particular, that a policy of control would also retard the growth of the road-related industries which could produce new employment opportunities for the workers and wealth for the customary small group. Early in 1918 the *Railway Gazette* observed:

> The motor lorry has become a standardised unit in the carrying trade and there is every reason to believe that they will become still larger users in the post-war period. The development of the lorry during the war has done in a few years what might otherwise have taken twenty-five. Discarded army lorries will be suitable for rural areas, collecting and delivering produce, and will be of great use to agriculture and save the need to build light railways.[7]

The petrol engine was the hope of thousands of demobilized soldiers looking for a way of earning a living and of making use of the skills learned in the army, and it was also a very promising field of expansion for capital. W. Joynson-Hicks, MP, Chairman of the Motor Legislation Committee, which represented road makers, the motor manufacturers and traders in Parliament, warned Local Government Boards about the threat, as he saw it, from a co-ordinated transport policy in a letter to *The Times* on 28 February 1919:

> The Minister will be responsible for showing a return on the enormous outlay represented by the railway system and if the Ways and Communications Bill were to be enacted he will be in the anomalous position of knowing that by assisting highway authorities he is assisting a competitor and thereby depreciating the economical value of railways. The result will inevitably be that either the local authorities will have to find more money or vital road work will remain undone.

This was overstating the case, since roads and lorries would still be required as part of the national system of transport, and taxes would be spent on them – though not in such large amounts as if the road hauliers had the field to themselves. So the road and car industry, young, aggressive, expanding, became the flagship of those opposed to state intervention. The over-capitalized, non-expanding and relatively unprofitable railways had a serious new competitor.

Clause 4 of the Ways and Communication Bill, which seemed to open the way for the nationalization of all but road transport, caused great concern among Conservative and Liberal MPs, even those whose party tag was prefixed 'coalition'; but they need not have worried. There was insufficient money to put the Geddes plan into effect, and the Government had no intention of carrying the clause through. In his Budget speech on 30 April 1919,[8] the Chancellor, Mr Austen Chamberlain, pointed out: 'I am not called upon to resume the civil spending that was interrupted under the stress of war but to provide the means within a few months or years for creating a new heaven and a new earth. I can work no such miracle.' He cited the high rate of inflation, the surfeit of paper money, the tiny gold reserve, the lack of real wealth and unimaginable depths of debt into which Britain had fallen because of the war.

As to the Government's intentions, the clause was simply an acknowledgement of, and a sop to, the intense feelings in favour of Socialism in a large section of the working classes; it was there to buy time for such feelings to die down, whereupon the powers, if granted, would not have been used. Bonar Law, the Conservative Leader of the

House, told an audience of 200 agitated Liberal and Conservative MPs on 15 May: 'There is nothing in the Bill involving Nationalisation. Nationalisation is a great evil [but] there must be some form of control of railways in order to secure the unification of transport – but not as a Department of Government.' He did, however, refer to the need for 'a comprehensive system of transport for the country as a whole'. Faced with the determined opposition of so many MPs, the clause was deleted on 6 May and the name of the Bill was changed to 'Ministry of Transport' in the Lords. Minus Clause 4, and with a Roads Advisory Committee to lobby on behalf of the road-building and motor industries, it received the Royal Assent on 15 August. Sir Eric Geddes was the first Minister of Transport. In November 1921 Herbert Asquith described the new Ministry as 'expensive and grandiose, undertaken wantonly'.

Throughout the year, the fight over Clause 4 of the Ways and Communications Bill had been paralleled by the railway unions' fight for an 8-hr day and a national, standard, pay-scale. During the war railwaymen's wages had remained frozen at 1914 levels but pay had been increased, at a rate well below the rate of inflation, by the war bonus, while their hours of work, for train crews particularly, were more or less whatever was required. Throughout the four years of war the munitions workers had struck work on numerous occasions for higher pay. Among the underpaid railwaymen there had been extreme discontent and even the occasional local strike, but generally, in four years of war half a million railwaymen and women had loyally kept the system running without striking, and they had been showered with praise – since words were cheap. In 1916 the ceramically smooth Lord Claud Hamilton had spoken of 'the loyal and ungrudging co-operation of the whole of the staff who have behaved splendidly throughout the course of the war'.[10] Sir Albert Stanley,[11] President of the Board of Trade, declared: 'The country owes a genuine debt of gratitude to all those employed on the railways for the immense amount of hard work they were doing and the long hours on which they were engaged.'[12] King George V and Queen Mary attended St Paul's Cathedral on 14 May 1919 for a service specifically 'in memory of those railwaymen who laid down their lives for their country in the Great War'.

On 1 February 1919 the 8-hr day became standard nationally for all railwaymen, but the question of a national pay-scale was unresolved. The atmosphere within the nation was frantic: every day that year there was an average of 100,000 men of all trades on strike, and the army was being demobilized as fast as possible because of the discontent and even Soviet tendencies within the ranks. Railwaymen in the large cities were ready to go on strike, and it was only through the efforts of the General Secretary of the NUR, J.H. Thomas, that they did not. On 2 March Bonar Law assured Thomas that standardization of wages would mean more money',[13] and with that several-times-repeated promise Thomas was able to delay a strike while he continued to press for some definite proposals. On 20 August the locomotive crews men were granted a national, standard pay-scale, which gave them a wage rise including the 33s war bonus they were then receiving, and stipulated 120 miles to be the standard of a day's work. It was a good settlement and the loco-men accepted it. On 19 September the Government placed before the executive of the NUR their first and final wages settlement for all other railway workers. The men were to lose their war bonus and be paid an amount equal to their 1913 wage. Since the cost of living was not less than 153 per cent above that of 1913, the 'genuine debt' owed by the nation to the railwaymen was to be cancelled with at least a 53 per cent decrease in the weekly amount the men would receive. Porters would lose 11s a week, guards would lose 4s to s a week, ticket-collectors, between 5s and 10s.[14]

The proposal was tantamount to a government invitation to strike, but still J.H. Thomas held them back. On 25 and 26 September he and his 'cabinet' of railwaymen met members of the actual Cabinet, all of whom had recently awarded themselves large pay rises through the Ministers and Secretaries Act:[15] Lloyd George who, only the day before, had admitted that in 1913 railwaymen were 'disgracefully paid'; Sir Eric Geddes, who had also had received a £50,000 'golden handshake' from the NER in February 1919;[16] Sir Robert Horne, Minister of Labour, whose £2000 a year salary was about to be raised to £5000, and Sir Auckland Geddes, Eric Geddes's brother, a Professor of Anatomy who was at the time filling the role of Acting-President of the Board of Trade. These men refused to withdraw the wage cuts – they were as essential to restore the competitiveness of British goods as were their own salary rises.

The union had no choice but to call a strike. The men stopped work at midnight on Friday 26 September. If the Government thought they had bought off the locomotivemen, they were mistaken: they came out in support, which assistance the NUR gratefully accepted. Thomas declined all other offers of sympathy strikes but he did accept gifts of money for the NUR fund. Lloyd George, fully aware of the months of negotiation wtih the exceptionally moderate J.H. Thomas, coolly announced to the nation that the strike 'was not for wages but has been engineered by a small group of subversives – the vast majority of trade unionists are opposed to the anarchist conspiracy'.[17]

The Times, Daily Express, Daily Mail and *Morning Post* were keen on the conspiracy theory, and abused the hitherto heroic railwaymen with assorted slanders. The NUR challenged Lloyd George to declare publicly that he did not intend to reduce railwaymen's wages, but he refused. The nation began to realize that if railwaymen's wages were reduced, so too would the earning of others. On 27 September the *Daily Express* published its opinion that there was 'no shadow or semblance of an excuse for a strike' and that the strike was 'an attack against the whole nation'; on 3 October, however, it carried the headline: 'The railwaymen have a case'.[18]

By 4 October there was the distinct possibility that other, non railway unions would come out on strike, and at 4.15 p.m. Lloyd George agreed that wages could stay as they were, complete with war bonus, until 30 September 1920. J.H. Thomas immediately caused telegrams to be sent out, calling off the strike as from 5 October, and the 'anarchist conspiracy' vanished. The 'subversive' railwaymen went back to work without even knowing the terms[19] of the settlement, trusting entirely to their union's General Secretary. Fomented deliberately by Lloyd George and Eric Geddes, the strike caused a loss to the Exchequer of £10 million[20] in non-receipt of various duties and taxes while the cost to business in lost production and exports must have been far greater. Sir Eric Geddes then announced that the men would not be paid for the week they had worked leading up to the strike on Friday midnight; at this even the *Daily Mail*, which had loyally abused the railwaymen throughout the strike, told him in a headline: PAY THEM WHAT THEY HAVE EARNED.

The railways were run down. On 26 March 1919 a group of Liberal Mps asked Sir Albert Stanley to order the railways to sell cheap tickets at Eastertide. Stanley replied: 'With the railways in their present condition it would be folly to encourage large numbers of people to use them . . . 25 per cent of locomotives are out of use because of lack of labour and materials to repair them.'[21] In the course of his Budget speech in May, Austen Chamberlain commented: 'Our roads, railways and machinery have suffered from the absence of ordinary upkeep during the war.' Reduced staff and shortages of materials and trained men created a dearth of locomotives and rolling stock, causing weeks of delay for freight traffic. Maintenance of the track and the rolling stock could not be carried out as comprehensively as before the war and yet they were being worked harder than ever before.

The national disgust at the 'profiteering' which took place during the war did not make an exception of the railway companies. The Third Report of the Select Committee on National Expenditure of 1918 acquitted the companies of the charge of profiteering but in so doing gave weight to the idea that the railways had not suffered loss as a result of their work for the nation:

> Since the companies are secured against loss no matter what their expenditure and since their management remains in their own hands there is an obvious danger of relaxation of control and increase in cost. We have investigated this and have found that no such results occurred. The desire of the Directors and their staff as good citizens to prevent extravagance from which the tax payer would suffer has prevented this.[22]

In 1919 the combined deficit in the capital accounts of all English, Welsh and Scottish railway companies amounted to £41.25 million, £6.25 million more than in 1913. On annual current account the total deficit for all railways for the financial year April 1919–20 was £45 million. Working costs took 100 per cent of gross income because government had not allowed railway charges to rise to reflect the cost of working. In spite of the government guarantee, given at the outbreak of war, that the companies' profits should be maintained at 1913 levels, it seems that dividends were less (in the case of the weak companies, much less) in 1919 than in 1913. Those which survived the war in the best condition were, not surprisingly perhaps, the GWR, L&NWR, MR and NER, who were able to put into depreciation funds the money they had not been able to spend on maintenance. At the end of 1917 the GWR Fund stood at £5,837,000, the L&NWR had £3,447,000 with £4,300,000 in the General Reserve, the NER had £4,812,000.[23] The lesser companies could only afford £10–20,000 and diverted the rest into day-to-day expenses, since they had problems with their cash-flow. All the companies were worried that after the war these funds would be insufficient for the purpose because the work would be done at inflated prices.

The SE&CR Working Union had been hard hit by the war. It had run its very heavy service for the war effort with only 80 per cent of its pre-war staff, which had been undermanned even then. The SER

Chairman, Mr Cosmo Bonsor, told the shareholders that their railway had been under enormous strain; had it not been for the money it had spent on strengthening the road, including bridges, between 1899 (when the Working Union was formed) and 1914, its routes would have broken down. The SE&CR was in such a bad way that Bonsor looked forward to government take-over, saying that if the undertaking was purchased under the terms of the 1844 Act – twenty-five years of the net income – it would be a very good bargain for the shareholders. Whatever happened, he said, he felt sure the Government would treat the railways with fairness.[24]

According to the Regulation of Forces Act of 1871, under which the railways had been taken over in 1914, the Government was obliged to hand them back to their owners in the same physical and financial state as existed when they were taken over. Since the Government had not permitted railway charges to rise in line with wartime inflation, large and inevitably unpopular increases were required to allow the companies to catch up and become profitable.

On 17 March Sir Eric Geddes told Parliament that the increased cost in 1919, compared with 1918, of running the railways would be £49 million, to which must be added the £43.5 million needed to maintain the dividend. Sir William Plender and Sir Albert Wyon, the government auditors, reported[25] that, in return for the guarantee, the railways had given transport services to the Government from 5 August 1914 to 31 December 1918 worth £112,043,808. Railway companies had also performed services with their steam-boats, docks and canals for which no charges were raised but which were estimated at £10–15 million. The total amount of the government guarantee paid to the railways between 5 August 1914 and 31 December 1918 was £95,313,607, which figure included allowances for deferred maintenance of track, rolling stock and plant, and left the railways out of pocket – without taking into account any provision for 'extra wear and tear', nor for the cost of replacing all manner of 'stores' which would have to be purchased at post-war inflated prices (see Appendix 16). The companies had also carried out much manufacturing for the war effort, at cost, and thus workshop machinery had been subjected to 'abnormal wear and tear'. The Report therefore estimated that the companies would have a claim for an additional £150 million. The 1914 Agreement had become an acute embarrassment to the Government. It was time to find ways of reducing the liability.

A Departmental Committee of the Ministry of Transport was established in September 1920, under the chairmanship of Lord Colwyn,[26] to investigate 'the possible extent of the State's liabilities under the terms of the 1914 Agreement, according to the interpretation that may be placed upon such Agreement', and to see what 'further steps should be taken to secure the interests of the State'.

In December, the country was six months into a severe trade depression, and the railways' income was depleted as they made their monthly claims for compensation, according to the 1914 Agreement. Among the 130 claims was one for £616,194 from the very hard-hit NBR: £186,000 was paid, and £430,000 was retained while the account was examined. The Furness, GNR and 'a number of other English companies'[27] suffered a similar short payment and examination of their claims. Six months later the accounts were still being examined, and the NBR was so short of funds that it could not pay any dividend or carry out proper maintenance. The NBR took the Government before the Railway & Canal Commissioners on behalf of itself and other cash-strapped railways, where it proved to the satisfaction of the Commission that their expenditure for December was equal to the figure claimed, and an interim injunction was given against the Ministry of Transport.[28]

The Ministry appealed to the Lord President of the Council, on the grounds that there was no legal obligation on the Minister to make monthly payments to the railway companies, and that, the NBR being a Scottish company, under Scottish legal *practice*, not law, such an interim injunction as had been issued was unknown.[29] This amounted not only to pillage but deviousness as well. The Lord President's opinion was that, on 12 October 1914, the Treasury had indeed agreed to pay the companies monthly 'on account'. He also agreed that the Railway Commissioners were entirely justified in seeking to bring to an end the 'interminable period of examination'.

The announcement that passenger fares and freight charges were to be increased by 100 per cent in July 1920 was greeted by howls of protest. The increases were necessary to comply with the law: the railways had to be as profitable when they were handed back to their shareholders as when they were taken away. Their total annual income, compared with that of 1913, was short by £54.5 million and there were only eleven months in which to close the gap.[30] The *Economist* opined:

> The Government has only itself to blame for the present outcry because it did not move earlier to make the railways' charges fit the cost of working.

A versatile press which runs 'government economy' as the 'stunt' of the week and 'holiday travel at the expense of the taxpayer' the next week – and a public which wants to travel cheap on the taxes – which it objects to paying – is a somewhat ridiculous picture.[31]

These huge rises created enormous trouble for the railways, driving traffic to the roads, while the growing recession reduced their traffic still further.[32] The price increases also gave the newspapers plenty of copy, 'proving' that the railways were 'up to their old tricks'. Business wanted cheap transport and believed they were not getting it; hence the myth of the 'feather-bedded' railways grew. As ever, the railways were assumed to be making profits at the expense of the rest. The Federation of British Industry was quoted in the *Railway & Shipping Journal* for December 1921: 'Everyone else is being made to reduce their charges in order to meet the needs of the present trade situation and the railways should not be sheltered from a similar necessity.' The railways actually did reduce by 25 per cent the rate for carrying iron ore and limestone, to cheapen the cost of iron and steel, whereupon the coal owners demanded cheap transport for coal – even though they absolutely refused to adopt high-capacity wagons which would have made a significant reduction in the railways' shunting and haulage costs and thus, have enabled the railways to reduce their charges to the collieries.

Answering the fare-rise furore, 'a railway officer' was quoted as saying, with great bitterness:

> The railways placed their entire resources at the disposal of His Majesty's Government. They scrapped their records to release men, they manufactured munitions at cost when others were making large profits, their steamships were used all over the world without payment – for what? A maintenance of pre-war revenue while all other concerns have increased their profits – even the Government has to pay more for its loans. All [the railways'] meritorious services are forgotten. They are told they are subsidised, that they cannot pay their way, when the fact is that their costs have been forced up by the Government. Even the economies we have effected by co-operative working are ascribed to government control. It was the merest act of justice to allow us to put up rates and fares.[33]

In July 1920 the Government issued its proposals for the future of railways.[34] Charles Saunders's and Samuel Laing's prophecy at Cardwell's 1854 Select Committee was to be fulfilled. There were to be seven 'groups', merged along the lines proposed by the companies –

and forbidden by Parliament – in the pre-war period. The companies agreed in principle but disliked the proposed Parliamentary groupings. Viscount Churchill, Chairman of the GWR and of the Railway Companies Association, commented: 'the RCA sees the need for Grouping which accords with past practice – but not State compulsory grouping. The RCA believe that one of the principle considerations should be financial equilibrium within each group.' He suggested a new grouping:

1. L&NWR, MR, NSR, L&YR, Furn.R, CR, G&SWR, HR
2. GCR, GNR, GER, HBR, NER, NBR, GNSR
3. GWR and Welsh
4. LB&SCR, SE&CR, L&SWR
5. London local railways

Parliament adopted this with the exception of Category 5. The White Paper also proposed that one third of the Boards of Directors of each company should consist of railwaymen. This was very much Sir Eric Geddes's idea – not that he had Soviet tendencies, since there was also the stipulation that none of these Worker–Directors could be a member of a trade union. Geddes maintained that if the workers could be told, by their own representatives, the financial effect on their Company – and thus on their jobs – of pay rises, they would moderate their demands. In making the proposal he was acknowledging the political significance of organized labour and that the workers should have a greater say in the management of their industry: he even referred to the 'semi-feudal' relations which then existed between railway management and workers. Viscount Churchill responded with outrage. The suggestion was 'quite unjustifiable and from every point of view objectionable'.

J.H. Thomas was in favour of Worker–Directors and for similar reasons to those of Geddes. 'Our conception of workers sharing in management', said Thomas mildly, 'is not that they should be merely trade union delegates whose only interest is in the wages and conditions of the men. Worker–Directors means something much bigger than that; it means a genuine contribution by practical men towards the solution of the difficulty common to the industry.'[35] Although on 29 November 1920 Thomas told the Government that railwaymen were 'absolutely united and determined' to have Worker–Directors, he was too optimistic.[36] Many of his members felt that, since such representatives could not be members of the union they would be 'company men', and thus not to be trusted by the railwaymen. So strong was this feeling that by April 1921 Thomas had to reverse his opinion. When the NUR and the companies met on the 29th, it was agreed that the idea of Worker–Directors would be dropped in return for the companies' allowing trade unionists to represent workers at disciplinary hearings, and that the companies would continue to support the existence of the National Wages Board as an arbitrator of wages.

The railway companies wanted the Act to empower them to engage in trade as road hauliers. The prospect of railway competition caused great concern among the free-wheeling Knights of the Road. The Road Haulage Association declared:

> Railway companies should confine their energies to the efficient working of railways and leave the carrying of goods by road to officially recognised road hauliers – the railways on roads should be resisted to the utmost as the natural tendency of railways would be to kill all private initiative and enterprise wherever met and to enjoy the monopoly they have enjoyed for so many years. Transport by road of light goods is infinitely preferable, being faster, cheaper, less damaging and with less likelihood of pilferage. Given road haulage powers the railways – with their dividends practically guaranteed [*sic*] – would no doubt at once begin to cut rates until private road haulage became impossible.[37]

A Departmental Committee was established to investigate the advisability of allowing railways to enter the road haulage business.[38] The report produced three opinions. The first stated that since railways had lost much traffic to the roads, they should be allowed to act as road carriers, provided there was legislation to control their charges; that their rates should be published and amalgamation between road and rail hauliers would be forbidden. The second concluded that traffic which went to road haulage did so as a result of better terms offered by road hauliers, and that traffic should always go by the fastest and cheapest route. The third report stated that it was entirely opposed to railways having road powers because the answer to the national transport problem was total nationalization of all transport. The outcome was that railways were forbidden to operate as road hauliers except in so far as they could 'feed' traffic to their rail-heads.

The financial advantage road transport had over railways was enormous. The formation of a motor manufacturing company did not require an Act of Parliament; but when, in 1918, the SE&CR had to strengthen and widen the Charing Cross bridge, a work of national importance, it could not proceed until the railway had obtained an Act. Not only did the Company have this burdensome expense in addition to the cost of doing the work; before Parliament would grant permission for this public improvement, it placed 'very onerous' (i.e. expensive) conditions on the Company for the railway's future operation.[39]

In February 1921 Lord Colwyn's Committee[40] reported its findings regarding the extent of the Government's indebtedness to the railways. He showed that the railway companies' shareholders had been 'protected from the loss they would otherwise have sustained as a result of post-war depression of trade', and concluded: 'We are of the opinion that it [the 1914 Agreement] has been an advantage to them'. Chapter 5 of the Report acknowledged that the companies had additional claims on the Government amounting to about £150 million to cover abnormal wear and tear and arrears of maintenance but it recommended that no such claims should be entertained. Chapter 8 stated: 'When the original Agreement was concluded it was the intention of the parties that the compensation should be exhaustive of the Government's liability.' Yet it was the case that the Act by which the railway came under government orders guaranteed that the undertakings would be handed back to their owners intact, and clearly this would not now be the case.

Under the Railways Act (Cap. 55) 19 August 1921 the 130 railway companies were grouped into four – the Great Western (GWR), Southern (SR), London, Midland & Scottish (LMSR) and London & North Eastern (LNER) – and handed back to their owners with a payment of £60 million between them as a final settlement of all government liability: less than half the amount Lord Plender had estimated they might be owed.

31

Advantage Road

A N OLD-HAND, GWR station-master whom I met when barely
out of my teens and working on the railway, told me that 'we
[the Company] had to fight the roads with one hand tied
behind our back'. Now, in my mid-fifties, having at last read the 1921
Act, my old friend's words seem remarkably fair comment. Section 20
established the Railway Rates Tribunal (RRT) which was to regulate
fares and charges in accordance with Section 58 of the Act: 'Charges
shall be such as will yield the Standard Revenue equivalent to the
aggregate net revenue of 1913 together with a sum equal to 5 per cent
on capital expenditure.' The Standard Net Revenue, which the four
companies together would be allowed to earn, amounted to
£51 million. If the annual net revenue of the four exceeded this amount,
80 per cent of the excess would be taken away from them through the
RRT's reducing their charges. Thus the railway companies were unable
to benefit from any economies they achieved through more efficient
working; the best they could hope for was static profits, index-linked
to inflation. The companies had wanted this 'claw-back' rule to apply
individually, by company, lest the good performance of one cause a
reduction in the charges of the others who were not earning so much
– but government insisted on looking at the earnings of the four companies as one.

Section 39 forbade outright any competition with coastwise shipping, although no such restriction was placed on road hauliers. The

Act allowed railways to compete with road haulage provided that the railway did not make discounts more than 40 per cent below the standard rate, which was itself so high that such a reduction still enabled the road haulier to undercut it. Such 'exceptional rates' would in any case have to be approved by the RRT; traders not in receipt of the reduction could then object, and while the railway was arguing its case with the RRT, the road haulier could (and did) drive away with the goods. Since the standard and the exceptional rates were, by law, public knowledge, the road haulier could easily undercut them while keeping his own prices a secret between himself and his customer.

Section 52 obliged companies to charge for goods traffic at the rate for the shortest route. The hope was that substantial economies could be effected by an absence of competition between companies and the standardization of equipment, especially with regard to electric traction; that there should be common-user rolling stock and generally co-operative working between companies – including the abolition of wasteful train services where two or more routes served the same places, and the closing of duplicated railway workshops and railway stations. The anticipated savings would not reward those who made them, but would be for the benefit of the nation at large.

The 1921 Grouping was, in fact, a disguised nationalization. The railway companies were earning government-decreed fares, which could only be lowered, never increased – presumably, for the good of society. All other industries continued to act in their own best interests, charging freely and beyond the rate of inflation, while demanding that railways reduce their rates. In 1922 the chief architect of the new system for railways, Sir Eric Geddes, took a seat on the Board of the Dunlop Rubber Company, where he directed the manufacture of motor car tyres and, as spokesman for the Federation of British Industry, demanded cheap railway freight rates for industrial produce.

To compensate themselves, in part at least, for granting reduced rates to industry, the railway companies lowered the wages of their men. The process began one year after the 1919 Agreement on pay, starting with the wages of signalmen and moving on to those of the footplate staff. Between August 1920 and March 1923 the combined wages bill for British railways was reduced by £43 million, with the acquiescence of the unions.[1] On 19 January 1924 the footplatemen went on strike, without the support of the NUR, returning on the 29th having obtained only an assurance that reductions in pay would be phased in, rather than introduced suddenly. Between 1920 and 1924, in the post-war boom and before the road hauliers really got into their stride, the railway companies increased their reserves and paid larger dividends to ordinary shareholders. The most profitable was always the GWR; from 1918 to 1927, with the exception of the General Strike year of 1926 (when income was halved), the Company paid its ordinary share-holders 7 to 8 per cent every year, making this the most profitable period in its history.

The GWR express train speeds and frequencies improved rapidly from 1919, thanks largely to the efforts of the underpaid locomotive crews, and the locomotive shed and workshop staff. Virtue brings its own reward, and the Company benefited from the men's personal pride in their work. The GWR had the advantage of a huge territory over which to run its standardized locomotives and carriages, and a very carefully ordered central factory where everything, from crank-shafts to cameras, was made for the Company. In 1904–6 the Chief Mechanical Engineer, Mr Churchward, had designed the powerful 'Saint' and 'Star' class 4–6–0 locomotives – which were years ahead of all other British engines for power and fuel efficiency. The Swindon works continued to turn out dozens of locomotives to standard designs; in 1923, the 'Castle' class appeared, developed from the 'Star', and in 1927 the 'King' class. Made to high standards of workmanship, these engines lasted many miles between repairs, which were carried out with a standard kit of parts at Swindon. By 1925 the GWR had more express trains, which could run faster than those of 1914. Thanks to the work of Churchward and his successors – who built on his work rather than overturning it – and to the commitment to the job of the footplate and shed staff, the GWR always had the most cost-effective of all steam-locomotive fleets.

The Southern only had one modern type of express passenger engine in 1921: the 'King Arthur' class 4–6–0, introduced by the L&SWR in 1918 – although there was also a modern, 'mixed traffic' type, inherited from the SE&CR and adopting Swindon precepts. In 1926 the Southern brought out the 'Lord Nelson' class 4–6–0, which was impressively large but no more powerful than the 'King Arthur' class.[2] The Southern was however, investing large sums in the electrification of its inner and outer suburban lines, extending even as far as Epsom and Caterham by 1928. Within the electrified areas pas-senger journeys and revenue increased and operating costs fell, while on its steam lines the converse was the case.

In 1925 the LNER was running at 1914 levels of performance, whereas the LMS's performance was decidedly slower than in 1914.[3] The LNER did not introduce a new express engine until Mr Gresley's A 1 class 4–6–2 of 1927; thus began the Gresley revolution, with a series of superbly powerful locomotives for the east coast main line and for East Anglian main lines. The LMS did not build a modern express engine until the 'Royal Scot' class 4–6–0 in 1927. However, these were only for the most important trains, and not until 1931 did LMS locomotive matters begin to improve, when the Company was fortunate to recruit W.A. Stanier, Churchward's deputy at Swindon. Thereafter, a standardized fleet of extremely powerful locomotives was developed, surpassing the power of their older cousins at Swindon. Before these improvements could take place and while the new fleets were being built, the locomotivemen did wonders with pre-war locomotives, using their great skill and physical endurance to run the heavier, post-war trains at pre-war speeds. The efforts of the footplatemen and especially the sooty fireman, shovelling an average of 50 lb of coal a minute on 60 mph express journeys lasting from 2½ to 5 hrs (and even as much as 7½ hrs on the LMS expresses Euston–Glasgow or Birmingham–Perth) make the much-lauded efforts of Olympic athletes running round in a circle look rather ridiculous.

Coal and minerals remained with the railways but from the 1920s the rising tide of consumer goods – gramophone records, electric light bulbs, vacuum cleaners, wirelesses, motor cars and their components, more contract traffic – brought competition from other quarters. The railways tried to capture the modern traffics by selling land for industrial estates and then offering rail connection, by running more express freight trains and guaranteeing overnight delivery. The road lorry was, however, a severe competitor in these areas, not only in matters of cost, but because it was thought by the consignors that lorries were less likely to damage the relatively fragile goods in transit.

The railways' capital burden for the replacement of aged locomotives and rolling stock, to strengthen bridges for heavier engines, widen tracks, electrify tracks and rebuild stations, was immense. Thirty years had passed since any railway company had been able to sell shares at a premium, and for years even railway Debentures had been sold at a discount. The road haulier was given his road in return for a licence-fee, and his business was very lightly taxed by the parochial rates – unlike the railways. How then were the railways now, with their 0 to 7 per cent dividends, to attract shareholders in competition with the motor car, lorry and petrol companies? Car companies in 1919 were paying dividends ranging from 10 to 30 per cent, yielding from £4 to £12 on a £1 share, while the railways were paying 1 to 6 per cent. Between 1922 and 1925 the total number of motor vehicles on the roads rose by 124 per cent and the number of commercial vehicles increased by 64.5 per cent. Meanwhile their total annual contribution to municipal rates and indirectly to road maintenance, was £7,826,603, or 19 per cent of their combined net revenue.[4]

While of course, hundreds of millions of passenger journeys were made by rail each year, and the Southern improved services on their electrified lines, the general trend from about 1924 was a decline, even before the trade depression set in. In July 1928 trade was falling into depression and Sir Felix Pole, General Manager of the GWR, told his Directors it was because of 'the large and growing number of unemployed people who have no money to spend on train journeys'. He also noted that 2500 new cars a week came on to the roads; in that month, 1,909,000 had been licensed, plus 662,000 motor cycles, 290,000 lorries and 87,000 taxis. He cited cases in South Wales where miners were clubbing together to pay for a taxi to work, in order to avoid the appallingly bad GWR carriages in which they would otherwise have to make the journey. GWR passenger train expenses were so high for a diminishing return that from 24 September the Company abolished seven expresses, including the 3.30 p.m. and 5 p.m. Paddington and the *Cheltenham Flyer*.[5] The public were outraged and all seven were reinstated, in spite of the worsening depression, on 1 March 1929. Paradoxically, throughout the same period the demand for holiday trains outstripped supply, and some very inappropriate carriages were pressed into service to 'strengthen' regular and extra trains.

The Railway (Road Transport) Bill promoted by the grouped companies was passed in August 1928, making it legal for the railway companies to own road haulage companies. The railways joined with existing bus companies to form large road passenger transport organizations, which resulted in combined road/rail tickets and bus and train co-ordination.[6] The road freight carriers Carter-Paterson and Hays Wharf Cartage were purchased by the four railway companies which brought the famous name of Pickfords into railway ownership and gave the combined railway companies 18 per cent of the road freight business. In 1929 the Local Government Act 'relieved' railways of 75 per cent of their parochial rates obligation. It was a strange 'relief because the money saved had to be passed on to industry by a reduction in freight rates to an amount equal to the saving. Industrial sites had already been given rate relief so industry was twice blessed. The Finance Act of 1929 'relieved' the railways of the tax on tickets sold, amounting to £370,000 per annum – but only so that the savings could pay the interest on government loans to the companies, thereby enabling them to undertake large-scale engineering works for the relief of unemployment, works which would improve railway routes and stations. Another Act – the Loans & Guarantees – was passed in 1929 and a similar measure came in in 1935, to enable the Government to lend the railways money, at interest, for the relief of unemployment. There was no question of road users having to take government loans to rebuild their local roads. The core of the railway companies' troubles was that the Government was using them as a conduit for subsidies to farming and industry.

In October 1928 the Heavy Motor Car Order of 1904 was modified to raise the speed limit of lorries from 12 to 20 mph; they were also ordered to fit rear-view mirrors. In December 1928 the easing of parochial rates on railway property enabled freight rates to be reduced on export coal, some agricultural traffic, iron and steel while 4d per gallon tax was imposed on petrol to go some way towards reducing the advantages enjoyed by the subsidized road haulage industry. Of course this was a two-edged sword, since the railways' road fleet used petrol too. In 1930 the tax was reduced by 2d a gallon, saving the GWR 10,000.

In 1928 the 'Country Lorry' system was introduced, and modest freight warehouses (no longer subject to a heavy rateable value) were erected at small town and rural stations. The long-distance goods came in by rail, in a container or in wagons, to be stored in the warehouses and distributed by the 'Country Lorry' service to the local traders, who could call in their wares daily or as they required them. The use of road/rail containers began in 1928, the GWR 'Green Arrow' service of trains running at passenger train speeds. The 'factory to shop' convenience and the speed of this service made it very successful at a time when income from conventional freight carrying operations declined.

The Depression began in earnest in 1929 with the crash on the American Stock Exchange. The worst-affected British railways were those who earned most from the old-fashioned heavy industries: coal, iron, shipbuilding and minerals. The LNER earned 60 per cent of its revenue from freight, the LMS 58 per cent, the GWR 51 per cent and

the SR 25 per cent.[7] In 1930 the GWR, LMS and LNER agreed to pool
their freight revenue and to reduce tolls paid to each other for the use
of certain strategic lines (the NLR, for instance). In spite of the
economies of amalgamation and the shedding of 104,000 jobs[8] between
1925 and 1932 – 35,000 during 1929 alone – the railway companies
became ever less profitable as the best traffic was lost to cheaper road
hauliers. Railway rates did not need to rise; what the railways needed
was the same commercial freedom and secrecy as the road hauliers. No
railway company ever achieved the 'standard net revenue' envisaged
by the Act. The GWR earned a gross revenue of £35,527,000 in 1928,
half a million less than 1927, while total working expenses were
£588,000 more. £22 million was paid in wages.[9]

   In August 1928 all British railwaymen and women were asked to
accept a temporary 2½ per cent wage cut if all railway Directors and
senior officers accepted an equal reduction in their fees/salaries. No
wage was to be reduced below 4s a week. The railwaymen agreed to do
this for a period of eighteen months when the cuts would be restored.
The average basic railway wage at that time was perhaps 55s a week at
a time, whereas the average wage in 'sweated' industries was 48s 10d
and about 20 per cent of railwaymen earned 46s a week or less. At the
end of the eighteen months' period, the companies asked the National
Wages Board to reduce railwaymen's pay by 4 per cent, which would
have brought the lowest wage to 38s a week. The railwaymen, who
were beginning to wonder where their co-operation with the companies might lead, became restless, and the threat of a national strike
loomed. The National Wages Board opted to keep the 2½ per cent cut
whereupon the companies withdrew from the National Wages Board
and agreed between themselves to implement as broad a co-operation
as possible, pooling all competitive revenue and sharing facilities
where possible, and closing those that became redundant thereby.

   In 1932, the worst year of the slump, the Ministry of Transport
established a Commission of eight men, four from the railways and
four from road haulage, chaired by Sir Arthur Salter. Their purpose
was to investigate how to 'place competition between road and rail on
an equal footing and how to allocate to each form of transport the
functions it can most usefully perform'. The Salter Report recommended that each class of road vehicle should pay its fair share of its
use of the road (the railways had wanted the wording 'full cost'); that
road hauliers should be licensed on the basis of the need for their
service; and that all licences should depend upon their providing fair

wages, and reasonable hours of work and conditions of service for their drivers.

The Road Traffic Act of 1933 translated the road vehicle safety recommendations of the Salter Report into law and established a system of Traffic Commissioners, whose purpose was to adjudicate between road and rail on matters of competition, and to which any road haulier would have to apply for a licence to run a bus or lorry – and to which application the railways could object on the grounds that they were already supplying the service. While the railways were subject to enormous safety costs imposed by law, and had a magnificent record on safety, the road hauliers skimped their costs, in spite of the law, to maintain their profits. In 1937 it was reported in Parliament[10] that there were 26,000 convictions against road hauliers, which included working their men excessive hours, having dangerous or unlicensed vehicles, or unlicensed drivers; another 7300 convictions were for speeding.

The SR did not join the 1930 or 1933 'poolings', and was the only company to attempt to economize through large-scale modernization of signalling and traction (although the GWR investigated the electrification of the main line and branches from Taunton westwards in 1927). The reason for not going ahead with this essential work is usually accepted to be the prevailing financial situation, yet between 1927 and 1929 the Southern had electrified its outer suburban routes as far as Windsor and Gravesend, and work costing £2.7 million for the Victoria, Brighton and Worthing line electrification continued throughout the Depression. This project was completed on 30 December 1932 with brand new trains, including Pullman electric cars whose bodies were nearly 9 ft wide and almost 70 ft long. The Southern then had 970 miles of electric railway, on which it saved £.4 million in operating costs while increasing passenger journeys. The programme of electrification continued up to the outbreak of war in September 1939.

The other railway companies produced remarkably good passenger services with steam-engines. The GWR ran powerfully from Paddington to Birmingham, Bristol and Newport, Plymouth, and Worcester at average speeds of around 60 mph, and from 1935 the 'Bristolian' was timed to cover the 118 miles to and from Bristol in 105 mins. In March 1933 the GWR inaugurated a passenger air service, using an Imperial Airways six-seater Westland 'Wessex', to fly between Cardiff and Plymouth. The plane was painted chocolate and

cream and had 'GWR' on the tail fin. In May the service was extended
to include Birmingham, and the LMS asked to join the scheme
Though the service was popular, the plane was too small to be profit
able and the companies ran it at a loss until May 1939.

In July 1934, the GWR introduced 80-mph streamlined diesel rai
cars, with lavatory and buffet, on the Birmingham–Cardiff route. The
made the 105-mile journey in 115 mins calling at three major station
The following year, the LNER ran its streamlined A 4 class 4–6–2 loco
motives with streamlined coaches on the *Silver Jubilee* at 100 mph, an
the LMS its *Royal Scot* express; from 1937, the latter also ran th
Coronation Scot, another streamlined train hauled by a streamline
'Duchess' class 4–6–2. From about 1934, the SR, LMS and LNE
caught up with and overtook the GWR in medium-powered loco
motives, and there was a general acceleration of secondary expresse
Even though the four companies never gave up the fight for traffi
never reduced their outlay on maintenance and, in 1938, restored t
their workers the pay cuts of 1928, they were unable to earn the annu
revenue to which, according to the Act, they were entitled. Withou
significant profits, railway could attract little or no investment fc
essential modernization.

In 1938, having been unable to move the Government in private, th
companies appealed to the public spirit of fair play, launching th
'Railways Demand a Square Deal Now' campaign for their comme
cial freedom. If the railways could not be as free as road hauliers t
pursue their business they would go bankrupt – this was the opinio
of Lord Stamp, President of the London Midland & Scottish Rai
way (LM&SR), Britain's greatest statistician and soon to be Chi
Economic Advisor to the Treasury.[11] Nothing, however, was don
In May 1939 the Minister of Transport, Captain Wallace, told th
Cabinet: 'It does not seem possible to accept that railways should b
put on the same footing as other transport.'[12] If government were t
release railways from their straitjacket, the companies could no long
act as a money pipeline to farming and industry.

The railways were taken over by the Government on 1 Septemb
1939 under the Emergency Powers (Defence) Act of that year. Th
Government agreed to 'give a definite undertaking that rates, fares ar
charges will be raised promptly to meet variations in costs'.[13] The con
panies wanted to be paid the 'Standard Net Revenue' of £51.4 millio
their legal entitlement under the 1921 Act. What they got was a gua
anteed net revenue of £40 million and the whole of the next £3

million they earned; any surplus thereafter, up to a limit of £56 million, was to be shared 50/50 with the Government. Anything above that was to go direct to the Treasury. The guarantee represented the average net revenue of the previous three relatively good years; but in justice (and perhaps in law also), the Government should have paid them their legal revenue, as laid down in the 1921 Act.

The *Economist* thought that the companies had been treated 'far too generously', since no one should make a profit out of their country in wartime – a noble thought, but not one that was taken seriously by the rest of British industry either in 1914–18 or in 1939–45. Herbert Morrison complained that, as a result of the Agreement, the value of railway stocks had risen 'by at least £100 million'.[14] But that was from a position at or close to zero for many railway stocks, and after all the years of government-imposed frugality, perhaps the companies deserved to earn a decent income. Petrol was, by February 1940, so strictly rationed that long-distance road haulage was reduced by 75 per cent and coastwise shipping was, for obvious reasons, not practical although food was still ferried across from Ireland – and Irish food ships were sunk by the Germans). The war meant that the railways were going to be worked harder than at any time since 1918, and a proper income would be needed to keep up with the costs of wages, fuel and repairs: to have merely the income of the pre-war era was patently insufficient.

In spite of their difficulties between 1921 and 1939, the companies had managed to restore their track, stations and rolling stock and achieve a high standard of maintenance – although nearly 40 per cent of locomotives were over thirty years old. They certainly took pride in the work: even though ill-paid, the trackmen kept the road pristine as any contemporary photograph will show. The railwaymen's high standards of training can be seen in the fact that between 1 and 4 September the railways ran 3823 special trains out of London, Liverpool and other large cities, and from East Anglia – places where bombing or invasion was expected – carrying 1,334,358 children away from danger. For the whole of September and into October the SR carried 102,000 troops and all their equipment to Southampton, for instance. In January 1940 temperatures reached 28 degrees below freezing with tremendous falls of snow. *The Times* reported that railway staff gave 'travellers and traders the best possible service' under these extraordinary difficulties.[15] In May 1940, with virtually no prior notice, the railways organized 183 trains to disperse the survivors of

Dunkirk from Dover and Southampton. In 1944 the railways ran 5<
per cent more ton-miles than in 1938 and carried 67 per cent more pas
sengers. It is worth recalling that all freight marshalling yards workec
at night in total darkness, or by the light of the moon. Years after the
war, the men and women who did the job were still justly proud o
their achievements.[16] Maintenance of the railways was, however
neglected because of shortage of staff, and the pressure to carry traffic

In June 1940, with a virtually unarmed Britain staring at disaste
poised to strike across the Channel, the Prime Minister Nevill
Chamberlain found himself blamed for the situation, lost the confi
dence of Parliament, and was obliged to resign his position. He wa
replaced by the prophet of Armageddon, Winston Churchill, deteste
by a Conservative establishment who still wanted to make a deal wit
Hitler. A coalition government was formed with two Liberal minister
and such great Labour figures as Attlee, Morrison and Bevin (whor
Churchill referred to as 'a friend of mine working hard for the publi
cause and a man who has much help to give').[17] With a strong Labou
Party contingent in the Cabinet, the 1939 agreement with the railway
was scrapped in favour of a 'rent' of £43 million a year and a trust fun
to allow for post-war reconstruction. The value of the new Agreemer
to the Government, and the loss to the railways, amounted betwee
January 1941 and December 1944 to £176 million. The railways effec
tively carried that much traffic free.[18]

In September 1940 the War Cabinet reneged on the 1939 agreemer
by directing the Chancellor and Ministry of War Transport not t
allow any railway price increases,[19] in order to control inflation. Si
Leonard Browett, Permanent Secretary to the Minister of Transpor
noted in 1941 that coal, iron, steel and timber cost 60 to 100 per cer
above 1939 prices,[20] although railway charges could not be hel
accountable, since they had not been increased. The Chancellor an
Minister of Transport pointed out to the Prime Minister that railway
should be maintained in a healthy economic condition, or else th
Government would be faced at some stage with the need to subsidiz
them, which would be inflationary.[21] The policy of holding dow
railway charges was adhered to, and in 1941 the guaranteed revenu
was reduced to £40 million and pegged down until 1946. During th
same period the companies' costs rose: 92 per cent for coal, 83 per cer
for materials and 75 per cent for labour.[22] The effect on the compani
was, of course, devastating, since they were carrying governmer
traffic for nothing while running their track and rolling stock into th

ground. Between 1940 and 1944, the LMS built 90 new carriages, out of a fleet of 22,000.[23] Compared with 1938 there were, in 1946, 32 per cent more locomotives, 92 per cent more coaches and 281 per cent more wagons out of use and awaiting repair.[24] Within that overall picture the GWR was in the best condition, followed by the SR, the LMS and, trailing last, the LNER. The backlog of repairs to locomotives, rolling stock and track in 1946 was so great as to affect the efficiency of the railways for another ten years.[25]

Nationalization and central planning had always been Labour Party policy but for years there had also been support from the Conservative and Liberal parties. People such as William Beveridge and J.M. Keynes wanted considerably to modify the capitalist system as a cure for the poverty, ignorance and ill-health which unbridled capitalism visited upon the ordinary people. Between 1940 and 1950, there was, among those who mattered, more or less a consensus on the benefits which would accrue from government planning. In 1947 the Conservatives revealed their 'Industrial Charter', written by a leading member of the party, R.A. Butler, architect of the 1944 Education Act. In this Charter Butler declared that, 'in the interests of efficiency, full employment and social security, modern Conservatism would maintain strong, central guidance over the operation of the economy'.[26] Never had this ideal been more popular among voters than in 1945, when on 5 July the Labour Party was voted into power, with a good majority,[27] to carry out its long-awaited programme including 'the public ownership and co-ordination of transport services by rail, road, air and canal. The railways, which had been used as a tool of government since 1921, were nationalized, together with roads and inland waterways, as from January 1948.

Epilogue

THE GREAT RECONSTRUCTION plan for Britain was formed during the darkest days of the war, and sprang from a universal determination to make a better world at the successful conclusion of the war – a hope that showed a great and idealistic faith, given the period in which the plan was made. After the war, the depth of the financial crisis which the country faced was greater than anyone could have guessed five years earlier, and most plans for spending on the railways were abandoned.

In 1953 the road haulage system was denationalized, which returned the railways to the same impossible position regarding road competition that they had occupied from 1921 to 1939. In 1959 the first motorway was opened, heralding a vast programme of major road building which undermined the position of railways still further money spent on roads was considered by the Government as 'an investment' but money spent on railways was known as 'a subsidy' and railways were now guilty of eating taxpayers' money. The cost effectiveness of railways was ignored, and indeed, they were accused of being inefficient. In fact they are exceedingly efficient carriers and therefore constitute a serious danger to the profits of the road, car and petrol industries. The cost to the nation of an anti-railway policy is in unemployment, and in an overburdening of the national infrastructure and the health service. The costs of the damage to roads and towns by the heavy lorries, the costs of essential bypasses and bridge strengthening was paid without demur from taxation. Between 1958 and 1967, 232,000 railway jobs and 5793 miles of route were abolished; where once there stood the largest marshalling yard in Britain, if not in Europe, employing a whole town of people, there now stands a huge prison. Still the railways 'did not pay'. The capacity for good, inherent in a national railway network, has been thrown away. The 1993 Railways Act was the formal abandonment of the last vestige of the humanitarian attitude, the idealistic faith that developed out of the hardships of two generations given life in 1945.

The certainty of British Railway's funding, the reliability of its manually operated services and equipment, contrast strangely with the complicated uncertainty of today's railway with its risk-laden finances and severely undermanned equipment. Point and train failures allied to lack of staff have an impact on the system unheard-of in former times. The old railway had men to deal promptly with equipment failures and spare capacity to cope with train failures or the lack of a driver – but now, away with staff and spare capacity; if there is a failure the passengers can wait or the train can be cancelled. The penalties imposed on the operators for not carrying out their promises are too mild to be a deterrent, while their reward for dispensing with jobs is greater profit.

The congestion caused by cars and lorries calls for a very strong railway system, but instead the railways have been comprehensively fragmented, running without an overall strategy. The break-up of the railway provided large fees for lawyers and others without assisting in laying one brick on the ground: a classic situation, which Robert Stephenson would recognize. The tenant operators have made huge promises to the nation, sometimes without a good basis of assets, and on borrowed money. They are running on a legacy bequeathed to them by the taxpayer, and one hopes they will replace it before they leave.

The railways have always been a microcosm of the nation and their present situation reflects the national situation and the prevailing philosophy: the blindness of self-interest replacing the faithful ideals of public service. The difficulties we face relating to employment, transport and the environment, and even the future of civilized society, will not be solved through individual self-interest but rather by attending comprehensively to the national problem. Enormous personal fortunes have been made from tricky financial deals and paper promises, leaving the railway operation to stand or fall by the result of a gamble. It is an enormous tragedy for the nation.

Appendices

Appendix 1
Declining Profits Following Expansion of Capital

AUTHORIZED RAILWAY CAPITAL AND LOANS 1844–1847

	1844	1845	1846	1847
Shares	£15,596,750	£44,876,770	£95,625,934	£34,152,520
Loans	£4,857,947	£14,622,682	£36,087,272	£10,060,619
Total	£20,454,697	£59,499,452	£131,713,206	£44,213,139

(Taken from Parliamentary Returns and published in *Railway Commercial Information*. See PRO, ZLIB 4/149.)

These figures are the amounts of capital and loans which were authorized to be raised by the railway companies in the Acts of Incorporation – which is not to say that these sums were actually raised. In many cases, a company estimated the cost of construction at, say, £2 million, but was authorized to raise £4 million. The scope for share creation, buying, selling and speculation in shares was enormous.

ACTS OF PARLIAMENT INCORPORATING RAILWAYS 1801–1848
MILES OF RAILWAY AUTHORIZED TO BE BUILT 1801–1848

1801–25	55 Acts throughout Great Britain
1826	11 Acts throughout Great Britain
1836	32 Acts throughout Great Britain

Up to 1835, 927 miles of railway were authorized in Great Britain, of which 815 were in England and Wales. In 1836, 875 miles were authorized in England & Wales.

Collapse of markets, 1836–7.

1838	3 miles new rly authorized in England & Wales
1840	2 miles new rly authorized in England & Wales
1841	5 miles new rly authorized in England & Wales
1843	41 miles (21 Acts)
1844	642 miles (48 Acts) £20,454,697*
1845	1665 miles (120 Acts) £59,499,452*
1846	3348 miles (277 Acts) £131,713,206*
1847	969 miles (196 Acts) £44,213,139*

* Capital authorized

Collapse of markets, 1847.

THE AVERAGE COST PER MILE OF BUILDING RAILWAYS IN EACH YEAR
1842: £34,690; 1843: £36,360; 1844: £35,670; 1845: £35,370; 1846: £31,860; 1847: 31,709; 1848: £34,234; 1849: £35,214; 1850: £35,229

These averages include such lines as the Waterloo Bridge Extension, which cost £500,000 per mile, the Blackwall (£300,000) and the Greenwich (£250,000). (Source: *Herapath*, 5 April 1851.)

Competitive lines took away traffic from each other even in the booming 1850s. The L&NWR share (%) of UK railway activity fell as shown below:

L&NWR RAIL ACTIVITY AS A PERCENTAGE OF THAT OF UK

	1851–2	% of UK	1858–9	% of UK
Passenger revenue	£1,480,221	18.5	£1,473,420	13.8
Goods revenue	£1,395,253	18.7	£2,234,853	16.0
Total	£2,875,476	18.6	£3,708,273	15.0
Capital (shares called & loans)	£30,134,818	12.1	£35,680,200	11.0
No. employed	8,592	13.2	14,891	12.8
Stations open	226	10.0	428	12.4

(Source: D. Gourvish, *Mark Huish and the London & North Western Railway*.)

The railways grew larger and thus employed more capital but they did not earn proportionately more money:

INCOME PER MILE P.A. AND EXTRA MILEAGE OPENED EACH YEAR

1842	£3118	–
1843	£3085	56
1844	£3278	194
1845	£3469	263
1846	£3305	593
1847	£2870	839
1848	£2556	975
1849	£2302	835
1850	£2227	591

Appendix 2
Financial Position of Companies, 1889–1902

THE ACTUAL CAPITAL EXPENDED BY RAILWAYS BETWEEN 1889 & 1897

	increase (capital)	increase (1889/97)	increase (gross rev.)	increase (net rev.)
GCR	£13,655,154	51.7%	19.8%	6.4%
GER	£5,415,234	13.3%	25.6%	15.5%
GNR	£7,886,449	21.3%	23.3%	10.7%
GWR	£9,044,687	11.6%	18.0%	1.7%
L&YR	£5,066,572	10.9%	18.6%	12.9%
L&NWR	£7,027,605	7.0%	13.1%	2.4%
L&SWR	£6,142,114	19.7%	33.1%	23.3%
LB&SC	£1,986,652	8.2%	19.1%	2.2%
LC&DR	£1,014,927	3.7%	14.7%	9.5%
MR	£12,404,534	14.5%	21.1%	9.6%
NER	£7,690,330	12.5%	17.3%	3.8%
SER	£2,388,499	10.1%	15.5%	6.0%

(The increase of capital excluding that raised for the London Extension was 19.3%. The London Extension had cost, by the end of 1897, £8,961,616. This sum included £650k as the interest on the loans raised to build the line.)

Out of the twelve major companies the best performance, 1889–97 was:

	L&SWR	GER	L&YR	GNR
gross exceeded net income	9.8%	10.1%	5.7%	11.6%
increase in profit	23.3%	15.5%	12.9%	10.7%

The worst performing during this period were the GWR and L&NWR, which had the smallest growth in gross revenue (13.1% and 18%) and the smallest increase in profit (1.7% and 2.4% respectively). In 1897, the GWR's gross income was £1,520,000 more than in 1889 and with that increase, the Company managed to add only £74,426 to its net receipts.
(Source: *Economist* (30 August 1898), p. 649.)

MILES OF TRACK PER £1000 INVESTED IN 1900

	miles	total paid-up capital	miles per £m
MR	1553	£204m	7.06
L&NWR	1969	£125m	15.75
GWR	3008	£99m	24.00
NER	1728	£81m	21.33
L&YR	591	£70m	8.40
GNR	863	£60m	14.38
L&SWR	966	£56m	17.25
GER	1133	£54m	20.98
GCR	757	£54m	14.00
SE&CR	629	{ SER £23m {LCD £30m	10.14
LB&SCR	454	£29m	15.65

(Source: *Herapath*, August 1900.)

The average cost of the money was 3½ per cent, so if the works completed by this extra capital did not produce a return of 3½% then the investment was a loss. This lack of return had a mildly depressing effect on share dividends and the market price thereof, so that the railways found it more difficult to raise money in the future, except by bank loans – which is the most expensive way of doing it.

FINANCIAL POSITION OF 12 MAJOR RLY COS, 2ND HALF OF 1890

	£ Gross	Wkg Expense	%	£ Net	Divd
L&NWR	6,209,286	3,323,519	53.5	2,885,767	7¾%
GWR	4,685,193	2,355,836	50.3	2,329,357	7¾%
MR	4,669,964	2,456,386	52.6	2,213,578	7%
NER	3,830,432	2,141,285	55.9	1,689,147	7¾%
L&YR	2,246,560	1,260,745	56.1	985,815	4½%
GNR	2,307,009	1,319,975	57.2	987,034	6%
GER	2,268,219	1,231,005	54.3	1,037,214	4%
L&SWR	1,849,465	999,266	54.0	850,199	7¼%
SER	1,268,089	618,489	48.8	649,600	6¼%
LB&SCR	1,350,543	588,697	43.6	761,846	9¾%
MS&LR	1,247,693	594,561	47.7	653,132	4¾%
LC&DR	783,061	400,112	51.1	382,949	(a) 4½%
NSR*	380,565	187,501	49.3	193,064	5%
Met	358,848	140,068	39.0	218,780	4¼%
NLR	280,719	145,448	51.8	135,271	7½%
Total	£33,735,646	£17,762,893	52.7	£15,972,753	6¼%

* North Staffordshire Rly

(a) On the 4½% Preference Shares; no divd on Ordinary Shares.

(Source: *Economist* (21 February 1891), p. 235.)

INCREASE/DECREASE SHOWN BY THE ABOVE FIGURES

	£ Gross	Wkg Expense	£ Net	Divd
L&NWR	+167,118	+195,286	−28,168	−¼%
GWR	+153,929	+161,085	−7,156	−¼%
MR	+236,843	+180,841	+56,002	+¼%
NER	+173,319	+221,875	−48,556	−¼%
L&YR	+78,895	+88,850	−9,955	−¼%
GNR	+67,810	+68,858	−1,048	−¼%
GER	+93,383	+96,393	+1,990	unchanged
L&SWR	+66,177	+59,249	+6,928	−¼%
SER	+2,574	+32,335	−20,761	−½%
LB&SCR	+23,250	+40,718	−17,468	−¼%
MS&LR	+28,582	+34,786	−6,204	−¾%
LC&DR	−5,854	+17,960	−23,814	unchanged
NSR	+16,713	+19,222	+2,509	unchanged
Met	+9,281	−4,181	+13,462	+¼%
NLR	+8,346	+8,550	−204	unchanged
Total	+£1,125,366	+£1,212,827	−£87,461	−2¾%

DIVIDENDS (%) TO ORDINARY SHAREHOLDERS 1889–1902

	1889	1897	1901	1902
GCR	3 1/8	0	0	0
GER	2	3 1/2	2 5/8	3 1/8
GNR	4 7/8	4 1/8	2 5/8	3 3/4
GWR	6 3/4	6	4	5
L&YR	4 1/2	5 7/8	3 5/8	4 3/8
L&NWR	7 3/8	7 3/8	7 1/8	5
L&SWR	6	6	7	5 1/2
LB&SCR	7 1/8	7 1/8	6 1/2	4 3/4
MR	6	6	6	4 5/8
NER	7 1/4	7 1/4	6 3/8	5 3/4
SER	4 7/8	4 7/8	4 7/8	2 5/16

Appendix 3
A Summary of the Career of W.H. Barlow

Mr William Henry Barlow, FRS (1812–1902). Son of Mr Peter Barlow, Professor of Mathematics, Royal Military Academy, Woolwich. 1832, worked for Maudslay & Field in Constantinople erecting re-casting and re-boring machinery for the guns of the Turkish army. 1838, Assistant Engineer to G.W. Buck, Manchester & Birmingham Railway; 1842, Resident Engineer, Midland Counties Railway and, from 1844, of the Midland Railway. Became Principal Engineer-in-Charge of the Midland Railway until 1857, when he moved into more general practice in London and became Consulting Engineer to the Company. From 1857 until 1866 he designed railways for the MR, and the MSL. He did work for Sir Joseph Paxton on the strength of the columns required for the Great Exhibition building of 1851. In 1860 he designed, in conjunction with Sir John Hawkshaw, the Clifton suspension bridge as a memorial and tribute to I.K. Brunel, FRS, 1806–1859, using the chains from the Hungerford (London) suspension bridge which had been designed by Brunel for the Clifton bridge in 1831. Barlow investigated the cause of the Tay bridge collapse and designed the new Tay bridge. He also took a leading part in the design of the Forth bridge by pointing out the necessity for the double vertical tubes in each cantilever. These verticals were not present in the original plan and without them the bridge would not have worked. He was a pioneer in the use of steel rather than wrought iron in bridges. Throughout his life he gave a great deal of thought and experiment to the theory of bridges and the strength of metals and read several very important papers to the Royal Society and other learned scientific societies on these matters.

He was also outstanding in his generation in that he never received a knighthood. He died at his home, High Combe, Old Charlton, on 12 November 1902.

(Taken from his Obituary in the Minutes of the Proceedings of the Institution of Civil Engineers, cli.)

Appendix 4
Sir Gilbert Scott

In 1857 the British Government established a competition for designs for a building to house the Foreign and War Offices between Whitehall and St James's Park. There were 218 entries, among them one from Gilbert Scott: a fantastic design of spires, turrets and coiling staircases. It did not convey the stern atmosphere that one might have expected for the departments of war, prisons and hanging, and, not surprisingly, he earned only a third prize.

He protested and lobbied against this and was actually appointed as the architect of the new offices and again put forward his Gothic plans. England in those days was not only staunchly Protestant but, in many quarters, it was fiercely anti-papist: to be a Catholic was still regarded as paramount to treason. Scott was unable to overcome the opposition of Lord Palmerston and, in 1861–8, was forced to design and supervise the erection of the very severe buildings now existing.

In his *Personal and Professional Recollections*, Sir Gilbert wrote: 'Having been disappointed, through Palmerston, of my ardent hope of carrying out my style in Government Offices I was glad to be able to erect one building in that style in London.'

Appendix 5
James Allport

James Allport was born in Birmingham in 1811. At the age of twenty-eight he was Chief Clerk to the Birmingham & Derby Junction Railway, then General Manager. He was one of the founders of the Railway Clearing House. On the formation of the MR he was made redundant and was sent by Hudson to the Newcastle & Darlington as General Manager. He helped this railway to grow and was in charge when it was amalgamated to become the York, Newcastle & Berwick. In 1850 he became General Manager of the MS&L and became General Manager of the MR in 1853. In March 1854 he was appointed to the Board of the MR, and in 1857 returned as General Manager. He retired in 1880 and was given a seat on the Board after the retirement of Edward Shipley Ellis, the Chairman. In 1877 the MR and GNR tried to buy up Watkin's MS&L as a joint line between them, but Watkin turned them down over half a per cent – a fact the shareholders must have come to regret in later years.

Allport retired from the Board in 1880 and was presented with a cheque for £10,000 by the shareholders. He was knighted in 1884 for his services to 3rd-class travellers.

Sir James commented, towards the end of his long career:

> If there is one part of my public life on which I look back with more satisfaction than on anything else it is with reference to the boon we conferred on third-class travellers. I have felt saddened to see third-class passengers shunted on to a siding in cold and bitter weather – a train containing many lightly clad women and children – for the convenience of allowing the more comfortable and warmly clad passengers to pass. When the rich man travels, or if he lies in bed all day, his capital remains undiminished and perhaps his income flows in all the same. But when the poor man travels he has not only to pay his fare but sink his capital, for his time is his capital and if he now consumes only five hours instead of ten in making a journey he has saved himself five hours of time for useful labour – useful to himself, his family and society. And I think with even more pleasure of the comfort in travelling we have been able to confer on women and children. But it took 25 years to get it done.

Allport was a typical, eminent Victorian of the best type: astute, forceful, but also genial and kind. He died in the Midland Grand Hotel, St Pancras, on 25 April 1892.

Appendix 6
Coal Production in England and Wales, 1855–1914

1855: 57m tons	1895: 161m tons
1865: 86m tons	1900: 192m tons
1870: 96m tons	1905: 200m tons
1875: 115m tons	1910: 223m tons
1880: 129m tons	1913: 245m tons
1890: 157m tons	

(Source: Mitchell and Deane, *Abstract of British Historical Statistics*, quoted in Simmons, *The Railway in England and Wales, 1830–1914*, p. 88.)

In 1888 the percentages of the total coal brought to London by rail were as follows: MR, 33.7%; L&NWR, 22.5%; GNR, 17.4%; GER, 13.5%; GWR, 11.5%. (Parliamentary Papers (1889), p. 500.)

AVERAGE ANNUAL TONS OF COAL TO LONDON, 1830–89

	Seaborne	Railborne	Total (tons)	Railborne (%)	Av. price per ton at ship
1830–9	2288m	0	2288m	0	22s
1840–4	2664m	0	2664m	0	20s
1845–9	3279m	19m	3298m	0.6	17s 10d
1850–4	3379m	451m	3830m	11.8	17s 10d
1855–9	3167m	1195m	4362m	27.4	18s
1860–4	3407m	1750m	5157m	33.9	18s
1865–9	3001m	3064m	6065m	50.4	18s 7d
1870–4	2940m	4609m	7549m	61.1	21s
1875–9	3257m	5559m	8819m	63.0	19s
1880–4	3952m	6701m	10653m	63.1	16s 2d
1885–9	4768m	7424m	12192m	60.8	15s 7d

(Figures end in 1889 because in that year the Corporation of London gave up its right to charge a toll on all coals passing their boundaries and thus the only combined statistics for all London were no longer kept.)
(Source: Mitchell and Deane, quoted in Simmons, *The Railway in Town and Country*, p. 44.)

Appendix 7
The Westinghouse Brake

AN EXPLANATION

Air is compressed by a steam pump and is fed at 70 lb psi through the driver's brake valve to the main reservoir on the engine and also, through the driver's brake valve, along the train pipe through the 'triple valve' to the auxiliary reservoirs, one on each vehicle. The train pipe is sealed airtight at each end of the train.

Each vehicle has a brake piston in a cylinder. Compressed air can be admitted to each cylinder from the auxiliary reservoir through the triple valve. Pressure on the brake piston drives it along the cylinder. A connecting rod from the piston to the brake blocks pulls the brake blocks against the wheels of the vehicle.

To apply the brake, the driver moves his brake handle to allow some of the train pipe pressure to exhaust to atmosphere, reducing the pressure in the train pipe and thus, that of the triple valve.

When pressure is reduced in the triple valve, the valve moves to permit air from the auxiliary reservoir (still at 70 lb psi) into the brake cylinder, driving the brake piston and forcing the brake blocks against the wheels. A reduction of 25 lb psi in the train pipe occurs during a full brake application.

When the driver closes his brake valve, air from the main reservoir enters the train pipe and restores the original pressure, causing the triple valve to close off the supply from the auxiliary reservoir and venting to atmosphere air pressure in the brake cylinder. A spring in the brake cylinder ensures that the brake piston moves back and releases pressure on the brake blocks.

If the train pipe should be broken, as in a crash or an accidental parting of the train, the pressure in the train pipe falls and the brakes are applied to all vehicles. Thus the system is 'fail-safe'. It has an inherent danger in that there is no brake if the air pressure on both sides of the piston is reduced to atmospheric. The driver must remember to charge his reservoir and train pipe before he starts.

Appendix 8
Francis Webb

Francis William Webb (1835–1906) was Chief Locomotive Superintendent of the L&NWR from 1871 until 1904. He was without a doubt a great manager and organizer but he ruled as a dictator: no one dared offer even the most justified and helpful criticism. As a result, for many years his locomotivemen had to suffer some very bad engines; there were some good ones but those Webb loved best – his 'Compounds' – were the worst designed and the cause of most trouble to their crews. Using these engines they had to keep time on the fastest and heaviest of L&NWR expresses, and if they lost time their wages were confiscated by the designer.

The L&NWR's Crewe locomotive works was the largest and most efficient in the world, thanks to Webb's single-minded grasp of both broad strategy and minute, practical detail, and employed 13,000 men. Webb was a brilliant production manager, engineer of locomotives, carriages and wagons, factory machinery and signalling equipment. He had a policy of self-sufficiency in all fields. At Crewe the L&NWR smelted ore and produced its own steel. Webb designed some fine, practical locomotives but he was also devoted to complicated, badly designed locomotives which were the bane of enginemen's lives.

The town of Crewe was very much the creation of the railway Company. It built the houses, provided the employment and paid most of the parochial rates. As the chief representive of the Company in the town and the Master of at least 5000 factory employees, Webb felt very strongly that he ought to take responsibility for the town and that the town ought to do as he said. He lived an austere, solitary life, the virtual Dictator of Crewe: Locomotive Carriage & Wagon Superintendent, Magistrate and Mayor. His brother, reputedly 'a bit odd' (there was some history of hereditary insanity in the family), was Vicar of Crewe.

Francis Webb was paid a salary of £2000 a year in 1871. In his previous post as Chief Indoor Assistant (Works Manager), he had received only £180 per annum. His salary was to increase to £7000 a year, more than that of the General Manager of the Company, Frederick Harrison (a source of some bitterness to the latter). From the royalties Webb received from the Company for his dangerous brakes and other patents, he amassed a huge fortune. After his death he left most of it to charitable causes: £10,000 for free nursing for the poor of Crewe; £9000 for church-run charities; money to endow a bed for a railway employee at University College Hospital; £1000 to the Railway Convalescent Home at Rhyl; £1000 to the Railway Servants' Orphanage at Derby; £2000 each to University College Liverpool and Manchester, to endow scholarships for the sons of L&NWR employees; £1000 to the Institution of Civil Engineers as the 'Webb Prize' for annual papers read on railway engineering; and £70,000 to build the Webb Orphanage for the children of deceased L&NWR employees. This was opened in 1911. His will stipulated that one of the Orphanage governors should be the current Locomotive Superintendent of the L&NWR.

(See: C.H. Ellis, *Twenty Locomotivemen*, pp. 146–7; O.S. Nock, *The London & North Western Railway*, pp. 79–80; B. Reed, *Crewe Locomotive Works and its Men*; and W. H. Chaloner, *The Social and Economic Development of Crewe*.)

Appendix 9
Advances in Interlocking

% OF DOUBLE LINES WORKED BY THE 'ABSOLUTE BLOCK' SYSTEM

England/Wales

1874	1876	1878	1880	1882	1884	1886	1888	1890	1892	1894
63	78	83	89	93	95	97	97	98.5	99.5	99.8

Scotland

33	51	61	71	85	95	97.5	99	100	100	100

% OF POINTS INTERLOCKED ON PASSENGER LINES

England/Wales

1875	1877	1879	1881	1883	1885	1887	1889	1891	1895
63	73	80	85	88	91	93	94	97	99.7

Scotland

35	52	61	67	71	77	79	83	88	99

% PROGRESS MADE BY SOME COMPANIES' INSTALLATION OF INTERLOCKING

	1877	1879	1881	1883	1885	1887	1889	1891	189
Met	100								
GWR	70	75	80	85	89	90	92	94	99
L&NWR	78	83	87	91	94	97	97	100	
MR	80	84	87	91	93	93	95	98	100
LB&SCR	93	98	100						
LC&DR	62	99	99	99	100				
NLR		100							

(Source: The Signalling Study Group, *The Signal Box*, p. 23, drawing on Board of Trade Returns

% OF ENGINES/CARRIAGES WITH BRAKES AS PER BOT REQUIREMENTS

0.6.83	30.6.84	30.6.85	30.6.86	30.6.87	30.6.88	30.6.89	30.6.90	30.6.91
0/38	44/44	49/47	52/52	52/54	61/62	75/72	83/81	86/86

% OF ENGINES/CARRIAGES WITH BRAKES NOT AS PER BOT
REQUIREMENTS

0.6.83	30.6.84	30.6.85	30.6.86	30.6.87	30.6.88	30.6.89	30.6.90	30.6.91
0/31	23/32	26/32	35/31	40/32	32/29	20/20	13/15	11/10

Source: Board of Trade ½-Yearly Return of Continuous Brakes from 30 June 1883 to 30 June
1891.)

Appendix 10
Railway Charges Justified

In 1888, the General Manager since 1866 of the GWR, James Grierson, wrote a comprehensive survey of British railway charges. He showed that the highest rate for the carriage of fish in Britain was for salmon, which travelled the 750 miles from Wick to London by express passenger trains, to arrive in prime conditions on the fishmonger's slab. For this service the railways charged ⅛d per lb. Salt herrings in barrels from Grimsby to London (160 miles) were carried for 1¼d per ton/mile. Fresh sole was charged slightly less than 3½d per ton/mile. Thus the railway charge for 112 lb of fresh sole at Owner Risk is 2s 4d per cwt, which was about what the housewife paid the fishmonger for one pound of the fish.[1] According to a Return given by the GER to the House of Commons in 1888, the GER carried 50–70,000 tons of fish a year, nearly half of it to London.[2] The price of fish in London was said to be high and the reason given the extortionate charges made by the railways. But that ignores the demands of the fishmongers: if the railways carried fish for free, would that bring down prices at Billingsgate? A box of prime fish at Yarmouth cost 10.42d per lb. Carriage to London and the return of the empty box amounted to ⅕d per lb, less than 2 per cent of the total cost of the fish. Out of their income the GER also paid for the maintenance and dredging of Lowestoft harbour.

Ackworth, *The Railways of England*, p. 253.
Ibid., p. 432.

HOW RAILWAY CHARGES ARE ARRIVED AT
The value of conveyance is not necessarily what it costs but what that conveyance is worth to the person who wishes his property to be conveyed. If an article is costly, for example silk or velvet, dealers in it can expect to pay more than if it was of low value. 1d per ton/mile would be prohibitive when carrying sand or lime, but insignificant in the carriage of silk. A distinction is made between tea and whisky, eau-de-cologne and coal. It would be more than some traffics could bear if they were charged by a set mileage rate, equal for all items. If the railway managers set rates with the sole object of obtaining the highest profit without regard to the interest of traders – while keeping within the statutory bounds – they might levy rates detrimental to the traffic and this would reduce the amount of traffic carried.
The 1845 Railway Clauses (Consolidation) Act ordered railway companies 'to accommodate the rates to the circumstances of the traffic'. This is what the managers have done. They have found the rate which best compromises between the good of the

railway and the traders. The railway rates policy has developed long- and short
distance traffic, and has aided the opening of new industries – fruit, vegetables, flowers
potatoes, milk, fish – [these] were all developed from markets 150 miles from London
thanks to sympathetic railway rates. The bringing in of all this extra traffic has kep
the modest dividends going although carrying the traffic has increased the companies
costs. If rates had been charged on a simple 'per ton/mile' basis much of the traffic
would not be able to be carried and the market would not have developed.

(Source: A.H. Tatlow, Goods Manager of the Glasgow & South Western Railway, *Railway
Magazine* (August 1901), p. 120.)

Appendix 11
Rehousing the Poor

The legally enforceable obligation of the railway companies to compensate owner
occupiers and tenants operated effectively in proportion to wealth: the wealthier yo
were the better chance you had of receiving compensation for the loss of your house
Until 1874 railway companies had no legal obligation to rehouse, compensate prop
erly (or compensate at all) those of the under-class who were made homeless by thei
constructions. In 1874 a Standing Order of the House of Commons required railwa
companies to provide alternative accommodation for the poorest people. The compa
nies ignored this. In 1885 a Royal Commission was set up on 'The Housing of th
Working Classes', and in 1890 a 'Housing of the Working Classes Act' was passed t
consolidate and amend Acts relating to artisans and labourer dwellings. Section
stated:

> Where an official representation as hereinafter mentioned is made to the loca
> authority that within a certain area in the district of such authority eithe
> (a) any houses, courts, or alleys which are unfit for human habitation or (b) th
> narrowness, closeness, and bad arrangement or the bad condition of the stree
> and houses or groups of houses within such area or the want of light, air, vent
> lation or proper conveniences or any other sanitary defects are injurious c
> dangerous to the health of the inhabitants and the evils cannot be effectuall
> remedied other than by an improvement scheme.

During the construction of Marylebone station and its approaches, in the 1890s, th
Great Central Railway displaced 6200 people, 4448 being 'of the labouring class'.[1] Th
GCR built six, 5-storey tenement blocks, known as Wharncliffe Gardens, to rehous
2690 of these people. In 1901 the L&NWR had an important Bill before Parliamen
for a wide range of improvements to its railway: the quadrupling of the Trent Valle
line, improvements to Holyhead harbour and its facilities, and works at Hammersmit
requiring the demolition of forty-three slum houses. A model clause had been inserte
in the Bill to ensure that those losing their rented housing would be rehoused by th
L&NWR.

The Bill was thrown out, despite the model clause, because the L&NWR's goo
intentions were in doubt. The Home Office and the Company were already in dispu
over this same issue of rehousing with regard to other properties they had taken. Th
Home Office had issued a writ claiming £16,000 penalties from the L&NWR for th
latter's non-compliance with its rehousing obligation in three London streets. The
matters had to be satisfactorily resolved before the Company were allowed to r
present their Bill.[2]

In 1907 the GWR failed to rehouse nearly 300 people out of 1028 made homeless y line widening near Paddington.[3]

A. Jackson, *London's Termini*, p. 354.
Herapath (3 May 1901).
The Builder (1907), quoted in J. Simmons, *The Railway in Town and Country, 1830–1914*, p. 35.

Appendix 12
Welfare Provision and Railway Militias

ir William Beveridge studied the administration of the GWR Medical Fund, when the Jational Health Service was under consideration, since it was one of the largest in the ountry. When the Swindon scheme was made redundant by the introduction of the IHS in 1948, the GWR Medical Fund was caring for 45,000 people.[1]

The Grand Junction Railway always declared, as a separate entry on their balance seet, the money they earned from Sunday travel.[2] Those Directors and shareholders hose conscience forbade them to profit from running trains on Sunday gave up about per share of their holding, and this money was put into a 'Sunday Travel Account' raise money for charitable purposes.

In June 1840 the Dowager Queen, widow of William IV, rode on the Grand Junction ailway in her own carriage, specially built for her by the London & Birmingham ailway. This was her first railway journey and she was so delighted that she gave £35 a donation to a charitable cause of the Directors' choice. This was added to the inday Travel Fund which was then renamed the 'Adelaide Charitable Fund'. The oney was distributed to various charities including an orphanage for girls.[3]

In 1842 the Grand Junction Railway instructed their Engineer, Joseph Locke, to iild a gothic Anglican church, Christ Church in Prince Albert Street, close to the comotive works. Other grants of money were made to enable to erection of 'esleyan and Roman Catholic places of worship. The Anglican church was conse- ated on 18 December 1845.

That same year the Grand Junction opened public baths alongside the railway at rewe. The facilities included eight baths with hot and cold water and a Turkish bath. he Company charged 1½d per bath. The baths were closed in 1862 because by that ne they could only be reached across several busy railway lines.[4]

A cottage hospital for Crewe, to save the necessity of going to Nantwich hospital, as mooted in 1883. In 1887 the L&NWR gave £10,000 to construct Queen's Park. iis was on rolling land and was very ably landscaped. In 1893 F.W. Webb persuaded e L&NWR Directors to give land on Victoria Avenue, Crewe, on which to build a ree-ward hospital for railwaymen and their families. Webb, and Yates Thompson, a irector of the L&YR, each gave £1000 towards building costs. The hospital was iened 7 August 1895 and was enlarged over the years.[5]

A. Peck, *The Great Western at Swindon Works*, pp. 73–4, 242.
N. Webster, *The Grand Junction Railway*, p. 109.
Ibid., p. 125.
B. Reed, *Crewe Locomotive Works and its Men*.
W.H. Chaloner, *The Social and Economic Development of Crewe*, pp. 181–2.

The Midland Railway does not appear to have built a hospital for their men at erby, probably because, unlike Swindon and Crewe, Derby was a town before the

railway came and thus the municipal authorities provided health care and other facil
ities. J.B. Radford, in his *Derby Works and Midland Locomotives* (p. 160), notes tha
it was not until June 1918 that an ambulance room was provided within the locomo
tive works, and then only because government regulations demanded it. In 1875 th
Midland did, however, open an orphanage called St Christopher's, for the children o
deceased railwaymen. Twenty children were living there in 1875. In 1877 a large
orphanage, consisting of several houses, was set up in Ashbourne Road with accom
modation for 600 children; obviously the intention was to be able to take in railwa
orphans from any railway company. The new building was opened on 20 July 188
and then housed 200 children. The maximum number was 285 in 1920. In 1982 one o
the houses was converted into flats for retired railwaymen or railway widows. In 199
it passed out of railway ownership and now forms student accommodation for Derb
University.[1]

The 11th (New Swindon) Rifle Volunteers, formed in April 1860, became the 4t
Battalion, Wiltshire Regt. (TA) in 1908.

In 1865 the 36th Cheshire Rifle Volunteers Unit was raised in Crewe with 400 mer
mostly railwaymen. It was disbanded in 1880. In 1887 F.W. Webb instigated the for
mation of a Railway Engineers Volunteer Corps. The Unit consisted of 24 Officer:
610 men: drivers, boilermakers, fitters, platelayers, signalmen, shunters, etc. It wa
renamed the 2nd Cheshire Engineer (Railway) Volunteer Corps. 285 of its Officer
and men took part in the Boer War, (1899–1902), building, repairing and operating rai
ways, driving rail locomotives and heavy traction engines of the Steam Road Transpor
Company and also stringing barbed wire for the system of fortified blockhouses o
the veldt and around the concentration camps for Boer families. During the Firs
World War the Railway Operating Division of the Royal Engineers employed thou
sands of railwaymen to operate trains in the war zones.

The Unit was taken into the Territorial Army in 1908 but local enthusiasm wane
numbers dwindled, and it was disbanded 17 March 1912.

1. Derby Local Studies Library.
2. A. Terry, *Historical Records of the 5th Administrative Battalion of the Cheshire Rif
   Volunteers*, quoted in Chaloner, *The Social and Economic Development of Crewe*, p. 273.

Appendix 13
Three Knights of the Railway

SIR JOHN FOWLER, KCMG, LL D
(1817–1898)
Born at Wadsley Hall, Sheffield, in 1834 John Fowler was apprenticed with N
Leather, a hydraulics engineer. He entered railway service in 1841 with J.U. Rastricl
to design the London–Brighton line, and rejoined Mr Leather in 1843 as tl
Assistant Engineer of the Stockton & Hartlepool Railway. He engineered the cor
struction of the Manchester, Sheffield & Lincolnshire line, railways in India, Irelar
and New South Wales, as well as the Metropolitan, the Metropolitan District, tl
first 'tube' railway (deep level) City & South London line, and the New Hollar
floating bridge. He had a natural genius for all branches of civil engineering cor
struction. President of the ICE in 1865 and 1866, he recommended in the latter yea
the idea of specialization and an intense, formal, technical training for engineer

later to be the norm. He was one of the greatest civil engineers of the nineteenth century.

Source: Proceedings of the Institution of Civil Engineers (1899), cxxxv.)

SIR BENJAMIN BAKER, KCB, KCMG, D.SC. LL D, MAI, FRS (1840–1907)

Born at Keyford, Frome, Benjamin Baker was apprenticed at sixteen to Neath Abbey iron works. He assisted W.H. Wilson in the building of Victoria station. In 1862 he joined Sir John Fowler's staff and rose to be his partner in 1875. The variety and magnitude of his works equal those of Fowler. They worked on many projects as partners, although Baker was also Senior Civil Member of the Ordnance Committee and contributed to the study of gun construction. He also gave advice as to the possible interference which might arise at Greenwich Observatory from the working of an electricity generating station nearby. He was Consulting Engineer of the Aswan Dam and designed the vessel to carry 'Cleopatra's Needle' to London and the system by which the obelisk would be raised upright on the Thames Embankment. He was elected President of the ICE in 1895.

Source: Proceedings of the Institution of Civil Engineers (1907), clxx.)

SIR WILLIAM ARROL, FRSE, MIME (1839–1913)

The son of a poor, crippled, cotton spinner in Renfrewshire, William Arrol went to work in a cotton mill at the age of nine, and was apprenticed to a blacksmith when he was eleven. He attended night school to learn mathematics and geometry. After his apprenticeship he was a casual blacksmith in a Clyde shipyard, and mended or made whatever was called for – including the men's porridge saucepans. Out of work, he tramped from factory to factory, town to town; he joined the army and came out again, and became Foreman of a bridge and boiler works at Laidlaw & Sons, Glasgow & Edinburgh. In 1870, having saved £85, he launched out as a contractor in his right. He bought a stationary steam-engine and boiler for £43 and some hand tools, and became steel-work erector. In 1872 he was able to build his famous Dalmarnock works, and three years later he invented a hydraulic riveting machine while engaged in the erection of a bridge across the Clyde for the NBR. He also devised a method of prefabricating cantilevered girders on land and rolling them from pier to pier over the water, which saved time, money – and lives.

In 1890 Arrol said that it saddened him to observe that, when men such as himself raised themselves to prosperity through herculean efforts, they gave their sons a very smart education and encouraged them to think of themselves as 'gentlemen', or to pursue some very light employment, rather than a trade: 'The result will be that in a few years we will be overstocked with clerks. Give them the best education you can but give them a trade as well.' He never forgot that he had started from poverty and was renowned for his kindness towards his working men.

Source: *The Engineer* (1913), cxv, p. 230.)

Appendix 14
Directors as MPs

RAILWAY DIRECTORS AS MEMBERS OF HOUSE OF COMMONS

	MP/Directors	On major Co. Boards
1865	157	41
1868–84	124	42
1885–91	83	36
1892–1905	73	40
1906–14	42	18

(Source: Simmons, *The Railway in England and Wales*, p. 245, quoting G. Alderman, *Th
Railway Interest*.)

Appendix 15
Mr Inskip's Letter to The Times

24 August 190

Sir,

Your Special Correspondent, whose communications command my interest an
sometimes my admiration has referred to me in terms of criticism.

Your Correspondent states that, in 1890, the Chairman of the TVR (Inskip) wa
'undoubtedly weak'. He is entitled to his opinion but it is not binding on me.

My reply is that subsequent experience and a wider knowledge of men and thing
have confirmed my belief that in 1890 a mistake was made in refusing to speak to M
Harford at an earlier stage. Had the meeting taken place the strike would probabl
have been averted.

At that time I was Chairman of a Joint Committee of TVR, Bute Docks (nov
Cardiff Railway), Barry and Rhymney Railways and all four Companies wer
involved in the strike. The daily mischief to thousands of helpless people was immens
My belief was that wages were a matter for negotiation and the workmen were as full
entitled to appoint an agent as was a land-owner or any other great person having t
exchange property for its value in another form.

At first the majority of my colleagues dissented from my view but placed no bon
upon me as an individual and the result was that all questions were settled and th
strike ended.

There was no great victory for the men. A few justifiable concessions were give
All my colleagues from all four Companies sanctioned my terms and it is therefore fai
for me to add that if I was 'undoubtedly weak' on that occasion then my colleague
were weaker.

But the late Mr Harford is charged with 'hoodwinking' me. In other words he wa
wicked while I was weak. On the contrary, he was very frank. I exonerate him fror
the odious part of hoodwinking me.

It is not desirable for me to discuss the merits of the present strike but the idea tha
workmen are the one class who may not appoint an agent is outworn and outmode
and ought to be abandoned. Whatever the merits of the present controversy it is lam
entable to reflect that the one step has not been taken which might have averted a dail
loss by hundreds of thousands falling on persons who have no part in the strike.

Appendix 16
Financial Position of Companies, 1913–1919

Capital raised up to 31 December 1913:

Ordinary shares	£452,784,000
Preference	£456,682,000
Guaranteed	£338,435,000
Total share capital	£1,247,901,000

Total overdraft of all companies to cover deficit in capital account: £35,000,000

Total capital employed: £1,283,000,000

Percentage of net income to total capital: 3.92

Deficit in capital accounts of major companies, covered by bank overdraft:

	1913	1919
GCR	£2,855,310	£2,611,499
GER	£1,520,129	£1,715,273
GNR	£662,756	£1,346,544
GWR	£1,747,671	£3,012,499
L&YR	£2,579,739	£2,706,096
L&NWR	£5,547,211	£6,149,600
L&SWR	£910,961	£1,508,018
LB&SCR	£927,242	£1,218,261
MR	£2,965,363	£3,921,587
NER	£4,570,614	£5,092,784

The interest to pay these overdrafts had to come from interest earned on the companies' reserve funds or on the deposits of the employees' savings banks or that part of employees' pension funds which had not been invested to produce the pensions. It was very unlikely, given the overspent state of the companies' finances, that they would be able to raise new capital at a sufficiently low rate of interest to make the investment profitable for the railway Company.

(Source: C.L. Edwards, Railway Capital Expenditure', in *Railway Gazette* (16 July 1920), p. 21. Edwards, CBE, FSAA, was Chief Accountant of the Great Northern Railway.)

Notes

1. Early Railways

1. J. Francis, *A History of the English Railway: Its Social Relations and Revelations, 1820–1845*, p. 16.
2. Ibid., p. 171.
3. Francis, *The English Railway*, p. 171.
4. C.F. Dendy Marshall, *A History of the Southern Railway*, p. 11.
5. R. Young, *Timothy Hackworth and the Locomotive*, p. 19.
6. *Annual Register*, 26 July 1805, in Dendy Marshall, *The Southern Railway*, p. 17.
7. Young, *Timothy Hackworth*, p. 22.
8. Ibid., pp. 38–41.
9. R.S. Watson, *History of the Newcastle Literary & Philosophical Society*, p. 144.
10. Young, *Timothy Hackworth*, p. 63.
11. Ibid., p. 50.
12. Supplied by Darlington Railway Museum.
13. 'On the Means of Procuring a Steady Light in Coal Mines without the Danger of Explosion', in Royal Society, Philosophical Transactions, ciii 200 and *Dictionary of National Biography* (1887), p. 370.
14. Watson, *Newcastle Lit. & Phil. Soc.*, p. 146.
15. Young, *Timothy Hackworth*, p. 72.
16. The coned blastpipe at the base of the chimney, concentrating exhaust steam into a powerful jet, for the purpose of drawing-up the fire, was the invention of Timothy Hackworth in 1827. This was acknowledged by Robert Stephenson in a letter to Samuel Smiles in 1858. However, a coned jet to send *live* steam up the chimney was patented by Nicholson in 1806. See E.L. Ahrons, *The British Steam Railway Locomotive from 1825 to 1925*, p. 8.
17. Young, *Timothy Hackworth*, p. 74.
18. John Birkenshaw of Bedlington Ironworks patented in 1820 a roller for T-shaped rails having a broad head as in modern practice.

19. R. Christiansen, *A Regional History of Railways*, vii, p. 32.
20. He built Trevithick's locomotive. In 1816 he made and erected a cast-iron road bridge over the Wye at Chepstow. In 1828 at his Stourbridge works he designed and constructed three locomotives for North America; one of the trio, the *Stourbridge Lion*, was the first steam-locomotive in America. In 1829 he built the *Agenoria* for the Shutt End industrial railway at Cannock.

2. The Stockton & Darlington Railway

1. Spearman's Inquiry (1729), quoted in W.T. Tomlinson, *North Eastern Railway*, p. 112.
2. Tomlinson, *North Eastern Railway*, p. 60.
3. Ibid., p. 61.
4. Revd Luke Prattman was a Congregationalist, who ministered at Barnard Castle. Prattman paid £800 in 1813 to have a 500-seat chapel built in Barnard Castle and preached there without payment. Butterknowle and Copley collieries, also known as Grewburn and Lynesack, covered 3000 acres and had four seams, the lowest 6 ft thick and 384 ft below the surface. Prattman died before 1855; the collieries were sold the previous year.
5. John Bowes (1769–1820), styled Lord Glamis until 1776, was the eighth Earl of Strathmore. He married, aged fifty-one, 'when nearly *in extremis*' on 2 July 1820, and died the next day, one hopes with a smile on his face.
6. Tomlinson, *North Eastern Railway*, p. 75.
7. Section 8: 'It shall be lawful for the said Company of Proprietors or any person or persons permitted by them . . . to make and erect such and so many loco-motive or moveable engines as the said Company of Proprietors think proper and expedient and to use and employ the same in or upon the said Railway or Tramroads . . .
8. But not in Ireland. By 1843 the Dublin & Kingstown, had a 4 ft 8½ in.-gauge, the Ulster Railway 6 ft 2 in. and the proposed Dublin & Drogheda intended 5 ft 2 in. The Board of Trade consulted George and Robert Stephenson and they recommended 'something between 5 ft and 5 ft 6 in.', whereupon 5 ft 3 in. was ordered to be the standard.

3. 'At Private Risk for Public Service'

1. Young, *Timothy Hackworth*, p. 102.
2. S. Smiles, *Brief Biographies* and *Lives of the Engineers*, quoted by A. Jarvis, in *Journal of The Railway & Canal Historical Society* (1993), pp. 176–83.
3. Institution of Civil Engineers Records, HEW 151.
4. He received £150 p.a., free house, candles and fuel (Young, *Timothy Hackworth*, p. 107).
5. Tomlinson, *North Eastern Railway*, p. 96.
6. 'The two Jameses and the two Stephensons', p. 47, quoted in Young, *Timothy Hackworth*, p. 149.
7. This bridge was constructed in preference to a plate girder bridge designed by Timothy Hackworth. The suspension bridge, by Capt. (Sir) Samuel Brown, had a span of 284 ft and was the first railway suspension bridge in the world. Under load it bent 9¼ in. at centre, so the wagons would 'follow the horse rather quick'. It was replaced by a rigid bridge in 1841 (ICE Records, HEW 717).
8. PRO, Rail 667/1043.
9. S. Smiles, *Lives of George and Robert Stephenson*.

10. Ibid.
11. *Practical Mechanics Journal*, iii (1850), p. 49.
12. Tomlinson, *North Eastern Railway*, p. 144.
13. PRO, Rail 667/17.

4. 'Perfect Liberty'

1. PRO, Rail 667/1009.
2. PRO, Rail 667/1025.
3. PRO, Rail 667/1062.
4. PRO, Rail 667/485.
5. PRO, Rail 667/1099.
6. PRO, Rail 667/17.
7. PRO, Rail 667/1122.
8. PRO, Rail 667/485.
9. PRO, Rail 667/17.

5. 'To Unite the Disjointed Parts'

1. PRO, Rail 667/1186.
2. PRO, Rail 667/160.
3. Young, *Timothy Hackworth*, p. 128.
4. Henry Pease at the S&DR Jubilee banquet, reported in the *Newcastle Daily Chronicle*, 28 September 1875.
5. PRO, Rail 667/4.
6. PRO, Rail 667/1025.
7. PRO, Rail 667/1139.
8. PRO, Rail 667/42.
9. PRO, Rail 667/1139.
10. *Regional History of Railways*, IV, *The North East* (K. Hoole), p. 134, and XIV, *The Lake Counties*, (D. Joy) p. 11.

6. The Liverpool & Manchester Railway

1. R.E. Carlson, *The Liverpool & Manchester Railway Project, 1821–1831*.
2. D.H. Porter, *Abolition of the Slave Trade in England, 1787–1807*, p. 3.
3. *An Account of the Liverpool & Manchester Railway* (1830), quoted in Carlson.
4. Baines, *History of Liverpool*, quoted in Carlson, *The Liverpool & Manchester*.
5. J.R.T. Hughes, *Liverpool Banks and Banking*, p. 2.
6. Ibid.
7. Ibid., p. 62.
8. Ibid., p. 4.
9. B. Falk, *The Bridgewater Millions: A Candid Family History*.
10. Young, *Timothy Hackworth*, p. 87.
11. Ibid.
12. See Carlson, *The Liverpool & Manchester*, p. 133.

7. The Triumph of George Stephenson

1. Carlson, *The Liverpool & Manchester*, p. 133.
2. Ibid., p. 193.

8. The Battle for the Locomotive

1. Carlson, *The Liverpool & Manchester*, p. 189.
2. Established in 1817 to lend money for public works employing large numbers of labourers.
3. *Civil Engineer and Mechanics' Journal*, 1 October 1863, quoted in Young, *Timothy Hackworth*, p. 85.
4. Stephenson approved of the rope-worked system employed on the London & Blackwall Railway, opened in 1840. This was a passenger shuttle, 3½ miles long with steep gradients and sharp curves. Carriages were hauled by a continuously moving rope. Speed was restricted to the speed of the rope, 20 mph. The system was abandoned for conventional traction in 1849.
5. Young, *Timothy Hackworth*, p. 175.
6. Ibid., p. 199.
7. Ibid.
8. N. Wood, *Treatise on Railroads*, 3rd edn, p. 316, quoted in Young, *Timothy Hackworth*, p. 196.
9. Young, *Timothy Hackworth*, p. 197.
10. Ibid., p. 234.
11. For a list of Hackworth's inventions, see ibid., p. 403.

9. Inter-city Turnpike Railway

1. E. Longford, *Wellington: Pillar of State*, p. 198.
2. Ibid., p. 277.
3. The Huskisson Memorial was a white marble tablet (smashed to bits by barbarians in recent years) set within a monumental wall, bearing the following legend:

> A tribute of personal respect and affection has been placed here to mark the spot when on 15 September 1830 the day of the opening of the rail-road

> THE RIGHT HONOURABLE WILLIAM HUSKISSON M.P.

> singled out by the decree of an inscrutable Providence from the midst of the distinguished multitude that surrounded him in the full pride of his talents and the perfection of his usefulness met with the accident that occasioned his death which deprived England of an illustrious statesman and Liverpool of its most honoured representative which changed a moment of the noblest exultation and triumph that science and genius had ever achieved into one of desolation and mourning: and striking terror into the hearts of the assembled thousands brought home to every bosom the forgotten truth that:

> 'IN THE MIDST OF LIFE WE ARE IN DEATH'

4. In 1842 UK railways carried 5 million tons of freight, 4 million of which was coal. In 1847, 17 million tons were carried including 10 million tons of coal. Nationally, the railways' income from freight did not exceed their income from passenger traffic until 1852. Rail-borne coal tonnages did not equal sea-borne tonnages until 1867 (Parliamentary statistics).
5. Most of these were local businessmen but they included the powerful forces of Edward Pease, George Stephenson, and Joseph Sandars of the L&MR (see P. Norton *Railways and Waterways to Warrington*).

10. Grand Junction Railway: Stephenson v. Locke

1. Locke's carefully thought out Theory of Gradients was expressed as a mathematical formula to find the optimum gradient, balancing first cost against future expenditure in fuel. To summarize, Locke stated that a dead level line is best but it ought not to be purchased where the interest on the excess capital expended to achieve the level line will exceed the cost of the increased fuel necessary to surmount the incline.

2. Stephenson quickly involved himself with collieries and quarries. He purchased collieries and sank new ones in Leicestershire and Derbyshire. He also bought Alton Grange colliery, near Coalville, in Leicestershire, paid good wages, designed and caused a 'model' village to be built, with a school, a church and chapel for Dissenters.

3. John Urpeth Rastrick (1780–1856) was apprenticed at the age of fifteen to his father, who was a machinist at Ketley in Shropshire. Rastrick was an extremely energetic civil and mechanical engineer whose activities ranged far and wide. He patented a steam-engine in 1814 and set up an engineering factory in Stourbridge, rail-rolling mills in England, Wales and France; he was a colliery owner and built stationary engines for colliery use. He built the cast-iron arch over the Wye at Chepstow in 1815–16 and was the engineer of the Stratford to Moreton tramway (1822–5) and the London to Brighton railway (1835–40), the latter with the famous Ouse Valley viaduct.

4. N. Webster, *Britain's First Trunk Line*, p. 30.

5. The dimensions of arches as given in the records of the Institution of Civil Engineers, which drew on BR (LMR) records. Lengths are those given in E.C. and W. Osborne, *A Guide to the Grand Junction Railway* (1838), p. 43.

6. Senior GJR Director James Heyworth's statement at the ceremony to mark the completion of the viaduct (Webster, *Britain's First Trunk*, p. 42).

7. Ibid.

8. Ibid.

9. Alfred Jee, of Liverpool. He became Locke's pupil in 1831; in 1838 he became Locke's Resident Engineer on the Manchester–Sheffield line, supervising Dinting and Etherow viaducts and the Woodhead tunnel. In 1851 the Spanish Government invited him to engineer the Santander Railway. He was killed on 30 August 1858 when the engine he was driving, on the inaugural train, overturned because of line subsidence (Minutes of the Proceedings of the Institution of Civil Engineers (1859), xviii, p. 193).

10. A. Helps, *Life of Thomas Brassey*, pp. 25–6.

11. Webster, *Britain's First Trunk*, p. 58.

12. Ibid., p. 81.

13. J. Devey, *the Memoirs of Joseph Locke*; Brassey's biography makes no mention of this commendable event.

14. He 'connived at slave labour' on his Argentinian contracts (see D. Mountfield, *The Railway Barons*, p. 83).

15. From 1841, the firm of Allcard, Buddicom & Co. built locomotives in France for French railways.

16. The line was quadrupled in July 1885, and the tunnel was opened out into a cutting, which revealed the misdirected burrowings.

17. R. Foster, *Birmingham New Street*, i, p. 38.

18. GJR Minutes, PRO, Rail 220/1.

19. Ibid.

20. Ibid.

21. Locke's track consisted of heavy, double-headed, wrought-iron rails wedged with wooden blocks or 'keys' into cast-iron 'chairs', the latter screwed to creosoted, timber

10 x 5 in. cross-sleepers. The intention of 'double-headed' rails was to turn them over when the first rail-head became worn down, but indentations in the underside head made this impractical. The system was denounced by experts such as Nicholas Wood, mine manager and author of an early, learned *Treatise of Railroads*, but within five years Locke's system became the accepted standard in Great Britain – I.K. Brunel always excepted. With the substitution of the single-head or 'bull-head' rail, Locke's design remained the basis of the British standard for 100 years.

22. C.H. Ellis, *British Railway History, 1830–1876*, i, p. 56.

11. A Natural Monopoly

1. M. Philips, *A History of Banks, Bankers and Banking in Northumberland, Durham and North Yorkshire.*

2. 'He intends his own gain and in this he is led as if by an invisible hand to promote an end which was no part of his intention.' (Adam Smith, *An Inquiry into the Wealth of Nations'*, iv, Ch. 2.)

3. Wealthy linen draper, MP for Ipswich 1836–45. His origins were very humble, and by 'industry, sagacity and integrity [he] achieved great wealth (*Dictionary of National Biography*).

4. Parliamentary Papers (1839), x.

5. It was incorporated on 26 August 1846 as the 'East & West India Dock & Birmingham Junction Railway', renamed 'North London Railway' on 1 January 1853.

6. Quoted in P. Bagwell, *The Railway Clearing House in the British Economy*, p. 29.

7. Ibid, p. 64, quoting Select Committee (1840) Minutes of Evidence, xiii, q. 2294.

8. Bagwell, *Railway Clearing House*, p. 68.

9. Ibid., pp. 69–70 (quoting contemporary reports).

10. Ibid., p. 26.

11. Ibid.

12. Ibid., p. 70.

13. Parliamentary Papers (1839), x.

14. List of Railway Acts, Appendix E.K.: Report of Royal Commission on Railways 1867 (quoted in C. Stevens, *English Railways and their Relation to the State*, p. 25.

15. 15 per cent on S&DR; 10 per cent on L&BR and GJR; 5 per cent on GWR.

16. B.R. Mitchell, 'The Coming of Railways and Economic Growth', in M.C. Reed (ed.), *Railways in the Victorian Economy*, p. 30.

17. The Committee was to 'consider whether any and what new Provisions ought to be introduced into such Railway Bills as may come before this House for the advantage of the Public and the improvement of the railway system' (Hansard (1844), lxxii, col. 232).

18. The son of a merchant banker, Henry Labouchere (1789–1869) was Liberal MP for Taunton, President of the Board of Trade (1839–41), and Chief Secretary to Lord-Lieutenant of Ireland (1846). He was responsible for repealing the Navigation Laws. His father, obliged by the ECR's Act of Incorporation to sell land to that Company, received £35,000 in compensation; after his father's death, Henry Labouchere repaid £15,000 to the ECR: a unique event in the annals of British railway history.

19. Lord Granville Somerset (1792–1848), Liberal MP for Monmouthshire (1828–48), Chancellor of the Duchy of Lancaster (1841–6).

20. The son of Edmund Denison, Chairman of the GNR, Beckett Denison became Lord Grimthorpe.

21. Lord Dalhousie (1812–1860) tenth Earl and first Marquis. Favoured by Prime Ministers the Duke of Wellington and Sir Robert Peel, he became Vice-President of the Board of Trade in 1843, President in 1844 and Viceroy of India (1848–56).

22. Samuel Laing (1812–1897) was Chairman of the LB&SCR (1848–55), Financial Secretary to the Treasury (1859–60), Minister of Finance for India (1855–1867), and again Chairman of the LB&SCR (1867–1896).
23. Select Committee on Railways (1844) xi.
24. Hansard (1844), lxxiv, col. 1324–5.
25. Hansard (1844), xxvi, quoted in Stevens, *English Railways*, p. 25.
26. Cap. lxxxv, Sec. 2.
27. Parliamentary Papers (1851), li, qq. 238, 252.

12. Hudson and the Great Railway Mania

1. Mitchell, 'The Coming of the Railway', in M.C. Reed (ed.), *Railways in the Victorian Economy*, p. 16.
2. For the same reason, Stephenson kept the North Midland Railway on the high ground east of Sheffield, bypassing the burgeoning industrial might of that place.
3. R.S. Lambert, *The Railway King*, p. 138.
4. Ibid., p. 60.
5. Bagwell, *Railway Clearing House*, p. 43.
6. Prior to the introduction of the Edmonson ticket, tickets were hand-written on paper. There was no standardization of method between companies, and the clerks could defraud the system.
7. *The Memoirs of Daniel Gooch*, quoted in A. Platt, *The Life and Times of Daniel Gooch*, p. 42.
8. Robert Stephenson in his presidential address to the Institution of Civil Engineers, January 1856, quoted in C. Grinling, *The History of the Great Northern Railway*, p. 57. Grinling gives the figure as £432,000.
9. On 30 August 1850; quoted in H. Pollins, 'Aspects of Railway Accounting before 1868', in M.C. Reed (ed.), *Railways in the Victorian Economy*, p. 140.

13. 'An Exaggeration of Enterprise'

1. Hansard (1844), lxxvi, col. 280. Brotherton was a wealthy cotton mill owner, a lay preacher, vegetarian and total abstainer.
2. Parliamentary Papers (1846), xvii.
3. A. Jackson, *London's Termini*, p. 192.
4. List of Railway Acts, Appendix E.K.: Report of Royal Commission on Railways 1867 (quoted in Stevens, *English Railways*, p. 25).
5. D. Morier Evans, *The Commercial Crisis, 1847–1848*, pp. 16, 38.
6. Parliamentary Papers (1846), xiii.
7. Ibid., qq. 475–80.
8. Ibid., Report, pp. 200–99.
9. Hansard (1846), lxxxv, col. 880.
10. Reported in the *Railway Times* (10 October 1846).
11. J. Clapham, *An Economic History of Modern Britain, 1820–1850*, p. 528.
12. Tooke, a contemporary economist quoted in Clapham, *An Economic History*.
13. But even in 1846 at least some of those who had gained their Acts were trying to abandon their powers.
14. Clapham, *An Economic History*, p. 524.
15. Ibid., p. 532.
16. Ibid.
17. In the American edition of his *Lives of the Engineers*, quoted by Adrian Jarvis in the *Journal of The Railway & Canal Historical Society* (November 1994).

18. *Dictionary of National Biography* (1896), xlvii, p. 250.
19. Minutes of the Proceedings of the Institution of Civil Engineers (1855–6), xv, pp. 122–54.
20. The *Economist*, throughout 1851.
21. Charles Austin (1799–1874) was a lawyer from 1826 to 1851. His diary shows his total income from 1826 to December 1843 as £65,817. From January 1844 to December 1847 he earned a total of £91,977 (Suffolk Record Office, Ipswich (Ref: 50.18.3)).

14. Repentance, Competition and Alliances

1. A. Peck, *The Great Western at Swindon Works*, pp. 54–5.
2. Railway Commercial Information, PRO, ZLIB 4/149.
3. Parliamentary Papers (1849), xvi.
4. Bagwell, *Railway Clearing House*, p. 251.
5. E.T. McDermott, *History of the Great Western Railway*, i, p. 133. (See also Foster, *Birmingham New Street*, i, pp. 58–60.)
6. McDermott, *Great Western Railway*, i, p. 190.
7. Opened 1 August 1852.
8. T. Gourvish, *Mark Huish and the L&NWR*, p. 245.
9. Ibid., pp. 293–4.
10. McDermott, *Great Western Railway*, i, p. 183.
11. Gourvish, *Mark Huish*, pp. 293–4.
12. Grinling, *Great Northern Railway*, p. 103.
13. 'Little', to differentiate it from the L&NWR.
14. The line was incorporated in 1846 and opened on 15 July 1850.
15. Grinling, *Great Northern Railway*, p. 123.
16. Parliamentary Papers (1852–3), xxxviii.
17. Hansard (1854), cxxxii, col. 590.
18. ECR Minutes (10 January 1861), PRO, Rail 186.
19. Gourvish, *Mark Huish* p. 210.
20. Ibid., p. 296.
21. Ibid., p. 230 and Table on p. 204.
22. Ellis, *British Railway History*, p. 235.
23. Ibid.
24. Gourvish, *Mark Huish*, p. 54.

15. Contractors and the Great Crash

1. One hundred and eighty-three financiers controlled fifty companies, the same men sitting as Directors on the various Boards. The PLM railway and Le Creusot steel works were closely allied under M. Schnieder; 53 per cent of iron and steel production was owned by eight companies – there were no trade unions. See R. Magraw, *France: 1815–1914: The Bourgeois Century*.
2. Clapham, *An Economic History*, p. 377.
3. D.M. Evans, *The History of Commercial Crisis, 1857–8*.
4. Clapham, *An Economic History*, p. 377.
5. G.P. Jones and R.G. Pool: *One Hundred Years of Economic Development*, p. 136.
6. *Economist* (14 January 1865; see Appendix 1).
7. C.J. Allen, *The Great Eastern Railway*, p. 30.
8. Ibid., p. 19.
9. P. Kay, *The London Tilbury & Southend Railway*, p. 16.

10. Ibid.
11. H. Pollins, in Reed (ed.), *Railways in the Victorian Economy*, p. 215–6.
12. The SER's Parliamentary route, from its London terminal of Bricklayer's Arms to Dover, was 87 miles. It used the London & Brighton Railway's line to Redhill before turning east for Ashford and Dover. The mail coach route, from London Bridge to Dover, via Dartford, Gravesend, Rochester and Canterbury, was 71 miles.
13. *Railway Times* (15 January 1853).
14. Pollins, in Reed (ed.), *Railways in the Victorian Economy*, p. 220.
15. A. Gray, *The London Chatham & Dover Railway*, p. 9.
16. *Economist* (16 June 1866), p. 697.
17. The idea of the barrister John Lloyd. The promise to pay was written on a piece of paper to which was attached the seal of the Company desiring the loan. Loans obtained under such circumstances were an act of desperation and were charged high rates of interest. See Hansard (1866), clxxxiii, p. 858.
18. Lord Overstone (1796–1883), banker and architect of the 1844 Bank Act, wrote to Col. Robert Torrens in January 1857: 'Precious metals alone are money. Paper notes are money because they represent metallic money. Unless so they are false and spurious pretenders.'
19. Quoted in J. Simmons, *The Victorian Railway*, p. 199.

16. Debt, Overwork and Democracy

1. MARKET VALUE OF ORDINARY SHARES

	November 1867 Highest/Lowest	November 1871 Highest
GER	35/25	47
NBR	40/27	60
GWR	56/38	163
MS&L	56/43	70
LB&SCR	91/48	70
L&NWR	120/108	145
GNR	122/104	138
MR	127/99	139
L&YR	132/118	156

(Source: *Economist*, November 1871.)

2. McDermott, *Great Western Railway*, ii, pp. 19–21.
3. Dendy Marshall, *The Southern Railway*, p. 222.
4. The amazingly optimistic 'Golden Valley Railway', 19 miles of single track, opened from Pontrilas to Hay in 1889, was intending to extend south to the Severn and north to the Mersey but closed nine years later, to be reopened by the GWR in 1901. Others included the Somerset & Dorset, the Midland & South Western Junction, Didcot, Newbury & Southampton, and the clutch of little companies which eventually formed the Midland & Great Northern Joint Railway.
5. 'British Investment in U.S. Railways' (*Herapath*, 7 January 1888).
6. S. Maccoby, *English Radicalism, 1852–1886*, p. 94, quoted in P. Bagwell, *The Railwaymen*, p. 36.
7. The punishment for a servant who broke his contract was prison under the 1823 Act. The amended Act made a fine the punishment for both master and servant. The master could now be punished with three months' hard labour if he beat his servant so severely that a fine would be an inappropriate punishment.
8. M. Sanderson, *Education, Economic Change and Society in England, 1780–1870*

p. 35.

9. In 1905 Imperial Tobacco, the largest, non-railway company, had a capital of £17.5 million. In 1855, the ECR had the same capital, the GWR had £22 million and the L&NWR £37.5 million (see Gourvish, *Mark Huish*, p. 267).

10. There were to be standard periods of validity of all companies' tickets; all return fares to be 50 per cent above the single fare; standard fares for dogs and commercial travellers' baggage. Everything possible was to be done to effect a continuous system of communication out of what had been built in an unplanned and even confrontational way.

11. Parliamentary Papers (1867), xxxviii.

17. The Midland Railway

1. The Birmingham & Derby Junction, Midland Counties, and North Midland were incorporated 1836; the Leicester & Swannington Railway (incorporated 1830) was absorbed into the Midland Railway on 27 July 1846 (see J. Gough, *The Midland Railway: A Chronology*).

2. 'The very heavy works of the MR has increased their mortgage and priority payments': 30 June 1864, £287,774; 30 June 1865, £307,984. Increase in working costs: 30 June 1864, £520,239; 30 June 1865, £562,484 (*Economist*, 2 September 1865, p. 1057).

3. ORDINARY DIVIDENDS PAID ANNUALLY

	MR	NER	GWR
1846	7		8
1847	7	–	7½
1848	5½	–	6½
1849	2¾	–	4
1850	2	–	4
1851	2⅝	–	4½
1852	3⅛	–	4
1853	3¼	–	4
1854	3⅝	2⅞	3
1855	3⅝	3	2¼
1856	4⅛	3⅜	2¾
1857	4⅝	4¼	1½
1858	4⅞	3⅞	1¼
1859	5⅝	4⅛	2¾
1860	6¾	4⅞	3¼
1861	6⅝	4⅝	2⅝
1862	6	4¼	1¾
1863	6⅜	4¾	2½
1864	7⅜	5⅞	3⅛
1865	6¾	6⅛	2

(Source: J.R.T. Hughes, *Liverpool Banks and Banking*, drawing on Stretton, Tomlinson and McDermott.)

4. E.G. Barnes, *The Rise of the Midland Railway, 1844–1874*, p. 141.

5. J. Simmons, *The Railway in England and Wales, 1830–1914*, p. 57.

6. Barnes, *Midland Railway*, p. 150.

7. Ibid., p. 169.

8. Ibid., p. 197.

9. Ibid., p. 194 (Allport's evidence to Parliament in 1863).
10. Ibid., p. 196 (Revd J. Campion's evidence to Parliament in 1863).
11. The Signalling Study Group, *The Signal Box*, p. 6.
12. Grinling, *Great Northern Railway*, p. 228.
13. *The Signal Box*, p. 6.
14. Barnes, *Midland Railway*, p. 175.
15. Ibid., p. 174.
16. Ibid., p. 171.
17. Grinling, *Great Northern Railway*, p. 229.
18. Gough, *The Midland Railway*.
19. Ibid., p. 356.
20. Ellis, *British Railway History*, i, pp. 331.
21. Joy, *Regional History*, VIII, *South and West Yorkshire*, p. 170.
22. Barnes, *Midland Railway*, p. 195.
23. Ibid., p. 193.
24. Ibid.
25. Jackson, *London's Termini*, p. 49. (See also Appendix 8.)
26. Barnes, *Midland Railway*, p. 242.
27. Jackson, *London's Termini*, p. 50.
28. Contemporary historian F.S. Williams, quoted in Barnes, *Midland Railway*, p. 218.
29. Jackson, *London's Termini*, p. 49.
30. Ibid., p. 51.
31. Ibid., p. 54.
32. Barnes, *Midland Railway*, pp. 253–5.
33. Jackson, *London's Termini*, p. 51.
34. Ibid., p. 58.
35. Barnes, *Midland Railway*, p. 267.
36. O. Carter, *An Illustrated History of British Railway Hotels*, p. 65.
37. Gough, *The Midland Railway*, p. 13.
38. Ibid.
39. W.M. Ackworth, *Railways of England*, p. 155.

18. The Cost of Intricacy

1. C.H. Ellis, *The Midland Railway*, p. 61.
2. Joy, *Regional History*, XIV, *The Lake Counties*, p. 46.
3. F.W. Houghton and W.T. Foster, *The Story of the Settle–Carlisle Line*, p. 27.
4. Parliamentary Papers (1872), xiii.
5. T.H. Farrer (1819–1899) became Lord Farrer and a Director of the Midland Railway. In 1901 he helped to modernize and improve MR express train services.
6. Parliamentary Papers (1872), xiii, qq. 148–52.
7. Houghton and Foster, *The Settle–Carlisle Line*; P. Baughan, *The Midland Railway North of Leeds*; F.S. Williams, *The Midland Railway: Its Rise and Progress*; D. Jenkinson, *Rails in the Fells*; D. Sullivan, *Navvyman* (1983), pp. 115–23.
8. Ellis, *The Midland Railway*, p. 62.
9. V.R. Anderson and G.K. Fox, *Stations and Structures of the Settle & Carlisle Line*, p. v. The lineside sign claimed 1169. Perhaps the last '6' fell off and was replaced upside down.
10. Gough, *The Midland Railway*, p. 353.
11. Anderson and Fox, *Stations and Structures*, p. iii.
12. Gough, *The Midland Railway*, p. 183.

3. Houghton and Foster, *The Settle–Carlisle Line*, p. 28.
4. Ibid., p. 34.
5. Gough, *The Midland Railway*, p. 183.
6. Carter, *Railway Hotels*, p. 65.
7. The Vicar of Horton-in-Ribblesdale said, after the blizzards of early 1947, 'The people of Horton owe a great debt of gratitude to the railwaymen. When the village was otherwise isolated for long, bitter weeks it was the railwaymen who brought our food, medical assistance and who distributed feed into the snow-covered lineside pastures so that our sheep and cattle might not perish' (Houghton and Foster, *The Settle–Carlisle Line*, p. 128).
8. Ibid.

19. The Great Western Railway

1. Brunel's private journal, Brunel Collection, Bristol University Library.
2. Ibid., p. 23.
3. L.T.C. Rolt, *Isambard Kingdom Brunel*, p. 67.
4. Ibid., p. 68.
5. Brunel's private journal, p. 28.
6. Ibid., p. 29.
7. Ibid.
8. Rolt, *Brunel*, p. 68.
9. McDermott, *Great Western Railway*, i, p. 72.
10. Ibid., p. 430.
11. Ibid., p. 106.
12. Ibid., p. 433.
13. 22½ miles from the original Paddington station.
14. Rolt, *Brunel*, i, p. 434.
15. Ibid., p. 431.
16. Ibid., p. 433.
17. Platt, *Daniel Gooch*, p. 7.
18. Platt, *Daniel Gooch*, p. 33, and McDermott, *Great Western Railway*, i, p. 377.
19. McDermott, *Great Western Railway*, i, p. 72.
20. Francis, *The English Railway*, quoted in Dendy Marshall, *The Southern Railway*, 55.
21. C. Hadfield, *Atmospheric Railways*.
22. McDermott, *Great Western Railway*, i, p. 109.
23. Ibid., ii, Appendix 4.
24. *Economist* (30 June 1866), p. 772.
25. McDermott, *Great Western Railway*, ii, p. 20.
26. Photocopy of original in author's possession.
27. *Economist* (8 June 1867).
28. McDermott, *Great Western Railway*, ii, pp. 25–38.
29. Ibid., ii, p. 303.

20. Speed, Comfort and Insanitary Practices

1. McDermott, *Great Western Railway*, i, pp. 341.
2. Ibid., i, p. 343.
3. Ibid., i, p. 103.
4. 'Railway Appliances and Public Health', in *The Engineer* (29 November 1861), quoted in Bagwell, *Railway Clearing House*, p. 196.

5. J.H. Russell, *A Pictorial Record of Great Western Coaches*, i, p. 17, Fig. 17.
6. Ibid., i, p. 9.
7. Ellis, *British Railway History*, i, p. 280.
8. McDermott, *Great Western Railway*, p. i, 445; see also Russell, *Great Western Coaches*, i, p. 9.
9. McDermott, *Great Western Railway*, ii, p. 304; see also Bagwell, *Railway Clearing House*, p. 58.
10. McDermott, *Great Western Railway*, i, p. 70.
11. Dendy Marshall, *The Southern Railway*, p. 301; McDermott, *Great Western Railway*, ii, p. 303.
12. McDermott, *Great Western Railway*, ii, p. 302.
13. Ellis, *British Railway History*, ii, p. 172.
14. C.H. Ellis, *Nineteenth-Century Railway Carriages*, p. 68.
15. O.S. Nock, *The London & North Western Railway*, p. 126.
16. Joy, *Regional History*, xiv, *The Lake Counties*, p. 71.
17. Ellis, *The Midland Railway*, p. 70.
18. Allen, *Great Eastern Railway*, p. 56.
19. Thomas Gethin Clayton started his career on the GWR at Wolverhampton works as a pattern maker. Alan Peck states that Clayton's personality was 'overbearing in the extreme' (*Swindon Works*, p. 69).
20. 'The Great Western is a very solid line which makes it progress in solid style; doing some great things and many small but all alike with the immovability of Jove', (D. Foxwell, quoted by McDermott in *Great Western Railway*, ii, p. 208).
21. McDermott, *Great Western Railway*, ii, p. 246.
22. Ellis, *The Midland Railway*, p. 73.
23. Ellis, quoting G.P. Neele, Superintendent of the L&NWR, in *British Railway History*, p. 173.
24. Nock, *London & North Western*, p. 105.

21. Standardization and Brakes

1. Bagwell, *Railway Clearing House*, p. 263 (quoting Parliamentary Papers (1872) xiii).
2. Court of Chancery 1858, E. and A. Prior (coal merchants) v. GNR, quoted in Bagwell, *Railway Clearing House*, p. 83.
3. Reed, *Victorian Economy*, p. 17.
4. J. Simmons, *The Railway in Town and County, 1830–1914*, ii, p. 45.
5. Ibid., p. 44.
6. Bagwell, *Railway Clearing House*, p. 85.
7. Ibid., p. 189.
8. Ibid., p. 207.
9. Ibid., p. 198 (quoting Proceedings of the Institution of Civil Engineers, clxxxix).
10. Bagwell, *Railway Clearing House*, p. 197.
11. *The Engineer* (9 October 1868), p. 270.
12. M. Robbins, *The North London Railway*, p. 24.
13. *The Engineer* (9 October 1868), p. 270.
14. Stevens, *English Railways*, p. 267.
15. *Punch*, lxv, p. 295, quoted in Simmons, *England and Wales*, p. 245.
16. Ellis, *British Railway History*, i, p. 377.
17. 'The Railway Interest: Its Organisation and Influence 1839–1914, in *Journal of Transport History* (November 1965), pp. 73–5.
18. Dendy Marshall, *The Southern Railway*, p. 345.

19. Ibid., p. 230.
20. McDermott, *Great Western Railway*, ii, p. 304.
21. Dendy Marshall, *The Southern Railway*, p. 134.
22. Ellis, *British Railway History*, ii, p. 65.
23. Rutherglen, 1881: 9 injured; Dalston Junction, 1881, 1 dead, 106 injured; Lockerbie, 1883, 8 dead, 30 injured.
24. Robbins, *North London Railway*, p. 24.
25. Bagwell, *Railway Clearing House*, p. 219.
26. C.H. Ellis, *Twenty Locomotivemen*, p. 101.
27. Bagwell, *Railway Clearing House*, p. 217.
28. O.S. Nock, *Historic Railway Disasters*, p. 61.
29. Robbins, *North London Railway*, p. 24.
30. Ellis, *Twenty Locomotivemen*, p. 105.

22. Guilty until Proven Innocent

1. Cap. xxv (1888), 'To be construed as one with the Regulation of Railways Act 1873'.
2. The Royal Commission on the Depression of Trade (1886) reported:

> We are beginning to feel the effects of foreign competition in quarters where our trade formerly enjoyed a monopoly. In every quarter of the world the perseverance and enterprise of the Germans is making itself felt. In the actual production of commodities we have few if any advantages over them. [In their] determination to obtain a footing whenever they can and a tenacity in maintaining it, they appear to be gaining ground on us. The Germans and the United States are dumping on us their surpluses at low prices (????).

British exports increased by 6.4 per cent between 1880 and 1900, but the USA increased exports by 42.8 per cent and Germany by 23 per cent. In 1880 British steel output was 1,020,000 tons, equal to a third of the world total. By 1902 British output had increased fivefold, but then constituted only a seventh of world production. Between 1880 and 1902, Britain dropped from its position as the premier steel producer in the world to third place behind the USA and Germany.

3. Evidence to Select Committee (1893–4), xiv, p. iv.
4. Ibid.
5. *Economist* (7 March 1891), p. 305, and (4 April 1891), p. 433.
6. *Economist* (16 December 1893), p. 1499.
7. Ibid.
8. Ibid. (quoting Parliamentary Select Committee on Railway Rates, 1893).
9. Cap. x (27 June 1892).
10. *Economist* (14 January 1893), p. 35.
11. *Economist* (16 December 1893), p. 1499 (quoting evidence in Parliamentary Select Committee on Railway Rates, 1893).
12. Nock, *London & North Western*, p. 85.
13. Stevens, *English Railways*.
14. H. Disney, *Carriage by Railway*, p. 63 (North Staffordshire Colliery Owners Assoc. v. N.S. Rly, 1908; Charlaw and Sacriston Colliery v. N.E. Rly, 1896. See also Ch. 16, 'Preference', p. 232).
15. Simmons, *England and Wales*, p. 117. Acts of Parliament intended to improve working-class housing in the great cities had been made since 1841. 'The Metropolitan Association for Improving the Dwellings of the Labouring Classes' was patronized by Prince Albert and Lord Shaftesbury. (See also Simmons, *Town and Country*, pp. 81–2.)

16. Dendy Marshall, *The Southern Railway*, p. 333.
17. A. Jackson, *London's Local Railways*, p. 28–9.
18. Ibid., p. 29.
19. Vic. 46 and 47, Cap. xxxiv: 'Fares not exceeding the rate of one penny a mile shall be exempt from duty. Duty shall be payable at 2 per cent on fares exceeding one penny a mile for conveyance between stations within one urban district. If sufficient workmen's trains at rates not exceeding one penny a mile are not provided the Board of Trade may order the Company to provide such accommodation.'
20. The Great Eastern trains ran at a loss unless at least 500 people travelled on each. The Chairman of GER is quoted in Simmons, *The Victorian Railway*, p. 326. See also Simmons, *Town and Country*, pp. 83–4.
21. Allen, *Great Eastern Railway*, p. 58.
22. Standing Orders 29–31 of 30 July 1874. No. 29 ordered any company taking fifteen houses or more to deposit in the Private Bills Office a statement of how many 'persons of the Labouring Classes' would be displaced. No. 30 ordered the company taking the houses to put up public notices to that effect in the streets concerned, six weeks before the demolition. No. 31 ordered: 'That in every such Bill a clause shall be inserted requiring the promoters to procure ... sufficient accommodation for persons of the labouring classes who will be displaced under the powers of the Bill'.
23. Parliamentary Papers (1884–5), xxx, p. 99.
24. Simmons, *Town and Country*, p. 34, and Parliamentary Papers (1884–5), xxx, p. 99.
25. Simmons, *Town and Country*, p. 34.
26. Housing of the Working Classes Act, Cap. lxx (18 September 1890; see Appendix 11).
27. Jackson, *London's Termini*, pp. 107, 155, 223, 229 *et seq.*
28. Reprinted from *The Statist* and published by that journal in London in 1902.
29. Simmons, *Town and Country*, p. 35. In 1908 Lloyd George appointed Paish to the Board of Trade Conference on railway charges and amalgamations.

23. The Forth Bridge, Strikes and the 'Golden Age'

1. Simmons, *England and Wales*, p. 240.
2. P.S.A. Berridge, *The Girder Bridge*, p. 77.
3. W. Westhofen, 'The Forth Bridge', in *The Engineer* (28 February 1890), p. 50.
4. Ibid., p. 59.
5. Ibid., p. 62.
6. Ibid., p. 50.
7. Ibid., p. 58.
8. Berridge, *The Girder Bridge*, p. 78.
9. Ibid., p. 79.
10. Ellis, *British Railway History*, ii, p. 31.
11. *The Engineer* (6 February 1891).
12. J. Thomas, *A Regional History of the Railways of Great Britain*, VI, Scotland, p. 247.
13. Bagwell, *The Railwaymen*, i, p. 140.
14. Ibid., p. 146.
15. Parliamentary Papers (1890–91), xvi.
16. A census taken on 6 June 1908 showed 1319 trains in 24 hrs (Thomas, *A Regional History*, VI, Scotland, p. 248).
17. W.H. Beattie (1843–1898) designed the 'Central', the 'Clarendon' and the 'Royal' hotels in Edinburgh and was the original promoter of the Edinburgh cable tramway (Carter, *British Railway Hotels*, p. 67).

18. Ibid., p. 89.
19. Ibid., p. 26.
20. Ibid.
21. McDermott, *Great Western Railway*, ii, p. 251.
22. The summit of the L&SWR Exeter–Plymouth line was at Sourton, approximately 925 ft; the summit of the GWR line was at Wrangaton, approximately 425 ft. Although the GWR route had some very severe inclines, they were of short duration. The L&SWR gradients were less severe but almost continuous for 30 miles.
23. Grinling, *Great Northern Railway*, pp. 383–4.
24. M&GN Joint Committee Accounts (in author's possession).
25. During the Great War it was used as a Red Cross hospital from 1915; the first patients were those wounded at Gallipoli.
26. Harry Allen (1879–1947) was the son of a poor farm labourer near Blakeney, Norfolk. He left school at twelve and worked as a labourer until he found a career on the M&GN. He became Chief Inspector of Signalmen, Alderman of Norfolk County Council, a member of Norfolk CC Education Committee and a Justice of the Peace.
27. M&GN Society, *The Midland & Great Northern Joint Railway*, p. 7.
28. Allen, *Great Eastern Railway*, p. 115.
29. D. Bradley and D. Milton, *Somerset & Dorset Locomotive History*, p. 38.
30. D. Bartholomew *The Midland & South Western Junction Railway*, i, p. 7.
31. *Economist* (5 September 1891), p. 1139.
32. *Economist* (21 February 1891), p. 235.

24. The Destructiveness of Self-interest

1. Simmons, *England and Wales*, p. 93.
2. Ellis, *British Railway History*, i, p. 315.
3. See Grinling, *Great Northern Railway*.
4. Ackworth, *Railways of England*, p. 254.
5. Ellis, *British Railway History*, i, p. 47, and Gray, *London Chatham & Dover*, p. 187.
6. Dendy Marshall, *The Southern Railway*, p. 220–21.
7. Ibid., p. 331.
8. Ellis, *British Railway History*, i, p. 309.
9. Ahrons, *British Steam Railway Locomotive*, p. 150; see also Dendy Marshall, *The Southern Railway*, p. 351, and Gray, *London Chatham & Dover*, p. 195.
10. O.S. Nock, *Great Locomotives of the Southern Railway*, p. 10.
11. Dendy Marshall, *The Southern Railway*, p. 334.
12. Ibid., p. 221.
13. Gray, *London Chatham & Dover*, p. 105.
14. *Herapath*, quoted by Bagwell in *Journal of Transport History* (November 1955), p. 70.
15. Dendy Marshall, *The Southern Railway*, p. 332 (quoting local press report).
16. Ibid., p. 304.
17. *Herapath* (11 August 1877), p. 832, and *Journal of Transport History* (November 1955), p. 70.
18. *Herapath*, quoted in *Journal of Transport History* (November 1955), p. 73.
19. C.E. Lee, *The Metropolitan District Railway*, p. 2.
20. Ibid., p. 6.
21. Simmons, *England and Wales*, p. 122.
22. *Railway News*, quoted in Lee, *Metropolitan District*, p. 12.
23. Dendy Marshall, *The Southern Railway*, p. 303.

24. Jackson, *London's Termini*, p. 355.
25. *Journal of Transport History* (November 1955), p. 77.
26. Ibid.
27. *Economist* (28 July 1900), p. 1065.
28. Ibid.

25. The Trade Unions

1. Bagwell, *The Railwaymen*, i, p. 175.
2. McDermott, *Great Western Railway*, i, p. 355.
3. Bagwell, *The Railwaymen*, i, p. 21.
4. Peck, *Swindon Works*, p. 53.
5. Ibid., p. 55.
6. Ibid.
7. Report of Investigation, PRO, Rail 186/62.
8. *Herapath* (16 September 1871), p. 907, quoted in Bagwell, *The Railwaymen*, i p. 47.
9. NUMBER OF MEN EMPLOYED ON RAILWAYS AND TRADE UNION MEMBERSHIP

	1881	1891	1901	1911	1913
Total no. employed	166K	223K	322K	378K	390K
Total membership of all rly TUs	10K	49.5K	82K	185K	326K

(Source: Board of Trade returns, quoted in Clapham, *An Economic History of Modern Britain, 1820–1850*, iv, p. 326.)

10. *The Times* (6 July 1862), quoted in Bagwell, *The Railwaymen*, i, p. 22. Gooch held one of two Parliamentary seats allotted to the Cricklade Division. He gained his seat in Parliament in 1865 when few, if any, railwaymen had the right to vote. In 1881 a Liberal, Storey Maskelyne, took one seat and Gooch the other, although Maskelyne had twice the number of votes. In 1884, when the franchise was extended to cover all railwaymen, there was then only one seat for Cricklade, and Gooch lost it to Maskelyne.
11. Bagwell, *The Railwaymen*, i, p. 73.
12. Michael Thomas Bass (1799–1884) was educated at Burton-on-Trent Grammar School. He was appointed Deputy-Lieutenant of Staffordshire in 1852, and served as Liberal MP for Derby from August 1848 to April 1884.
13. Reginald Windsor Sackville-West (1817–1896), MA, was Rector of Withyam Sussex (1841–65), and Chaplain to Queen Victoria (1846–65). He became Earl de la Warr in 1873.
14. Bagwell, *The Railwaymen*, i, p. 53.
15. Royal Commission Report on the Poor Laws, Parliamentary Papers (1909), xxxvii (see Bagwell, *The Railwaymen*, i, p. 77).
16. Ellis, *Twenty Locomotivemen*.
17. Parliamentary Select Committee on Railway Servants (Hours of Labour) (1891), xvi, qq. 9440–44, 9466, 9690; see Bagwell, *The Railwaymen*, i, p. 158.
18. The original Minutes of the meeting in author's collection.
19. P. Wood, *The Price of a Cigar*.
20. Bagwell, *The Railwaymen*, i. p. 698.
21. Ibid., p. 144.
22. Ibid., p. 147.

23. Directors on Committee: E. McNeill, Ballycastle Railway; J. Wilson, Glasgow Central Railway; G.R. Vernon, Lanarkshire & Ayrshire Railway and Caledonian Railway; H. Gladstone, Wrexham, Mold & Connah's Quay Railway; Gathorne-Hardy, South Eastern Railway; H. Maxwell, Great South Western Railway; Hicks-Beach, Collingbourne & Avon Valley Railway; Jo Pease, North Eastern Railway.

24. Parliamentary Papers (1892) xvi, q. 2353.

25. Parliamentary Papers (1890–91) xvi; see Bagwell, *The Railwaymen*, i, p. 159.

26. 'We the undersigned enginemen and firemen of the Great Eastern Railway hereby reiterate our protest against the interference of the Legislature with our hours of labour both as a denial of the assertion that has been made to the Committee that our previous signatures were obtained by jobbery and as conclusive proof [that] it was a spontaneous act of our own. Signed E. Smith, E. Buttons [or Duttons], J. McNess and 596 others' (Appendix 20 of the Committee's Report, Parliamentary Papers (1891), xvi).

27. 'The operations carried on by goods guards, brakesmen, permanent-way men and shunters represent a far more dangerous trade than any trade or process subject to State control – except merchant shipping . . . The chief causes of the large number of accidents are: the nature of the coupling gear necessitating the use of the shunting pole, inadequate or non-existent lighting, wires across the ground or other obstacles over which the men trip or run into or are knocked against – and a disregard for safety owing to pressure of work' (Select Committee on Accidents to Railway Servants, Parliamentary Papers (1900), xxxvii).

28. Original overtime sheets in author's collection.

29. Parliamentary Papers (1890–91) xvi, q. 1337.

30. Select Committee of Railway Servants (Hours of Labour), Special Reports 111, Parliamentary Papers (1892), xvi.

31. Cap. xxix (27 July 1893).

32. Bagwell, *The Railwaymen*, i, pp. 189–95.

33. James Inskip, born 21 January 1839 at Arlsey, Beds, was a solicitor in Bristol (1862). He became an Alderman of the City, and was a pillar of the 'Protestant League' and a lay preacher.

34. Bagwell, *The Railwaymen*, i, p. 209.

35. Ibid., p. 216.

36. Court hearing TVR v. ASRS (9 December 1902), qq. 2747–849, quoted in Bagwell, *The Railwaymen*, i, p. 216.

37. Ibid.

38. Ibid., p. 220.

39. The leaflet was headed 'Strike on the Taff Vale Railway'. The text declared: 'There has been a strike on the Taff Vale Railway since Monday last. Management are using every means to decoy men here who they employ for the purpose of blacklegging the men on strike.
Are you willing to be known as a
BLACKLEG?
If you accept employment on the Taff Vale that is what you will be known by. On arrival at Cardiff call at the above address where you can get information and assistance' (Bagwell, *The Railwaymen*, i, p. 220).

40. Ibid., p. 213.

41. Cap. xlvii. Its single most powerful clause is in Section 4: 'An action against a trade union whether of workmen or of masters against any members or officials thereof on behalf of themselves and all other members of the trade union in respect of any tortuous act alleged to have been committed by or on behalf of the trade union – shall not be recognised in any court.'

26. Competitive Excellence

1. *Economist* (25 April 1903), p. 732.
2. *Herapath* (23 February 1900).
3. *Economist* (25 April 1903), pp. 731–2.
4. In the period 1893–7, the total cost of materials used in repairing locomotives of all British railways increased by 105 per cent; coal/coke increased by 88 per cent when train mileage increased by 32 per cent (*Economist* (22 October 1912), p. 792).
5. Those carriages on the electric traction sections of the London Underground were electrically lit and the Great Northern & City underground trains had all-steel coaches from 1907. The LYR produced all-steel coaches for their Manchester–Southport service in 1913. The LB&SCR had electric lighting to supplement oil-pressure lamps in their Pullman cars as early as 1881. Mr Stone's axle-driven electricity generator was invented in 1900 and was at once adopted by the Great North of Scotland Railway and the London, Tilbury & Southend Railway, but the major companies did not like it. The generator was driven from the carriage axle, which increased the work of the loco-motive and used more coal.
6. Royal Commission on Accidents to Railway Servants (1900), quoted in Bagwell, *The Railwaymen*, i, p. 100.
7. E. Mason, *The Lancashire & Yorkshire Railway*, p. 41.
8. In the published report of the case, the magistrate ruled: 'Those persons in a carriage which is full have a legal and moral right to keep the door closed to prevent the carriage being over-crowded and the sooner the public understand that the better' (see *Railway Magazine* (February 1900), p. 186).
9. Allen, *Great Eastern Railway*, p. 158.
10. Dendy Marshall, *The Southern Railway*, p. 144.
11. *Railway Magazine* (April 1899), p. 311.
12. Ibid., p. 317.
13. R. Christiansen and R.W. Miller, *The Cambrian Railway*, ii, p. 135.
14. Ibid., p. 75.
15. *Railway Magazine* (July–August 1947), p. 205.
16. Houghton and Foster, *The Settle–Carlisle Line*, p. 87.
17. *Railway Magazine* (July–August 1947), p. 205.
18. Mason, *Lancashire & Yorkshire Railway*, p. 44.

27. Individualism on Wheels

1. Report of Ontario Commission on Railway Taxation 1905, quoted in EWR *Rating of Railways* (1908), p. 3.

2. PERCENTAGE INCREASES OF NET RECEIPTS AND RATEABLE VALUE OF ALL RAILWAYS IN BRITAIN COMPARING THE YEARS BELOW WITH 1870

	Net receipts	Rateable value
1894	56.1%	£184.8
1899	80.6%	£220.0
1906	94.4%	£258.4

The amount raised for parochial rates in England and Wales in 1904 – excluding money raised from railways – was 65.5 per cent more than was raised in 1894.

(Source: GWR, *Rating of Railways*, pp. 27, 31.)

3. In May 1901 Middlesex County Council went to Parliament for an Act to extend the tramway system from Tottenham to Wood Green and Friern Barnet, the first

'cross-country' tramway system. Another route was to run from Highgate Archway to Whetstone, and from Highgate railway station to the Muswell Hill entrance of the Alexandra Palace and Park, costing £½ million, to be built by North Metropolitan Tramways Co.

4. G. Gibbon and R. Bell, *History of London County Council*, pp. 165–70.

5. Simmons, *The Victorian Railway*, p. 331 (quoting L&NWR to Parliamentary Select Committee, Parliamentary Papers (1910).

6. Jackson, *London's Local Railways*, pp. 280–87.

7. The first electrically hauled transport in Britain were Magnus Volk's tramway along the beach at Brighton, opened on August 1883, and the Giant's Causeway, Portrush & Bush Valley Tramway, opened on 28 September 1883. The latter used hydro-electric power. (See Hamilton Ellis, *Railways of Britain*, ii, p. 150.)

8. From 1892 until 1906 there raged the 'Battle of the Bridges' whereby first the tram companies and then the LCC tried to obtain access across the Thames. The great philosopher and Liberal politician Lord Richard Haldane (1856–1928) led the opposition to this improvement to the tram system. A contemporary cartoon showed Haldane as 'Horatius guarding the bridge' and being told by a Londoner to 'Come into the 20th century'.

9. R.J. Irving, *The North Eastern Railway, 1870–1914*.

10. Report of shareholders' meeting (14 February 1913), in PRO, Rail 278.

11. Sixteen of the NLR's 24 Directors were appointed by the L&NWR; two-thirds of its capital was subscribed by the L&NWR (Robbins, *North London Railway*, p. 2.)

12. L&NWR Reports to shareholders, PRO, Rail 410/4.

13. WORKING COSTS

	1905	1906	1907	1908	1909	1910	1911	1912
GWR	64%	60%	61.3%	60.9%	60.9%	61%	62%	66.6%
L&SWR	57%	57%	58.7%	59.6%	59.6%	59.6%	60%	62%

14. The District Railway by that time extended as far west as Wimbledon, Richmond and Ealing.

15. Ellis, *British Railway History*, ii, p. 152.

16. Lee, *The Metropolitan Railway*, p. 16.

17. The Act was obtained on 6 August 1897 to build from Kensington to Piccadilly with a power station at Lots Road, Chelsea.

18. Hansard (1896), xlii, cols. 438 and 446.

19. The LB&SCR's all-Pullman *Southern Belle* was, perhaps, an attempt at the chic.

20. Hansard (30 June 1896), xlii, col. 445.

21. Tarmac's net profit was £16,295 in 1918 and £83,099 in 1924 (J.B.E. Earle, *Black Top: A History of the British Flexible Road Industry*, p. 20).

22. Between 1 January 1903 and 31 December 1913, 68,248 people were killed on the roads and 2,108,000 were injured. There were 144,000 cars registered in 1910 (HMSO, Road Accident Report, 1946).

23. W. Plowden, *The Motor Car and Politics*, p. 44. In 1907 the Liberal Prime Minister Herbert Asquith declared: 'A tax on motor cars would be an ideal tax because it is a tax on a luxury which is apt to degenerate into a nuisance' (ibid., p. 13).

24. *The Times* (11 August 1905), p. 12.

25. Earle, *Black Top*, p. 13.

26. Basic road statistics (British Road Federation, quoted in Earle, *Black Top*, p. 14).

28. The Companies Close Ranks

1. Departmental Committee on Railway Agreements and Amalgamations (1911) Para. 59, Command 5631.
2. Hansard (1895), xxxiv, col. 618.
3. *Economist* (12 August 1905), p. 1313.
4. *Economist* (18 August 1906), p. 1369.
5. WORKING COSTS AS A % OF GROSS INCOME

	1909	1910	1911	1912
GWR	60.9	60.9	62	66.6
(Large increases in route mileage)				
L&NWR	62.6	61.5	62.5	63.4
L&SWR	59.6	59.4	60	62.1
MR	60	59	61	60.4
NER	–	–	62.4	61.8
GCR	65.5	65.5	65.8	65
GER	–	–	60.75	64.3
(Serious floods 1912)				
GNR	63.1	62.7	62.5	63.8

(Source: *Economist* for relevant years.)

6. Report of Inquiry into Earnings and Hours of Labour of Workpeople in the UK (BPP, cviii).
7. Bagwell, *The Railwaymen*, i, p. 266.
8. Ibid., p. 270.
9. Ibid., p. 273.
10. Ibid., p. 280.
11. Hansard (1909), iii, col. 1282.
12. Hansard (1908), clxxxiii, cols. 1612–42.
13. Ibid., col. 1630.
14. Ibid., col. 1632.
15. Ibid., col. 1637.
16. Ibid., col. 1638–9.
17. Ibid., col. 1639.
18. Ibid., col. 1641.
19. Ibid., col. 1644.
20. Ibid., col. 1647.
21. *Economist* (25 November 1905), p. 1870; (18 August 1906), p. 1370; (19 March 1910), p. 60.
22. Bagwell, *The Railwaymen*, i, p. 286.
23. Ibid., p. 275.
24. Ibid., p. 286.
25. Command 5631 (1911).
26. Bagwell, *The Railwaymen*, i, p. 290, quoting from *Liverpool Daily Post* of 9 August 1911.
27. General Railway Workers Union.
28. Bagwell, *The Railwaymen*, i, p. 289, quoting from *The Times* of 15 August 1911.
29. Bagwell, *The Railwaymen*, i, p. 292.
30. Ibid., p. 295, quoting from Parliamentary Papers (1911), xlvii, p. 730.
31. PRO, Kew; catalogue entry for File HO/45 (closed for 100 years) lists 'Bayonet wounds inflicted at Llanelli 1911'.

2. The German gunboat *Panther* was sent to Agadir on 1 July 1911, ostensibly to
protect German interests during a rising by the Moroccans against the French
invaders, but in reality as part of a longstanding campaign to force the French to hand
over to Germany large tracts of the Congo then under French occupation. The
Germans achieved this in November 1911.
3. GWR Staff Records (PRO, Rail 264).
4. *Economist* (21 February 1914), p. 395.

29. Railwaymen, Loyalty and Sacrifice

1. Some very small lines – the Mid-Suffolk Light and the Garstang & Knott End for
instance – were taken under control. The 2 per cent not taken over, a total of 499 miles,
included all the London Underground lines, the Bishop's Castle, the Ravenglass &
Eskdale, the Tal-y-llyn, and the Wolverhampton & Cannock Chase.
2. Sir Herbert Walker, General Manager of the L&SWR, became Chairman in April
1914. His Executive consisted of the following General Managers:

D.A. Matheson	Caledonian Railway
Sir Sam Fay	Great Central Railway
C.H. Dent	Great Northern Railway
F. Potter	Great Western Railway
Sir Robert Turnbull	London & North Western Railway
J.A.F. Aspinall	Lancashire & Yorkshire Railway
Sir Guy Granet	Midland Railway
Sir A.K. Butterworth	North Eastern Railway
F.H. Dent	South Eastern & Chatham Joint Committee

3. Bagwell, *Railway Clearing House*, p. 270.
4. Command 1132 (1921).
5. In August 1914 Lord Kitchener said it would last three years and need a million
men. The Foreign Secretary Sir Edward Grey thought the idea 'unlikely, if not incredible' (J. Stevenson, *British Society, 1914–1945*, p. 49).
6. Sir Herbert Walker, to Wilson–Fox Committee (9 October 1918), quoted in the
Economist (13 September 1919), p. 427.
7. Bagwell, *Railway Clearing House*, p. 274.
8. E. Pratt, *British Railways and the Great War*, i, p. 100.
9. Lord Faringdon (18 December 1916), PRO, Rail 226.
10. Pratt, *The Great War*, ii, p. 1016.
11. Ibid., ii, p. 1009.
12. Ibid., i, p. 103.
13. Ibid., p. 114.
14. PRO, Rail 250/590.
15. Pratt, *The Great War*, i, p. 924.
16. Ibid., i, p. 273.
17. Ibid., ii, p. 1049.
18. Ibid., i, p. 305.
19. Ibid., i, p. 306.
20. H.A. Vallance, *The Highland Railway*, p. 101.
21. Ibid., pp. 105–6.
22. Ibid., pp. 106–7.
23. Ibid., p. 102.
24. Pratt, *The Great War*, i, p. 64.
25. Pratt, *The Great War*, i, p. 63, and Jackson, *London's Termini*, p. 204.

26. The standard trains provided in the first instance by these companies: GCR, GER, 3; GWR, 5; L&YR, 2; L&NWR, 6; L&SWR, 3; MR, 2.
27. Pratt, *The Great War*, i, p. 134.
28. *Economist* (15 February 1919), p. 230.
29. *Railway Review*, quoted in Bagwell, *The Railwaymen*, i, p. 345.
30. Not until early in 1918 was extra food supplied by the Government to engi sheds for enginemen without food. The allowances and prices were:

Meat	4 oz	6½d
Cheese	2½ oz	2½d (a man could not buy meat and cheese)
Biscuits	1 lb	6d
Jam	4 oz	2½d (no bread supplied to go with jam)
Tea	1 oz	2d

(Source: *Railway Gazette* (29 March 1918), p. 370.)

31. Bagwell, *The Railwaymen*, i, p. 345.
32. Ibid., p. 347.
33. James Henry Thomas (1874–1949), was a locomotive cleaner on the GW Newport line (1889). He became National President of the ASRS (1904), and Labo MP for Derby in 1910. In 1917 he became a Privy Councillor, in recognition of h success in preventing a national railway strike; he was also General Secretary of t NUR (from 1918) and President of the British TUC and International TUC (1920)
34. Bagwell, *The Railwaymen*, i, p. 347.
35. Pratt, *The Great War*, i, p. 128.

30. Broken Promises

1. *The Times* (8 December 1919).
2. Eric Geddes, Conservative MP for Cambridge (1918). He coined the legenda phrase: 'We will squeeze Germany like a lemon until the pips squeak'.
3. P. Rowland, *Lloyd George*, p. 450.
4. C.L. Mowatt, *Britain between the Wars*, p. 7.
5. *The Times* (28 February 1919), p. 6.
6. *Financial Times* (3 July 1919), p. 5.
7. *Railway Gazette* (22 February 1918).
8. *Financial Times* (1 May 1919).
9. *Financial Times* (16 May 1919).
10. *Railway News* (3 October 1916).
11. Sir Albert Stanley, General Manager of the Underground, became President of t Board of Trade; Sir Guy Granet, General Manager of the Midland, became Direct General of Movements and Railways; Sir Guy Calthorp, General Manager of t L&NWR, became Controller of Coal Mines; Sir Sam Fay, General Manager of t GCR, was put in charge of the Department of Military Railways; Sir Vincent Rave Chief Mechanical Engineer of the NER, was in command at Woolwich Arsenal.
12. Hansard (1918), cvi, cols. 391–2.
13. Reported in the *Daily Herald* (29 September 1919); quoted in Bagwell, *Th Railwaymen*, i, p. 383.
14. Bagwell, *The Railwaymen*, i, p. 383.
15. Ministers and Secretaries Act (ibid., p. 386.)
16. Hansard (1919), cxiv, col. 1099.
17. Bagwell, *The Railwaymen*, i, p. 393.
18. Ibid., p. 395.
19. Wages to remain static until 30 September 1920. Negotiations on the national wag

ates to be complete by 31 December 1919. No adult railway to receive less than 51s a week so long as cost of living is 110 per cent above 1913. Strikers and those who did not strike to work harmoniously together. No victimization by unions or management.

0. Hansard (1919), cxx, col. 275.
1. *Railway Gazette* (22 February 1918), p. 213.
2. Parliamentary Papers (1918), iv.
3. *Financial Times* (19 February 1919).
4. Ibid.
5. Command 1132 (1921).
6. Frederick Smith was an India rubber and cotton manufacturer, a Director of Martins Bank, and, from 1917, first Baron Colwyn.
7. *Railway & Shipping Journal* (1 July 1921), p. 22g, quoting the Lord President.
8. Ibid.
9. Ibid.
0. *Economist* (14 August 1920), p. 258.
1. *Economist* (24 July 1920), p. 138.
2. August 1921: 115,128,460 passengers (21 per cent down on August 1920); passenger revenue down 51 per cent, passenger train mileage increased by 3.86 per cent. Freight tonnage reduced by 15 per cent, freight train mileage reduced by only 10.7 per cent. The average wagon in August 1921 carried 5.3 tons and an average train load was 123 tons, compared with the August 1921 figures of 5.38 and 132.3 tons. The net ton/miles per engine hour in August 1921 was 423, compared with 433 in August 1920 *Economist* (14 August 1921), p. 258).
3. *Railway Gazette* (27 August 1920), p. 268.
4. Command 787 (1920).
5. Bagwell, *The Railwaymen*, i, p. 408.
6. Ibid., p. 410.
7. *Railway & Shipping Journal* (August 1921).
8. Command 1228 (1921).
9. *Railway Gazette* (22 February 1918).
0. Command 1132 (1921).

31. Advantage Road

1. *Railway Review* (18 May 1923), quoted in Bagwell, *The Railwaymen*, i, p. 434.
2. Nock, *Great Locomotives*, p. 151.
3. M. Bonavia, *A History of the LNER*, i, p. 40.
4. National Wages Board Report (9 December 1925), Para 37, quoted in Bagwell, *The Railwaymen*, i, p. 443.
5. PRO, Rail 250/455.
6. 'We [the GWR] have now formed the "Western National Omnibus Co" 50/50 with the National Omnibus & Transport Co. to take over passenger road services in Devon and Cornwall hitherto run separately by the GWR and N.O. Co. A similar agreement with "South Wales Commercial Motors" is being negotiated' (PRO, Rail 50/455).
7. Bonavia, *History of the LNER*, i, p. 46.
8. Bagwell, *The Railwaymen*, i, p. 518 (quoting *Ministry of Labour Gazette* for October 1933).
9. PRO, Rail 250/454 and 455.
0. E.A. Gibbins, *Blueprints for Bankruptcy*, p. 14.
1. Ibid., p. 15.

12. PRO, MT 6/2876, quoted in Gibbins, *Blueprints*, p. 21.
13. PRO, MT 47/276 quoted in Gibbins, *Blueprints*, p. 20.
14. Bagwell, *The Railwaymen*, i, p. 575.
15. *The Times* (January 29–31 1940), quoted in Bagwell, *The Railwaymen*, i, p. 547
16. Gourvish, *British Railways*; p. 3, and Bagwell, *The Railwaymen*, i, p. 573.
17. P. Addison, *The Road to 1945*, p. 106.
18. Bagwell, *The Railwaymen*, i, p. 576.
19. PRO, MT 47/276, quoted in Gibbins, *Blueprints*, p. 21.
20. Ministry of Transport Memoranda to Cabinet, PRO, MT 47/276, quoted i Gibbins, *Blueprints*, p. 22.
21. Quoted in Gibbins, *Blueprints*, p. 22.
22. Gourvish, *British Railways*, pp. 3–4.
23. Ibid., p. 5.
24. Ibid.
25. Ibid., p. 4.
26. R.A. Butler, *The Art of the Possible*, p. 146.
27. Labour 47.8 per cent of total vote (393 seats); Conservatives 39.8 per cent of tot vote (213 seats).

Bibliography

Periodicals and Newspapers

The Engineer
Economist
Financial Times
Herapath's Railway Journal (Herapath)
Journal of the Railway & Canal Historical Society
Journal of Transport History
Newcastle Daily Chronicle
Railway Commercial Information
Railway Gazette
Railway Magazine
Railway News
Railway Review
Railway Times
Suffolk Chronicle
The Times

The above are available at the British Library, Colindale, London.

Public Record Office References, Kew, London

GCR Minutes, Rail 186
LCR Minutes, Rail 226
JR Minutes, Rail 220
WR Minutes, Rail 250
LNWR Minutes, Rail 410
LDR Minutes, Rail 667

Bibliography

Parliamentary Records

Command 787 (1920)
Command 1228 (1921)
Command 1132 (1921)
vol. x (1839)
vol. xi (1844)
vol. xvii (1846)
vol. li (1851)
vol. xxxviii (1852–3)
vol. xxxviii (1867)
vol. xiii (1872), p. xxiv
vol. xiii (1872), q. 148–52
vol. xiv (1893–4), p. iv
vol. xxxvii (1909)
Hansard

Other Records

Institution of Civil Engineers Records
Minutes of the Proceedings of the Institution of Civil Engineers
Newcastle Literary & Philosophical Society
Royal Society, Philosophical Transactions, ciii 200
Suffolk Record Office, Ipswich (Ref.: 50.18.3)

Secondary Sources

Ackworth, W.M., *Railways of England* (London, 1899).
Addison, P., *The Road to 1945* (London, 1975).
Ahrons, E.L., *The British Steam Railway Locomotive from 1825 to 1925* (Londo 1927).
Allen, C.J., *The Great Eastern Railway* (London, 1967).
Anderson, V.R. and Fox, G.K., *Stations and Structures of the Settle & Carlisle Li* (Poole, 1986).
Bagwell, P., 'The Rivalry and Working Union of the South Eastern and Londo Chatham & Dover Railways', *Journal of Transport History* (November 1955), p. :
——, *The Railwaymen*, 2 vols (London, 1963).
——, *The Railway Clearing House in the British Economy* (London, 1968).
Baines, T., *History of Liverpool* (Liverpool, 1852).
Barnes, E.G., *The Rise of the Midland Railway, 1844–1874* (London, 1966).
Bartholomew, D., *The Midland & South West Junction Railway* (Didcot, 1982).
Baughan, P., *The Midland Railway North of Leeds* (Newton Abbot, 1987).
Berridge, P.S.A., *The Girder Bridge* (London, 1969).
Bonavia, M., *A History of the LNER*, 3 vols (London, 1984).
Bradley, D. and Milton, D., *Somerset & Dorset Locomotive History* (Newton Abb 1973).
Butler, R.A., *The Art of the Possible* (London, 1971).
Carlson, R. *The Liverpool & Manchester Railway Project* (Newton Abbot, 1969).
Carter, O., *An Illustration History of British Railway Hotels* (St Michael's, Lan 1990).

Bibliography

aloner, W.H., *The Social and Economic Development of Crewe* (Manchester, 1950).

ristiansen, R., *A Regional History of Railways*, vii (Newton Abbot, 1973).

—, and Miller, R.W., *The Cambrian Railway*, 2 vols (Newton Abbot, 1971).

apham, J., *An Economic History of Modern Britain, 1820–1850* (Cambridge, 1938).

ndy Marshall, C.F., *A History of the Southern Railway* (London, 1963).

vey, J., *The Memoirs of Joseph Locke* (Bentley, 1862).

sney, H., *Carriage by Railway* (London, 1915).

rle, J.B.E., *Black Top: A History of the British Flexible Road Industry* (Oxford, 1974).

is, C.H., *Nineteenth-Century Railway Carriages* (London, 1949).

—, *The Midland Railway* (London, 1955).

—, *Twenty Locomotivemen* (London, 1958).

—, *British Railway History, 1830–1876*, 2 vols (London, 1960).

—, *Railways of Britain*, ? vols (London, 1960).

ans, D.M., *The Commercial Crisis, 1847–1848* (London, 1848).

—, *The History of Commercial Crisis, 1857–8* (London, 1859).

lk, B., *The Bridgewater Millions: A Candid Family History* London, 1942).

ster, R., *Birmingham New Street*, i (Didcot, 1997).

ancis, J., *A History of the English Railway: Its Social Relations and Revelations, 1820–1845* (London, 1851).

bbins, E.A., *Blueprints for Bankruptcy* (Alsager, 1995).

bbon, G. and Bell, R., *The History of London County Council, 1889–1939* (London, 1939).

ooch, E. (ed.), *Dairies of Sir Daniel Gooch* (London, 1892).

ugh, J., *The Midland Railway: A Chronology* (Mold, 1989).

urvish, T.R., *British Railways, 1948–1973: A Business History* (Cambridge, 1986).

—, *Mark Huish and the L&NWR* (Leicester, 1972).

ay, A., *The London Chatham & Dover Railway* (Rainham, 1984).

inling, C., *The History of the Great Northern Railway* (London, 1903).

dfield, C., *Atmospheric Railways* (Gloucester, 1985).

lps, A., *Life of Thomas Brassey* (London, 1872).

ole, K., *A Regional History of the Railways of Great Britain*, IV, *The North East* (Newton Abbot, 1970).

ughton, F.W. and Foster, W.H., *The Story of the Settle–Carlisle Line* (Huddersfield, 1965).

ughes, J.R.T., *Liverpool Banks and Banking* (London, 1906).

uxley, R. *The Rise and Fall of the Severn Bridge Railway* (Gloucester, 1984).

ing, R.J., *The North Eastern Railway: An Economic History, 1870–1914* (Leicester, 1976).

—, *London's Termini* (Newton Abbot, 1969).

ckson, A., *London's Local Railways* (Newton Abbot, 1978).

vis, A., 'Engineering the Image: The Censoring of Samuel Smiles', *Journal of the Railway & Canal Historical Society*, xxxi (November 1993), pp. 176–85.

y, D., *A Regional History of the Railways of Great Britain*, XIV, *The Lake Counties* (Newton Abbot, 1983).

ay, P., *The London Tilbury & Southend Railway* (Teignmouth, 1996).

mbert, R.S., *The Railway King* (London, 1934).

e, C.E., *The Metropolitan District Railway* (Lingfield, 1956).

ngford, E., *Wellington: Pillar of State* (St Albans, 1975).

&GN Society, *The Midland & Great Northern Joint Railway* (London, 1989).

cDermott, E.T., *History of the Great Western Railway*, 2 vols (London, 1964).

agraw, R., *France, 1815–1914: The Bourgeois Century* (London, 1984).

ason, E., *The Lancashire & Yorkshire Railway* (London, 1954).

Mitchell, B.R. (ed.), 'The Coming of the Railway and Economic Growth', in M.C
    Reed (ed.) *Railways in the Victorian Economy* (Newton Abbot, 1969).
Mountfield, D., *The Railway Barons* (London, 1979).
Mowatt, C.L., *Britain between the Wars* (London, 1955).
Murray, A., *The Forth Bridge: A Celebration* (Edinburgh, 1983).
Nock, O.S., *The London & North Western Railway* (London, 1960).
——, *Historic Railway Disasters* (London, 1966)
——, *Great Locomotives of the Southern Railway* (London, 1983).
Norton, P., *Railways and Waterways to Warrington* (Cheshire, 1984).
Peck, A., *The Great Western at Swindon Works* (Poole, 1983).
Philips, M., *A History of Banks, Bankers and Banking in Northumberland, Durha*
    and North Yorkshire (London, 1894).
Platt, A., *The Life and Times of Daniel Gooch* (Gloucester, 1987).
Plowden, W., *The Motor Car and Politics* (London, 1971).
Pollins, H., 'Aspects of Railway Accounting before 1868', in M.C. Reed (ed
    Railways in the Victorian Economy, p. 140.
Porter, D.H., *Abolition of the Slave Trade in England, 1784–1807* (Connecticut, 197C
Pratt, E., *British Railways and the Great War*, 2 vols (London, 1921).
Reed, B., *Crewe Locomotive Works and its Men* (Newton Abbot, 1982).
Reed, M.C., *Railways in the Victorian Economy: Studies in Finance and Econom*
    Growth (Newton Abbot, 1969).
Robbins, M., *The North London Railway* (South Godstone, 1953).
Rolt, L.T.C., *Isambard Kingdom Brunel* (London, 1957).
Rowland, P., *Lloyd George* (London, 1975).
Russell, J.H., *A Pictorial History of Great Western Coaches* (Oxford, 1982).
Sanderson, M., *Education, Economic Change and Society in England, 1780–18;*
    (London, 1991).
Signalling Study Group, *The Signal Box* (Poole, 1986).
Simmons, J., *The Railway in England and Wales, 1830–1914* (Leicester, 1978).
——, *The Railway in Town and Country, 1830–1914* (Newton Abbot, 1986).
——, *The Victorian Railway* (London, 1991).
Smiles, S., *Brief Biographies* (Boston, MA, 1860).
——, *Lives of George and Robert Stephenson* (London, 1862).
——, *Lives of the Engineers* (Boston, MA, 1864).
Smith, A., *An Inquiry into the Wealth of Nations* (London, 1966).
Stevens, C., *English Railways and their Relation to the State* (London, 1915).
Stevenson, J., *British Society, 1914–1945* (London, 1984).
Thomas, D. St J., *The North British Railway* (Newton Abbot, 1969).
——, *A Regional History of the Railways of Great Britain*, VI, *Scotland* (Newto
    Abbot, 1971).
Tomlinson, W.T., *North Eastern Railway* (Newton Abbot, 1969).
Vallance, H.A., *The Highland Railway* (Newton Abbot, 1963).
Vaughan, A., *Isambard Kingdom Brunel: Engineering Knight-Errant* (London, 199I
Watson, R.S., *History of the Newcastle Literary & Philosophical Society* (London, 1897
Webster, N., *Britain's First Trunk Line* (Bath, 1972).
Wood, N., *Treatise on Railroads* (Science Museum Library, London, 1838).
Wood, P., *The Price of a Cigar* (London, 1996).
Young, R., *Timothy Hackworth and the Locomotive* (Shildon, 1975).
Williams, F.S., *The Midland Railway; Its Rise and Progress: A Narrative of Moder*
    Enterprise (London, 1888).

Index

Index

Boer War: damaging effect of on railway wages, 261

boiler: single-flue, 9, 24; return-flue, 70; multi-tubular, 70

Bolton & Leigh Railway: 52; free coal at opening, 77, 78

Bonomi, Ignatius: and Skerne bridge, 23

Bonsor, Cosmo, 247, 320

Booth, Henry: L&MR Secretary, 58, 59; suggests multi-tubular boiler to R. Stephenson, 70

Booth, Thomas: on L&MR Committee, 49

Bore, Richard: L&NWR Carriage Superintendent, 202

Borough Bank of Liverpool: failure of, 139

Bosanquet, Henry: ECR Chairman, 109

Bouch, Sir Thomas: and Tay bridge, 224

Bouch, William: report on S&DR locomotives, 41

Bournemouth Belle, 236

Brace, Under-Secretary, 314

Bradshaw, Robert: Bridgewater Canal Superintendent, 47–9; attacks L&MR, 51, 55, 56

brakes: Westinghouse air, 198, 208–9, 210; Kendall's air, 207; automatic vacuum, 192, 209; introduction opposed by companies, 207, 210; trials of at Newark, 208–9; chain, 208; simple vacuum, 208; Bill in Parliament for, rejected, 210; standard pipe end adopted, 211

Brandreth, Thomas: invents horse-driven treadmill haulage, 69

Brassey, Mrs Thomas, 86

Brassey, Thomas: contractor, 82; and Penkridge viaduct, 82, 85, 86; sees railways as government department, 97, 98; and Peto, 140, 141; and London, Tilbury & Southend Railway, 143; and General Credit & Finance Co., 145, 150; builds Leicester–Hitchen line, 159; and 'Canada' works, 240

Braythwaite, John: engineer, 69

Bridgewater, Duke of: 46–7; Canal, 46–7, 79; threat of railway reduces prices by, 56, 77; abuse of monopoly, 57

Bright, John: defends free market on railways, 99

Bristol Railway: proposed by Brunton and Price (1832), 178; Brunel refuses to make cheapest route, 179; Brunel and William Townsend appointed surveyors, 180; title changed to Great Western Railway, 181

Bristol & Exeter Railway (B&ER): 186; poor station at Bristol, 186

Bristol & Gloucester Railway (B&GR), 187

Brompton & Piccadilly Circus Railway, 285

Brougham, Lord: criticizes parliamentarians over railway mania, 119

Browett, Sir Leonard, 336

Brunel, Isambard Kingdom: 61, 66, 85, 118, 139; complains of free market chaos, 98; civil engineer, 178; and Daniel Gooch, 178, 185; opposes competition for cheapness, 179; 'the best, not the cheapest', 179; appointed Surveyor of Bristol Railway, 180; creates title Great Western Railway, 181; route a strategic masterpiece, 181, 185; proposes 7-ft gauge, 181–2; Paddington terminal his third choice, 182; his reasons for broad gauge, 183; designs carriages and track badly, 183; modifies designs, 184; bad specifications for locomotives, 185; architectural effects, 185; Engineer of B&ER, 186; economy in bridge design, 188; engineer of Oxford, Worcester & Wolverhampton Railway, 188–9; experiments with 'atmospheric' propulsion, 189; carriage for Queen Victoria, 194

Brunel, Marc: Rotherhithe tunnel, 307

Brunton, William: proposes Bristol–London railway, 179